GLENVIEW PUBLIC LIBRARY

3 1170 00233 5242

W9-CBP-299

The
Art of
MEXICAN
COOKING

Books by Diana Kennedy

The Cuisines of Mexico
Mexican Regional Cooking
The Tortilla Book
Nothing Fancy

The
Art of
MEXICAN
COOKING

TRADITIONAL MEXICAN COOKING
FOR AFICIONADOS

Diana Kennedy

PHOTOGRAPHS BY MICHAEL CALDERWOOD
PHOTOGRAPH STYLING BY DIANA KENNEDY
ILLUSTRATIONS BY SUSANA MARTINEZ-OSTOS

641.5972
KEN

BANTAM BOOKS
NEW YORK · TORONTO · LONDON · SYDNEY · AUCKLAND

Glenview Public Library
1930 Glenview Road
Glenview, Illinois

THE ART OF MEXICAN COOKING
A Bantam Book / November 1989

All rights reserved.
Copyright © 1989 by Diana Kennedy.
Book design by Barbara Cohen Aronica.
No part of this book may be reproduced or transmitted
in any form or by any means, electronic or mechanical,
including photocopying, recording, or by any information
storage and retrieval system, without permission in
writing from the publisher.
For information address: Bantam Books.

Library of Congress Cataloging-in-Publication Data

Kennedy, Diana.
The art of Mexican cooking.

Includes bibliographical references.
1. Cookery, Mexican. I. Title.
TX716.M4K44   1989   641.5972   89-17649
ISBN 0-553-05706-5

Published simultaneously in the United States and Canada

Bantam Books are published by Bantam Books, a division of Bantam Doubleday
Dell Publishing Group, Inc. Its trademark, consisting of the words ''Bantam
Books'' and the portrayal of a rooster, is Registered in U.S. Patent and Trademark
Office and in other countries. Marca Registrada. Bantam Books, 666 Fifth Avenue,
New York, New York 10103.

PRINTED IN THE UNITED STATES OF AMERICA

DH   0 9 8 7 6 5 4 3 2 1

OCT 3 1 1989

TO ALL MY MEXICAN FRIENDS,
COOKS AND GOOD EATERS ALIKE

CONTENTS

ACKNOWLEDGMENTS

None of my books could have come into being without the help of many Mexican friends—housewives, cooks, teachers, restaurateurs, scholars, etc. —each of whom has contributed to my culinary education over the years in one capacity or another. A very special thank you to all of them; and to name a few: Hortensia Cabrera de Fagoaga, Ana María Guzmán de Vázquez Colmenares, Livier Ruiz de Suarez, María Dolores Torres Izábal, Margarita Martínez de Porter.

My deep gratitude to my much valued editor and friend, Frances McCullough, who has held my hand through the pangs of book-birth on five occasions; also to the totally (unwittingly) British crew of Michael Calderwood, the photographer, and artist Susana Martinez-Ostos. Also to my painstaking copy editor Chris Benton (*non*-British). All were a joy to work with. A special thank you to Janet Long-Solis, whose doctoral thesis and subsequent book, *Capsicum y Cultura—La historia del chilli*, greatly enlightened me (and other recent writers on the subject) on the complexities of the culture and history of that most fascinating of plants.

My congratulations to the designer, Barbara Cohen Aronica, who made visual sense out of a highly complicated manuscript. My thanks and sympathy to my managing editor, Diane Shanley, and to my excellent and sorely tried proofreaders, Margaret Benton and Rose Ann Ferrick. And for all of his help on the botanical details, my appreciation to Alejandro de Avila. I would also like to express my gratitude to Harper & Row for allowing me to use several recipes from my earlier books, albeit in a somewhat modified form.

Finally an acknowledgment of my debt to those wonderful cooks who, if judged by the excellence of their food, should all be published authors: the Annes, Augustins, Frans, Loises, Jerries, and Robertas, for they with others have kept my books alive and thriving. I should like to include for them a quote from Poppy Cannon (in her introduction to *Aromas and Flavours* by Alice B. Toklas):

"Little by little I began to understand that there can be value in giving a fine performance of another's compositions . . . that an exquisite interpretation can be in its own way just as creative, just as imaginative as an invention."

INTRODUCTION

This book devotes itself to the traditional popular foods of Mexico: those distinctive and delicious everyday dishes that for me sum up this remarkable cuisine. Even five years ago it wouldn't have been possible to write this book—in terms of the sophistication of cooks and availability of ingredients. I've placed special emphasis on the necessity for the right ingredients and how to prepare them using traditional methods. Cooking techniques are not complicated—unlike many of those in the French cuisine, for instance—and they are the result of my 32 years of living, traveling, and learning in Mexico. My teachers have been women and men from all walks of life—some with little formal education—but who share an immense appreciation of their regional foods and how they should be prepared to bring out the very special flavors and textures that make them authentic. This book does not pretend to be a definitive work, which would require many more years of study and several volumes, but rather a selection of particularly important dishes.

These popular, traditional foods are so regionally diverse, and so varied within those regions themselves, that they defy a cohesive, all-embracing definition. A certain homogeneity has indeed come about through improved transportation and other communications. But the basic differences remain, perhaps more because of the inability to reproduce the same *chiles* and herbs unique to one area in another (owing to climatic and topographical conditions) rather than from the strong dictates of local cultures. They vary in levels of sophistication from those that are wild and gathered at random—often eaten raw—to dishes that call for a number of nonindigenous ingredients requiring more intricate methods of preparation. But while peasants and urban gourmets alike can lick their lips over a snack of grilled grasshoppers or a *taco* of *colorín* (coral tree) flowers with a sauce of grilled *tunas* (prickly pears), the peasants would go hungry rather than eat, say, a *crêpe* of sautéed sweetbreads in a *pulque*/cream/*pasilla* sauce, or a chicken breast stuffed with *cuitlacoche* in a cream of squash flower sauce *à la nouvelle*. Nor would a Sonorense or Campechana necessarily delight in a *chichilo negro* from the Oaxacan coast, redolent of charred *chiles* and avocado leaves.

These foods, most of them unique to Mexico, can be seen at many different levels that do not necessarily coincide with the social or economic conditions of the consumers, and a taste for them varies little between large urban centers, provincial towns, and villages. There are the hunted or gathered wild and seasonal foods that I have mentioned in other books: *iguana*, *armadillo*, migrating ducks and doves (*canates* and *huilotas*), insects like *chapulines* (grasshoppers from Oaxaca), *jumiles*, a type of beetle often eaten alive in Morelos, *escamoles* (ant larvae) from Hidalgo and neighboring states; *colorín* (coral) and yucca flowers, flowers and fruits of various cacti, wild greens and herbs like lamb's-quarters (*quelite cenizo*) and wild anise (*anis del campo*) among many, many others.

There are the hearty country meats, most often prepared by local experts on weekends for country markets and for the townsfolk whose *dia del campo* (day in the country) would hardly be complete without tacos of *carnitas* (browned pork) or pit-barbecued lamb with its accompanying stuffed stomach, *montalayo*, or pit-barbecued ox head in maguey leaves (picturesquely referred to as *rostro*, which means "face" or "countenance" in Spanish) with a rustic, rough-textured *chile* sauce and a bowl of the concentrated juices from the cooking pit.

The early morning brings women to the entrance of the marketplaces or to strategic street corners with their *tamale* steamers and earthenware pots of *atole* (corn-based gruel), and later on in the morning those who serve a restorative tripe soup, *menudo*, guaranteed to cure the worst of hangovers.

Many of the same cooks return later in the day with the street food of the evening—*pozole* (a pork and hominy soup/stew) or *masa antojitos*, *sopes*, *quesadillas*, *enchiladas*, etc.—made up while you wait for the charcoal under the *comal* to settle down to a healthy glow. Next would come the eating stands of the marketplaces with their long wooden tables and benches, akin to the *cocinas económicas*, modest little holes-in-the-wall that serve simple *comidas* to market and office workers and well-dressed *aficionados* alike. It will be home-cooked, honest food: rice or pasta soups; unsophisticated stews of *chiles,* meat, and vegetables; or vegetable fritters in a tomato broth, all followed without fail by some soupy beans. It is the same food that might be served in more affluent homes, where more protein, richer sauces, and the regional touches of the household's cook would undoubtedly be included.

Tourist hotels are finally catching on, and breakfast and Sunday lunch buffets of regional foods have become commonplace. Banquets for diplomats and other grand occasions have for the most part (with the great exception of those prepared by Señora Mali Quijano and her famous mother) remained European in content.

Generally, and sensibly, the main meal, *comida,* is served anytime after two o'clock in the afternoon, after a sustaining mid-morning brunch (*almuerzo*), with a light supper to finish off the day's eating—a hearty meal of rice and *mole* would be unthinkable just before going to bed.

The foods of regional Mexico are in a gastronomic world of their own, a fascinating and many-faceted world, but alas, far too many people outside Mexico still think of them as an overly large platter of mixed messes, smothered with a shrill tomato sauce, sour cream, and grated yellow cheese preceded by a dish of mouth-searing sauce and greasy, deep-fried chips. Although these *do* represent some of the basic foods of Mexico—in name only—they have been brought down to their lowest common denominator north of the border, on a par with the chop suey and chow mein of Chinese restaurants 20 years ago. These dishes can be wonderful when cooked with care and presented in their correct culinary context, but instead, they have been transformed into a cheap culinary "fix."

On the other hand, to be fair there *are* some significant, positive changes going on across the United States as a small, but growing, number of specialty restaurants are attempting—and with no small measure of success—to change this image by presenting Mexican regional foods, interpreted in an American or southwestern style, with light adaptations and grilling as prominent features. Perhaps they have found the answer with this happy medium, for it is not always easy or even feasible to present the authentic day-to-day meals of a country and people so different in climate, temperament, and eating patterns from those of the United States, where sophisticated restaurant-goers and food writers are constantly in search of "something new" to satisfy their culinary curiosity. This is great in more ways than one, but I sometimes wonder just how much is being distorted or lost in this enthusiasm for the new. Fredy Girardet says, "We must preserve our regional cuisines because they are our culinary foundations." And Poppy Cannon, in her introduction to *Aromas and Flavours* by Alice B. Toklas, notes, "I began to comprehend a little the French resentment against *change without reason* (italics are mine). It began to dawn upon me that certain dishes like sonnets or odes cannot be brought into being without obeisance to classic rules and restrictions." The talented young chefs in America today are creating some wonderful dishes— but also some culinary misalliances with Mexican ingredients. I'm sure it wouldn't occur to them to put cilantro and jicama into their *coq au vin* or add *pozole* corn and cumin to desecrate their *bouillabaisses.* They've studied the French, Italian, and Chinese cuisines seriously but use Mexico's exciting ingredients without due regard for the traditional cooking processes and balances that make a great Mexican dish, with its many-faceted or layered depths of flavor. It's this depth and character that I find so often missing in these "new" dishes, and it's one of the reasons I've included detailed instructions on techniques and ingredients. My aim in all my books is that expressed by a Finnish designer, Antti Nurimeineim: "I am interested in continuity and refinement. I want to perfect things, not always to make new ones."

So often the new dishes hit only the high notes and miss the satisfying complexities altogether. For instance, a blended raw *chile* sauce tastes blatant, without the subtleties of, say, charring the *chiles* to round out the flavor. Nor should dried *chiles* be soaked endlessly or skinned and blended to a smooth, watery liquid. Colorful, yes, but the flavor is unidentifiable. They should be lightly toasted, as a general rule, soaked for the required time, and then blended to a specific texture with other balancing ingredients—without, for instance, the shocks of pineapple juice or chocolate in a table sauce. And cumin! Used in microscopic quantities in some Mexican cooked sauces, as it should be, it is pleasant, but added as it is *con bravura* in many southwestern-type recipes, it has a sweaty taste. And what about those beans, *al dente* and saltless to boot? Apart from being very gassy and innocuous, they bring to mind the admonition in a little cookbook written to the *campesina* (country-woman): "If you eat beans, they should be well cooked and with salt." (And it also gives this advice: "A little pig will bring pleasure to your home.")

It is heartening to see the great increase in the availability of ingredients for these and other regional recipes across the country. Of course, the Southwest—especially California—and the Chicago area, still lead the way, catering to their large Hispanic populations. But to see a new food chain like the Tianguis markets in California (of Von's parentage), for instance, devoting itself to the needs of those populations, with an increase in the variety of *chiles,* fresh produce, and staples, is a "happening" in the world of food. It will also make a large proportion of these recipes cookable; a few may be more difficult to reproduce but not to the *aficionado,* who in my experience will beg, borrow, grow, or mail-order in order to re-create faithfully the authentic flavors of this compelling and addictive food. I have no doubt that letters will soon be arriving to tell me about flourishing *hoja santa* bushes, American sweet potatoes being sun-seasoned in the Mexican style, or some little tricks to cultivate *epazote* the year round—not to mention the discovery of a homespun corn grinder for the *nixtamal.* It is for them and the other *aficionados* of honestly authentic Mexican food—wherever they may be in the world—that I have written this book.

NOTE ON COOKING TIMES

The cooking times given in the following recipes should be considered an approximate guide since actual cooking times will be influenced by a number of factors. Food cooks faster on a professional range or heavy counter-top burners with the same high gas pressure than on an ordinary domestic stove. Heavy pots and pans will transmit the heat more efficiently than lighter ones, while wider pans will reduce sauces faster than deep, narrow pans. Altitude is also important, since of course liquids boil at a lower temperature the higher the altitude.

In Mexico these factors also apply, of course. Mexican meat and poultry tend to be more compact than their American counterparts, so cooking times should be extended by about one third to one half.

NOTE ON SPANISH AND ENGLISH TRANSLATION

Although it's inconsistent, for the sake of clarity and easy reference, in the recipes the Spanish title appears first while in all other cases the English appears first.

CORN
(Maíz)

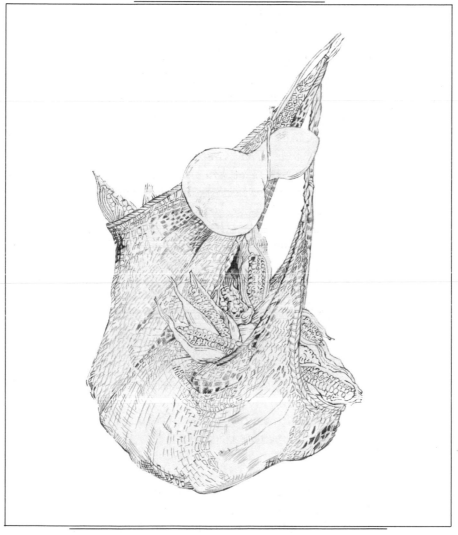

"With each rising of the sun man became more like the corn and with each moon the corn became more like man; and both began to take on the likeness of the Gods."

TORTILLAS AND TORTILLA DISHES

"There was an intimate relationship between the Otomis (known as the Men of Corn and the first inhabitants of the central highlands of Mexico), a dependence, a symbiosis, a living together with bonds of affection between these two living beings: man and plant. Both grew on this earth to provide for one another: man laboring, planting, irrigating, and fertilizing the corn. The corn providing man with tortillas, tamales *and* atole.*"*

I f you have lived in Mexico as many years as I have, you will agree, romantic as the notion is. It is particularly true in the case of the small farmers, whose lives and activities center around the cultivation of their corn—even if it is just enough for the family's consumption, *para el gasto,* as they put it. Planting, except in the case of nonseasonal irrigated corn, begins just before the rains start toward the end of May. Then the first longed-for rain eventually falls, and the corn sprouts and grows; there is the first weeding, *la descarda,* to be done. As the rains continue and the corn grows apace, new weeds spring up and thicken around the base of the corn, and the *segundando,* the second weeding, takes place. It is a backbreaking job for the laborer, who squats with his knees almost up to his chin, coaxing out the weeds with the tip of his curved *machete* so as not to hurt the young corn plant. Then there is the fertilizing and afterward the anxious watch for mealybugs that burrow through the heart of the sprouting ears, until the first tender *elotes* (ears of corn) begin to form. In their green husks they are sold to be roasted over charcoal or the kernels shaved off for the fresh corn *tamales* or *atole* (gruel). The corn silk is dried and made into a tea used as a *remedio* for the kidneys; the long, dark green leaves are cut from the stalk for wrapping the intricately bound *corundas* (triangular *tamales* in Michoacán); the plumelike flower at the top of the plant is shaken and the seeds collected to be toasted and ground for *tamales de espiga* (a specialty of eastern Michoacán), while the bulbous, silvery-skinned mushroom *cuitlacoche* that sometimes grows on the ears provides an epicurean treat.

3

Then comes the long wait throughout the autumn as the corncobs dry out on the stalk. If the rains continue, the stalks are bent over so that the water will run from stem to tip of the fully sheathed corn husks. The dried ears of corn are harvested at the beginning of December, a time when the whole family will turn out with hemp slings over their shoulders in which to collect them. Once the corn is stored in rustic bins made of dried reed, the work is almost finished except for cutting and raking in the dried cornstalks for fodder for the cattle. According to the village or region, each and every one of these stages will be marked with a ceremony—blessing the crops, scaring away evil spirits, exhortations for rain, blessing the new corn, and then the harvest—all of them rooted in the pre-Hispanic customs and beliefs of the past.

As work in the field slackens, the dried grains of corn are shaved from the cobs (one of the most rustic but efficient instruments for this shaving is the *elotero* illustrated on page 29, made up of tightly packed and tied old dry corncobs; I am told that it lasts for years) and stored in bags until needed for the next batch of *tortillas*. And as spring approaches, the stubble is burnt to ashes, the land tilled and left fallow until the advent of May, when the cycle begins all over again.

All kinds and colors of corn are grown, depending on local preferences and prejudices, climate and soil. *Cachuazintle,* broad white hominy (confusingly in Michoacán there is a small brownish corn that goes by the same name), is used for *pozole,* or *tamale* flour. There are the medium-sized *ancho* (broad) corn and *punteado*, shaped like a thin, tapering tooth. All colors of the rainbow are represented: creamy and canary yellow, mauve, mulberry, greenish, or bluish-black (*prieto*). There is corn of variegated colors called *pinto,* and there are many shades in between. There is a plentiful choice for making exotic-colored *tortillas* and *atoles.* (These are not always in favor; I know of a small country restaurant near Jungapeo where *capitalinos,* people from Mexico City, walk out when they see *tortillas* of these multicolored corns, favoring the whitish, clean look of the ones they are expecting— although ironically the Mexico City *tortillas* are a dirty yellow, tough and leathery in contrast to Don Ignacio's tender handmade ones.)

To sum up, the cooking of corn in Mexico with all its elaborations and ramifications is, and always has been, within the realm of the highest culinary art, beyond that of any other country.

TORTILLAS DE MAÍZ *(Corn Tortillas)*

"The tortilla would puff up as if alive, as if it wished to fly, as if Ehecatl [the Aztec God of Wind] had blown into it himself."
Salvador Novo

I wrote at some length in *The Cuisines of Mexico* about the history and regional differences of *tortillas* (there are about 30 types in Oaxaca alone, according to the latest research on the subject), so I will not dwell on these aspects here. Suffice it to say that the corn *tortilla* was for centuries, and still is in the country areas, the sustaining bread of the Mexican people, with the exception of those in the northern states. In *The Tortilla Book* I mentioned its versatility: a wrapper for countless ingredients—*tacos* and *enchiladas*; a pasta—*chilaquiles* and dry soups; a scoop—*totopos*; a plate—a *tostada*; dried and ground to a flour, it is re-formed and made into *antojitos* or small balls for soups, to mention just a few of its uses.

The simplest food is always the most difficult to prepare, for there are no predominant flavors to mask bad or indifferent ingredients or the careless handling of those ingredients. The corn *tortilla* provides the best example of this idea that I know. The ideal *tortilla* is made of carefully selected dried corn; just the right amount of lime (calcium oxide) should be added to the cooking water—too much will make for a dull yellowish, bitter-tasting *tortilla* with an acrid smell. If the corn is left too long over the heat, the dough will be sticky and impossible to make into *tortillas*.

Without doubt, a hand-patted *tortilla* is the best; it is soft edged and tender. But as I have written elsewhere, the patting out of *tortillas* is a dying art, so one has to opt for the next best: those pressed out individually with a *tortilla* press and then cooked if possible on an earthenware *comal* (bakestone) over a wood fire. (I have described the alternative methods on page 11).

A superbly made *tortilla* almost melts as you bite into it and when properly stored lasts some time without drying out. But the perfect *tortilla* is hard to come by nowadays, even in Mexico City, let alone in the United States. In my teaching travels in the United States recently I have seen some excellent *tortillas*, especially in California, Detroit, and Chicago, and while Texas (particularly Houston) is improving, Arizona and the South still have a long way to go.

WHAT TO LOOK FOR IN A GOOD *TORTILLA*

It should be of white corn (let's forget blue for the moment), opaque, mealy, neither too thin nor too thick, and speckled with brown to give some indication that it is cooked (many look half raw).

TYPES OF *TORTILLAS* TO AVOID

- The much-touted American handmade ones (from San Francisco and else-where) that are far too thick and clumsy.
- Those dirty-yellow, bitter-smelling ones. Too much lime has been added to the cooking water.
- *Tortillas* that are too thin, transparent, and chewy, which means that wheat flour has been added to the *masa*.
- *Tortillas* made of blue cornmeal that crumble at a glance. The corn for the cornmeal has not been treated in an appropriate way for making *tortillas*.
- Frozen *tortillas* that turn out to be as stiff as cardboard.

With these criteria in mind, there are multiple good choices.

CHOICES OF *TORTILLAS*

- Buy good frozen *tortillas* (avoid those with additives).
- Buy good packaged *tortillas* from a supermarket or *tortilla* factory if you live in an area with a Mexican population.
- Buy frozen *masa*, now widely available in many Mexican markets, and make your own.
- Buy fresh *masa* from a *tortilla* factory and make your own.
- Buy dried corn and make your own *nixtamal* for the *tortilla* factory to grind and make your own *tortillas*.
- Do the above but grind it yourself.
- Use Quaker Masa Harina, mix with water, and make your own.

Note: If you are buying fresh *masa* and making your own *tortillas*, the *masa* will probably be sold to you still hot in a tightly tied plastic bag. Undo it as soon as possible. Set aside what you want to use right away, divide the rest up into, say, four portions, weigh each portion, form into a flat cake (more convenient for storing), and wrap for the freezer with the weight clearly marked on it. Fresh *masa* tends to sour if left in the refrigerator for more than a day or two.

A final note: Sour *masa* will not hurt you. It just has a vaguely unpleasant taste and smell.

Lime (Cal)

This chemically pure lime, calcium oxide, is used in the preparation of dried corn for making *tortilla* and *tamale* dough. It is generally sold in rocklike lumps of varying sizes. To use it in this state, break off a piece about as large as a golf ball (once you have some experience you can estimate more accurately) and crush it down as much as possible. Sprinkle well with cold water. It will then start to slake, or burn as the Mexicans say, and it does just that. It starts to crumble with a slight sizzling noise, sending off a vapor. If you put your hand over the bowl you are using, you can feel the heat emanating from it. When the action has subsided, it is now slaked; stir again and pour the milky liquid through a strainer into the pot with the corn and water (page 8). Take a taste of the water; it should have a slightly acrid taste or, as the Mexican expression goes, "grab your tongue." If the water is very strong and bitter, add more cold water to dilute the corn water. If it is too weak, pour more water through the strainer containing the lime residue and try again.

Since one usually buys lime by the pound at the very least, it can be broken up into smaller pieces and stored in closed jars, but with time it will naturally slake on its own with the natural moisture in the air. It is still usable, although it will have broken down to a powder containing some small lumps. When you add water to it for the *nixtamal*, it will not burn.

Note: When handling lime, be careful not to get any near your eyes and always use a noncorrodible container for diluting it.

Preparation of Dried Corn and Making of Masa (Nixtamal y Masa de Maíz)

Nixtamal is the name given to dried corn kernels that have been cooked in a solution of lime and water. After this step, the kernels are ground to a fine dough called *masa* that is ready to be made into *tortillas, antojitos,* or some *tamales.*

CHOOSING THE CORN

When buying dried corn of whatever color or size, always make sure that it is not *picado* (perforated) by weevillike insects that burrow into the kernels, eating the starchy content inside. If the corn is already packaged, you can easily see this by a powdery residue at the bottom of the bag.

The kernels should be free of any musty odor—such an odor indicates that it has been stored in a damp place—which will affect the flavor of the *tortillas.*

PREPARATION

MAKES ABOUT 2 POUNDS OR 3¾ CUPS MASA

1 pound (2½ cups) dried corn kernels
1 cup water
2 rounded teaspoons powdered lime (see page 7)

First run the dried corn kernels through your hands to pick out any small stones, pieces of chaff, etc. Rinse thoroughly in cold water and drain.

Put the rinsed corn into a pan and add enough water to come at least 1 inch above the surface of the corn. Stir 1 cup of water into the powdered lime (be careful of your eyes; it burns) and pour the mixture through a fine strainer into the pan, pressing out any soft lumps with the back of a wooden spoon and discarding the hard residue. Stir the corn well.

Set the pan over medium heat. As soon as the mixture heats up, the outer skin of the corn kernels will turn bright or dull yellow, depending on how much lime is used. Cook until small bubbles appear on the surface—the mixture should not boil. Lower the heat and continue cooking until the yellow skin can easily be sloughed off the kernels—test by rubbing a few kernels between your fingers. This should take about 15 minutes more. Set the corn aside in the warm liquid for at least 12 hours and up to 48. Drain, rinse in cold water—it is not necessary to rub off all the skins for this type of *masa*—and send to the mill to be ground (see page 10 for additional information on grinding utensils).

The important thing to look for when making your own *nixtamal* is that the corn should not be overcooked, or it will make a tacky *masa,* practically impossible to handle for making *tortillas.*

Equipment for Making Corn Tortillas

TORTILLA PRESS

The natural *tortilla* press is, of course, the hands, but the art of patting out a *tortilla* is dying. The second method, also handmade, is on the wane, too, except for a few isolated places in the low hot country. A ball of *masa* is pressed onto a piece of banana leaf—which has now almost totally given way to plastic—and patted out with one hand while the other turns the leaf in circular fashion to ensure that the *tortilla* will be round. Both these methods are rapid and carried out with amazing dexterity.

But with the modern age has come the *tortilla* press. The wooden press (illustrated on page 7) is certainly picturesque but is also clumsy and tends to slide around. By far the most efficient is the heavy cast-iron press made in Mexico; these vary in size—from 6 to 7 inches in diameter is a good size for general use. Care needs to be taken as they tend to rust, despite their noncorrosive paint finish. They need no curing, just a rinse. Be sure the plates are thoroughly dry before making the *tortillas;* you will also need a plastic liner for each plate so that the *masa* does not stick to the metal. The smallest (1 quart, although it seems too small) Alligator Baggie is my choice hands down—no zips and locks and fancy flaps. After being used (think ecologically) they can be wiped clean, folded, and stored with the press. After you use it, the press should also be wiped clean and dried thoroughly; place paper toweling between the plates to prevent any moisture from forming and corroding the metal.

There have been a couple of fancier presses made in the United States—one elegant enameled heavy one that seems to have faded from view and a sleek, light aluminum one, easy to clean but too light for the job, which tends to snap under heavy pressure.

CORN MILL (MOLINO DE MAÍZ)

In Mexico the only corn-grinding utensils for centuries were the black basalt *metate* (grinding stone) and the *mano* or *metlapil* (muller). Of course they are still used today in remote villages or when the electricity fails at the local country mill. The *nixtamal* is stone-ground at the country mill, although I have noticed some places in the southeast of the country where the mill is of metal—the resulting *masa* is much coarser.

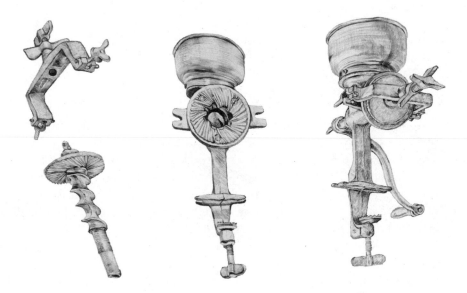

There are now small *tortilla* factories almost everywhere in the United States—there is even one in Alaska—and it is possible to go and buy *masa* if you want to make your own *tortillas*. However, for the dedicated do-it-yourselfers there are alternatives. You can prepare your own *nixtamal* (see page 8) and take it to the *tortilla* factory. Or you can buy a grinder like the one illustrated and grind your own corn. For that you must tighten the blades as far as possible, and even then the *masa* will be fairly coarse. This last method will require patience and a very strong arm.

COMAL OR GRIDDLE

The *comal* (the name comes from the Nahuatl word *comalli*) is a thin, circular "griddle" used for cooking *tortillas*. There are several types to choose from, as well as substitutes, depending on what is available where you live (if you travel to Mexico unencumbered, you can always bring the real thing back with you) and what sort of cooking facilities you have.

The traditional *comal*, still used in the villages for cooking over wood or charcoal (I use it over gas), is a disk of thin, unglazed earthenware. Before being used it must be cured, or the *tortillas* will stick to it. Dilute some powdered lime with cold water and stir to form a thin paste. Spread the cooking surface of the *comal* with a thick coating and place over the fire. When the white lime turns a cream color after it has dried out, brush off the excess powder, and the surface will be ready for cooking *tortillas*. Every time you want to use this type of *comal* for *tortillas* or *masa antojitos* the process will have to be repeated.

A heavy tin or light metal *comal* is the most commonly used in Mexico, often made with the recycled lids of old oil drums. It can be used over any type of fire, although it tends to warp when used over an electric burner. The advantage of this type of *comal* over the others that follow is its thinness, so that the heat cooks the dough fast, an important requisite for a tender *tortilla*. And also the heat can be adjusted quickly. A light rubbing with oil is all the curing that is needed. It can be washed with soap and water if messy, and any substances sticking to it can be scoured with a pumice stone. The important thing is to dry this *comal* thoroughly after washing as it rusts easily. A heavy iron griddle can be used quite successfully over gas or electricity, but it takes longer to transmit the heat to the dough, and the heat is not as easily controlled. Follow manufacturer's instructions for curing.

A heavy frying pan with a black surface could be used, but you can burn your hands on the hot sides and the high heat will probably spoil the pan's surface.

If you have one of those glass-topped stoves, you can make *tortillas* right on the surface, although I don't know whether the manufacturer would approve!

For making good *tortillas* the surfaces to avoid are those highly polished metals—aluminum, stainless steel, Teflon, etc.—that reflect the heat. Your *tortillas* made in them will tend to be dried out, pale, and underdone.

Making a Tortilla by Hand

Knead the *masa* well until it is completely smooth. Moisten your hands with water. Take a small piece of dough and roll it into a ball about 1½ inches in diameter. Press it out a little between your hands and then begin patting it out and extending it with each pat first on one palm and then the other, turning your hands over as you do so, until you have a thin disk of *masa* with a smooth circumference, about 5 inches in diameter. (It takes about 33 pats to extend it, I am told—although I always lose count.)

TORTILLAS MADE WITH PREPARED MASA

MAKES 15 5-INCH *TORTILLAS*

1¼ pounds (about 2½ cups) prepared corn *tortilla masa* (page 8), approximately
water if needed

If the *tortilla masa* has been freshly made, it will probably be the right consistency for working immediately—a soft, smooth dough. If the *masa* has been sitting around and drying out a little, then add a very little water and knead until it's smooth and pliable, not the slightest bit crumbly.

Divide the dough into 15 equal parts (each one should weigh just over 1 ounce) and roll into smooth balls about 1½ inches in diameter. Place all but one of the balls under plastic wrap so that they do not dry out.

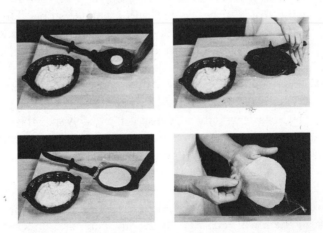

Heat an ungreased *comal* or griddle over a medium flame. Open up the *tortilla* press and place a small Alligator Baggie on the bottom plate. Place a ball of the dough on the bottom Baggie, a little off center toward the hinge rather than the pressing lever (it presses too thin on that side), and press it out with your fingers to flatten a little. Cover with the second Baggie and press down firmly but not too fiercely (or the dough will be too thin and you will never be able to pry it off the Baggie in one piece). Open the press, remove the top Baggie, lift the bottom Baggie up in one hand, place the dough onto the fingers of your other hand, and very carefully peel the Baggie off the flattened dough. Do not try to peel the dough off the bag. Keeping your hand as horizontal as possible, lay the *tortilla* flat onto the *comal*. There should be a slight sizzle as the dough touches the surface of the *comal*. Leave for about 15 seconds; the underside will have opaque patches and be slightly speckled with brown. Flip the *tortilla* over onto the second side and cook for a further 30 seconds; the underside should now be opaque and speckled. Flip back onto the first side again and cook for 15 seconds more. If you have done all the correct things and the *comal* is the correct heat, the *tortilla* should puff up, showing that the extra moisture has dried out of the dough. If the *tortilla* doesn't puff up and it's necessary in order to make *panuchos*, for example, then press it gently on the last turn with your fingers or a towel.

As the *tortillas* are made, they should be placed one on top of the other in a basket or gourd lined with a cloth to preserve the heat and keep them moist and flabby. They can also be wrapped in foil packages and frozen.

TORTILLAS MADE WITH QUAKER MASA HARINA

MAKES ABOUT 15 5-INCH *TORTILLAS*

2 cups (10½ ounces) Quaker *Masa Harina*
1⅓ cups water, approximately
2 1-quart Alligator Baggies for pressing *tortillas*

Mix the *masa harina* with the water and work well so that it is evenly distributed through the flour and forms a cohesive mass when pressed together. The dough should be of medium consistency, neither too firm nor wet and sticky.

Follow the instructions for making *tortillas* in the preceding recipe.

Methods for Reheating Corn Tortillas

If you are cooking on a gas range or a wood or charcoal fire, simply throw the *tortilla* onto the grill and heat for a few seconds on each side. They may char a little, but no matter—it adds great flavor and couldn't be more authentic. But serve immediately; these won't hold.

For a gas or electric range, wood or charcoal fire: heat a *comal* over the fire, place *tortillas* on it, and reheat for a few seconds on either side. Serve immediately, or they will harden.

If the *tortillas* have been made ahead, wrapped in foil packages, reheat them for about 20 minutes in a 325° oven. Or reheat them in a microwave oven: place a dozen or so in plastic wrap and heat for 30 seconds (approximately, as each oven varies), turning the package over and heating for another 30 seconds. Timing will also depend on the thickness of the *tortillas*.

If you are using frozen *tortillas*, it is better to defrost them first and then reheat them in one of the ways suggested above.

To add a little folklore to this more technical advice: I like to heat a pile of *tortillas, en famille* of course, following the method taught me by a Mexican artist/craftsman, Feliciano Bejar:

TO REHEAT A SMALL PILE OF *TORTILLAS*

This is the "kitchen" way of reheating *tortillas*, which can be done over a gas or electric burner or over an open grill. If they char a little around the edges, no matter; that adds flavor.

Place a *tortilla* on an open burner to heat for about 5 seconds (longer if it is a thick one) and turn over, putting another one on top; leave for a further 5 seconds, turn both over together, and place another one on top, continuing until the whole pile is heated. Wrap in a cloth and bring to the table.

A friend and great cook from Hidalgo, Señora Lara, once after a meal presented her guests with crisped tortilla *halves sprinkled with salt. "Even if you think you have no room, eat it; it aids the digestion," she said.*

TORTILLA RECIPES

Tortilla Pieces (Totopos)

TOTOPOS FRITOS I *(Fried Tortilla Pieces)*

Small fried squares of dried corn *tortillas*, *totopos* are sometimes used as a crisp topping for a bowl of soup. In Mexico, they are used for *frijoles puercos* (page 181—Michoacán version) and Michoacán *chilaquiles* (page 31). They can also be tossed into a salad just before serving, added to melted cheese dips, scrambled with eggs, or just served by themselves as snacks. You can also make delicious *totopos* from whole-wheat flour or a mixture of corn and wheat *totopos* (pages 17 and 18).

It is best to use a thin *tortilla* for *totopos*. Stack about 4 of them together and cut off the curved parts to form a large square. Then cut them again into small squares, about ½ inch. Spread them out on a rack to dry, in the sun, in an airy place, or, if you are in a hurry, in a 325° oven for about 40 minutes.

Heat about ½ inch of oil in a small pan (a large one uses too much oil) and fry the *tortilla* squares a few at a time—they will fry more evenly and more quickly if you don't overcrowd the pan. Turn them over from time to time until they turn a deep golden brown—about 3 to 4 minutes (depending on the thickness of the *tortilla*). Transfer with a perforated spoon, briefly holding them over the pan to drain off some of the oil, to a double layer of paper toweling. Strain the oil and store in the refrigerator for another use.

When the *totopos* have cooled off, they can be used as suggested above; any left over can be frozen in an airtight container. Although they will remain crisp in the freezer, they need a little freshening up to look shiny and appetizing. There is no need to defrost them. Either heat them for about 5 minutes in a toaster oven or heat them in an ungreased frying pan with a lid so that you can toss them for a few seconds over fairly high heat.

TOTOPOS FRITOS II *(Fried Tortilla Pieces)*

When you're presenting a large bean roll or dip, the *totopos* should be triangular to act as scoops. Cut each *tortilla* into 6 triangles and follow the procedure above.

TOTOPOS SALADOS Y FRITOS
(Fried Salted Tortilla Pieces)

If you wish to have salted *totopos*, make a solution of salt and water—about 3 tablespoons salt to 1 cup water—stirring until the salt has dissolved. Quickly submerge the *tortilla* pieces in the water, strain and shake well, and then immediately throw into very hot oil. It splatters a lot and no doubt breaks down your oil—but it is for a good cause.

TOTOPOS TOSTADOS (Crisp Baked Tortilla Pieces)

If you wish to cut down on your fat intake, then prepare the *totopos* by toasting, not frying, the dried *tortilla* pieces. Cut the *tortillas* into the required size, dry them off, then crisp them and let them brown slightly in a 325° oven for about 40 minutes, turning them over from time to time. Cooking time will depend on the thickness of the *tortillas*.

TOSTADAS (Fried Whole Tortillas)

Tostadas, often erroneously called *chalupas* in the Southwest, are corn *tortillas* that have been fried flat until crisp. They are then topped with various ingredients dictated by regional likes and dislikes. It is best to have a not-too-thin *tortilla* for these, or your *tostada* may collapse at first bite and the topping fall all over the place. Oil to a depth of ¼ inch in the pan should be sufficient to fry the *tostadas*. They are pan-fried, not deep-fried, until crisp and a deep golden color. They should be eaten as soon as possible after frying; if not, they can be reheated in a 350° oven on a paper toweling–lined tray that will absorb some of the excess oil.

RASPADAS (Thin, Crisp Tortillas)

The *raspadas* of Jalisco, the *totopostes* of Chiapas, and the *tlayudas* of Oaxaca all have one thing in common: while of slightly different sizes, they are large, almost transparent, crisp-dried *tortillas*. In this condition they can be stored indefinitely and carried on long journeys, ready for toasting or frying to accompany a meal.

The *raspadas* are made in an interesting way. The cook begins by making a 6-inch *tortilla* in the normal way; she then lets it dry out, rather than take on color, on a huge, thin metal hot plate heated by gas. After about 2 minutes the bottom of the *tortilla* is dry enough for the uncooked top layer to be scraped off. This she does with a length of ½-inch metal tubing. As the dough is scraped off it forms a wrinkled oval shape referred to as a *pachola*—the same name given to the ground meat patties that are rolled off the *metate*. (You may wonder what happens to those uncooked layers of dough: in Tequila, there is always a pig or two hovering in the background to absorb that waste.)

The thin *raspadas* are now completely dried off on the second side, again without browning, for about 30 seconds. They are then cooled off and sold in the hundreds to the restaurants of Guadalajara and even sent far afield to homesick Jaliscienses.

TORTILLAS DE MAÍZ Y TRIGO
(Corn and Wheat Tortillas)

MAKES ABOUT 11 5-INCH TORTILLAS

A considerable amount of wheat is grown in the colder central highlands of Mexico, and often in country marketplaces there you can find *tortillas* made with corn *masa* mixed with an equal proportion of wheat. There is some debate as to whether this came about from taste or necessity, to spin out the corn toward the end of the season, when it becomes infected with weevils. This mixture makes a slightly heavier-textured *tortilla* with an excellent taste.

Wheat that has been picked over and rinsed well is then sent along with the *nixtamal* (the corn cooked in lime water) to the mill, and they are ground together to make a fine *masa*. Since very few people have a mill that will crush the corn and wheat together in a wet mix, or access to one, I have given an alternative method that works very well.

It is best to try to buy a rather roughly ground whole-wheat flour for this recipe—certainly not a brown pastry flour for instance.

You will need to press the dough harder in the *tortilla* press than for normal corn *tortillas;* cooking time will be slightly longer as will reheating time.

When you're cooking the *tortilla* on the *comal*, the wheat in the dough tends to stick, so it may be necessary to grease the *comal* very lightly.

½ pound (about 1 cup) prepared corn *tortilla masa* (page 8)
⅔ cup whole-wheat flour (see note above)
3 to 4 tablespoons water

Mix all the ingredients together and work well so that the flour is distributed evenly through the *masa*. The dough should be smooth but fairly firm and pliable—add a little extra water only if necessary to obtain this consistency.

Cover the dough with plastic wrap and set aside for the wheat particles to soften for at least 2 hours in a cool place. If the weather is hot and humid and you are leaving it for a longer resting period, refrigerate the dough. But always bring it up to room temperature before making the *tortillas*.

Follow the instructions for making corn *tortillas* (page 12), but increase the cooking time by about 1 minute on each side and add a few seconds on the final turn.

Note: If you are starting from scratch with access to the right type of mill, prepare 1 part corn and ¾ to 1 part wheat berries.

Enchiladas

There are two main methods for cooking *enchiladas*: (1) frying the tortilla lightly, dipping it into a warm cooked sauce, filling, and rolling; (2) dipping a tortilla into a raw sauce, frying it, then filling and rolling. Detailed instructions for both methods are given in the following recipes.

ENCHILADAS PLACERAS
(Enchiladas Served in the Central Plaza)

SERVES 4 TO 6

These little *enchiladas* are served every evening in the main plaza of Xicotepec de Juarez in the northern part of the Sierra de Puebla that adjoins the state of Veracruz.

Traditionally a serving consists of 4 small—about 3½-inch—*tortillas*. The tomato sauce should be of a consistency that thinly covers the *tortillas*. While the dish should be eaten the moment it is assembled, the component parts can be prepared ahead.

These *enchiladas* are sometimes filled with refried black beans instead of shredded meat, a good vegetarian dish.

¼ cup, approximately, melted lard or safflower oil for frying
16 3½-inch *or* 12 4½- to 5-inch corn *tortillas*
1¼ cups *salsa de jitomate, Sierra de Puebla* (page 339), kept hot
1 cup *res deshebrada* for *Salpicón* (page 298), kept hot
¼ cup finely chopped white onion
¼ cup finely grated *queso anejo* or Romano cheese

Have ready a tray lined with paper toweling.

Heat a little of the lard to cover the bottom of a frying pan and fry 2 of the *tortillas* at a time for about 5 seconds on each side, adding more lard as necessary. They should not become crisp around the edge; drain on the paper toweling.

Immerse the *tortillas* in the hot sauce for a few seconds. Fill each one with a scant tablespoon of the shredded beef, roll the *tortillas* up, cover with a little of the sauce, sprinkle with onion and cheese, and serve immediately.

ENCHILADAS DE SANTA CLARA

SERVES 4 TO 6

This is one of many recipes given to me by Señora Hortensia Fagoaga. Although born in the Sierra de Puebla, she has had the opportunity of living in many parts of the republic and is keenly interested in good regional Mexican food. She has exceptional *sazón* (flavoring), as the Mexicans say, and has generously allowed me to cook with her and eat with the family on countless occasions.

The origin of the recipe is unknown, and she is not sure to which Santa Clara it refers.

While the sauce could be prepared ahead, the *enchiladas* should be eaten as soon as they are ready, or they will become soggy.

4 *chiles anchos*
1 cup water, approximately
1 garlic clove, peeled and roughly chopped
1 rounded teaspoon (or to taste) sea salt
2 large eggs
½ cup, approximately, melted lard or safflower oil for frying
12 4½-inch corn *tortillas*
½ pound *queso fresco* or a substitute (see pages 445–447), cut into 12 slices
about ¼ inch thick

Have ready a tray lined with a double thickness of paper toweling.

Remove the stalks, if any, from the dried *chiles*, slit them open, and remove seeds and veins. Toast the *chiles* lightly by pressing them down onto a warm *comal*; the inside surface will turn an opaque tobacco brown. Remove and allow to soak in hot water for about 15 minutes or until reconstituted but not mushy.

Put 1 cup of water, the garlic, and the salt into a blender jar and blend until smooth. Transfer the *chiles* to the blender jar with a slotted spoon and blend until the sauce is absolutely smooth—about 8 seconds. Break up the eggs with a fork and stir them into the sauce.

Heat enough of the lard to cover the bottom of a small frying pan. Before you begin frying, make sure that the oil is at medium heat; if it's too hot and smoking, then the *chile* sauce will burn.

Dip one *tortilla* at a time into the *chile* sauce to cover it thickly and fry for about 10 seconds on each side. Using tongs and a spatula, carefully remove the *tortilla* from the oil and drain on the paper toweling. The egg/*chile* sauce will look uneven and lumpy (that's okay; all the more appetizing). Place a slice of the cheese on one side of the *tortilla* and double over—the cheese should begin to melt with the heat of it. Continue with the rest, adding lard as necessary and working as fast as you can, and serve immediately. Although the *enchiladas* are traditionally served alone, you could accompany this dish with a lightly dressed tomato and lettuce salad.

ENCHILADAS VERDES (*Green Enchiladas*)

SERVES 4 TO 6

Although there are many versions of this dish with slight regional differences, this recipe is more typical of the central area of Mexico, in and around Mexico City.

Although traditionally eaten at suppertime, *enchiladas* in fact make a great lunch dish accompanied by a salad, or with a light appetizer—like *ceviche*— they make a substantial main course for dinner.

Enchiladas without exception must be eaten the moment they are assembled, or the *tortillas* tend to become soggy.

THE SAUCE
1 pound (about 22 medium) *tomate verde*, husks removed, rinsed
2 *chiles serranos*, stalks removed, rinsed
1 garlic clove, peeled and roughly chopped
1 tablespoon lard or safflower oil
⅓ cup chicken broth
sea salt to taste

THE REST
¼ cup safflower oil, approximately, for frying
12 corn *tortillas*
1½ cups *pollo deshebrado para tacos* (page 218)
½ cup finely chopped white onion
½ cup *crème fraîche* or sour cream
⅓ cup *queso fresco*

Have ready a warm serving dish into which the *enchiladas* will just fit in one layer, or individual plates, and a tray lined with paper toweling for draining the fried *tortillas*.

Put the *tomate verde* and fresh *chiles* into a saucepan, barely cover with

21

water, and bring up to a simmer. Continue simmering until the *tomates* are just soft—about 8 minutes. Remove from the heat, drain, reserving ¼ cup of the cooking water, and transfer to a blender jar. Add the garlic and reserved cooking water and blend until smooth.

Heat the lard in a frying pan, add the sauce, and cook over medium heat, stirring from time to time, for about 5 minutes. Add the broth and salt to taste and continue cooking until the sauce has reduced to about 2 cups— about 5 minutes more. Set aside, but keep hot while you prepare the *enchiladas*.

Heat about 2 tablespoons of the oil in a frying pan, immerse one of the *tortillas*, holding it down in the oil with a spatula for about 1 minute, turn it over, and fry on the second side for about 30 seconds—the *tortilla* should be well heated through but not crisp. Drain on the paper toweling while you continue with the rest of the *tortillas*, adding more oil as necessary. Dip one of the fried *tortillas* into the green sauce, spread a little of the shredded chicken across the center, add a sprinkling of onion and a little cream, roll up, and place on the warmed dish. Continue with the rest of the *tortillas*. Pour the remaining sauce over the *enchiladas*, spread with the remaining cream, sprinkle with more of the onion and the cheese, and serve immediately.

ENJOCOCADAS I
(Tortillas in a Sauce of Cheese and Cream)

SERVES 6 TO 8

I was introduced to this dish for the first time by a good friend and wonderfully intuitive cook, Señora Livier Ruiz de Suarez, who was born in Valle de Juarez, a rich dairy-farming area on the borders of Michoacán and Jalisco. She has most generously spent countless hours traveling with me and teaching me about the very diverse regional cooking of Michoacán.

The word *enjococadas* means *tortillas* immersed in *jocoque—jocoque* can mean soured milk, cream, or yogurt in other areas, but here it refers to the cream skimmed off raw milk that has been left at room temperature overnight. It is collected over a period of several days and stored in an earthenware jug. It has a pleasant acidity, and although very thick, it is often whipped lightly before being used on *uchepos* (page 86) or *corundas* (page 70).

This is a very unusual and delicate-tasting dish depending totally on the quality of the *tortillas*—which should be freshly made and rather thin—and an excellent *crème fraîche*, which should be used instead of the *jocoque*. While the

22

cheese traditionally used is the salty, rather grainy *añejo* or *cotija*, I prefer to use a rather dry *queso fresco*.

Enjococadas are usually served as a "dry soup" or first course by themselves, but they could well serve as a main dish—and a vegetarian one at that—with a lightly dressed salad.

Traditionally, *enjococadas* are assembled and then immediately reheated in a fireproof dish that is gently shaken over the flame. An oval copper *gratin* dish would be ideal for this, but an alternative is to put them into an ovenproof dish and cover it loosely with foil so that the cream does not dry up.

I am sorry, but there is nothing you can do in advance; this is last-minute, pan-to-mouth food.

¼ cup safflower oil, approximately
12 thin corn *tortillas* (see note above)
2 cups crème *fraîche*
1¼ cups finely grated *queso añejo* or *queso fresco* (see note above)
¾ cup finely chopped white onion, approximately

Heat oven to 350° (if using alternative method).

Have ready a flameproof or ovenproof dish into which the rolled *tortillas* will just fit in one layer and a tray covered with two layers of paper toweling.

Heat enough of the oil to cover the bottom of a small frying pan and fry the *tortillas* one by one, adding more oil as necessary, until they are soft and well heated through but do not become crisp around the edge. Drain on paper toweling. Meanwhile, in another pan heat the cream until it bubbles and reduces for about 5 minutes. Immerse each *tortilla* in the hot cream, put about 1 tablespoon of the cheese and a little of the onion across the center of each *tortilla*, roll them up, and place side by side on the bottom of the dish. Pour over the remaining cream and the rest of the cheese and shake the pan over the heat until the *enjococadas* are well heated through and the cream is just bubbling (or heat in the oven for about 10 minutes). Serve immediately.

ENJOCOCADAS II
(Casserole of Chicken Tacos and Green Sauce)

SERVES 6 TO 8   JIQUILPAN, MICHOACÁN

This absolutely scrumptious recipe was prepared for me by the famous Mexican artist and craftsman Feliciano Bejar. It comes from his native Jiquilpan, in the northern part of Michoacán, which is a rich dairy-farming area.

It is really a rich casserole (although I hate that word as it has too many sloppy connotations in Mexican-American food) of layered *tacos* filled with chicken and *chorizo*/egg filling, with green sauce and cream. It is a meal in itself and is best served with a very lightly dressed salad. While all the component parts can be prepared ahead, the final assembling and baking of the dish have to be done at the last minute, or the *tortillas* will become soggy and disintegrate.

The size of the baking dish is important: it should be at least 2 inches deep and large enough to accommodate two layers of 10 small *tacos*—about 9 inches by 9 inches is ideal.

The layers of *tacos* should just be covered with, not drowned in, the sauce and generously but not too thickly topped with cream.

⅓ cup safflower oil, approximately, for frying
20 5-inch corn *tortillas*
1½ cups thick *crème fraîche*
2 cups well-seasoned *pollo deshebrado para tacos* (page 218), warmed through
2 cups *chorizo*/egg filling (page 320), warmed through
2 cups *salsa verde* (recipe follows), warmed through

Heat the oven to 375°. Have ready a tray covered with two layers of paper toweling.

Put a little of the oil into a small frying pan—it should be about ⅛ inch deep—and heat. When the oil is hot but not smoking, immerse a *tortilla* until thoroughly warmed through and softened, about 10 seconds, but do not allow the edge to become crisp. Drain on paper toweling and repeat until all the *tortillas* have been fried.

Meanwhile, heat the cream and allow to bubble and reduce for about 5 minutes. Immerse one of the *tortillas*—the cream should lightly coat it. Fill with the chicken, roll, and set onto a warmed dish. The second *tortilla* may be filled with the *chorizo* filling. Continue immersing in cream and filling a total of 10 *tortillas*—alternately with chicken and *chorizo*—to form the first layer. Spread with 1 cup *salsa verde* and a little of the remaining cream. Continue with the second layer until all the *tortillas* have been used up. Top with the remaining sauce and *crème fraîche* and bake in the top part of the oven until bubbling, about 15 to 20 minutes. Serve immediately.

SALSA VERDE PARA ENJOCOCADAS II
(Green Sauce for Enjococadas II)

MAKES 2 CUPS

This simple sauce can also be used for *corundas* (page 70).

1 pound *tomate verde* (about 22 medium)
3 (or to taste) *chiles serranos,* stems removed
1 garlic clove, peeled and roughly chopped
1½ tablespoons safflower oil
sea salt to taste

Remove the papery husks from the green tomatoes and rinse briefly. Put into a saucepan, cover with water, and add the *chiles*. Bring the water to a simmer and cook for about 10 minutes. Remove the pan from the heat and let the tomatoes and *chiles* sit in the water for about 5 minutes longer.

Transfer the *tomate verde* and *chiles* with a slotted spoon to a blender jar, add the garlic, and blend until smooth (no extra water should be necessary).

Heat the oil in a frying pan, add the sauce, and cook over fairly high heat, stirring from time to time, until the sauce has reduced—about 3 to 4 minutes. Season with salt as necessary.

TOSTADAS DE APATZINGÁN

On a recent trip to the hot country of Michoacán I came across the perfect *tostada*. Apatzingan is a thriving agricultural center where a lot of street eating goes on, especially in the open-air Mercado de Aguates. It opens early in the morning and has a brisk trade with *menudo* and *tamales*, progressing through the day with pork stew served with *morisqueta* (boiled rice) and *antojitos* of various types (despite the great heat), ending with the evening *pozole*.

The crowd was thinning out as we arrived one evening to search out local food. We stopped at a *tostadería*, specializing as its name implies in *tostadas*. They were not exceptional. We tried a bit of this and that but were still hungry when we returned to the hotel. In the dining room we saw people eating most impressive *tostadas* piled high with various layers, including one of very luscious-looking shredded pork.

The *tostadas* were made of very large corn *tortillas* that had been fried crisp (you can toast them crisp in the oven to avoid so much grease; see page 16) and topped with the following layers:

a thin layer of *frijoles refritos* (page 180)
a thick layer of finely shredded lettuce
a thick layer of *carne de puerco cocida y deshebrado* (page 248)
2 tomato slices
2 tablespoons sour cream or *crème fraîche*
some thinly sliced radishes
sliced white onions, wilted in lime juice as for *cebollas encurtidas para tatemado* (page 364)
2 tablespoons *Michoacán* tomato sauce (page 340)
a sprinkling of grated *queso añejo* or Romano cheese

And served on the side for those who like it more *picante*:

salsa de chile de árbol (page 344)

You will need both hands and a liberal supply of paper napkins.

FLAUTAS DE GUADALAJARA

Flautas (flutes) are the large crisp-fried *tacos* of Jalisco. The *tortilla* used is usually about 6 to 7 inches in diameter. When they are freshly cooked, the *telita*, or top layer that puffs up, is removed, leaving a very thin *tortilla*.

Various traditional fillings for *flautas* follow. A large spoonful is put along the center of the *tortilla*; then it is tightly rolled, secured with a toothpick, and fried in lard or oil until quite crisp and a deep golden color. After being drained on paper toweling they are served on a bed of shredded lettuce seasoned with lime juice, thin slices of radishes, about 2 tablespoons of *salsa de plaza* (page 348), and, if available, Tamazula sauce (see page 346), but it is not absolutely necessary.

This is pan-to-mouth food. *Flautas* must be filled, fried, and eaten right away, or they become tough.

Fillings for Flautas

POLLO DESHEBRADO (*SHREDDED CHICKEN*)

MAKES ABOUT 1¼ CUPS TO FILL 6 FLAUTAS

2 tablespoons melted lard or safflower oil
3 tablespoons finely chopped whole onion
½ pound (about 1 large) tomato, unskinned, finely chopped
2 *chiles serranos*, cut into rounds
2 cups *pollo deshebrado para tacos* (page 218)
sea salt to taste

Heat the lard in a frying pan. Add the chopped onion, tomato, and fresh *chiles* and fry gently for about 5 minutes, stirring the mixture from time to time so that it does not stick to the pan. Add the shredded chicken and salt and continue cooking until the mixture is well seasoned and almost dry.

RAJAS DE CHILE POBLANO (*POBLANO CHILE STRIPS*)

MAKES ABOUT 1 HEAPED CUP TO FILL 8 TO 10 *FLAUTAS*

3 tablespoons safflower oil
3 tablespoons finely chopped white onion
1 cup prepared *rajas* (see page 471) of *chile poblano*
½ pound (about 1 large) tomatoes, finely chopped, unpeeled
sea salt to taste
8 heaped tablespoons crumbled *queso fresco*

Heat the oil in a frying pan, add the onion and *chile* strips, and fry gently until the onion is translucent. Add the tomatoes and salt and continue cooking until the sauce has reduced and is well seasoned—about 8 minutes.

Fill the *flautas* with the *rajas*, and before rolling add a good tablespoon of the cheese.

PAPAS GUISADAS (*POTATOES WITH TOMATOES*)

MAKES ABOUT 1 HEAPED CUP TO FILL 8 *FLAUTAS*

This sounds too simple for words, but it is delicious.

½ pound (3 medium) cooked red bliss potatoes, unpeeled
3 tablespoons melted lard or safflower oil
3 tablespoons finely chopped white onion
¼ pound (about 1 small) tomatoes, roughly chopped, unpeeled
sea salt to taste

Mash the potatoes roughly with their skins—they should have some texture.

Heat the lard in a frying pan, add the onion, and fry gently until translucent, about 3 minutes. Add the tomato and cook over medium heat, stirring and scraping the bottom of the pan, for 3 minutes more. Add potatoes with salt to taste and cook until the mixture is almost dry and well seasoned.

PICADILLO BLANCO (GROUND MEAT)

MAKES ABOUT 2 CUPS TO FILL ABOUT 1 DOZEN *FLAUTAS*

½ pound ground beef, medium-fine grind with some fat
3 tablespoons finely chopped white onion
¼ pound (about 1 small) tomatoes, finely chopped, unpeeled
¼ cup roughly chopped Italian parsley
sea salt to taste

Spread the meat over the bottom of an ungreased heavy frying pan and cook over low heat until the fat starts to exude; this will take about 10 minutes, and it will be necessary to stir the meat from time to time and scrape the bottom of the pan to prevent sticking. Add the chopped onion and cook for 3 minutes longer over medium heat. Add the tomato, parsley, and salt and cook until the mixture is fairly dry—about 8 minutes.

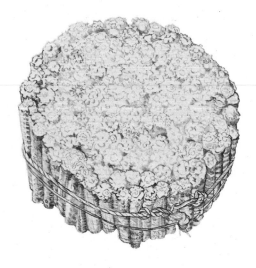

TACOS DE REQUESÓN (*Ricotta Tacos*)

MAKES 6 TACOS

This is a most unusual recipe that was given to me by one of the old families of Patzcuaro. The contrast of textures and the taste of sharp sauce against the rather bland ricotta are surprising and quite delicious, the perfect vegetarian snack. They must be eaten right away, or they will become leathery.

THE SAUCE
⅓ cup fresh lime juice
sea salt to taste
⅓ cup finely chopped radishes
¼ cup finely chopped white onion
1 *chile perón,* black seeds removed and roughly chopped, or any hot green
    chile, chopped with seeds
1 tablespoon roughly chopped *cilantro*

THE *TACOS*
1 cup drained and lightly salted ricotta cheese
6 thin 5-inch corn *tortillas*
6 toothpicks
safflower oil for frying

Have ready a tray lined with a double thickness of paper toweling.

First make the sauce. Put the lime juice and salt into a glass bowl, mix in the rest of the ingredients, and leave for at least 30 minutes to marinate. This should make about 1 cup.

Spread 1 tablespoon of the ricotta over half of each *tortilla.* Fold over and secure with a toothpick.

Put oil to a depth of ¼ inch in a large frying pan and heat. When hot but not smoking, add a few of the *tacos* and fry, turning once until they are a golden color and quite crisp. Continue with the rest, adding oil if necessary.

Drain the *tacos* well on paper toweling and remove as soon as they are cool enough to handle. With a toothpick, ease them open and insert about 2 tablespoons of the sauce. Serve immediately; they cannot wait.

EFIGENIA'S CHILAQUILES

SERVES 4   MICHOACÁN

Making a dish of *chilaquiles* is a simple and delicious way of using up stale *tortillas*, any leftover sauce, and some cheese. It is a national dish, and while ingredients and methods do vary from region to region, they do not vary that much. They are served mostly at brunch time, *almuerzo*, with eggs or grilled meat, accompanied by refried beans. This is Mexican soul food . . . and beware, it is addictive! This is how Efigenia, my housekeeper, prepares them, and while it is a very simple recipe, much will depend on the quality of the corn *tortillas*, the ripeness of the tomatoes, and the richness of the cream used.

¾ pound (about 2 medium) tomatoes, broiled (see page 450)
2 *chiles serranos*, broiled (see page 472)
2 garlic cloves, peeled and roughly chopped
sea salt to taste
⅓ cup safflower oil, approximately
6 large corn *tortillas* cut into 1½-inch squares and dried overnight
¼ cup finely chopped white onion
2 heaped tablespoons roughly chopped *epazote*
⅓ cup crumbled *queso fresco*
⅓ cup sour cream or *crème fraîche* (optional)

Have ready a tray lined with two layers of paper toweling.

Blend together the tomatoes (unskinned), fresh *chiles*, garlic, and salt to taste. Set aside.

Heat about half the oil in a frying pan and fry some of the *tortilla* pieces until slightly crisp and a pale gold color. Remove and drain. Fry the rest of the *tortilla* pieces, adding more oil as necessary.

Drain off all but 2 tablespoons of the oil from the pan, return the fried *tortilla* pieces, add the sauce, and stir well over medium heat for about 2 minutes.

Sprinkle the onion and *epazote* over the top, cover, lower the heat, and cook, shaking the pan from time to time to prevent sticking, for about 8 minutes. By this time the onion should be transparent and the *tortillas* softened but not mushy. Sprinkle with the cheese and cream and serve immediately.

CHILAQUILES DE TEQUILA

SERVES 4 TO 6

This recipe comes from an old Tequila family. Although now the *chilaquiles* are made with a tomato sauce, the daughters of the family tell me that they used to be made with the large, red, smooth-skinned *chilacate* used so much in Jalisco. (I suggest using a dried Anaheim or New Mexican *chile* as a substitute.) *Chilaquiles* are generally eaten for brunch, often to accompany eggs or broiled meats.

6 large *chilacates* or a substitute (see note above)
2 cups water (to cover)
2 garlic cloves, peeled and roughly chopped
½ teaspoon (or to taste) sea salt
⅓ cup melted lard or safflower oil, approximately
3 cups dried corn *tortilla* squares or diamonds (about 15 small *tortillas*)

THE GARNISH
¼ cup finely chopped white onion
⅓ cup finely crumbled *queso adobera* (in Jalisco), *queso añejo*, or Romano cheese

Remove stalks from the dried *chiles*, wipe with a damp cloth, slit open, and remove seeds and veins. Put the water into a saucepan, bring to a simmer, add the cleaned *chiles*, and simmer for 5 minutes. Put 1½ cups of the cooking water into a blender jar, add garlic, salt, and *chiles*, and blend as smoothly as possible. Pass the sauce through a fine sieve or strainer (the *chile* skins are very tough), pressing down well. Discard the *chile* debris and set the sauce aside.

Using a heavy 10-inch frying pan (ideally), heat about one third of the oil and fry one third of the dried *tortilla* pieces over medium to low heat until they are a light golden brown, remove with a slotted spoon, and drain on paper toweling. Add a little more oil and proceed with the rest of the *tortilla* pieces, one third at a time, adding more oil as necessary.

When you have finished frying, drain off all excess oil, return the *tortilla* pieces to the pan, add the sauce, and cook over fairly high heat until the sauce has reduced—about 8 minutes. Adjust seasoning, sprinkle the top with the onion and cheese, and serve immediately.

Note: The sauce should be of medium consistency, neither too dry nor too soupy. Add a little more water if necessary during the blending or cooking time to adjust.

TORTILLAS CON ASIENTO (A Oaxacan Tortilla Snack)

SERVES 1

Walking along the streets of Oaxaca any hour of the day or evening, you are likely to see women on the sidewalks selling what resemble turnovers made of large, soft *tortillas*. They are, in fact, the large, white, soft *tortillas* called *blanditas* doubled over and toasted in the pork drippings that seep through the dough. As you bite into them they are textured and *picante*, rich and luscious all at once, the heartiest *tortilla* snacks that I know of.

Try to find really large (7- to 8-inch) corn *tortillas* for this recipe, but if they are not available, use the normal-sized ones, reducing the filling slightly so that it does not ooze out and scorch on the *comal* or griddle.

This snack lends itself to many innovations; they can be prepared ahead of time and taken on a picnic to be toasted on the barbecue grill or on a griddle over an open fire.

1 5½- to 7-inch corn *tortilla*
1 rounded tablespoon *asiento* (see Ingredients, page 275)
1 tablespoon *frijoles fritos Oaxaqueños* (see Filling, *Tamales de Frijol,* page 75)
a thin layer of finely shredded cabbage
1 tablespoon crumbled *queso fresco*
1½ teaspoons (or to taste) *salsa de chile pasilla de Oaxaca* (page 342) or other hot *chile* sauce

Spread the *tortilla* with the *asiento* and the rest of the ingredients in layers. Set on a hot *comal* or griddle for about 2 minutes, until it is well heated but not crisp. Double the *tortilla* over and press the edges together very firmly. Toast the *tortilla* for about 2 minutes on each side or until crisp and eat with your hands using a large paper napkin to protect your clothes.

ENFRIJOLADAS *(Tortillas in Bean Sauce)*

SERVES 4 TO 6

A typical Oaxacan dish, *enfrijoladas* are served for *almuerzo*, the Mexican brunch, accompanied by broiled or fried *tasaja*, air-dried beef, or as a main meal with *pollo con orégano* (page 220).

If avocado leaves are not available, either fresh or dried, then add *epazote*— not a substitute but an acceptable alternative. While the bean sauce may be prepared ahead and stored or even frozen, the frying of the *tortillas* and the assembly of the dish should be done at the last minute before serving; preparing ahead and reheating will produce a sad, soggy mess.

THE BEAN SAUCE
2 tablespoons lard or safflower oil
½ medium white onion, thickly sliced
2 *chiles de árbol,* left whole, stems removed
a small bunch of tender avocado leaves *or* 5 large mature leaves *or* 4 baby
    stems of *epazote* (see note above)
5 small garlic cloves, charred and peeled (see page 439)
½ cup water
3 cups black *frijoles de olla* (page 179) with their broth
sea salt to taste

THE REST
¼ cup safflower oil, approximately
12 5½- to 6-inch corn *tortillas*
1 medium white onion, cut into fairly thick rings
¾ cup crumbled *queso fresco*
rajas con limón (page 359) or *chiles jalapeños en escabeche* (page 356)

First make the sauce. Heat 1 tablespoon lard in a frying pan, add the ½ onion and dried *chiles,* and fry over medium heat until slightly golden. Transfer with a slotted spoon to a blender jar, reserving the lard. Hold the bunch of avocado leaves over an open flame or place on a hot *comal* and let them sizzle and singe slightly. Crumble the leaves, but not the thick stalks and veins, into the blender jar. Add the garlic and water and blend until smooth. Gradually add the beans and their broth and blend until smooth— you may have to do this in two batches, adding a little water to make the blades work efficiently.

Add a second tablespoon of lard to the pan and heat. Stir in the bean puree and cook over medium heat, stirring and scraping the bottom of the

34

pan from time to time to prevent sticking, until thickened and well seasoned—about 8 to 10 minutes. Adjust salt. Set aside and keep warm, covered, or the bean puree will form a crust on top.

Meanwhile, heat the ¼ cup oil in a small frying pan and fry the *tortillas* one at a time for a few seconds on each side until well heated through—they will probably puff up—but not crisp around the edge. Drain the *tortillas* on paper toweling.

Reheat the bean sauce, which may have thickened too much. Test by immersing a *tortilla;* the sauce should lightly cover it. If it is too thick, add about ½ cup hot water and stir until smooth. Bring to a simmer, immerse the *tortillas* one by one in the sauce, and fold into four. Sprinkle each serving with onion rings and cheese; serve the pickled *chiles* on the side.

ENTOMATADAS *(Tortillas in Tomato Sauce)*

SERVES 4 TO 6

Entomatadas are a popular dish in Oaxaca for *almuerzo*, brunch, accompanied by some broiled air-dried beef, called *tasajo*. They are really simple *enchiladas*, but the *tortillas* are folded into four, and the tomato sauce has decided Oaxacan characteristics.

This dish lends itself to many interpretations for a light meal, accompanied by some broiled chicken or meat and a salad. It is best to use large corn *tortillas*, if available, so that they can be folded more easily.

The sauce may be prepared ahead, but the frying of the *tortillas* and assembly of the *entomatadas* should be done at the last moment, or the dish will turn into a soggy mass of indistinguishable elements.

THE SAUCE
2 tablespoons safflower oil
½ medium white onion, thickly sliced
4 small garlic cloves, peeled
2 whole allspice
2 *chiles serranos* (see page 471) or *chiles de agua* (see page 463), broiled
   (optional)
½ cup cold water
1½ pounds (about 3 large) tomatoes, broiled or stewed (see pages 450 and 451)
3 small leafy stems of *epazote*
sea salt to taste

THE REST
¼ cup safflower oil, approximately
12 5½- to 6-inch corn *tortillas*
1 medium white onion, cut into thick rings
¾ cup crumbled *queso fresco*
a small bunch of tender, flat-leaf parsley, torn into small sprigs

First make the sauce. Heat 1 tablespoon oil in a frying pan, add the onion and garlic, and fry over medium heat, stirring from time to time, until they are slightly golden. Remove the onion and garlic with a slotted spoon and put into a blender jar with the allspice, optional fresh *chiles*, and water and blend until smooth. Gradually add the unpeeled tomatoes and blend until smooth—you may have to do this in two batches. Add another tablespoon of oil to the pan in which the onion was fried and heat well. Add the sauce, the *epazote*, and salt to taste and cook over fairly high heat, stirring and scraping the bottom of the pan until slightly thickened and well seasoned—about 10 minutes. Set aside and keep warm.

Heat ¼ cup of oil in a small frying pan and fry the *tortillas* one by one for a few seconds on each side until well heated through—they will probably puff up—but not crisp around the edge. Drain the *tortillas* on paper toweling.

Reheat the sauce, which may have thickened too much. Test by immersing a *tortilla*; the sauce should lightly cover it. If too thick, then add about ⅓ cup of water and bring up to a simmer. Immerse each *tortilla* in the sauce and fold into four as for *enfrijoladas*. Sprinkle each serving with a few onion rings, crumbled cheese, and a few small sprigs of parsley—serve immediately.

PAPADZULES *(Tortillas in Pumpkin Seed Sauce)*

MAKES 12 *PAPADZULES* TO SERVE 4 TO 6   YUCATÁN

A dish of well-made *papadzules*—from the Mayan words "food for the lords"—is as fascinating to taste as it is beautiful to look at: the rolled *tortillas* covered with a pale green sauce, the vivid accent of color given by the tomato sauce, and then the pools of green oil—squeezed from the pumpkin seeds— that add depth and sparkle to the whole. *Papadzules* could hold their own in any international gastronomic display.

Because this dish relies on few ingredients, they must be of the highest quality to allow you to appreciate the delicacy of flavor—although this concentrated pumpkin seed sauce is quite an acquired taste.

It is rare to find this dish well executed commercially because none but the most exacting cooks will bother to extract the oil that gives the *toque final* (special finishing touch), for appearance and contrast of flavor.

Although all the component parts of this dish may be prepared ahead, the final assembly will have to be done at the last moment, especially the sprinkling of the oil, which should be done seconds before serving, or it will sink back into the sauce.

The dish is usually served warm as a first course by itself.

Although it's relatively simple to execute there are some points to watch:

When toasting the pumpkin seeds, toss or stir constantly; they should swell and turn a slightly different color, but do not allow them to brown, or the sauce and oil will be brownish instead of green. Do not grind them to a flour; they should still have a texture, although slight.

Add the broth gradually; you may not need ¼ cup, depending on the freshness of the seeds.

Take care when heating the sauce; keep the heat low and keep stirring and scraping the bottom of the pan. If the heat is too high, the sauce will stick to the pan and become grainy. If that happens, put the sauce back into the blender with a little warm water and blend briefly.

2½ cups water
2 large leafy stems of *epazote* (no substitute)
1 scant teaspoon (or to taste) sea salt
½ pound (about 1⅔ cups) hulled raw pumpkin seeds
12 freshly made corn *tortillas,* kept hot
5 hard-cooked eggs, shelled, roughly chopped, and salted to taste
1 cup *salsa de jitomate Yucateca* (page 341)
2 additional large hard-cooked eggs, whites and yolks separately chopped finely,
 for garnish
12 *epazote* leaves, for garnish (optional)

Have ready a warmed, not hot, serving dish onto which 12 rolled *tortillas* will fit with a little space around them for the extra sauce.

Put the water, *epazote,* and salt into a pan, bring to a simmer, and continue simmering for about 5 minutes. Set aside and keep hot. Spread the pumpkin seeds over the bottom of a heavy frying pan and toast them over low heat, tossing and stirring until they swell up and turn a more intense green, about 3 minutes—but do not allow them to brown. Spread onto a large plate to cool. When cool, put a small quantity at a time into an electric spice grinder and grind for about 5 to 6 seconds to a fine but textured consistency. Turn out onto a plate with a slight ridge around it.

Measure out ¼ cup of the hot *epazote* broth. Sprinkle the ground seeds with a little of the broth, kneading them together until they form a crumbly paste—you may not need all the broth. (If you add too much water, you will get a pale green sauce instead of a darkish green paste. If that should happen, you will have to add some more ground seeds and knead the mixture well.) Almost immediately the paste will take on a shiny surface; keep on kneading and squeezing. Tip the oil into a small container. If you have resolve, you should be able to extract between ¼ and ⅓ cup.

Strain about 1½ cups of the hot broth into a blender jar, crumble the paste into it, and blend until smooth. Return to the frying or other heavy pan and stir in the remaining broth. Heat the sauce over very low heat, stirring and scraping the bottom of the pan almost continuously, until the sauce thickens slightly. Dip one of the *tortillas* into the broth; it should coat the *tortilla* well. Put a little of the chopped egg across the middle of the *tortilla* and roll it up loosely on the serving dish. Continue with the rest of the *tortillas.* By the time you have finished the sauce will have thickened, so add a little more warm water if necessary and pour the remaining sauce over the *papadzules.* Pour the tomato sauce in a thick band in the middle of the *papadzules,* sprinkle with bands of white and yolk of the extra eggs, and decorate with the extra *epazote* leaves. Last of all, decorate with small pools of the green oil. Serve immediately.

ANTOJITOS OF CORN MASA

Chalupas ("Canoes")
Quesadillas
Molotes
Chorizo y Papa (Chorizo and Potato Filling)
Carne Deshebrada (Shredded Beef Filling)
Molotes Oaxaqueños (Oaxacan Molotes)
Sopitos Colimenses (Little Sopes from Colima)
Tlacoyos
Cazuelitas
Polkanes ("Snake's Head" Snack)
Pintos
Chochoyotes (Small Dumplings)
Panuchos

As the last rays of the sun make long shadows of the buildings and dusk begins to fall, many a Mexican street corner comes alive. It is like watching a play as the crowd steals on silently, the main figures carrying charcoal braziers and *comals*, followed by a string of children with buckets of *masa* and water, small bowls with fillings to be reheated, sauces and chopped onion, *cilantro* and *chiles*. The buckets and bowls in brilliantly colored plastic, each with its blue enamel spoon, are the hallmarks of the modern Mexican kitchen. The air is filled with the unmistakable smell of resinous pine (*ocote*) that suddenly bursts into flame and sets the charcoal smoking. It is not long before the *comal* is sizzling with oil and the first *antojitos* are patted out and coaxed into shape—round, oval, thick, thin, stuffed, or mixed with beans . . . whatever the local specialty may be. These are *picadas* from Jalisco, *tlacoyos* from Hidalgo, *garnachas* from Veracruz, *gordas* from the Bajio, *sopes*, *pelliscadas* *pintos*, pinched up at the edge or in the middle—an infinity of shapes and flavors.

These *antojitos* (little whims) are snacks made of corn *tortilla* dough. Sometimes they're served at the beginning of the midday meal, but they are mainly considered evening food and at their best when eaten with the fingers, standing up, in the company of others, and if it isn't in the street, eaten in the kitchen with everything hot from the stove.

CHALUPAS *("Canoes")*

MAKES 12 CHALUPAS

No, they are not flat and fried; those are *tostadas*. And no, they did not originate in California. *Chalupas*, oval-shaped *masa* snacks, are named for the small canoes, *chalupas*, that have been used since pre-Columbian times in the waterways between the *chinampas*, the floating gardens of Xochimilco.

Chalupas are regional *antojitos*, found only in and around Mexico City, as far away as Puebla.

There are two methods of forming *chalupas*, depending on whether you like your dough thin or thick.

Like other *masa* snacks, they should be trimmed and eaten as soon as they are cooked; otherwise they tend to become heavy and tough.

¾ pound (1½ cups) prepared corn *tortilla masa* (page 8)
melted lard or safflower oil for reheating (optional)
2 Alligator Baggies for pressing *tortillas*

THE TOPPING
1½ cups *pollo deshebrado para tacos* (page 218), warmed
¾ cup *salsa verde cruda* (page 336)
6 heaped tablespoons finely chopped white onion
6 tablespoons finely crumbled *queso fresco*

Work the *masa* well until it is soft and smooth. Divide it into 12 equal portions and roll each into a ball about 1¼ inches in diameter. While you work with one, place the rest under a damp towel or piece of plastic wrap to prevent the *masa* from drying out.

Set an ungreased *comal* over medium heat.

Roll one of the balls into a thin cylinder about 3 inches long. Open the *tortilla* press and line it with Baggies as you would for making *tortillas* (page 12). Place the cylinder on the bottom Baggie and press down with the top plate of the press, but not too hard, so that the *masa* is pressed out to a thin oval shape. Lift up the bottom Baggie. Place the dough on the fingers of your other hand and peel off the Baggie (just as in making *tortillas*) and place the dough carefully onto the hot *comal*. Leave it there until the underside of the dough is patchily opaque—about 1 minute. Remove it from the *comal* and pinch the dough around the edge to form a low rim. Replace the *chalupa* on the *comal* and cook on each side for another 1 or 2 minutes, until the dough is cooked through and lightly speckled with brown spots. Trim, add toppings, and serve immediately (see below), or when all have been made, heat them through in a lightly greased pan, smearing a little lard over the surface of the *chalupa*, before topping them.

Shaping Chalupas, Method 2

Take one ball of the dough and roll it into a bobbin shape (see photo). Make a deep impression in the center with your index finger to form a canoelike shape. Cook it on an ungreased *comal* for about 5 minutes on bottom and top and then a further 1 minute on each side. The dough should be opaque and speckled with flecks of brown.

Place enough melted lard in a frying pan to cover the bottom and reheat the *chalupas* briefly on all sides—they should not become crusty and brown—then trim and serve.

For lack of space on top of *chalupas* made following method 2, a generous half portion of the topping ingredients should be sufficient.

QUESADILLAS

MAKES 12 4½-INCH *QUESADILLAS*

In many places *quesadillas* have degenerated since I first went to live in Mexico; they were never a doubled-over flour *tortilla* with melted cheese inside. They are, in fact, an *empanada* of corn *masa* filled with one of the fillings given below. While the more traditional cooks still cook them on a lightly greased *comal*, when made commercially in large numbers they are fried crisp in oil or lard.

Like other *antojitos* of this type, they should be served the moment they come off the heat; otherwise they will be tough. They are served without a sauce or other topping and make a great accompaniment to a bowl of soup.

lard or safflower oil for the *comal*
¾ pound (1½ cups) prepared corn *tortilla masa* (page 8)
2 Alligator Baggies for pressing *masa*

Heat the *comal* or griddle over a medium heat and grease it lightly.

Work the *masa* well with your hands for a few moments, until very soft and smooth. Divide it into 12 pieces and roll each into a ball about 1¼ inches in diameter. While working with the first ones, keep the rest under a damp cloth or plastic wrap to prevent the *masa* from drying out.

Press out one of the balls to a diameter of about 4½ inches in the lined *tortilla* press as if making a *tortilla* (page 12). Remove the top Baggie, put one tablespoon of the filling (see below) on one half of the dough, double the other side over the filling, and press the edges of the dough together.

Cook on the *comal* until the underside of the dough has become opaque and speckled with dark brown spots—about 5 minutes. Turn the *quesadilla* over and cook on the second side for 5 minutes. When properly cooked, the *masa* will have a slight crust on the outside and be soft but not raw on the inside. Serve immediately.

Fried Quesadillas

If you prefer to have crisp fried *quesadillas*, heat the oil, or better still melted lard, to a depth of about ¼ inch. Fry to a deep golden color, about 2 to 3 minutes on each side. Drain on paper toweling and serve immediately.

Fillings for Quesadillas

1. *The* most traditional of fillings is a strip of *queso Oaxaca*, or string cheese, a strip of peeled fresh *chile poblano*, and one or two *epazote* leaves. For 12 *quesadillas* you will need about 6 ounces of cheese, 12 strips of *chile*, and 12 *epazote* leaves.
2. 1½ cups *flor de calabaza* (page 150), when in season
3. 1½ cups cooked *cuitlacoche* (page 168), when in season
4. 1½ cups *hongos al vapor* (page 164)
5. 1½ cups *chorizo y papa* (page 46)

MOLOTES

MAKES 12 MOLOTES   SIERRA DE PUEBLA

Molotes—there is no good translation for the word in this context—are small fried bobbins of *masa*, filled with shredded meat, or *chorizo* cooked with potato. They are eaten hot and plain, without sauce.

While the *molotes* may be filled and shaped ahead, they should be kept under a damp towel or plastic wrap so that the *masa* does not form a hard crust on the outside. They are served as soon as they come out of the pan; if they have to stand around or be reheated, they become tough.

½ pound (1 cup) prepared corn *tortilla masa* (page 8)
2 tablespoons softened lard
1 teaspoon (or to taste) sea salt
2 Alligator Baggies for pressing *masa*
carne deshebrada or *chorizo y papa* (recipes follow)
⅓ cup, approximately, melted lard or safflower oil for frying

Mix the *masa*, lard, and salt together until you have a smooth, pliable dough that does not stick to your hands. Divide the dough into 12 pieces, rolling each into a ball about 1 to 1¼ inches in diameter; cover with a damp cloth or plastic wrap. Line the *tortilla* press with Baggies.

Roll one ball at a time into a cylinder about 2¼ inches by ¾ inch. As if you were making *tortillas* (page 12), press the dough out lightly to form an egg shape about 4 inches long. Remove the top Baggie, lift the bottom Baggie, and transfer the dough to the upper part of the right or left hand, whichever way you work. Carefully peel off the Baggie. Place 1 tablespoon of the filling down the center of the dough, then press the edges together, covering the filling completely. Roll the dough between your hands (lightly grease your hands if dough is sticking to them) and form the filled dough into a bobbin shape (see photos).

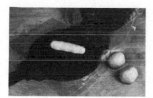  

Continue with the rest of the dough, placing the formed *molotes* back under the damp cloth while the lard is heating. Heat the lard in a small frying pan (the lard should be about 1 inch deep) and fry the *molotes* a few at a time, turning them over until they are an even, deep gold color and cooked through—about 3 minutes on each side over medium heat. Then increase the heat and allow them to fry for a minute or so more to become a very deep brown color. Drain on paper toweling and serve immediately.

CHORIZO Y PAPA (CHORIZO AND POTATO FILLING)

MAKES ABOUT 1 LOOSELY PACKED CUP TO FILL 12 MOLOTES

1 tablespoon lard
2 ounces (1 small link) *chorizo*
¼ pound (about 2 small) red bliss potatoes, diced and cooked
sea salt to taste

Heat the lard in a small frying pan. Skin and crumble the *chorizo*, discarding the skin. Fry over very low heat until the fat has rendered out of the *chorizo* and it is just about to become crisp. (If the *chorizo* you are using is very fatty, you may want to drain off some of the excess fat, leaving just enough to fry the potato.) Add the potato, mash roughly into the *chorizo*, and cook over slightly higher heat for about 3 minutes. Taste for salt.

CARNE DESHEBRADA (SHREDDED BEEF FILLING)

MAKES 1 WELL-PACKED CUP TO FILL 12 MOLOTES WITH PROBABLY A LITTLE LEFT OVER FOR A COUPLE OF TACOS

2 tablespoons melted lard or safflower oil
2 tablespoons finely chopped white onion
3 (or to taste) *chiles serranos,* finely chopped
¼ pound (about ¾ cup) ripe tomatoes, finely chopped
1 cup *carne deshebrada* (the meat) for *Salpicon de res* (page 298)
sea salt to taste

Heat the lard in a medium frying pan. Add the onion, fresh *chiles,* and tomatoes and fry over fairly high heat for about 3 minutes, turning the mixture over from time to time to prevent sticking. Add the shredded beef, mix well, and continue cooking until the juice of the tomatoes has been absorbed. Taste for salt. When the beef is shiny and just beginning to fry—in about 5 minutes—remove it from the heat and keep warm.

MOLOTES OAXAQUEÑOS *(Oaxacan Molotes)*

MAKES 12 MOLOTES

The *molotes* from Oaxaca are virtually the same as the ones given in the previous recipe; the *masa* and filling *are* the same, but in Oaxaca they are served differently.

I was shown a different way of forming them in Oaxaca. The dough is pressed out to a thin disk in the *tortilla* press. The *molotes* are then formed and fried in the usual way. Each *molote* is served on a romaine lettuce leaf, the top spread with a little black bean paste and sprinkled with crumbled *queso fresco*. *Salsa de chile pasilla de Oaxaca* is passed separately.

½ pound (1 cup) prepared corn *tortilla masa* (page 8)
2 tablespoons softened lard
1 teaspoon (or to taste) sea salt
2 Alligator Baggies for pressing *masa*
⅓ cup, approximately, melted lard or safflower oil for frying
chorizo y papa (page 46)
12 romaine lettuce leaves
¾ cup *frijoles fritos Oaxaqueños* (see Filling, Tamales de Frijol, page 75)
6 tablespoons crumbled *queso fresco*
salsa de chile pasilla de Oaxaca (page 342)

Mix the *masa*, lard, and salt together until you have a smooth, malleable dough that does not stick to your hands. Divide the dough into 12 pieces and roll each into a ball about 1 to 1¼ inches in diameter. Cover with a damp cloth or plastic wrap to prevent them from drying out.

Press out one of the balls of dough in the *tortilla* press, following the instructions for making *tortillas* (page 12). Remove the top Baggie and put a small spoonful of the filling across the center of the dough. Lifting up the bottom Baggie, with dough, etc., begin to roll the dough off the Baggie so that it covers the filling well. Then (greasing your hands lightly if necessary) roll into a tapered cylinder shape, just like a bobbin. Place under the damp cloth and form the rest of the *molotes*.

Heat the lard or oil (it should be about ½ inch deep) and fry a few of the *molotes* at a time—they should not touch in the pan, or they will not brown properly. Turn them over from time to time until they are a deep golden color. Drain on paper toweling and serve as suggested. They should be eaten immediately as the dough tends to get tough if held.

SOPITOS COLIMENSES *(Little Sopes from Colima)*

MAKES 24 2½-INCH *SOPITOS*

Sopes are one of the popular snacks of central Mexico; they are small cakes of corn *masa*, pinched up around the edge when half cooked to form a rim—presumably to stop the sauce from running off the edge. These *sopitos*, or little *sopes*, have a different topping and sauce from those prepared elsewhere.

Señora Yolando Alcaraz, who gave me this recipe, was brought up in Colima. An avid cook, she has seriously studied her regional food, particularly that which is traditionally served for *fiestas*, banquets, and baptisms.

According to Señora Alcaraz, these small *antojitos* should be about the size of the top of a water glass (about 2½ inches in diameter). The sauce made to go on them is unusual because it is fairly thin, diluted with pork stock, and not fried or reduced.

THE MEAT TOPPING
1 pound very finely ground pork, with some fat left on
¼ cup finely chopped white onion
1 whole allspice, crushed
4 peppercorns, crushed
1 whole clove, crushed
1 garlic clove, peeled and finely chopped
sea salt to taste
4 cups pork broth (page 248) or lightly salted water

THE SAUCE
1 pound (about 22 medium) *tomate verde*
2 *chiles de árbol,* lightly toasted, stems removed, crumbled
2 cups reduced pork broth (page 248)
sea salt to taste

THE *SOPITOS*
1¼ pounds (about 2½ cups) prepared corn *tortilla masa* (page 8) *or* 2 cups
   masa harina mixed with approximately 1⅓ cups warm water
2 Alligator Baggies for pressing *masa*

THE FINAL TOPPING
1 cup finely chopped white onion
1 cup finely sliced red radishes
3 cups closely packed, finely shredded cabbage, soaked 1 hour in 3 cups lightly
   salted water mixed with ¼ cup fresh lime juice
1 cup finely ground *queso añejo* or a substitute (see pages 444–445)

The Meat Topping

The meat should be finely ground. Have the butcher pass it twice through the grinder or process it in a food processor, adding the rest of the ingredients except the broth and processing until well incorporated.

Divide the mixture in half and roll each portion into a large ball.

Heat the pork broth or lightly salted water, and as it comes up to a simmer add the meatballs. Cook over gentle heat for about 20 minutes. Remove from the heat and let the meatballs sit in the water for a further 10 minutes. Remove and drain. Return the broth to the saucepan and reduce to 2 cups over high heat.

Crumble the meat with your hands or in a *molcajete* (Señora Alcaraz says the stone enhances the flavor) and set aside in a warm place.

The Sauce

Remove the husks from the *tomate verde*, rinse, put into a pan, cover with water, and cook until tender but not falling apart—about 10 minutes, depending on size. Drain, discarding the cooking water.

Put the drained *tomates*, crumbled dried *chiles*, and broth into a blender jar and blend for a few seconds, until almost smooth. Set aside and keep warm.

The Sopitos

Work the *masa* well with your hands, adding a little more water if necessary to make it smooth and pliable. Divide the dough into 12 pieces and make 2 1-inch balls of each piece. Cover those already made with a damp cloth to prevent them from drying out. Using a *tortilla* press and Baggies as for making *tortillas* (page 12), flatten the dough out to make a disk about 3 inches in diameter. Place on a well-greased *comal* for about 3 minutes on the first side or until the dough is opaque and speckled with brown, then flip them over to cook for about 2 minutes on the other side.

Press the *masa* up around the edge to form a shallow ridge and return it to the *comal* for a minute or 2 longer. The *masa* should still be moist but not raw. Serve each *sopito* topped generously with about 1 tablespoon shredded meat, a little chopped onion, and a few radish slices; smother with shredded cabbage, sprinkle with cheese, and finish off with about 2 tablespoons sauce. Serve immediately.

Note: Sopitos can be served "soft" as above or, after cooking on the *comal*, fried in lard until very slightly crisp on the outside.

TLACOYOS

MAKES 12 *TLACOYOS*

Tlacoyo is the Nahuatl name for this oval-shaped *antojito* of corn *masa* filled with mashed cooked beans or other pulses. They are made in slightly different forms in the states of Mexico, Puebla, and Hidalgo. While they are generally cooked on a well-greased *comal*, they can also be fried in lard.

These particular *tlacoyos* are made of white *masa*, while perhaps the most spectacular ones of all are those made on the sidewalks of the villages around Toluca on market days: thick oval shapes of blue *masa*, about 5 inches long, with a wide yellow band of mashed dried fava beans in the middle. While *tlacoyos* can be prepared ahead, they tend to toughen while waiting around.

½ pound (1 cup) prepared corn *tortilla masa* (page 8), not too damp
2 tablespoons softened lard
1 teaspoon (or to taste) sea salt
1 cup dried black, white, or fava beans, cooked and mashed or refried
lard for greasing *comal* or frying *tlacoyos*
1¼ cups *salsa de tomate verde, cocida* (page 337)
6 tablespoons finely chopped white onion, approximately
6 tablespoons grated *queso añejo* or a substitute (pages 444–445), approximately

Mix together the *masa*, lard, and salt and work until you have a smooth, malleable dough that does not stick to your hands. Divide the dough into 12 balls about 1½ inches in diameter. Line the *tortilla* press with the Baggies. Roll the balls into cylinders (see photo, page 41) about 2½ inches by 1 inch and press out with a *tortilla* press or with your hands to an oval shape about 3½ by 3 inches. Place 1 tablespoon of the mashed beans along the center of the dough, press the edges of the dough together to cover the filling, and gently flatten the shape between your hands to form an oval shape.

To cook the *tlacoyos* on a griddle: Liberally grease the surface of the *comal* with lard, taking care that the fat does not slide off into the flame. Place some of the *tlacoyos* on the griddle and cook over medium heat for about 4 minutes on each side—when cooked, the surfaces should be opaque and speckled with brown while the inside is still moist but not raw.

To fry the *tlacoyos*: Heat ½ cup of lard in a small frying pan and fry the *tlacoyos* a few at a time until very lightly golden with a tender crust on the outside and moist but not raw inside. Drain on paper toweling.

Heat the green sauce. If it has thickened while standing, add a little water to dilute to a medium consistency that lightly coats the back of a wooden spoon. Just before serving, immerse the *tlacoyos* for 1 minute, no more. Put them on the plates with a little more sauce on top and sprinkle with onion and cheese.

CAZUELITAS

MAKES 12 CAZUELITAS   SEÑORA BERTA G. DE MORALES DORIA

Cazuelitas are from the northern state of Nuevo Leon. These delicious little snacks have been so named because they are formed to resemble small *cazuelas*, the Mexican earthenware cooking casseroles. There they accompany the "dry soup" rice course. They make a wonderful hors d'oeuvre, albeit a very filling one, because you really cannot stop after the first. *Cazuelitas* may be filled with either *chorizo* or zucchini cooked with tomato, both with grated cheese on top. Like so many other *masa antojitos*, they must be eaten the moment they are fried, although they can be formed ahead and kept under a damp towel or plastic.

about ½ pound (1 scant cup) prepared corn *tortilla masa* (page 8)
¼ pound (about 2 small) red bliss potatoes, cooked with their skins
⅓ cup grated *Chihuahua* cheese or medium-sharp Cheddar
sea salt to taste
lard or safflower oil for frying

Put the *masa* into a bowl and crush the potatoes with their skins into it. Add the cheese and salt to taste and mix well—the dough should be lumpy but soft and pliable. Add a little water if it seems dry. Divide the dough into 12 pieces and roll into balls about 1¼ inches in diameter. Take one of the balls, press your thumb into the middle to form a well, and gradually work the dough out into a flared cup—or *cazuela*—shape. The dough will be about ¼ inch thick around the sides and slightly thicker on the bottom.

Put enough melted lard or oil into a frying pan to measure about ½ inch deep. When hot, carefully put the *cazuelitas* into it face down and fry for about 5 minutes, then turn them over and fry for about 8 minutes or until they are crusty and a deep golden color. The dough inside the crust should be soft but not raw. Drain on paper toweling, fill, and serve immediately.

Fillings for Cazuelitas

½ pound *chorizo*, skinned, crumbled, and fried, plus ⅓ cup finely grated Chihuahua cheese or 1½ cups *calabacitas guisadas* (page 152)

51

POLKANES *("Snake's Head" Snack)*

MAKES 10 *POLKANES*

Polkan is the Mayan word for the head of a snake—these little snacks consist of *tortilla* dough wrapped around beans, chives, and toasted pumpkin seeds and formed like a snake's head. They are then fried and served with tomato sauce. They make perfect "grazing" food and are vegetarian to boot. Of course, if you are not up on your snakes, make them into any form; that of *molotes* (page 44) might be the best.

In Yucatán fresh *ibis*, flattish tender beans, are used but could be adequately replaced by small lima beans. Unhulled pumpkin seeds and a flat-leaf chive called *cebollina* in Yucatán are used. They should be eaten as soon as they are made, or they will turn leathery.

½ pound (1 cup) prepared corn *tortilla masa* (page 8)
4½ teaspoons flour
½ teaspoon (or to taste) sea salt
lard or safflower oil for frying
2 Alligator Baggies if you're using a *tortilla* press
½ cup cooked lima beans
rounded ¼ cup ground toasted unhulled pumpkin seeds
3 tablespoons finely chopped chives
sea salt to taste
1 cup *salsa de jitomate Yucateca* (page 341)

Mix the *masa* with the flour and salt. Divide the dough into 10 pieces and roll each into a ball about 1¼ inches in diameter. Cover all but the ball you are going to use with a damp cloth so that the dough will not dry out. Heat lard to a depth of ½ inch in a small pan over low heat.

Using either your hands (see photos) or a *tortilla* press, as for *molotes*, press the ball of dough out to a disk about 3½ inches in diameter. Put a few beans, ground pumpkin seeds, chives, and a sprinkling of salt in the center, then fold the dough over and all around, covering the filling completely. Form into snake's heads or what you will and fry until golden brown and crisp all over—about 7 minutes. Drain on paper toweling. Serve immediately with a little of the sauce.

PINTOS

MAKES 12 *PINTOS*

Pintos are a favorite *antojito* around Xicotepec de Juarez in the Sierra de Puebla. Black beans are used almost exclusively in the area, and they should be cooked but still whole and not mushy (not *al dente* beans, please!); salt, and nothing else, is added toward the end of the cooking time.

The *tortilla masa* should not be too moist. It can be mixed with the rest of the ingredients ahead of time, but the *pintos* should be eaten the moment they are made or, like other *masa* snacks, they will become tough in reheating.

¾ pound (1½ cups) prepared corn *tortilla masa* (page 8)
3 tablespoons softened lard
1 teaspoon (or to taste) sea salt
2 Alligator Baggies if you're using a *tortilla* press
¾ cup *frijoles negros de olla* (see note above and recipe, page 179)
1¼ cups *salsa de jitomate, Sierra de Puebla* (page 339), kept hot
6 tablespoons finely chopped white onion
¾ cup finely grated *queso añejo* or Romano cheese

Heat an ungreased *comal* over medium heat. Mix the *masa* with the lard and salt to make a smooth, pliable dough. Carefully mix in the beans, taking care not to break them up. Divide the dough into 12 pieces and roll each piece into a ball about 1½ inches in diameter. Press out the ball in a *tortilla* press (page 12) or between your hands to make a thickish *tortilla* about 3½ inches in diameter.

Place several of the *pintos* on the *comal* and cook over medium heat for about 5 minutes. (If the *comal* is too hot, the dough will be burned on the outside and raw inside.) By this time the dough should be opaque and slightly browned and come easily from the surface of the *comal*. Turn the *pintos* over and cook for 3 minutes longer. Remove the *pintos* from the *comal* and, when cool enough to handle, press the dough up to form a slight ridge around the circumference. Pass each *pinto* through the warming sauce and serve immediately, putting a little more sauce on the top and sprinkling it with the onion and cheese.

Note: As an alternative, serve the *pintos* topped with *chile macho* (page 360) and sprinkled with cheese and onion as above.

CHOCHOYOTES *(Small Dumplings)*

MAKES 18 1¼-INCH DUMPLINGS (THEY GROW IN COOKING)   OAXACA

Chochoyotes, or *chochoyones* (called *ombligitos* in Veracruz), are small dumplings with a deep indentation in the middle that are cooked in soups, stews,
or beans in Oaxaca. *Asiento,* the dark, fatty residue from making *chicharrón,* is
usually used for making them, but since it is difficult to obtain, unless you
live in Oaxaca or make friends with a *chicharrón* maker, the substitute suggested
should be used.

> ½ pound (1 cup) prepared corn *tortilla masa* (page 8)
> 2 heaped tablespoons *asiento* or a substitute (page 275)
> sea salt to taste

Mix all the ingredients together and divide the dough into 18 equal
pieces. Roll each piece into a small ball about 1 inch in diameter. Then (see
photo), taking one of the balls in the palm of one hand, press a well in the
center—but not through the dough completely—with the index finger of your
other hand and rotate until you have a circular shape on the outside, with the
dough about ½ inch thick in the well. Set aside and continue with the rest of
the balls.

To cook, carefully place the *chochoyotes* in the simmering broth, sauce,
or beans, push down gently to cover as much as possible, and cook for about
15 to 20 minutes.

PANUCHOS

The popular evening snacks in Yucatán are *panuchos;* they are rich but wonderful. A slit is made in a puffed-up tortilla to form a pocket; it is stuffed with black bean paste and a slice of hard-cooked egg, fried, and then topped with chicken in escabeche or other shredded meats or used with shark (*pan de cazón,* page 210) and liberally strewn with soused onions. In fact, they lend themselves to many innovations. As with any *masa antojito,* they are much better fried in lard, but oil can be substituted.

You can prepare them ahead up to the point of stuffing and then fry and top them at the last moment. After being stuffed they can even be frozen.

about ½ pound (1 scant cup) prepared corn *tortilla masa* (page 8)
12 rounded tablespoons *frijoles colados y fritos a la Yucateca* (page 186)
12 slices hard-cooked egg
lard or safflower oil for frying
1½ cups shredded *pollo en escabeche rojo* (page 238) or any shredded meats
  or shark, approximately
1½ cups *cebollas en escabeche* (page 363)

Divide the *masa* into 12 pieces and roll each into a ball about 1¼ inches in diameter. While you work with one, keep the rest under a piece of plastic wrap or a damp towel to prevent drying. Follow the instructions for making a *tortilla* (page 12), making sure that it puffs up. If it doesn't look very promising, then press the dough very lightly with a towel. It should then puff up enough at least to make a slit about one third of the way around the edge of the dough on the side that has puffed up.

Put a very full tablespoon of bean paste into the pocket that has been formed, then a slice of egg. Press down and continue with the rest. *Alternatively,* cook all the *panuchos,* cutting the skin for the pockets and then filling them all together.

Heat the lard in a medium frying pan. Have ready a tray lined with a double layer of paper toweling. Heat the shredded meat and have the onion rings at hand. Put one or two of the *panuchos* flat in the frying pan and fry for a few minutes on each side until golden and the edge is slightly crisp. Drain first over the pan and then on the paper toweling. Top with plenty of the shredded meat and soused onion rings and serve immediately, just as they are, with nothing else.

TAMALES

The *tamales* of Mexico warrant a study of their own, so varied are their shapes, wrappings, ingredients both rare (alligator tail) and mundane (chicken), flavors, and textures. A delicate *tamale* made with care is a gastronomic delight.

There are *tamales* of the thinnest *masa*—a mere film of dough is spread on the banana leaf—like those of *mole* from Oaxaca, and of the thickest, gelatinous *masa*, like the *colados* from Yucatán, the puffy white ones from central Mexico, and the rough-textured *sacahuil*, either savory or sweet, from the Huasteca. But most of these differences depend on the way in which the corn is prepared for the *masa*.

Many coastal areas use an ordinary *tortilla masa* for making their thin *tamales* wrapped in banana leaves, while the thicker ones wrapped in corn husks are usually made with corn that has been *refregado*, cleaned of all the transparent skins, and less finely ground. As you will see, the dough for *tamales colados* (page 68) is very different again. The corn is not cooked, just soaked with lime, then the dough is strained and cooked with lard and water to make a fine, gelatinous *masa*. The corn used for the Huastec *sacahuil*, as well as that used for the Oaxacan barbecue, is just broken up, *martajado*, while in the hot country of eastern Michoacán, *masa* of dark corn is left to sour overnight.

The word *tamal, tamale* in English usage, covers more than one suspects. In fact, it refers to anything wrapped and cooked in a corn husk: small fish or embryo frogs seasoned with tomato and *chile*; a pasty mess of wild cherries; a spongy wheat flour dough flavored with the toasted and ground seeds of the corn flower, resembling Chinese steamed buns and called a *tamal de espiga*; spongy yellow ones made of rice flour and butter stuffed with raisins, known as *canarios* (resembling British steamed pudding); and so on.

Tamales, with few exceptions, are usually served alone—no sauce, no topping. The exceptions are mostly in Michoacán: *corundas*, unfilled, and *uchepos* are served with sauce and cream, and the *tamales* on the Michoacán/ Jalisco border, served as they are with a tomato sauce and crisp vegetables, would make the central Mexican purist frown.

There are some marked regional differences in the preparation of *masas*, or doughs, for *tamales*. The most highly esteemed ones in the central area around Mexico City are white and spongy, made from specially prepared flour for which the recipe follows. Several years ago a commercially made and distributed *tamale* flour of high quality was on the market in Mexico. Now that has disappeared, and a totally inferior yellow one is being touted to the unknowing. Why can't cornmeal be substituted? Because it is too granular, and the parched corn has not undergone the soaking in a lime solution that gives it a special quality and flavor.

Substitutions in the following recipes will be suggested where feasible and acceptable.

MASA REFREGADA SPECIALLY PREPARED FOR TAMALES

MAKES ABOUT 3½ POUNDS MASA

Tamales made with the following *masa* are not as spongy as those made with flour but are spongier than those made with *tortilla masa.* Each recipe will indicate which should be used.

2 pounds dried white corn
2½ quarts cold water, approximately
5 teaspoons powdered lime (see page 7)

Put the corn into a stainless-steel or enamel pan. Cover with cold water and set over low heat. Dilute the lime in 1 cup of water and add to the pan, pressing out the lumps through a fine strainer. Stir well. The skins of the corn kernels will almost immediately turn bright yellow. Bring the corn up to a simmer—about 20 minutes. Remove from heat, cover the pan, and set aside overnight or for about 8 hours.

The following morning, strain the corn and put into fresh water, rubbing it through your hands to remove the yellow skins. Strain and cover with fresh water and repeat the rubbing process. It will take about 4 or 5 changes of water and about half an hour's work to rub off all the yellow skins, leaving the corn white. Drain well and grind or send to the mill to be ground to a textured dough, not as fine as that for *tortillas.* The *masa* can be used at once or frozen and stored for future use. It should keep for several months.

TEXTURED CORN FLOUR FOR TAMALES

MAKES ABOUT 1 POUND, 10 OUNCES

The whitest, spongiest *tamales* of central Mexico are made of a textured flour of ground hominy. This flour is still available in and around Mexico City and sold loose in some grocery stores. (There used to be an excellent brand that was widely distributed by Nabisco, but I have not seen it around in recent years. Avoid at all costs the very inferior packaged yellow type of flour masquerading as *tamale* flour.) However, if you have the patience and access to a (dry) grain mill, you can always make your own. You could make it in quantity and keep it in a hermetically sealed container in the refrigerator; it should keep well for several months.

The nearest substitute for this flour would be white grits that have been more finely ground.

2 pounds dried whole hominy or white corn
2½ quarts cold water, approximately
5 teaspoons powdered lime (see page 7)

Put the corn into a stainless-steel or enamel pan. Cover with cold water and set over low heat. Dilute the lime in 1 cup water and add to the pan, pressing out the lumps through a fine strainer. Stir well. The skins of the corn kernels will almost immediately turn bright yellow. Bring the corn up to a simmer—about 20 minutes—and continue to simmer for about 7 minutes longer. Cover the pan, remove from the heat, and set aside for about 1 hour. Strain corn and put into fresh water, rubbing it through your hands to loosen the yellow skins. Strain and cover with fresh water, repeating the rubbing process. It will take about 4 or 5 changes of water and about half an hour's work to rub off all the yellow skins, leaving the corn white.

Spread the corn out on a fine-mesh wire rack to dry, turning it over from time to time. If it is put into the full sun, it will take about 2 days to dry, but you can also put it into a very low oven, or in an airy warm place, or near an electric fan and dry it out in less time, for about 1 day.

Grind to a textured consistency like fine grits or cornmeal—take care not to overgrind to a powder. Pass through a fine sieve to extract all the tough pedicels that remain after the grinding.

Use immediately or store in a cool place as suggested.

TAMALE WRAPPERS

The choices are: corn husks fresh and dried, banana leaves, corn leaves, and reed leaves.

Fresh Corn Husks

Fresh green husks are used to wrap *tamales* made of fresh corn, *tamales de elote, uchepos* in Michoacán, *cuichis* in northern Veracruz (green corn *tamales* in the United States), or by whatever name they are known. These tough green leaves provide an effective, colorful, and waterproof covering for the *tamales* and add their own special flavor to the dough. For these you will need to find fresh field corn (sweet corn does not contain enough starch), neither too young nor too starchy and dry; when you dig your nail into the kernel, a milky juice will spurt out. Buy them with their sheath of leaves still intact, and if possible buy a few extra leaves to replace any torn ones and to line the bottom of the steamer and cover the stacked *tamales*. Before attempting to remove the husks, cut around the base of the leaves as close to the stem as you can, but still permitting you to unfurl the leaves with their cupped bases intact (see photo, page 86). Rinse well in cold water (they may have some residues of insecticides on them), shake dry, and stack overlapping in a line. They are now ready to use. The only example I know of where they are first blanched is for making *uchepos de cuchara*, a recipe not given in this book.

Dried Corn Husks

Dried corn husks bought in the Mexican markets, or given me by my neighbors who grow their own corn, are left whole with the cupped leaf base intact. This makes the wrapping of a *tamale* much easier than when using the neat, cut-off leaves commercially packed in the United States. If you're using the latter, the top edge has to be folded down and secured with a tie. I know that often the top is left open by cooks in the United States, but there is always a danger that the condensed steam will get in, and come to think of it, I have never had a decent *tamale* cooked that way. If the corn husks are thin and pliable, they need only to be immersed a few moments in water, shaken dry, and then used. If they are tough and brittle, you will have to soak them for about 15 minutes. Again, shake them dry or pat them dry on a thick towel and stack them as illustrated for fresh corn husks, in equitant fashion, overlapping so that they can be separated easily when the business of filling *tamales* starts. If they are needed, ties for *tamales* may be made by stripping the husks into narrow strands and then soaking them for about 10 minutes for greater strength and flexibility.

Banana Leaves

There are many *aficionados* of Mexican food living in the southwestern part of the United States who can, for most of the year, grow banana leaves for *tamales* (not to be confused with bird of paradise leaves, which are poisonous). If you have a choice, cut those that are newer, a lighter green, and more tender as opposed to the coarser, darker ones. Lay the leaf flat and with a very sharp knife cut one side of the leaf off the hard central rib (see photo below). But always begin at the top of the leaf and cut *with* the grain as opposed to starting at the base, which is against the grain and will tear the leaves. Discard the rib and cut up the leaf into the required sizes. Notice that the underside of the leaf is smooth—that is the side you always spread the dough on, as opposed to the upper side of the leaf, which is slightly ridged. At this point the pieces of leaf are not flexible enough to wrap around a *tamale*, so they have to be wilted, which is best done over an open, high flame (or if you have an electric stove, get the burners very hot). Draw a piece of the leaf slowly across the flame—you can see it changing color and becoming flexible— then turn it over and do the same thing again, moving it around so that it is evenly wilted. A tender leaf should take about 4 seconds on the first side and 2 seconds on the second, while a tougher one should take about 5 to 6 on the first side and 3 on the second. But be careful not to burn the leaf, or you'll have to start again with more.

 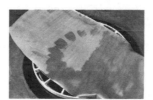 

Set the pieces of leaf out to cool, because if you try to spread the *tamale masa* onto it while it is still hot, the *masa* will run, and all your beating will have been to no avail. I know of a woman who makes *tamales costeños* commercially, and she ties all the banana leaf pieces together and boils them in water for about 30 minutes. This may be simpler and quicker in the end, but there is a distinct loss of the flavor that would normally be imparted to the dough.

When I was cooking in Yucatán, I was told by a Mayan cook to be sure to cut leaves only from the *platano manzano* plant. I forgot to ask her why, but mention it as a gastronomic curiosity and have relegated the information to the files of esoterica.

If you need ties for your *tamales colados*, for instance, wilt extra pieces of leaf and then shred them across the width, along the grain, into narrow strips. Tie two or three together to make ties of about 20 inches.

For the many who do not have fresh banana leaves on hand, neatly packed frozen ones from the Philippines are now on sale in most Asian and some Latin American markets. They are dark green and tough, presumably picked to withstand the freezing and storage, but they are perfectly adequate— much more so, in fact, than the browned, sorry-looking ones often sold in Puerto Rican markets around New York. These leaves, after defrosting, need to be wilted for a longer time—5 seconds or more—on each side before they are pliable enough to wrap the *tamales* snugly.

Corn Leaves

The long leaves of the corn plant, as distinct from the husks, are used for the intricate wrapping of *corundas*—the typical five-pointed sextahedron shape of a first-class six-sided *corunda* in Michoacán. The tough, uneven base of the leaf should be cut off, the leaf rinsed and shaken dry. With the center rib still attached, they are wound, rather clumsily, around the *corunda* dough; or, flattened and bent into short lengths, they are used to support the flat, disk-shaped *corundas* of the eastern part of the state. But, more expert yet, by pulling the center rib, *starting at the center of the leaf* (see photo, below), and this is important, you will have two soft strips of leaf. Held together at the base, they are cunningly wound around a lump of *corunda* dough. Don't worry; there's an easier method of wrapping it into a simple triangular shape, and both methods are illustrated in photos (page 7). Not only does the leaf serve as a wrapper; it also imparts a delicate flavor to the dough.

STEAMERS

It took me an inordinately long time to realize that the conventional steamers, Chinese or otherwise, are not suitable for the efficient cooking of a dense mass of *tamales*: they take forever except in small quantities. And, since *tamales* generally freeze well (except where indicated) and setting up for them is a fairly elaborate business, it is not worth making fewer than 20 at a time.

The Mexicans are masters of steaming and have been since pre-Columbian times. Today the little old ladies who dispense *tamales* at an early hour daily outside practically every marketplace in central Mexico use a steamer improvised from a square, shiny alcohol can, about 18 inches high, with a homemade wire rack near the bottom. Although there is very little water in the bottom, it never seems to evaporate much with the solid mass—at least 100 *tamales*—stacked closely, but not squeezed, into the space above.

Steamers like the one illustrated are sophisticated by comparison. While this one was factory-made in one of the big cities, any local *hojalatero* (tinsmith) in a smaller town or village will be happy to oblige and make a fair, if somewhat rustic-looking, copy. The steamer is well designed, practical, and efficient. It is also used as a labor-saving *barbacoa* for lamb, goat, or *mixiotes* (seasoned meat wrapped in the tough membranous skin of the maguey leaf), and steaming meat in it simulates in texture, if not wholly in flavor, the pit-barbecued meats of Mexico.

In some areas of northwest Mexico *tamales* are actually boiled, and the giant *sacahuil* of the Huasteca is cooked in an *adobe* oven, but elsewhere some sort of improvised arrangements are made for steaming the *tamales*. The Mayan cooks I knew, when making the *tamales colados* in great number, put to use every pot and pan in the kitchen, deep or shallow, with broken bits of the thick banana leaf stems laid across the water to hold the *tamales* and anything flat serving as a lid. If you want to improvise, the important thing is a deep pot, metal rather than earthenware for speed of cooking, with a rack set just above the level of the water. You should have a lid or pot to fit tightly on top and something heavy to rest on it to prevent steam from escaping.

Preparing the Steamer

The level of the water you put into the bottom of a commercial steamer is often indicated by the manufacturer. However, if you are improvising, first look at the expected cooking time of the *tamales*; if it is short, say 1 hour, you will not need the same depth of water as for those that take 2½ hours to cook. It may take a bit of guessing at first.

It is important to remember that the water must be boiling by the time you put the assembled *tamales* into the steamer and that the water must never go off the boil, or the *tamales* will be heavy. Always keep a pot of boiling water at hand just in case. Drop a coin or two into the water; you can then tell when the water comes to the boil, and when their jiggling around and rattling ceases, you will know that the water is dangerously low or going off the boil because the heat is too low. Just above the level of the water, set a rack on which the *tamales* are going to sit and put in a couple of layers of corn husks—or banana leaves, whichever you're using with the *tamales*—to line the rack. There should also be enough of these to place over the top of the stacked *tamales* when the steamer is finally packed. I put a terry-cloth towel over the top of the leaves to absorb the condensation and—something I have seen only recently—a heavy plastic bag (not the thin Saran Wrap) stretched over the top of the *tamales* and tucked down around the edge. This ensures that as little of the steam as possible is allowed to escape, thus concentrating the heat and providing for more efficient and even cooking. Finally you'll need a lid, which should be weighted down with the heaviest practical object you have in the kitchen—I use an ancient *molcajete*.

Stacking the Tamales in the Steamer

Once the steamer has been assembled and is ready, it should be put over low heat so that the water is boiling by the time the *tamales* are ready to be packed in. *Tamales* with a very soft, batterlike mixture are usually laid flat or slightly inclined so that the dough does not slip to the bottom of the husk. Some cooks allow the bottom layer of these *tamales* to "set" first—about 10 minutes—before stacking the rest on top of them. The only trouble is that you cannot go ahead and fill all the husks; if you do, in the case of *uchepos* the mixture will separate, and the *canarios* will flatten out. Flattish *tamales*, like those of fish and *costeños*, wrapped in banana leaves, are always laid in horizontal layers—without the cooking of the first layer—and so are the bulkier *colados*.

The *tamales de flor de calabaza* and others like them wrapped in dried corn husks are stacked upright, also in layers, and care must be taken not to crowd them too much, or there will be no room for the dough to expand.

Testing for Cooking Time

To test a *tamale* to see if it is done after the specified cooking time has elapsed, remove a small part of the plastic and towel covering them and lift one out with tongs (without letting the water go off the boil), helped along with a spatula so that you are not left with an empty husk in the tongs and a collapsed *tamale* making a mess over the rest of them. Open up the leaf. The dough at the edges should come cleanly away from the leaf or husks and appear completely set.

If you are not going to serve the *tamales* at once—when they are at their best—allow them to cool off before packing loosely in foil (not plastic bags, since they tend to collect moisture) and keep in the refrigerator for no more than 2 days; after that they should be frozen, because the *masa* tends to dry out.

When reheating a small quantity, put them in a shallow steamer—I use a vegetable steamer in a shallow pot—with boiling water for about 5 minutes. For a large quantity I use the conventional steamer. Take care not to steam them too long, or they will become watery and lose their flavor. To reheat *tamales* that have been frozen, *do not defrost*, as they become too watery; put them frozen into a steamer with boiling water.

Tamales colados do not freeze well. They tend to become very sloppy on top, and the chicken becomes tasteless and stringy when reheated. However, if you have to, put them still frozen into a 350° oven in loose foil packages for about 20 minutes or until well heated through.

TAMALES COLADOS *(Yucatecan Strained Tamales)*

Tamale making in Mexico is a high art, and the leading example of that art is without doubt the *tamales colados* of Yucatán. They rank first in complexity of flavor, texture, and technique. The last time they were made for me at a friend's house there were at least 12 members of an extended family in the kitchen, not counting the children. Six pounds of *masa* were used, every suitable table from the large rambling house was brought into the kitchen for the "assembly line," and every pot and pan was converted into an improvised steamer. By the time the *tamales* were ready the news had spread like wildfire, and yet another eight people had appeared. If making them had been short work, the disposal of them was even faster, as a steaming pile of *colados* were gone in a flash. Those who had eaten five or even eight loosened their belts or discreetly stretched out their *achiote*-stained *huipiles* to hide their swelling stomachs, and there was a lot of burping and nodding in the heat of that Yucatecan afternoon.

These are rich and filling and wonderful, but don't attempt to make them alone or for a hundred guests. It is a labor of love, a gastronomic adventure and culinary exercise *par excellence.*

The *masa*, which is strained (hence the name *colado*), is made in an unusual way, and that method follows for the purists; they can also be made, less delicately, with ordinary *tortilla masa* and can come in a poor third with *masa harina.*

TRADITIONAL METHOD FOR PREPARING CORN FOR TAMALES COLADOS

MAKES ABOUT 2¾ POUNDS MASA

  5 cups water
  1 heaped tablespoon powdered lime (see page 7)
  2 pounds dried white corn

Put the water to boil in a stainless-steel or enamel (not aluminum) pot. As it is heating, add the powdered lime through a fine strainer, pressing out the small lumps. As soon as the water is boiling, add the corn, stir well, turn off the heat, cover the pot, and leave the corn to soak overnight.

The following day, drain the corn and rinse in fresh water. Then rub the corn through your hands as if you were washing clothes until as many as possible of the (now) yellow skins are removed—this is laborious and can take up to 25 minutes. Then grind the corn as finely as for *tortillas* (see page 10).

COOKED MASA FOR TAMALES COLADOS

MAKES ENOUGH MASA FOR ABOUT 28 TAMALES

2½ pounds *masa refregada* (page 58) or prepared corn *tortilla masa* (page 8)
4 cups water
2 teaspoons sea salt, approximately (to taste)
1 cup melted lard

Put 2 pounds of the *masa* and the water into a bowl, reserving the rest of the *masa*, and rub between your hands until all but the very small lumps have dissolved. Pour through a fine strainer, pressing out the lumps with a wooden pestle or bean masher, into a heavy, wide pan. Discard the debris—called *xixito (shishito)* in Mayan, a much more romantic word. Put the pan over medium heat, add the salt, and continue cooking for a few minutes; the mixture will start to thicken at the bottom of the pan. Keep stirring and scraping the bottom of the pan until the whole *masa* takes on body. At that point start adding a little of the lard, stirring until it is all absorbed before adding more, and continue adding little by little until it is all absorbed and the mixture is thick and shiny. Keep stirring until it becomes hard work and as you stir the mixture holds its shape. This whole process should take 15 to 20 minutes. Turn the *masa* out onto a tray with sides or a roasting pan and spread evenly so that it is ½ to ¾ inch thick. Set aside to cool and "jell." When firm, cut into 28 rectangles or squares.

TAMALES COLADOS
(Yucatecan Strained Tamales)

THE CHICKEN FILLING
1 3- to 3½-pound chicken, cut into 8 pieces
1 small head of garlic, unpeeled and charred (see page 439)
1 teaspoon crumbled dried Yucatecan oregano *or* ½ teaspoon ordinary dried
  oregano
3 tablespoons *recado rojo* (page 428)
1 tablespoon bitter orange juice or vinegar
¼ teaspoon freshly ground black pepper
sea salt to taste

THE *ACHIOTE*-FLAVORED GRAVY
1 cup *masa* reserved from preceding recipe
1½ tablespoons flour
3 cups reduced broth from cooking chicken

Put the chicken pieces into a pot and barely cover with water. Add the
garlic cloves, oregano, *achiote* paste diluted with the juice, pepper, and salt;
bring to a simmer. Continue simmering until the chicken is just tender—
about 25 minutes. Strain and set the chicken aside to cool off. Return the
broth to the pan and reduce over high heat to 3 cups.

When the chicken is cool enough to handle, strip the meat from the
bones and shred coarsely together with some of the skin—makes about 3½
cups. Set aside.

The Gravy

Put the *masa* and flour into a bowl. Gradually stir in 1 cup of the hot
broth, pressing out any lumps with the back of a wooden spoon until
completely smooth. Gradually stir in the rest of the broth and strain again
back into the pan. Cook over low heat, stirring constantly and scraping the
bottom of the pan until the gravy completely covers the back of a wooden
spoon without falling off the sides. Set aside to cool. It should "jell."

Assembling the Tamales

Prepare the steamer (see page 64) and set over low heat while you
assemble the *tamales*.

28 cooked *masa* squares
32 (just in case) pieces of banana leaf, 9 by 7 inches, wilted (see page 61)
the gravy
the cooked chicken
2½ cups plum tomatoes, approximately, sliced lengthwise
⅔ cup loosely packed, roughly chopped *epazote* leaves, approximately
1½ cups closely packed, thinly sliced purple onions, approximately

Put a square of the *masa* on each piece of banana leaf and add 1 tablespoon of the gravy, some chicken, 2 tomato slices, a few *epazote* leaves, a few onion slices, and a little more gravy if you have any left over. Fold the leaves over the filling, long side first, then the shorter side, to form a package, and tie securely. Place in the steamer horizontally (the water should be boiling and the coins rattling) and cover with the odd bits of leftover leaves, a towel and/or a piece of plastic, and the lid. Add a weight to hold it down and keep in as much of the steam as possible. Cook until the *masa* can be separated easily from the banana leaf but, in the case of these *tamales*, is still soft—about 1½ hours.

CORUNDAS (Michoacán Triangular Tamales)

MAKES 21 TO 24 3-INCH CORUNDAS

One of the most popular street foods in parts of Michoacán is a dish of *corundas* with thick cream and a red or green tomato sauce. *Corundas* are puffy white *tamales* cunningly wrapped in a corn leaf (not husk) (see page 62) or reed leaf (below) in the form of a sextahedron—with six sides and five points. The corn leaf gives a distinct yet subtle flavor to the dough, although the reed leaf is easier to handle for wrapping the *corunda*. *Corundas* can also be stuffed with meat in a *chile* sauce or cheese, but they are so good plain that they hardly need it.

In the eastern part of the state *corundas* have degenerated into a flat disk, rather rubbery at that, made of corn prepared with ash.

I am afraid there are no good substitutes for the *masa* that should be prepared of white corn. When the corn is sent to the mill, the instructions should be: *martajar* (crush roughly) the corn and do not grind smoothly as if you were making *tortillas*. It should also be kept as dry as possible and should be mealy.

I have been given dozens of recipes for *corundas*. Most cooks insist that the secret of good ones is *en la batida*, in the beating, but I would lay the emphasis on the preparation and grinding of the corn. Some cooks add baking powder (which is not necessary if you beat it enough), some add milk, others water, and some even half vegetable shortening, but the flavor will not be the same. Here is the recipe that I think works best.

If you are not going to eat the *corundas* right away or the next day, it is best to freeze them to prevent them from drying out. They will keep very well in the freezer for a month or so. When it comes to reheating, do not defrost; put them into the steamer still frozen and reheat for about 30 minutes or more, depending on the efficiency of your steamer.

Any left over can be sliced and used in the following recipe, a delicious "dry soup" with *chile* strips, cream, and cheese. *Corundas* are best served with plenty of *crème fraîche* and a fairly *picante* red (page 339) or green tomato sauce (page 25).

The narrow, elongated, triangular reed leaves from a native Mediterranean plant, *arundo donax,* are also used to wrap *corundas* when fresh corn leaves are not available. This plant was introduced into Mexico, where it thrives and is used mostly for basket making. While reed leaves do not impart the flavor that corn leaves add to the *tamale* dough, they are much more manageable as a wrapper.

30 corn leaves (see page 62) or reed leaves (see note on page 70)
14 ounces lard
2 pounds (about 3¾ cups) *masa refregada* (page 58), ground as dry as
  possible
⅔ cup milk or water, approximately
1 scant tablespoon sea salt

Set the prepared steamer (see page 64) over low heat and line the top
with extra leaves or corn husks.

Beat the lard until very light and fluffy—about 5 minutes. Gradually beat
in the *masa* and a little of the milk or water with each addition; retain at least
half of the liquid until you test the consistency of the dough when all the
masa has been incorporated—it should have good body but plop fairly easily
off the spoon. If it appears stiffer than that, add a little more liquid. Now beat
the *masa* for about 10 minutes. Put a small dab of it into a glass of water. It
should immediately float to the top; if not, continue beating.

Take one of the leaves and form a pocket as shown in the photo, fill
with about ⅓ cup of the dough, and fold as illustrated, in the modified way
to form a triangle. As soon as the water in the steamer is boiling, arrange
the *corundas* in layers, not crowding them since they should have room to
expand. Cover with more leaves or a terry-cloth towel and steam until the
dough is spongy and easily comes away from the leaf when unwrapped—about
1 hour.

SOPA SECA DE CORUNDAS (Casserole of Corundas)

SERVES 6 TO 8

SEÑORA GUADALUPE ALCOCER DE MENDOZA,
PATZCUARO, MICHOACÁN

Like the *sopa seca de uchepos,* this is a delicious way of using up any leftover *corundas* and to my mind is worth making a batch of them especially for this dish. It is served alone as the dry soup, or pasta, course. Actually, with a salad it makes a wonderful lunch dish and is excellent on a brunch buffet. While it does not freeze well, all the component parts may be cooked ahead. Fry the *corundas* and assemble the dish just before putting it into the oven. Cube the *corundas* carefully as they tend to crumble when cold.

> 6 tablespoons unsalted butter, approximately, plus additional for greasing the dish
>
> 5 cups (about 16) cubed ½-inch *corundas,* leaves removed
>
> 1 cup *rajas,* either 8 *chilacas* or 6 *poblanos,* charred, peeled, cleaned, and cut into strips (see pages 464 and 470)
>
> 2 cups *salsa de jitomate,* cooked version (page 339), blended with 1 small white onion, sliced
>
> 1 cup *crème fraîche*
>
> ½ cup grated Chihuahua cheese or medium-sharp Cheddar

Have ready a lightly buttered ovenproof dish or casserole, ideally 9 by 9 by 2 inches deep. Heat oven to 350°.

Melt about 1½ tablespoons of the butter in a large frying pan, add one quarter of the *corunda* cubes, and fry, turning them over from time to time until they are golden and slightly crusty. Continue frying the *corundas,* adding more butter as necessary. Spread half of the fried *corundas* over the bottom of the dish and sprinkle with two thirds of the fresh *chile* strips plus half of the sauce, cream, and cheese. Spread with the remaining cubes and top with the rest of the sauce, cream, cheese, and finally *chile* strips.

Bake until hot and bubbling, about 15 minutes. Do not overcook, or the *corundas* will become mushy and fall apart. Serve immediately.

TAMALES COSTEÑOS *(Chicken Tamales from the Coast)*

MAKES ABOUT 18 5- BY 3-INCH *TAMALES*   REINA OLVERA, VERACRUZ

These *tamales* are thin and delicate. Wrapped in banana leaves and seasoned with *achiote*, they reflect the cooking of the southern part of Veracruz that borders on Campeche. There are two typical fillings: chicken and half-dried shrimps seasoned with tomatoes and fresh *chiles jalapeños*. Since these shrimps are difficult to come by other than in certain coastal areas at specific times of the year, I am compromising with a mixture of fresh and dried shrimp. If you use all dried, the flavor of them overwhelms the *tamale* and proves far too strong for many palates, including mine.

Always cook the filling first, giving it time to cool off before making the *masa* and assembling the *tamales*. Tying them is optional. These *tamales* freeze very well for several weeks.

THE CHICKEN FILLING
3 tablespoons rendered chicken fat (page 217)
½ medium white onion, finely sliced
1 pound (about 2 large) tomatoes, peeled and roughly chopped
1½ cups *pollo deshebrado para tacos* (page 218), roughly shredded
sea salt to taste

Heat the chicken fat in a frying pan, add the onion, and fry gently without browning for 1 minute. Add the tomatoes and continue frying over fairly high heat, stirring from time to time, until the mixture has reduced and thickened a little—about 8 minutes. Stir in the chicken and salt to taste and warm through for about 5 minutes to season the chicken. Set aside to cool.

THE SHRIMP FILLING
3 tablespoons safflower oil
½ medium white onion, finely sliced
1 pound (about 2 large) tomatoes, peeled and roughly chopped
16 small, pitted green olives, approximately
1¼ cups peeled raw medium shrimps
¼ cup (about 2¼ ounces) peeled dried shrimps, soaked in warm water for 20
   minutes and drained
sea salt to taste

Heat the oil in a frying pan, add the onion, and fry gently without browning for 1 minute. Add the tomatoes and continue frying over fairly high heat, stirring from time to time, until the mixture has reduced and thickened a little—about 8 minutes. Stir in the olives and shrimps, adjust salt, and continue cooking over medium heat for 5 minutes. Set aside to cool before assembling the *tamales*.

THE *TAMALES*
¼ pound lard, plus additional for greasing the leaves
1 pound (about 2 rounded cups) prepared corn *tortilla masa* (page 8), not too dry
1 rounded teaspoon (or to taste) sea salt
1 tablespoon plus 1 teaspoon *recado rojo* (page 428)
18 pieces of banana leaf, 9 by 7 inches, wilted (see page 61)
the chicken or shrimp filling
3 *chiles jalapeños*, each cut into 6 strips with veins and seeds
18 ties (optional) (see page 62)

Set the prepared steamer (see page 64) over low heat. Line the top with the leaf scraps left over after cutting the right sizes. Beat the lard with an electric mixer until white and fluffy—about 5 minutes. Gradually beat in the *masa*, salt, and *recado rojo*. After all the *masa* has been incorporated, beat for a further 2 minutes. The mixture should be smooth but a good deal drier than other *tamale* doughs. Divide the *masa* into 1½ inch balls.

Liberally grease the center portions of the leaves with lard. Take one of the balls and flatten it onto one of the leaves, spreading the dough as evenly as possible with the heel of your hand until it covers a rectangular area roughly 5 inches by 4 inches and about ⅛ inch thick. Spread 1 heaped tablespoon of the filling over the center of the dough, add 2 of the fresh chile strips, fold the long side closer to you over to cover two thirds of the *tamale*, and fold the second long side over that and then the ends over to form a rectangular package about 5 inches by 3 inches. Tie if desired as shown on page 85. Place the *tamales* horizontally, folded edges up, overlapping in layers in the top part of the steamer and steam until the dough slides easily away from the banana leaf and is set—about 1 hour.

TAMALES DE FRIJOL *(Bean Tamales)*

MAKES 14 TO 15 TAMALES   OAXACA

Almost every region of Mexico has its own version of *tamales* filled with pureed beans, some more complex than others. This recipe from Oaxaca is simple to make and delicious. The *tamales* can be served just with a *salsa de chile pasilla de Oaxaca* (page 342) or can accompany a stew or *mole*.

The dough can either be pressed out by hand like the *costeños* (page 73) or put into the *tortilla* press as illustrated.

Avocado leaves, or even sprigs of *epazote*, may be used instead of the *hoja santa*, and they may be wrapped either in dried corn husks or, for a better flavor, in the long corn leaves.

Like all *tamales*, these are best eaten fresh from the steamer, but they can be reheated in a steamer or frozen and reheated as suggested in the instructions on page 65.

HAVE READY:
the prepared steamer with dried corn husks or corn leaves lining the top part
14 dried corn leaves or husks, approximately, rinsed and shaken dry
14 pieces *hoja santa,* about 3 by 2 inches, or halved avocado leaves
salsa de chile pasilla de Oaxaca (page 342)

THE FILLING
2 tablespoons lard or safflower oil
1 small white onion, thickly sliced
6 avocado leaves
8 small garlic cloves, charred and peeled (see page 439)
½ cup water
about 3½ cups *frijoles negros a la Oaxaqueña* (page 184), with broth
sea salt to taste

THE DOUGH
1 pound (about 2 cups) prepared corn *tortilla masa* (page 8)
3 ounces lard
sea salt to taste
3 tablespoons chicken broth if necessary
2 Alligator Baggies for pressing the *masa*

First make the filling. Heat the lard in the frying pan, add the onion slices, and fry, turning them over until golden. Transfer with a slotted spoon to a blender jar.

Put the avocado leaves onto a hot *comal* (if they're in a spray, just hold them over the flame) and let them sizzle and char slightly for a few seconds. Crumble the leaves into the blender jar, discarding the stalks and tough ribs. Add the garlic and water and blend until smooth.

Gradually add the beans and their broth, blending well after each addition until smooth, adding more water only if necessary to release the blades of the blender.

Reheat the lard remaining in the frying pan and add the pureed beans to the pan. Cook over fairly high heat to reduce, stirring and scraping the bottom of the pan to prevent burning, until the mixture is thick and barely plops off the spoon. Season and set aside to cool.

Mix the dough with the lard and salt, adding the chicken broth only if it is still rather stiff. Divide the dough into 14 equal pieces and roll each into a ball about 1½ inches in diameter.

Line the *tortilla* press with Baggies exactly as you would to make *tortillas* (see page 12). Place a ball of the dough on the bottom plate, cover with a second Baggie, and press down with the top plate until you have a disk about 6 inches in diameter. Lift up the top Baggie, simply to loosen it, replace, and turn the whole—Baggies and dough—over. Lift the (now) top Baggie. Spread 1 tablespoon of the bean paste over the surface of the dough as evenly as possible, leaving a border of about ½ inch. Starting from the right (or left if you are left-handed as I am), lift up the Baggie and fold the dough two thirds of the way over the filling. Do the same with the left side so that the dough covers the beans completely. Then fold over the top and bottom to about ½ inch in depth to form a rectangular shape about 3½ by 2 inches. Place the piece of *hoja santa* or avocado leaf on top, transfer carefully to the corn husks or leaf, and fold as indicated in the photo. If using corn husks, place the *tamale* flat, seam side down, into the cupped base of the leaf and fold the pointed end over it, doubling the husks, then folding the two sides in. If using the corn leaf, just put the *tamale* on the base and double over. Halfway down the leaf, fold diagonally until you cover the sides of the dough or use another whole leaf to wrap the sides.

Place the *tamales* horizontally in the top of the steamer and cook for about 40 minutes. Test by opening one; the dough should easily and cleanly separate from its wrapper. Serve with the *salsa*.

DZOTOBICHAY
(Yucatecan Chaya Leaf Tamales)

MAKES 18 *TAMALES*   YUCATÁN

Dzotobichay is a small Yucatecan *tamale* wrapped in *chaya* leaves (see page 79) and filled with hard-cooked egg and ground toasted pumpkin seeds. A tomato sauce is served with it. While it is traditional, and more flavorful, to use lard in the corn *masa*, vegetable shortening can be used instead to make the perfect vegetarian dish.

In some cases the name *dzotobichay* is erroneously given to the larger *tamale* of *chaya*-flecked dough with the same filling but wrapped in banana leaves, which is in fact *brazo del indio* (*brazo*, arm, is always applied to rolled foods, either savory or sweet, like a jelly roll).

Although spinach is often recommended as a substitute for the *chaya*, I prefer Swiss chard, which has more substance, forms a better wrapper, and has an excellent flavor when combined with the corn dough.

In Yucatán the very small, fat pumpkin seed is used. Because it is not available elsewhere, I have included a proportion of hulled seeds.

If you are using real corn *masa* from the *tortilla* factory, see if they have some that is not as finely ground—that they use for some types of *tamales*. Failing that, use any available *tortilla* dough.

Dzotobichay is served as a separate course, and one per serving should be sufficient. For a main course serve two, allowing about ¼ cup tomato sauce per serving.

Although always better eaten right away, the *tamales* can be reheated in a steamer for about 15 minutes or frozen and reheated, not defrosted, for about 25 minutes.

HAVE READY:
a prepared steamer lined with extra chaya *or* Swiss chard leaves
16 *chaya* leaves *or* 8 large Swiss chard leaves, well rinsed and stems removed
1 cup *salsa de jitomate Yucateca* (page 341)

THE FILLING
½ cup raw, unhulled pumpkin seeds
¼ cup raw, hulled pumpkin seeds
3 hard-cooked eggs, each cut into 6 pieces lengthwise
sea salt to taste

THE DOUGH
¾ pound (about 1½ cups) prepared corn *tortilla masa* (see note above and
   page 8)
4 ounces lard
sea salt to taste

First make the filling. Put the unhulled pumpkin seeds into a heavy, ungreased frying pan and heat over fairly high heat, turning them over and shaking the pan until the husks are just turning color, about 5 minutes. Add the hulled seeds and continue mixing them around, so that they do not burn but color evenly, for 5 minutes. Spread out on a flat surface to cool off.

When they have cooled, grind them in an electric spice/coffee grinder, a small quantity at a time, until they resemble fine crumbs. Set aside.

Set the prepared steamer (see page 64) over medium heat, and as the water in the bottom begins to send off steam put 2 of the Swiss chard leaves at a time into the top section for a few seconds, until they wilt and are more flexible. Lay them out to cool.

Beat the *masa* together with the lard and salt for about 1 minute. Divide into 8 equal parts and roll each into a ball about 1½ inches in diameter.

Lay one of the Swiss chard leaves or 2 overlapping chaya leaves as illustrated on the table in front of you and press one ball of the dough out until thin and approximately 4 inches by 3 inches. Sprinkle the surface of the dough with 1 tablespoon of the ground seeds, arrange 2 slices of the egg end-to-end along the center of the dough, and then start to roll the whole thing, including the leaf, into a small "jelly roll." Double the protruding parts of the leaf over at the ends and lay horizontally into the steamer. Cover with a piece of terry-cloth toweling and steam for about 1 hour. Test by breaking one open to see if the dough is cooked right through. If you are making a larger quantity, the cooking time will be a little longer.

Serve with the tomato sauce over the top and a final sprinkling of additional ground seeds.

TAMALES DE ACELGAS *(Swiss Chard Tamales)*

MAKES ABOUT 24 TAMALES   EASTERN MICHOACÁN

This is a most unusual and delicious *tamale* that I have never found anywhere but in the eastern part of Michoacán. It has a distinctly Lebanese touch, possibly because there are many longtime resident Lebanese families in this part of Mexico. The *tamales* are easy to prepare and cook, and if there are any left over they freeze successfully. Although they're delicious served by themselves, sometimes I put a small spoonful of *salsa ranchera* (page 338) on each one—but *never* smother them with sauce.

Although the *picadillo* made locally is usually simpler, I use one given to me by Señora Fagoaga, whom I have mentioned many times before.

They can be served alone as a first course, say before a fish dish, or as a first course with a salad.

MEAT FOR THE FILLING
1½ pounds pork with some fat, cut into 1-inch cubes
½ white onion, roughly sliced
1 garlic clove, peeled
3 peppercorns
1 teaspoon (or to taste) sea salt

SEASONING FOR THE FILLING
2 tablespoons lard or safflower oil
3 tablespoons finely chopped white onion
2 garlic cloves, peeled and finely chopped
4 small (about 10 ounces) tomatoes, finely chopped, unpeeled
1½ tablespoons roughly chopped almonds
2 heaped tablespoons raisins
5 *chiles serranos en escabeche*, roughly chopped
2 tablespoons *chile* juice
sea salt to taste

THE *TAMALES*
24 large Swiss chard leaves, plus additional leaves for lining the steamer
1 pound (about 2 cups) prepared corn *tortilla masa* (page 8)
5 tablespoons lard
rounded ½ teaspoon (or to taste) sea salt
½ cup warm broth from the meat, approximately

First prepare the meat for the filling. Put the pork, onion, garlic, peppercorns, and salt into a pan, cover with water, and bring to a simmer.

Continue simmering until the meat is tender but not too soft—about 25 minutes. Set aside to cool off in the broth for about 15 minutes, then drain, reserving the broth. When the meat is cool enough to handle, shred and then chop it roughly. Strain the broth and set aside.

Heat the lard, add the onion and garlic, and fry over medium heat for about 2 minutes—they must not brown. Add the tomatoes and fry for 5 minutes more, until reduced. Add the chopped meat, almonds, raisins, *chiles*, *chile* juice, and ⅔ cup of the reserved broth and cook over fairly high heat, stirring and scraping the bottom of the pan until the mixture is almost dry and shiny—about 10 minutes. Season and set aside to cool.

Rinse the Swiss chard leaves well and trim off the stalks up to the base of the leaves. Blanch each one for only 2 seconds in boiling water to soften them. Set aside to drain and cool.

Fill the bottom of the steamer with water and put in a coin or two so that they will rattle when the water is boiling. Line the top of the steamer with the extra leaves and put over low heat while you prepare the *tamales*.

Beat the *masa*, lard, salt, and broth together well for about 5 minutes. Spread 1 heaped tablespoon of the dough thinly over the center of the prepared leaves. Spread another tablespoon of the filling over it and double the leaves over (see center photo). Lay the *tamales* in horizontal layers in the top of the steamer, sprinkling each layer lightly with salt. Cover the top of the *tamales* with another layer of leaves, a cloth, and the lid. Cook for about 1 hour. Test by breaking one of the *tamales* open; the dough must be cooked through.

TAMALES DE PESCADO, TAMAULIPAS
(Fish Tamales from Tamaulipas)

MAKES 20 TO 24 TAMALES

These *tamales* are light and delicate in flavor and texture, especially appealing to those who like the strong anise flavor of the *hoja santa*. Avocado leaves can be substituted (although the former are edible and the latter are not) since they do leave a somewhat similar flavor in the *masa*.

This recipe was given to me some years ago by a friend and great cook, María Emilia Farías, who was born in Tampico. The dough and form of the *tamales* are essentially the same as for those from Veracruz (printed in *The Cuisines of Mexico*), but made with fish and green sauce as opposed to meat and red *ancho* sauce. You will need thin fillets of a non-oily fish like flounder, sole, or catfish.

It is not really necessary to tie each *tamale* if after folding them you turn them face down, then turn them over, face up, and stack carefully in the steamer, overlapping them slightly in layers. These *tamales* freeze well, but since they are so thin and delicate it is best not to resteam them; rather, heat them briefly in a foil package in a moderate oven.

HAVE READY:
24 pieces of banana leaf, 9 by 7 inches, wilted (see page 61)
24 ties (optional) (see note above and instructions, page 62)
extra leaf pieces to line the steamer

Set the steamer over low heat while you prepare the tamales.

THE DOUGH
¼ pound lard
1 pound (about 2 cups) prepared corn *tortilla masa* (page 8)
⅔ cup lukewarm chicken broth
½ teaspoon (or to taste) sea salt

THE FILLING
1 pound fish fillets (see note above), skinned, boned, and cut into pieces roughly 3 inches square
2 cups *salsa verde* (recipe follows)
24 *hoja santa* leaves, about 3 inches square, tough ribs removed, *or* 24 halved avocado leaves

First make the dough. Beat the lard with an electric mixer until white and fluffy—about 5 minutes. Gradually beat in the *masa*, broth, and salt to taste, beating well after each addition. When the ingredients have all been beaten in, the mixture will be soft but not runny. Spread 1 heaped tablespoon of the mixture in the center of each piece of banana leaf to cover an area roughly 4 inches by 3 inches; it should be ⅛ to ¼ inch thick. Place a piece of fish on each with about 1½ tablespoons of the sauce, cover with *hoja santa* or avocado leaves, and wrap, lengths first and then the sides, to form a rectangular package. Place face down while you fold the rest. When they have all been wrapped, carefully transfer them to the steamer, with the openings up, overlapping in horizontal layers. Steam for about 1 hour and test; if the *tamales* are cooked, the *masa* will have set and will slip easily away from the leaf.

SALSA VERDE PARA TAMALES DE PESCADO
(Green Sauce for Fish Tamales)

MAKES ABOUT 2 CUPS

1 pound (about 22 medium) *tomate verde*, papery husks removed, rinsed
4 (or to taste) *chiles serranos*, stalks removed
¼ medium white onion, roughly chopped
1 heaped tablespoon firmly packed *epazote* leaves
2 tablespoons safflower oil
sea salt to taste

Put the *tomates* and fresh *chiles* into a saucepan, cover with water, and set over medium heat until the water comes to a simmer; continue simmering for about 10 minutes or until the *tomates* are soft but not falling apart. Remove and strain, reserving a little of the cooking water. Transfer cooked *tomates*, *chiles*, and ¼ cup of the cooking water to a blender jar. Add onion and *epazote* leaves and blend until smooth. Heat the oil in a frying pan, add the sauce, and fry, stirring from time to time and adding salt to taste, until the sauce has reduced and thickened—about 8 minutes. Set aside to cool before assembling the *tamales*; if hot, it will make the *masa* runny.

TAMALES DE FLOR DE CALABAZA
(Squash Flower Tamales)

MAKES ABOUT 25 3-INCH *TAMALES*   SEÑORA GLORIA VILCHIS, ZITÁCUARO

When I first tried these *tamales* some years ago, I was struck by how delicious they were and how different from any I had come across before. Nobody seemed to know where they came from or if they were a specialty of this area, where many cooks make them but with slight differences in *masa* and ingredients.

To try to find out I first went to my *Diccionario de Cocina*, 1845 edition. There were scathing remarks about *tamales* in general: Did decent families really want to know how to make them, as they were the food of "the lower orders"? But *La Cocinera Poblana* (1877 edition) did have a recipe for *tamales de flor de calabaza*. In it, eggs as well as lard were beaten into the *masa*, and then it was mixed with flowers, *epazote*, and *chiles*. In a 1901 book from the state of Hidalgo, the same method is used but with a simpler *masa* mixed with squash, *epazote*, and cheese. I suspect this recipe was copied again in a 1954 book but in a slightly more elaborate fashion.

It is interesting to see how a recipe travels and evolves, or degenerates, how each cook adds her own touch, and even I have added crisp, fresh corn kernels to this recipe from Señora Vilchis. While cooks here use *masa refregada* (page 58) for the dough, they can be made with ordinary *tortilla masa* plus a little baking powder to make them spongy. The dry, salty *anejo* is the cheese called for, but a roughly crumbled *queso fresco* is very good, too, and occasionally instead of *chile serrano* I use chopped strips of peeled *chilaca*, the regional chile here. If squash flowers are not available, leave them out; you will still have delicious *tamales*. These *tamales* freeze well and can be kept for about 2 months.

¼ pound lard
1 pound (about 2 cups) *masa refregada* (page 58) or prepared corn *tortilla masa* (see note above and page 8) plus 1 scant teaspoon baking powder
¼ cup pork or chicken broth
¼ pound (approximately 1 cup) *queso añejo* or *fresco*, crumbled (see note above)
1 teaspoon (less if *añejo* is used) sea salt
½ cup zucchini in ¼-inch cubes
rounded ½ cup *carne de puerco cocida y deshebrado* (page 248)
1 heaped cup closely packed, chopped zucchini flowers
¼ cup closely packed, roughly chopped *epazote* leaves

3 *chiles serranos,* cut into thin rounds with seeds and veins *or* ⅓ cup skinned
and roughly chopped *chiles poblanos* or *chilacas*
rounded ½ cup corn kernels (optional)
25 dried corn husks (see page 60), lightly greased with lard
25 dried corn husk ties (optional)

With an electric mixer, beat the lard until white and fluffy—about 5
minutes. Gradually beat in the *masa* and broth alternately with the baking
powder and stir in the remaining ingredients, except husks, thoroughly; the
masa will be very stiff. Put 1 overheaped tablespoon of the mixture down the
center of the corn husk; do not flatten, but fold the husk over loosely to allow
for expansion. Fold the ends in the usual fashion tie (optional) and place
upright in the top of the steamer. Cover with more husks, a towel, and a
piece of plastic; steam until the dough comes away cleanly from the husk—
about 2 hours.

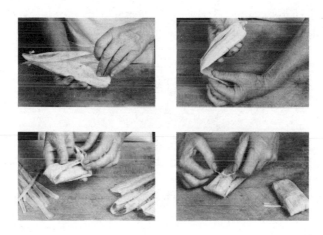

UCHEPOS *(Michoacán Fresh Corn Tamales)*

MAKES ABOUT 20 *UCHEPOS*   MICHOACÁN

While each region of Mexico has its own version of fresh corn *tamales* (known as green corn *tamales* in the United States), those of Michoacán, known as *uchepos,* are by far the most delectable and delicate. Although they may be filled with a shredded pork and tomato filling, they are most often served with a green or red tomato sauce, thick soured cream, like *crème fraîche,* and slightly melted *queso fresco;* when well made and served like this, they are sublime.

To make them to the right consistency you will have to find field corn: not too tender, not too starchy. The best test is to push a fingernail into the kernels—they should be slightly firm but still juicy.

The fresh corn husks should be cut off as near the base as possible but permitting each leaf to be unfurled whole. They should then be stacked, overlapping in a line ready to be filled. *Uchepos* freeze very well.

20 fresh corn husks (see note above)
5 cups field corn kernels (see note above)
¼ cup milk
3 tablespoons sugar
3 tablespoons unsalted butter, softened
3 tablespoons *natas, crème fraîche,* or thick cream
1 rounded teaspoon sea salt
1½ cups *salsa de jitomate,* cooked version (page 340), kept warm
½ pound *queso fresco,* cut into slices about ¼ inch thick
½ cup *crème fraîche*

Put the prepared steamer (see page 64) over low heat and line the top part with a layer of fresh corn husks.

Put half of the corn into the container of a food processor, add the milk, and process until the corn has been reduced to a textured pulp—about 1½ minutes. Add the rest of the corn and continue processing until the corn has been reduced to a loose, finely textured purée—about 2½ minutes. Add the sugar, butter, and cream and process briefly. Stir in the salt.

Shake the husks to get rid of any surplus water and place 1 heaped tablespoon of the mixture along the center, starting just below the cupped end, extending it for about 2 inches. Do not flatten. Fold the sides of the leaf over the mixture, leaving room for expansion, turn the pointed end up on the side opposite to the seam (see photo), and place one layer horizontally in the top of the steamer. Cover and leave to cook for about 10 minutes or until the mixture is just beginning to set. Give the mixture a good stir, fill the rest of the leaves, always mixing and stirring as the corn tends to separate from the juice, and place in horizontal layers in the steamer. Cover with more of the leaves, a terry-cloth towel, a sheet of plastic (see page 65), and the lid, well weighted down so that the steam cannot escape; cook for about 1 to 1½ hours, depending on how efficient your steamer is.

Serve hot, 3 *uchepos* per person, on a warmed plate. At one side put ¼ cup of the warmed sauce with a slice of cheese in the middle and 1 heaped tablespoon of the *crème fraîche*.

SOPAS DE UCHEPOS

This is typical *comida casera*, home cooking. If there are a few *uchepos* left over, not enough to make the recipe that follows, crumble a couple of them into a bowl with some soft butter and a little *salsa verde* or a red tomato sauce. This is called *Sopas* locally. Best eaten alone and with a spoon.

SOPA DE UCHEPOS
(Casserole of Fresh Corn Tamales)

SERVES 6   MICHOACÁN

This is a wonderfully rich casserole for using up any leftover *uchepos*—or it is even worthwhile making a batch especially for it. Since this is a typically Michoacán recipe, it is of course better with the green *chilacas* (long, spindly, dark green *chiles*); *poblanos* make a very good substitute but with less bite. Use 6 *poblanos* or 8 *chilacas*.

This dish should be eaten as soon as it comes out of the oven; it does not freeze successfully. It is served alone as a dry soup or pasta course.

3 tablespoons unsalted butter or safflower oil
1 medium white onion, finely sliced
1 cup *chilacas* or *chiles poblanos*, charred, peeled, cleaned, and cut into strips
   (see note above and page 469)
sea salt to taste
22 freshly made or frozen *uchepos*, husks removed
1 cup thick *crème fraîche*
¼ pound *queso fresco*, crumbled (1 cup)

Have ready an ovenproof dish into which the *uchepos* will just fit in two layers—9 by 9 by 2 inches deep is ideal. Heat the oven to 375°.

Heat the butter or oil in a frying pan, add the onion, and fry gently until translucent—about 2 minutes. Add the fresh *chile* strips and salt to taste. Cover the pan and cook over medium heat, shaking the pan from time to time, until the *chiles* are tender but not soft—about 5 minutes. If they tend to be very juicy, uncover the pan and cook for a few more minutes to reduce the liquid.

Cover the bottom of the dish (there is no need to butter it) with one layer of the *uchepos*, spread the *chile* strips evenly over the *uchepos*, and cover with half the cream and half the crumbled cheese. Put a layer of the remaining *uchepos* over the top and finish off with the rest of the cream and cheese. Bake until well heated through and bubbling.

TAMALES DE ELOTE Y MIEL
(Fresh Corn and Honey Tamales)

MAKES ABOUT 20 3-INCH TAMALES   SEÑORITA ELIVA CARRILLO OLIVARES,
COATEPEC

These are rather unusual *tamales*, spongy but moist, with a wonderfully fresh taste of fresh corn and honey. They are eaten at suppertime with a glass of milk or reheated for breakfast in place of *pan dulce*. (They—and the *tamales canarios*—remind me so much of British steamed puddings that I am always tempted to serve them hot with a *crème Anglaise* quite strongly flavored with tangerine, orange, or lime.) The type of corn and the *masa* each one produces is well known in Mexico, but it takes some explanation for those less familiar with them to produce the best results—so bear with me.

First, you need field corn—as for all *tamales*, corn puddings, and the like in these recipes—half of it very mature and starchy and the other half mature but still juicy. In Mexico the corn is ground—actually crushed—between the metal blades of the corn grinder illustrated on page 10—indispensable to the serious Mexican cook. No *one* modern electric appliance quite does the job alone, so I have given a compromise below, and if you can be bothered to follow it—actually it's very easy—your *tamales* will come out with the correct texture. (A food processor will never break down the skins sufficiently, and the blender alone would take too long.)

4 cups fresh field corn kernels (see note above)
⅓ cup clear honey
1 scant teaspoon ground cinnamon
pinch of salt
½ teaspoon baking soda
⅛ teaspoon whole aniseed (optional)
22 fresh corn husks (see page 60), insides lightly buttered

Set the prepared steamer (see page 64) over low heat while you prepare the *tamales*. Put 2 cups of the tender corn into the container of a food processor and process for about 2 minutes or until the kernels have been broken down and the juice has exuded. Add the rest of the corn and process for 2 minutes longer. Transfer about ¾ cup of the puree to a blender jar and blend for a few seconds at low speed and then for about 30 seconds at high speed, until the tough skins of the kernels have been thoroughly broken down and the mixture resembles a textured, loose paste. Turn into a bowl and continue with the next batch. When all the corn has been ground in this way, stir in the remaining ingredients except husks and mix thoroughly.

Put 1 overflowing tablespoon of corn down the center of the prepared husks, in a line about 3 inches long; do not flatten. Fold the leaves over to allow for expansion. Stack the *tamales* horizontally or slightly angled in the top of the steamer—by now the coins should be rattling to show that the water is boiling below. Cover with more husks, a towel, and a sheet of plastic before the lid is weighted down. Steam, without letting the water go off the boil, until the dough of the *tamale* is spongy but not sticky and rolls easily away from the husk—about 1½ hours.

TAMALES CANARIOS *(Canary Tamales)*

MAKES ABOUT 20 SMALL *TAMALES*   EASTERN MICHOACÁN

You don't come across these little, sweet *tamales* very often (although I have found mention of them in cookbooks of other central Mexican areas), but in the eastern part of Michoacán they are served on festive occasions with *atole* or hot chocolate. They are pale yellow—hence their name—and spongy, the color varying with the intensity of the color of the yolks. Although the quantities of ingredients are more or less standard, cooks can never agree about whether the egg whites go in as well. I learned from a respected cook here to use just one white to soften the batter. A similar recipe from a nineteenth-century cookbook calls them *tamales de arroz* (rice *tamales*) and calls for a proportion of lard as well as butter and mixes rice flour with *tamale masa*.

Although they're usually wrapped in dried corn husks, I have seen them also in fresh corn husks, which I think give a slightly better flavor.

¼ pound (rounded ¾ cup) rice flour
1 teaspoon double-acting baking powder
¼ pound (½ cup) unsalted butter at room temperature, plus additional for
    greasing husks
3½ ounces (scant ⅔ cup) sugar
4 large egg yolks
1 large egg white
3 tablespoons milk
3 ounces (approximately ½ cup, heaped) raisins
22 rinsed, dried (see page 60) corn husks, insides well buttered

Put the prepared steamer (see page 64) over low heat.
Sift the flour and baking powder together and set aside.
Beat the butter and sugar together to a cream. Beat in the yolks one at a time with a dusting of the flour. Finally, beat in the egg white, milk, and flour and mix well. The batter should be creamy and barely plop off the beaters. Put 1 heaped tablespoon of the mixture down the center of the husk, starting near the cupped end; do not flatten. Press 4 or 5 raisins into the batter and fold the husks over loosely, turning up the pointed end on the opposite side. Make sure the water in the steamer is boiling, then place the folded *tamales* horizontally in layers in the steamer. Cover with more husks, a towel, and the lid; steam for about 15 minutes. Test one at the end of the cooking time; the puffy dough should roll easily away from the corn husk. Eat immediately or store in the freezer.

SOUPS AND BROTHS

(Sopas y Caldos)

Caldo o Consomé de Pollo (Chicken Broth)
Sopa de Bolitas (Masa Ball Soup)
Sopa de Fideos y Acelgas (Vermicelli and Swiss Chard Soup)
Sopa de Fideo en Frijol (Vermicelli in Bean Broth)
Sopa de Albóndigas (Meatball Soup)
Crema de Flor de Calabaza (Cream of Squash Flower Soup)
Pipián de Oaxaca (Oaxacan Pumpkin Seed "Soup")
Sopa de Flor de Calabaza (Squash Flower Soup)
Sopa de Cuitlacoche (Corn Fungus Soup)
Whole Hominy for Soups
Pozole Verde (Green Pozole)
Menudo Blanco Sonorense (White Sonoran Menudo)
Sopa de Habas (Dried Fava Bean Soup)
Frijol Blanco con Camarón Seco (White Bean and Dried Shrimp Soup)
Caldo de Camarón Seco (Dried Shrimp Broth)
Sopa Tarasca (Tarascan Soup)
Cross-reference: Hongos de Vapor en Caldo

Soups play an indispensable part in the main meal of the day in Mexico, either in the home or in the smaller, more typical eating places. Whatever the climate, soups open up the appetite and comfort the soul.

Two of the most popular, hearty soups play different roles: *menudo* (tripe soup) is served for *almuerzo* (brunch), and a large bowl, steaming and spicy, is a great restorative. *Pozole*, with its pork and whole hominy in a rich broth with lots of crisp toppings, is the soup of the evening and will sustain you through the night.

Mexican and Asian soups have quite a lot in common: many have a thin broth base with pasta or crisp fresh vegetables to add texture and flavor contrast.

It is a pity that soups do not play a more important part in the diet north of the border. But perhaps too many Americans have unpleasant memories of commercial soups—not only from cans but on planes and in cafeterias—thick and glutinous with strong, salty flavoring masking overcooked ingredients.

I go along with Lewis Carroll: "Soup of the evening, beautiful soup!"

CALDO O CONSOMÉ DE POLLO (*Chicken Broth*)

MAKES ABOUT 10 TO 12 CUPS

In many cultures chicken broth is considered a panacea, a comforter, sustenance for invalids. In Mexico it is all of that and more. It is a constant in the restaurant or home kitchen: in itself a soup, a base for many soups of other ingredients, a medium for poaching chicken or cooking rice. There is always a lot of it around, particularly in the small, popular restaurants or *puestos* in the marketplace, because so much chicken is consumed: shredded for *tacos* or other *antojitos* and in stews and *moles*. In a simple meal at one of these *changarritos*—as these fast-food stands are popularly known—you are offered *consomé* to start the meal, *sopa aguada* or brothy soup, as opposed to the rice or dry soup, *sopa seca*. It may have a little rice in it, a suspicion of carrot or zucchini, perhaps some shredded chicken, and it might be served with quartered limes, chopped white onion, *chiles serranos*, and *cilantro* or with a piece of *chile chipotle* floating in it and a few cubes of avocado. Or it can be ordered as a main course with a large portion of chicken in the broth and of course corn *tortillas* broken to form little pincers to pluck the meat off the bone—far more effective than using a knife and fork to pursue the piece of meat sliding around in the broth.

The broth is always a "white" one; the meat, bones, and vegetables are not browned first. There should be only a hint of carrot—more would make the soup too sweet—and just enough onion and garlic. All edible parts of the chicken go into the broth (except for the liver, which is too strong and could be bitter): intestines, unlaid eggs, gizzard, heart, head and neck, plus the skinned feet.

4 pounds chicken parts or a large hen (see note above) and giblets
1 small carrot, scraped and sliced
1 medium white onion, roughly chopped
2 garlic cloves, peeled
4 peppercorns
sea salt to taste

Crack the main bones of the chicken and put into a pot with the rest of the ingredients. Add enough water to come about 3 inches above the meat and bring to a simmer. Continue simmering, uncovered, for about 4 hours. Set aside in a cool place overnight for the gelatinous properties of the bones to exude. Skim off any fat that has formed a layer over the top, reheat to a boil, and strain. Degrease once more if necessary. If you are not using the broth right away, then reduce it (to save storage space), measure, and freeze in ice trays. When it's solid, transfer it to plastic bags.

95

SOPA DE BOLITAS (*Masa Ball Soup*)

SERVES 6   FELICIAN BÉJAR, MICHOACÁN

This is a simple but very good soup. The base is essentially the same as that for *tortilla* soup, or *vermicelli* and Swiss chard soup: a thick broth enriched with tomato. The little *masa* balls add the special touch; they can be served in the soup or handed round separately with more grated cheese if desired. (The balls themselves, by the way, could be served as a very inexpensive cocktail snack.) However, a warning: if you are using *tortilla* dough, spread it out and dry it a little before adding the other ingredients. If you are making up dough from *masa harina,* use half the quantity of water specified. If the dough is then too wet and cannot be rolled, form the balls between two small spoons, and if they turn out to be rather rough-looking, no matter; they will have more fried surface, and that's always good.

If the tomatoes you are using are really ripe and red, blend them raw with the onion and garlic; if underripe, broil them; if they are rather dry, stew them—what matters is to bring out the best in whatever products you have.

THE SOUP
½ pound (about 1 large) tomatoes, roughly chopped, unpeeled (see note above)
1 tablespoon finely chopped white onion
1 small garlic clove, peeled and roughly chopped
¼ cup water
1 tablespoon safflower oil
sea salt to taste
6 cups reduced chicken broth (page 95)
2 leafy stems of *epazote or* 4 *cilantro* sprigs

THE *MASA* BALLS
1 *chile ancho,* cleaned of seeds but not veins
1 small egg
1 teaspoon (or to taste, depending on how salty the cheese is) sea salt
5 tablespoons grated *queso añejo* or Romano cheese
10 ounces (1¼ cups) prepared corn *tortilla masa* (page 8)
lard or safflower oil for frying

Put the tomatoes, onion, garlic, and water into a blender jar and blend until almost smooth. Heat the oil in a frying pan, add the blended ingredients with a little salt to taste, and fry over fairly high heat until reduced and seasoned—about 8 minutes. Add this to the chicken broth with the *epazote or cilantro* and cook over medium heat for about 10 minutes. Set aside to season while you make the *masa* balls.

Cover the dried *chile ancho* with hot water and leave to soak for about 15 minutes. Put the egg and salt into the blender jar, add the *chile,* torn into pieces, and blend until smooth. Add the blended ingredients and the cheese to the *masa* and work well until the dough is smooth and the *chile* evenly distributed through it. With lightly greased hands, form the dough into balls about ¾ to 1 inch in diameter. Meanwhile, heat lard to a depth of about ¼ inch in a small frying pan and fry a few *masa* balls at a time, turning them over until they are crisp and brown. Drain on paper toweling and keep them warm. Serve the soup as suggested above.

SOPA DE FIDEO Y ACELGAS
(Vermicelli and Swiss Chard Soup)

SERVES 6   SEÑORA HORTENSIA FAGOAGA

This recipe was given to me by Señora Hortensia Fagoaga, and neither she nor her friends who make this soup know where it came from. It is unusual and delicious. Traditionally a soup of this type is not *picante*, but you can add a small piece of *chile serrano* when blending the tomato if desired.

¾ pound (about 2 medium) tomatoes, roughly chopped, unpeeled
1 garlic clove, peeled and roughly chopped
¼ small white onion, roughly chopped
a small piece of *chile serrano* (optional)
1 tablespoon lard or safflower oil
6 cups well-seasoned chicken broth (page 95)
½ pound Swiss chard, washed, stems removed, roughly chopped
sea salt to taste
2 medium eggs, separated
3 ounces fine *vermicelli*
3 tablespoons finely grated *queso añejo* (optional)
safflower oil for frying

Put the tomatoes, garlic, onion, and optional fresh *chile* into a blender jar and blend until smooth. Heat the lard in a soup pot, add the blended ingredients, and fry, stirring from time to time and scraping the bottom of the pan, until reduced and thickened—about 4 minutes. Add the broth and bring to a boil. Add the Swiss chard and simmer for about 10 minutes. Taste for salt.

Meanwhile, beat the egg whites until stiff but not dry. Beat in the yolks one at a time with a pinch of salt. When the yolks are well incorporated, crumble the uncooked vermicelli into the beaten eggs and add the optional cheese. Stir until the vermicelli is well coated with the egg.

Heat safflower oil about ¼ inch deep in a frying pan and when hot add large spoonfuls of the egg/vermicelli mixture. When they are a pale golden brown on the underside—about 1 minute—turn them over and fry on the second side (if they become too brown, lower the heat). Drain on paper toweling. There should be about 12 *tortas*, each about 3 inches in diameter. Add them to the broth and simmer, turning them carefully once so they do not break open—about 12 to 15 minutes.

Serve in deep bowls, 2 *tortas* per person with a lot of the broth.

SOPA DE FIDEO EN FRIJOL (*Vermicelli in Bean Broth*)

SERVES 6

This is an interesting variation of the more popular soup of *vermicelli* in a tomato broth. It is a great cold weather soup and may be made with either *pinto* or black beans. Although it is better eaten the day it is made, it will keep for a day or two in the refrigerator. It will thicken up considerably, so you will have to dilute it with more bean or chicken broth.

The *vermicelli* should be fairly soft, not *al dente* Italian style. Although it's not traditional, I like to pass finely chopped white onion to sprinkle on top of the soup and a dish of pickled *chipotles* or *moras* on the side.

1 small tomato (about ¼ pound), roughly chopped, unpeeled
2 tablespoons finely chopped white onion
1 small garlic clove, peeled and chopped
3 tablespoons safflower oil or melted chicken fat
⅔ cup *frijoles de olla* (page 179)
5 cups broth from *frijoles de olla*
4 ounces fine *vermicelli*, broken into 4-inch pieces
sea salt to taste
1 leafy stem of *epazote* or flat-leaf parsley

THE TOPPING
⅓ cup finely grated *queso añejo* or Romano cheese
⅓ cup finely chopped white onion (optional)
pickled *chipotles* (optional)

Put the tomato, onion, and garlic into a blender jar and blend until smooth. Heat 1 tablespoon of the oil, add the tomato puree, and fry over fairly high heat, stirring and scraping the bottom of the pan until it has reduced and thickened—about 3 minutes. Set aside.

Put the beans and bean broth into the blender jar and blend to a smooth puree; set aside. Put the remaining oil in a heavy saucepan, add the *vermicelli*, and fry, stirring and turning it over until it is a deep golden color—about 3 minutes. Drain off the excess oil. Add the tomato puree and fry, stirring and scraping the bottom of the pan until the mixture is dry. Add the bean puree and salt to taste, cover, and cook over medium heat for about 10 minutes. Add the *epazote* or parsley, cover again, and cook until the pasta is soft—about 5 minutes more. Sprinkle each serving with some of the cheese and pass the onion and *chiles* separately.

SOPA DE ALBÓNDIGAS (*Meatball Soup*)

SERVES 6

This light and satisfying soup is a great favorite in Mexico and particularly good as a mid-morning pick-me-up or part of a brunch. It can be made a day or two ahead if necessary, but it does not freeze well.

THE MEATBALLS
1 tablespoon unconverted long-grain rice
6 ounces ground pork with a little fat (medium grind)
6 ounces ground beef with a little fat (medium grind)
1 small egg
⅛ teaspoon cumin seed, crushed
3 leaves fresh or dried mint
⅛ teaspoon dried oregano, Mexican if possible
⅓ cup roughly chopped white onion
4 peppercorns
sea salt to taste

THE BROTH
½ pound (about 1 large) very ripe tomatoes
1 heaped tablespoon roughly chopped white onion
2 small garlic cloves, peeled and roughly chopped
1 tablespoon lard or safflower oil
6 ounces (about 3 medium) carrots, trimmed, scraped, and cut into ¼-inch
   cubes
6 ounces (about 1½) zucchini, trimmed and cut into ¼-inch cubes
2 cups chicken broth (page 95) or homemade beef broth
4 cups water, approximately
3 yellow wax (Fresno) *chiles*
2 large fresh mint or *cilantro* sprigs

Cover the rice with boiling water and leave to soak for 20 minutes.

Mix the meats together well in a bowl. Put the remaining meatball ingredients into a blender jar and blend until smooth. Stir this into the meat and work the mixture in with your hands to make sure it is well incorporated. Drain the rice and stir into the meat mixture. Roll small portions of the mixture into balls about 1 inch in diameter; there should be about 24 balls. Set aside while you prepare the broth.

Put the tomatoes into a pan, cover with hot water, and cook for 5 minutes. Drain and cool, discarding cooking water. When cool enough to handle, remove skin and base where stem is attached and transfer to the blender jar. Add onion and garlic and blend until smooth. Heat the lard in a wide, heavy pan, add the tomato puree, and fry over high heat until reduced and slightly thickened—about 4 minutes. Add the carrots, zucchini, broth, and water; bring to a simmer. Carefully add the meatballs. Make two cuts in the form of a cross in the base of the fresh *chiles* and add them with the mint or *cilantro* to the broth. Cook over low heat until the meatballs are cooked through, the vegetables soft, and a thin film or sheen appears on the surface—about 50 minutes.

CREMA DE FLOR DE CALABAZA
(Cream of Squash Flower Soup)

SERVES 6

This is a wonderfully delicate soup, best eaten the day it is made. It will work only if the flowers are very fresh and there is a large ratio of petals to green calyxes (see page 150).

3 tablespoons unsalted butter
2 tablespoons finely chopped white onion
1 small garlic clove, peeled and finely chopped
1 pound *flor de calabaza*, cleaned and finely chopped (see page 150)
sea salt to taste
4 cups light chicken broth (page 95)
⅔ cup *crème fraîche* or heavy cream

THE TOPPING
2 *chiles poblanos*, peeled, cut into strips or squares and sautéed (see page 471)
crisp-fried *totopos* (optional) (page 15)

Melt the butter in a large frying pan, add the onion and garlic, and fry gently until translucent but not browned—about 3 minutes. Add the chopped flowers and a touch of salt to flavor, cover the pan, and cook for 5 minutes more. Remove the lid and cook for about 10 minutes or until the calyxes are just tender and the mixture is moist but not too watery. (If the flowers are rather dry, you will need to add about 3 tablespoons of water and cover for the whole of the cooking period, shaking the pan from time to time.)

101

Set aside ½ cup of the flowers for final garnish; add the rest to a blender jar with 1½ cups of the broth and blend until smooth. Return the blended mixture to the pan, add the remaining broth, and simmer over low heat for about 8 minutes. Stir the cream into the soup and heat through gently until it reaches a simmer. Adjust seasoning and serve with the unblended flowers, *chiles*, and optional *totopos*.

PIPIÁN DE OAXACA *(Oaxacan Pumpkin Seed "Soup")*

SERVES 4 TO 6   OAXACA

It is hard to give a succinct title to this recipe because it does not, like some other Mexican dishes, fit into recognized categories of foods in other, more familiar cuisines. This *pipián* from Oaxaca is a delicately flavored chicken in broth thickened with ground unhulled pumpkin seeds and sprinkled as a final touch with some fiery crumbled *chile piquín*. It is customarily served for breakfast the morning after *fiestas*—weddings and baptisms in particular—to signal the guests that the celebration is over and it is time to go home.

This is a personal favorite of mine and I think well worth the bother of careful grinding and straining. I serve it in individual soup cups, putting some shredded chicken, heated separately, in the bottom of each one to make sure it is evenly distributed.

The *pipián* can be made ahead; it keeps well and freezes successfully. After defrosting it is better to blend it for a few seconds before reheating.

HAVE READY:
5 cups reduced chicken broth (page 95), approximately, cooked with a large
   leafy stem of *epazote* or a mint sprig
1½ cups *pollo deshebrado para tacos* (page 218), kept warm
crumbled *chile piquín*

THE SOUP
6 ounces (1¼ cups) raw, unhulled pumpkin seeds
¼ cup *chile* seeds
1 whole clove
1 whole allspice
1 garlic clove, charred and peeled (see page 439)
sea salt to taste

Put the pumpkin seeds into a heated large frying pan and cook over fairly high heat, without oil, stirring and tossing them until they begin to pop around (some will open up) and are well browned—about 8 minutes. Spread out on a flat surface to cool. In the same pan, toast the *chile* seeds, stirring and shaking the pan until they are a deep golden color. Transfer to a blender jar. When the pumpkin seeds have cooled off thoroughly, put a small quantity at a time into a coffee/spice grinder and grind as finely as possible. When all the pumpkin seeds have been finely ground, set them aside.

Add ½ cup of the chicken broth to the *chile* seeds in the blender jar and blend together with the clove, allspice, and garlic until smooth, adding a little more broth if necessary to release the blades of the blender. Put the contents of the blender jar into a saucepan, add the ground pumpkin seeds and the remaining broth, and bring to a simmer. Continue to cook for about 8 minutes or until the soup is just beginning to thicken. Pass through a fine strainer, pressing the debris of the husks down well—there will be about ½ cup left in the strainer. Continue to cook the soup over low heat, adjusting salt, until it thickens slightly—about 5 minutes. Put some of the shredded, warmed chicken into each of the soup cups, pour the hot soup over it, and sprinkle with *chile* to taste.

SOPA DE FLOR DE CALABAZA *(Squash Flower Soup)*

MAKES 6 CUPS

This is quite a rustic soup compared with the preceding more elegant recipe. It can be prepared well ahead, even the day before, but it does not freeze successfully.

2 tablespoons unsalted butter
2 tablespoons finely chopped white onion
1 garlic clove, peeled and finely chopped
1¼ pounds *flor de calabaza,* cleaned and finely chopped (see page 150)
5 cups light chicken broth (page 95)
⅔ cup zucchini in ¼-inch cubes
⅔ cup corn kernels
2 small leafy stems of *epazote*
sea salt to taste
2 *chiles poblanos,* peeled, cut into strips or squares and sautéed (see page 471)

Heat the butter in a frying pan, add the onion and garlic, and fry gently without browning for about 2 minutes. Stir in the flowers (it will seem an enormous quantity but will reduce rapidly to less than half the volume), cover the pan, and cook over medium heat for about 5 minutes. If the flowers are very fresh, the mixture will be juicy; remove the cover and continue to cook until the calyxes of the flowers are tender and the juice has been reduced—about 10 minutes. If the flowers tend to be dry, add 3 tablespoons water and cook, covered, for the whole period.

Put 1 cup of the flowers into a blender jar with ⅔ cup of the broth and blend until smooth. Transfer to a saucepan. Add the rest of the flowers and broth, zucchini, and corn kernels; cook over medium heat until the vegetables are tender—about 10 minutes. Add the *epazote,* taste for salt, and continue to cook for 5 minutes more. Garnish with *chile* strips.

SOPA DE CUITLACOCHE (*Corn Fungus Soup*)

SERVES 6

This is perhaps the only black soup in the world's cuisines and is very popular in central Mexico when *cuitlacoche* is at its best, during the rainy season. Take care not to overcook the *cuitlacoche*; it should have a good crisp texture. Blending the ½ cup to give body to the broth is optional.

This soup can be cooked a few hours ahead, but it is best eaten the same day that it is made. It does not freeze successfully.

3 cups cooked *cuitlacoche* (page 169), omitting *chiles* and *epazote*
4 cups chicken broth (page 95)
2 *chiles poblanos,* charred, cleaned, and cut into strips or squares (see page 47)
2 leafy stems of *epazote*
sea salt to taste
6 large tablespoons *crème fraîche*

Put ½ cup of the cooked *cuitlacoche* and 1 cup of the chicken broth into a blender jar and blend until smooth. Transfer this puree to a saucepan. Add the rest of the *cuitlacoche,* the remaining broth, the *chile* strips, and the *epazote;* simmer for about 10 minutes. Adjust seasoning. Before serving it, put a large blob of *crème fraîche* into each bowl.

WHOLE HOMINY FOR SOUPS

MAKES ABOUT 3½ TO 4 CUPS

The large white dried corn kernels known as *cacahuazintle* in Mexico, whole hominy, are used in many of the substantial soups, like *pozole*, some *menudos*, and *gallina pinta*, the hearty soup of Sonora. This corn is sold in Mexico and in Mexican markets either *con cabeza*, with pedicel (the small fibrous base of the kernel), or *descabezado*, with pedicel removed. Although the latter eliminates some of the cleaning work, the kernels have been cut with a machine and do not flower as well, and they still have to be treated with lime to remove the skin. So it is best to buy the *con cabeza* corn and prepare your own.

Of course you can buy canned hominy, but it is already cooked and tends to become mushy; besides, you will not have the cooking broth for enriching the soup. In almost all Latin American markets and supermarkets where there is a Latin American population you can find prepared hominy, ready for the final cooking and flowering, in the refrigerator or freezer cases. But choose your brand carefully; some tend to overdo the preservatives that give a slightly distorted taste to the corn.

The cooking and "flowering" of the corn is not complicated, but it's a little time-consuming until you are practiced in it. You can prepare a large batch up until the final cooking and freeze what you don't use.

While the corn is usually cooked with nothing but water, there are some exceptions, where salt, onion, and garlic are added.

Eight ounces of dried whole hominy, or large white corn kernels, measures about 1½ cups and when cooked will yield between 3½ and 4 cups, depending on quality.

½ pound whole dried hominy, with pedicel (*con cabeza*)
1½ rounded teaspoons powdered lime (see page 7)

Put the whole hominy into an enamel or stainless-steel pot and add enough cold water to come about 2 inches above the surface of the corn. Set over medium heat. Dilute the powdered lime with about ½ cup cold water and add to the pot through a fine strainer, pressing out the lumps with a wooden spoon. The water will become slightly milky. Cook the corn until it comes to a simmer (the skins of the kernels will now be bright yellow) and continue cooking, covered, until the skin can easily be slipped off the kernels—about 20 minutes. Remove from the heat and set aside to cool off. When the corn is cool enough to handle, drain and put into cold water, rubbing the kernels through your hands until the skins have been cleaned off. Skim off the skins and discard; rinse the corn once more. With the tip of a paring knife or a strong thumbnail, remove the pedicels.

When all the corn has been cleaned, add enough fresh water to come about 3 inches above the surface of the corn, cover, and bring to a fast simmer. Continue cooking until the corn is tender and has opened up like a cupped flower—about 1½ to 2 hours, depending on how old the corn is. When cooked, always reserve the cooking water and add it with the corn to the soup.

You may use a pressure cooker for this last step. Bring up to pressure, lower the heat, and cook slowly for about 30 minutes.

POZOLE VERDE (Green Pozole)

SERVES 4   GUERRERO

This is one of those rare recipes, surprising in its flavors and wonderful in its simplicity—an out-and-out favorite of mine. I found it in a little book dedicated to the cooking of Chilapa, in the state of Guerrero. It calls for 20 leaves of *axoxoco*, an intriguing name that turns out to be a wild sour-grass, also called *lengua de vaca* (cow's tongue) or *oreja de liebre* (hare's ear) or more prosaically in the state of Mexico, *vinagrera*, describing its sharp acidity.

During the rainy season I can find this wild green growing alongside the irrigation ditches, but since it wasn't raining when I was cooking this recipe, I substituted sorrel.

The toppings or garnishes for *pozoles* in Guerrero are different from those of other regions; while they call for finely chopped onion and dried oregano, which are normal, they also include cubed avocado and small pieces of *chicharrón* (fried pork skin), all of which provide a wonderful contrast to the soup. Chopped *chiles serranos* and limes are also part of it, but I think they tend to exaggerate the heat and acidity of this particular *pozole*. I have listed them as optional.

Leaving aside the *chicharrón*, this seems to me to be the perfect vegetarian dish; crisp-fried *totopos* (page 15) can be substituted for the *chicharrón*.

½ cup hulled, raw pumpkin seeds
9 ounces *tomate verde*, husks removed, rinsed and quartered (about 2 cups)
1½ cups water
10 large sorrel leaves, rinsed, stems removed, roughly chopped
finely chopped *chile serrano* to taste
2 tablespoons safflower oil or melted lard
3 to 3½ cups cooked hominy (preceding recipe), with ¼ white onion and 2
    peeled garlic cloves added
1 quart hominy cooking water
1 large leafy stem of *epazote*
sea salt to taste

THE TOPPINGS
finely chopped white onion
dried oregano, Mexican if possible
1 large avocado, peeled, pit removed, and cubed
2 ounces *chicharrón*, broken into small pieces
lime quarters (optional, see note above)

Put the pumpkin seeds into an ungreased frying pan and heat through over medium heat, shaking the pan from time to time, until they begin to pop around and swell noticeably; do not let them brown. Spread them out on a flat surface to cool. When cool, grind them finely in a coffee/spice grinder.

Put the *tomate verde* into a pan with ½ cup of the water.

Cook over medium heat until soft and mushy—about 15 minutes (there should be hardly any liquid in the pan; if there is, drain them). Transfer mixture to a blender jar. Add the chopped sorrel leaves, fresh *chiles*, and remaining 1 cup water and blend until smooth.

Heat the oil in a heavy pan and add the blended ingredients through a fine strainer, pressing down to extract as much of the juice as possible without the stringy veins, etc. Fry over fairly high heat, stirring from time to time, for about 5 minutes. Stir in the ground seeds and cook for 10 minutes longer, stirring and scraping the bottom of the pan until the broth has thickened slightly and is well seasoned—about 10 minutes.

Add the hominy and the 1 quart water in which it was cooked. Add the *epazote* and salt to taste and cook for another 10 to 15 minutes.

Serve in deep bowls and pass the toppings separately in small bowls.

MENUDO BLANCO SONORENSE
(White Sonoran Menudo)

SERVES 8 TO 10

Menudo is usually a deep, earthy red broth with tripe in it and, depending on the region, with or without hominy. But the *menudo* of Sonora is "white," or whitish, and of all the comfort foods this is number one in my book. It is also the one dish that has carried across the border with any fidelity—although the lemon served with it up north is too strong. My friend María Dolores, who was born in Sonora, tells me that her mother made it this way, with a sprig or two of *cilantro* in the broth, and served it plain with crumbled *chile piquín*. Nowadays you are offered finely chopped white onion, chopped *cilantro*, and lime quarters. It is served in deep bowls with wheat flour *tortillas*; there should be about 1 cup of broth per person.

Read the comment on buying tripe (page 311) before marketing. The calf's foot gives an added richness to the broth. You may need to give the butcher advance notice for both items.

This *menudo* can be eaten the day after it is made; in fact it keeps well for a few days in the refrigerator. It freezes remarkably well for several weeks.

1 small (about 2 pounds) beef or calf's foot, split horizontally and cut into 6 pieces
1 small head of garlic, unpeeled and cut in half horizontally
1 medium white onion, roughly sliced
1 scant tablespoon sea salt
2 pounds tripe
¾ pound (4½ to 5 cups) dried hominy, cooked and flowered (page 106) plus cooking water

TOPPING
crumbled *chile piquín*
finely chopped white onion
roughly chopped *cilantro*
lime quarters

Put the calf's foot pieces, garlic, onion, and half the salt in a large pan. Put the tripe on top with the remaining salt, cover the pan, and cook over very low heat so that it simmers for about 3 hours.

Strain the meat, reserving the broth, and cut the tripe into small squares—about 1½ inches. Remove the bones from the calf's foot and chop the flesh roughly. Return the meats to the pan with the broth, the flowered hominy, and the hominy cooking water. Taste for salt and continue cooking over very low heat for 1 hour. Serve in deep bowls with flour *tortillas*, passing around the topping for each to serve *al gusto*.

SOPA DE HABAS *(Dried Fava Bean Soup)*

SERVES 4 TO 6   CENTRAL MEXICO

When I was going back through old notebooks of recipes given to me during my first years in Mexico, I found this delicious way of cooking a Lenten soup of dried fava beans.

Always buy the peeled yellow fava beans, not the unpeeled chocolate-colored ones, which are better for planting than for cooking. Cooking time will depend on the age and dryness of the beans, how long they have been stored, etc. These factors can also affect the amount of water used in cooking.

This soup can be made ahead; in fact it develops flavor and thickens considerably, so it may have to be diluted with water or a light chicken broth.

A friend from the Sierra de Puebla tells me that in her family they spread a *tortilla* or *tostada* with the jellied—for that's how it is the next day—fava bean soup and sprinkle it with toasted *chiles moritas* and *queso añejo*.

½ pound dried peeled fava beans
3 to 3½ quarts water
1 small white onion, roughly chopped
1 garlic clove, peeled
4 peppercorns
¼-inch cinnamon stick
3 whole cloves
sea salt to taste
3 tablespoons olive oil
1 medium tomato (about 6 ounces), finely chopped, unpeeled
1 to 2 (to taste) *chiles serranos*, finely chopped
2 tablespoons roughly chopped *cilantro*, plus additional for garnish
1 large mint sprig

Rinse the fava beans, drain, and put into a large pan. Add 3 quarts of the water, the onion, garlic, peppercorns, cinnamon, and cloves. Cover the pan and bring to a simmer. Continue simmering, stirring the mixture from time to time, until the beans begin to soften—about 1½ hours. Add salt, more water if necessary, and cook for another hour. Meanwhile, heat 1 tablespoon of the oil in a frying pan, add the tomato and fresh *chiles*, and fry over fairly high heat, stirring and scraping the bottom of the pan, until you have a reduced and textured sauce—about 8 minutes. Add this, the *cilantro*, and the mint and continue cooking until the soup has thickened and all the flavors have blended well together.

This soup is not smooth; there will still be pieces of the beans that do not entirely disintegrate. To each serving of the soup, add a teaspoon of the remaining oil and a sprinkling of additional *cilantro*.

FRIJOL BLANCO CON CAMARÓN SECO
(White Bean and Dried Shrimp Soup)

MAKES 9 CUPS TO SERVE 6   OAXACA

If there is one unforgettable sight in Oaxaca's central Juarez market, it is the enormous piles of dried and semidried (moist and orangey in color) shrimps from minute ½-inchers to large 3-inch prawns.

While dried and semidried shrimps primarily form an important part of the Lenten food throughout Mexico, in Oaxaca there is always a plentiful supply and they are consumed the year round.

This dish has a fascinating combination of flavors, with the small white beans, the half-dried shrimps, and the anisy *hoja santa* with stewed tomatoes. Although not a soup in the Oaxacan context—it is a main dish—it makes an excellent one. I suggest the following substitutions for reproducing it in the United States: Choose the smallest dried white bean you can find; fennel leaves and fennel seeds could be used instead of *hoja santa* with a mixture of half dried and half fresh shrimps. I also like to use a light olive oil instead of vegetable oil for frying the tomato puree.

This is a hearty dish and should be served in deep bowls with plenty of *tortillas* or French bread to accompany it.

It is better made the day before or at least left some hours to mature in flavor; if you do this, add the fresh shrimps just before reheating.

THE BEANS
½ pound dried white beans
a small head of garlic, charred (see page 439)
½ small white onion, charred (see page 455)
¼ teaspoon sea salt (not much, as the shrimps are salty)
2 quarts hot water, approximately

THE REST
¼ pound dried shrimp
¾ pound (about 2 medium) tomatoes, broiled or stewed (see pages 450 and 451)
5 small garlic cloves, peeled
½ small white onion, roughly chopped
¼ cup water
3 tablespoons light olive oil
2 *hoja santa* leaves or fennel leaf sprays and ¼ teaspoon fennel seed
¼ pound medium-sized fresh shrimps, unshelled

112

Run the beans through your hands to make sure there are no stones or lumps of earth in them. Rinse well and then put them into a slow cooker or bean pot. Add the garlic, onion, and salt; cover with the water (always having extra on the side to add when necessary). Bring to a simmer and continue to cook slowly for 3 to 5 hours, depending on the age and dryness of the beans. Meanwhile, cover the dried shrimps with warm water and allow to soak for about 10 minutes. Drain and set aside.

Put the tomatoes, garlic, onion, and water into a blender jar and blend until smooth. Heat the oil in a frying pan, add the puree, and cook at a fast simmer for about 15 minutes, until the puree is thickened and well seasoned.

When the beans are soft, add the tomato puree and dried shrimps and cook for about 10 minutes. Add the *hoja santa* or fennel and fennel seeds, fresh shrimp, salt if necessary. Add water to bring the total quantity up to 9 cups. Cook for 10 minutes. Serve 1½ cups per person.

CALDO DE CAMARÓN SECO (*Dried Shrimp Broth*)

MAKES ABOUT 8 TO 9 CUPS

This is a wonderfully colorful and substantial soup most often prepared during Lent by El Vergel restaurant in Zitácuaro, Michoacán. The locals consider it an effective restorative in cases of bad hangovers. Señora Guadalupe Muniz, owner/chef of El Vergel, uses a pork knuckle to further enrich the broth, but this is optional and certainly not Lenten. Substitute a good tablespoon of rich olive oil stirred into each bowl for a smooth richness.

You can't serve this in dainty portions. A large bowl of this dried shrimp soup, accompanied by crusty French bread (or *bolillos* like those baked daily in the wood-fired ovens of the many small bakeries dotted around the town) and followed by a salad, is a meal. Or perhaps you could serve a few *antojitos* to start.

You can, of course, use canned chick-peas, but these have been partially cooked and tend to turn mushy; besides, by cooking your own, you have the broth to add to the soup and give an extra hint of flavor.

Finding the large dried shrimp that are sold in Mexico may prove a problem. If so, use small ones. And yes, you do crunch through the shells and tail!

The soup can be served with lime (not lemon) quarters and chopped white onion if preferred.

¼ pound dried shrimp (see note above)
1–1½ ounces (about 10) *chiles guajillos*
1 pound (about 2 large) ripe tomatoes
2 large garlic cloves, peeled
2 tablespoons safflower oil
⅔ cup cooked chick-peas (page 187)
6 ounces (3 medium) carrots, scraped and cut into ½-inch slices
6 ounces (3 small) red bliss potatoes, peeled and cut into ½-inch cubes
5 cups water, approximately
sea salt to taste

THE GARNISH
⅓ cup olive oil (optional; see note above)
½ cup chopped white onion
8 lime quarters

Remove heads and legs from the shrimps, if any (leaving tails and shells intact), and grind them to a fine powder in an electric spice grinder. Set both the whole shrimps and the shrimp powder aside.

Wipe any dust or dirt off the dried *chiles* with a damp cloth. Remove the stems and discard. Slit them open, removing veins and seeds. Discard the seeds and set veins aside. Tear the *chiles* into small pieces.

Cover the tomatoes with water and bring to a simmer. Simmer for about 5 minutes. Drain, discarding the cooking water. Transfer the unskinned tomatoes to a blender jar (do not use a food processor as it is not as effective in this case), add the garlic, and blend until smooth. Add the *chile* pieces and blend again until the puree is as smooth as possible, adding a little water if necessary to do a more efficient job. Press the puree through a fine strainer or sieve and discard the *chile* skin debris.

In a large saucepan, heat the oil, add the tomato/*chile* puree, and cook over high heat, stirring and scraping the bottom of the pan from time to time to prevent sticking, until reduced—about 10 minutes. Add the chick-peas, whole shrimp, shrimp powder, carrots, potatoes, water, and salt to taste; set over low heat to simmer for about 1 hour. By this time the shrimps will be soft, the vegetables tender, and all the flavors amalgamated. Dilute with 1 cup water if too concentrated. Top with olive oil, onion, and lime.

Note: If cooking with pork knuckle, have butcher cut one large or two small knuckles into several pieces, cover them with water, and simmer for about 2 hours. Strain, discard the knuckles, reserve the broth, and reduce or make up to 5 cups. Use instead of water in soup.

SOPA TARASCA *(Tarascan Soup)*

SERVES 6

There are two soups with the name *sopa Tarasca* in and around the Pátzcuaro/Morelia area. The version given here bears a close resemblance to *tortilla soup* and is more commonly found in restaurants there. The other version, known as *tipo conde*, is made with a base of pureed beans, and the recipe was published in *The Cuisines of Mexico* some years ago.

This soup can be made ahead and, in fact, improves as it stands; the *tortilla* strips, fried *chile ancho*, and cheese are added a few seconds before serving.

½ cup water
6 ounces (about 1 medium) tomatoes, roughly chopped, unpeeled
1 small slice white onion
1 garlic clove, peeled and roughly chopped
1 small *chile ancho*, cleaned of veins and soaked in hot water for 10 minutes
1 corn *tortilla*
1 tablespoon safflower oil
5 cups chicken broth (page 95)
1 large leafy stem of *epazote* (optional)
sea salt to taste
⅛ teaspoon dried oregano, Mexican if possible
6 corn *tortillas*, cut into narrow strips and fried crisp
3 *chiles anchos*, cleaned of seeds and veins, flattened out, torn into thin strips, and fried crisp
6 tablespoons finely grated *queso añejo* or Romano cheese

Put the water into a blender jar and add the tomato, onion, garlic, dried *chile ancho*, and *tortilla*. Blend to a fairly smooth puree. Heat the oil in a soup pot, add the puree, and fry over fairly high heat for about 8 minutes. Add the chicken broth, optional *epazote*; cook over medium heat until well seasoned— about 10 minutes. Taste for salt and add oregano.

Put some of the fried *tortilla* pieces into each cup, pour the soup over them, top with pieces of fried *chile ancho* and cheese, and serve immediately.

PASTA AND RICE DISHES

(Sopas Secas)

Arroz a la Mexicana (Mexican Rice)
Arroz Blanco (White Rice)
Arroz Verde (Green Rice)
Morisqueta (Plain Boiled Rice)
Morisqueta con Chorizo (Boiled Rice with Chorizo)
Arroz con Caldo de Frijol (Rice with Bean Broth)
Arroz con Zanahoria y Chayote (Rice with Carrot and Chayote)
Sopa de Espageti con Queso y Crema (Spaghetti with Cheese and Cream)
Macarrón con Jitomate (Macaroni with Tomatoes)
Sopa de Macarrón y Acelgas (Macaroni with Swiss Chard)
Cross-Reference:
Budín de Uchepos
Budín de Corundas
Efigenia's Chilaquiles
Budín de Cuitlacoche
Crepas de Cuitlacoche

If you are invited to a family *comida* (meal), or are eating in a small provincial restaurant in Mexico, it is always assumed that you will eat a *sopa seca* after the *botana*, or appetizer, and before the main course. It is the equivalent of the pasta course in an Italian meal and is generally served alone. In many cases it is not *picante*, but then there is always a *salsa* or some pickled *chiles* on the table for those who cannot eat without them.

Seven times out of ten the *sopa seca* will be a dish of rice, while on other occasions it may be a pasta, *macaroni, espageti, tallarines (tagliarini)*, or *coditos* (elbow macaroni) being the most popular, cooked in a simple tomato sauce or just with cream and cheese. A *budín* (savory pudding) or *tortillas* or *crêpes* layered between sauced meat, or vegetables with cheese and *chile* strips, or a dish of *crêpes* filled with wild mushrooms or squash blossoms baked with cream and cheese would appear in a more upscale meal. *Tamales* too play their part, sliced and layered between *mole* and shredded meats or vegetables and tomato sauce; they make an excellent *sopa seca*, while in Michoacán leftover *uchepos* and *corundas* are deliciously used up in this way (see recipes, pages 86 and 70). While these *sopas* form only part of a traditional meal, they can easily be incorporated into brunch or lunch menus or served with a salad to make a light dinner—an unusual one at that!

RICE *(Arroz)*

Rice plays quite an important role in Mexican food today—although not as important as the rather extravagant claims of the *Diccionario de Cocina*, 1845 edition: "This grain is used so much that there is hardly a dish, savory or sweet, in which it is not employed."

Rice was introduced into Mexico early in the colonial period, brought from the Philippines to Acapulco in the famous galleon the *Nao de China*. Spices and other luxuries were brought not only to the Spaniards living in Mexico, but for transshipment to Spain, whose sea routes to the East had been cut off by the Portuguese and the Turks.

While a dish of savory rice is the most important of the *sopas secas*, it is also used in various desserts; ground into flour, it is used in cakes, *budines* (vegetable puddings), *tamales*, different-flavored *atoles* (gruels), and the cooling drink *horchata*. Reading through my old cookbooks, I am fascinated to see the rather complicated recipes, both savory and sweet, in which rice figured at the turn of the century, practically all of which have been dropped from even the most traditional of tables.

The rice used and grown in Mexico is a long-grained one; it is not overrefined and thus still has the white fleck of the germ. When cooked, it will expand to four times its original bulk, thus absorbing more liquid than the rice distributed in the United States.

Brown rice, *arroz integral*, is sometimes seen in the supermarkets, but it is found mostly in health food stores for vegetarians and has not really captured the general public. In my earliest cooking days in Mexico, 30 years ago, I was taught to soak the rice for quite a long time (this softens the rice and it not only cooks more quickly but absorbs the flavors of the other ingredients better), fry it to a deep golden color, and then cook it in an earthenware *cazuela*, uncovered—*cazuelas* did not and still do not have covers. Like everything else in that span of time, the preparation has been modified, but not that much. The quality of the rice has no doubt changed, and the soaking period is much shorter; now I finish off the cooking by covering the *cazuela* with a towel and a lid. Many cooks I know now cook rice with the lid on all the time; I reserve this for *morisqueta* (page 124).

While the rule of thumb in the United States is 1 cup of rice to 2 cups of water, in Mexico it is 1 to 2½ or 3—so it is best to experiment with different brands of rice, quantities, etc., as they do act differently. The type and shape of pot, the length of storage, quality of packaging, and even the humidity in the air will affect the absorption point of the rice. Choose a heavy pot for cooking the rice; it will be less likely to scorch on the bottom. The shape of the pot is also important; if it is too wide, the water will cook off too quickly and the rice will not be as tender; if it is too deep, it is liable to be mushy at the bottom. For all of these reasons it is necessary to experiment a little. When cooked, every grain should be soft but stand apart. And one last word of advice: do not use precooked, preseasoned, or converted rice. These types of rice will not absorb the flavors or produce the right texture.

Any rice left over will freeze well. I always advise storing it in rather thin packages of heavy foil. It can be reheated just as it is, without even bothering to defrost, in a 350° oven for about 30 minutes, depending on the size of the package, of course. I do not recommend steaming to reheat, as the flavors tend to leach out into the water below.

ARROZ A LA MEXICANA (*Mexican Rice*)

SERVES 6

Without doubt this is the most popular way of cooking rice and the most ubiquitous "dry soup" in Mexico as a whole. It is not Spanish rice, as so many restaurant menus would have you believe, and the orangey-red color of it is from tomatoes, not saffron.

While often served alone, it is sometimes accompanied by a fried egg or pickled *chiles: jalapeños, anchos,* or *chipotles.*

It is quite common to find the rice flavored with a few vegetables: slices of carrot, a few peas, or diced zucchini; perhaps a sprig of flat-leaf parsley or a whole *chile serrano* or two—not to make it *picante* but to give flavor. Giblets from the chicken broth—heart, gizzard, etc.—are quite often roughly chopped and added, and among my neighbors in Michoacán, chicken fat is melted and used to fry the rice.

1½ cups (about 10½ ounces) unconverted long-grain rice
1 cup (½ pound) finely chopped unskinned tomatoes
2 tablespoons finely chopped white onion
1 garlic clove, peeled and roughly chopped
⅓ cup safflower oil, melted chicken fat, or melted lard
3½ cups light chicken broth (page 95), approximately
⅓ cup carrot rounds (optional)
½ cup fresh peas or diced zucchini (optional)
½ cup chopped giblets (optional)
sea salt to taste

Put the rice into a bowl and cover with very hot water. Stir and leave to soak for about 10 minutes. Drain, rinse in cold water, and drain again.

Put the tomatoes, onion, and garlic into a blender jar and blend until smooth. Set aside.

Heat the oil in a heavy pan. Give the rice a final shake and stir into the fat. Fry over fairly high heat until it begins to turn a light golden color. Strain off any excess oil, stir in the tomato puree, and fry, scraping the bottom of the dish to prevent sticking, until the puree has been absorbed— about 8 minutes. Stir in the broth, vegetables, and giblets, if used, add salt to taste, and cook over fairly high heat, uncovered, until all the broth has been absorbed and air holes appear in the surface. Cover the surface of the rice with a towel and lid and continue cooking over very low heat for about 5 minutes longer. Remove from the heat and set aside in a warm place for the rice to absorb the rest of the moisture in the steam and swell—about 15 minutes. Dig gently to the bottom and test a grain of rice. If it is still damp, cook for a few minutes longer. If the top grains are not quite soft, sprinkle with a little hot broth, cover, and cook for a few minutes longer.

Before serving, turn the rice over carefully from the bottom so that the flavored juices will be distributed evenly.

ARROZ BLANCO (*White Rice*)

SERVES 6

Arroz blanco is cooked and served in the same way as *Arroz a la Mexicana* (page 120), as a dry soup, often alone and sometimes with pickled *chile* strips on top—*jalapeños* (see page 356), *anchos* (see page 355), *chipotles* (see page 358)—with *cazuelitas* in the manner of the North, or with strips of fried plantain.

Vegetables are sometimes added, but sparingly; occasionally a branch of parsley or a couple of whole *serranos* are added—not to make the rice *picante* but to give flavor. In Michoacán diced zucchini is often added.

1½ cups (about 10½ ounces) unconverted long-grain rice
⅓ cup safflower oil, melted chicken fat, or melted lard
3 tablespoons finely chopped white onion
1 garlic clove, peeled and finely chopped
3½ cups light chicken broth (page 95), approximately
1 cup fresh corn kernels *or* ⅓ cup carrot rounds plus ½ cup fresh peas (optional)
1 parsley sprig *or* 2 whole *chiles serranos* (optional)
sea salt to taste

Put the rice into a bowl and cover with very hot water. Stir once and leave to soak for 10 minutes. Drain, rinse in cold water, and drain again.

Heat the oil in a heavy pan. Give the rice a final shake and stir into the fat. Fry over medium heat for about 5 minutes, stirring almost continuously. Add the onion and garlic and continue frying until the rice is just turning a pale gold and the onion is transparent—about 3 to 5 minutes longer.

Pour in the broth and, if used, the vegetables and parsley or fresh *chiles*, add salt to taste, stir once again for the last time, and cook over fairly high heat, uncovered, until all the broth has been absorbed and air holes appear in the surface. Cover the surface of the rice with a towel and lid and continue cooking over very low heat for 5 minutes more. Remove from the heat and set aside in a warm place for the rice to absorb the rest of the moisture in the steam and swell—about 15 minutes. Dig gently to the bottom and test a grain of rice. If it is still damp, cook for a few minutes longer. If the top grains are not quite soft, then sprinkle with a little more hot broth, cover, and cook for a few minutes longer.

Before serving, turn the rice over from the bottom so that the flavored juices will be distributed evenly.

ARROZ VERDE (Green Rice)

SERVES 6 TO 7

You would be hard put to find *arroz verde* in a restaurant; it is essentially a home-cooked version of Mexican rice with each cook exercising her preferences as to what greens she will use—or what there is to use around the kitchen.

I have cooked this recipe with a puree of pure *epazote* and *cilantro* but prefer the balance that the parsley gives. I also prefer to use the *poblano* in strips rather than blended with the rest of the greens, as it tends to have a rather bitter flavor. Serve with some pickled *chiles—jalapeños*, *chipotles*, etc.—and quarters of hard-cooked egg if desired.

1½ cups (about 10½ ounces) unconverted long-grain rice
⅓ cup safflower oil, melted chicken fat, or melted lard
3 tablespoons finely chopped white onion
2 chiles poblanos, charred, peeled, and cut into strips (see page 470)
4 cups chicken broth (page 95)
1 garlic clove, peeled and roughly chopped
1 cup firmly packed, roughly chopped flat-leaf parsley
½ cup firmly packed, roughly chopped *epazote* or *cilantro*
sea salt to taste

Put the rice into a bowl and pour very hot water over to cover; stir and set aside for 10 minutes. Drain in a strainer and rinse in cold water; drain again and set aside.

Heat the oil in a heavy pan, stir the rice into it, and fry over fairly high heat, stirring and scraping the bottom of the pan, for about 5 minutes. Add the onion and *chile* strips and continue frying for 4 minutes or until the onion is translucent.

Meanwhile, put 1 cup of the broth into a blender jar; add the garlic, parsley, and *epazote* and blend until smooth. Add this to the frying rice and continue frying and reducing the puree over quite high heat, stirring and scraping the bottom of the pan, until the rice is dry. Stir in the rest of the broth, add salt to taste, and cook over fairly high heat, uncovered, until the liquid has been absorbed and there are air holes in the rice. Cover with a towel and lid and continue cooking over low heat for 5 minutes. Remove from the heat and set aside, still covered, in a warm place for the rice to swell up. Before serving, turn the rice over with a fork from the bottom where a lot of the flavor and oil will have settled.

MORISQUETA *(Plain Boiled Rice)*

MAKES 2½ TO 3 CUPS

When you see a Spanish word like *morisqueta,* you know it has something to do with the Moors, and here it refers to plain boiled rice, steamed until fluffy and generally unseasoned. You find *morisqueta* in parts of west central Mexico— Colima, parts of Michoacán and Jalisco—where it is considered comfort food for sick days, rainy days, every day. One family in Jalisco always had it with some bean broth on it as a snack on arriving home from school. Another remembers the cheesecloth bag hanging in the broth from the neck of the *olla* where the *cocido* was cooking, while others remember the perforated aluminum ball—like a tea ball but larger—in which the *morisqueta* was steamed. (An enterprising German who until recent years was still selling high-class kitchen things had it made for the market in Mexico.) While generally eaten unsalted, *morisqueta* is often lightly salted; as in Chinese cooking, the sauces and seasoned meats eaten with it have flavor and salt enough.

I like to cook my *morisqueta* in a small earthenware bean pot—it has broad shoulders and a narrow neck so that the condensed steam falls back into the rice, thus keeping it moist—but any heavy pot will do.

1 cup (about ½ pound) unconverted long-grain rice
2 cups cold water
a touch of sea salt (optional)

Put the rice into a bowl, cover with very hot water, and leave to soak about 8 minutes. Drain, rinse well, and set aside. Put 2 cups water in a heavy pot or earthenware bean pot, bring to a boil, sprinkle in the rice, and return to the boil. Cover the pan, turn the heat to the lowest possible point, and cook until all the water has been absorbed by the rice, shaking the pot from time to time so that it does not stick. Test the rice after about 15 minutes; if soft but not mushy, turn off the heat and leave the rice sitting, still covered, for a further 5 minutes. Very carefully loosen the rice with a fork, fluffing it up. Cover again and leave to sit for another 15 minutes. Add salt if desired.

The rice can be accompanied by the cooked Michoacán *salsa de chile pasilla* (page 343) and grated *queso añejo.* It can also go on top of *espinazo de puerco con albóndigas* (page 260) or *frijoles guisados* and crumbled *queso añejo* (page 444).

MORISQUETA CON CHORIZO
(Boiled Rice with Chorizo)

SERVES 4   HUETAMO

This is a savory way of serving *morisqueta*, making use of the excellent *chorizo* that is available in Huetamo, an isolated town in the hot country of Michoacán, where traditional eating customs have been very much preserved.

2 tablespoons lard or safflower oil
6 ounces 3- to 4-inch *chorizo*, skinned
3 tablespoons finely chopped white onion
½ pound (about 1 large) tomatoes, finely chopped, unpeeled (about 1 cup firmly packed)
3 cups cooked *morisqueta* (page 124)
sea salt to taste

Heat the lard in a large frying pan, crumble the *chorizo* into it, and cook over low heat, stirring from time to time, until it is well heated through and beginning to fry. Remove with a slotted spoon and set aside. Remove all but 3 tablespoons of the fat or add fat to make that amount. Add the onion and fry for 1 minute or until transparent but not browned. Add the chopped tomatoes and cook, stirring from time to time, over fairly high heat until reduced—about 3 minutes. Stir in the *chorizo* and rice, add salt to taste, and keep turning over carefully until the rice is well heated through and all the flavors are combined. Serve as a dry soup—alone.

ARROZ CON CALDO DE FRIJOL
(Rice with Bean Broth)

SERVES 4 TO 6   OAXACA

This recipe is a classic one from Oaxaca and was published in *Tradiciones Gastronómicas Oaxaqueñas*, 1982. This is an intriguing way of cooking rice, especially if you have an avocado leaf to give it that anisy flavor. This rice tends to stick, so it may be better to do the final cooking in the oven than on top of the stove. This sort of dish can be prepared well ahead and reheated in a water bath to prevent scorching.

1 cup (about ½ pound) unconverted long-grain rice
3 tablespoons lard or safflower oil
1½ cups broth from *frijoles negros a la Oaxaqueña* (page 184)
½ cup water, approximately
½ cup *frijoles negros a la Oaxaqueña* (page 184), drained
2 small garlic cloves, peeled
¼ small white onion
1 small avocado leaf, toasted (see page 449)

THE TOPPING
½ cup *crème fraîche*, approximately
⅔ cup crumbled *queso fresco*

Put rice into a bowl, cover with very hot water, and leave to soak for 10 minutes; rinse in cold water and drain again.

Heat the lard in a heavy pan and stir in the rice so that the grains become as evenly coated with it as possible. Fry the rice over fairly high heat, stirring it from time to time, until it is just beginning to turn golden—about 4 minutes. Strain off any extra oil and return the rice to the pan. Heat the oven to 325°.

Put the bean broth into a blender jar. Add the water, beans, garlic, and onion and crumble in the toasted avocado leaf. Blend until smooth. Stir the bean puree into the rice, cover the pan, and either cook over the lowest heat (see note above) or put into the oven until all the liquid has been absorbed and the rice is soft but not mushy—about 20 minutes. Serve with *crème fraîche* and crumbled cheese.

ARROZ CON ZANAHORIA Y CHAYOTE
(Rice with Carrot and Chayote)

SERVES 6 TO 8   OAXACA

Devoted as I am to the more classical way of cooking Mexican rice, this recipe came as a welcome surprise when a Oaxacan cook prepared it for me recently. It is a perfect vegetarian dish that lends itself to many adaptations.

Of course, if you don't have *chayote* readily available, zucchini or any other tender squash can be used in its place.

Don't take fright at the amount of garlic; the cloves used in Oaxaca are very small and delicate in flavor, and the taste is not overwhelming if you use the small purple garlic cloves.

Serve this either alone as a separate "dry soup" course or with *salsa de chile pasilla de Oaxaca* (page 342).

1½ cups (about 10½ ounces) unconverted long-grain rice
½ medium white onion, roughly chopped
6 small garlic cloves, peeled
½ cup cold water
¼ cup safflower oil
2 *chiles de agua* or any large green *chile*
4 cups loosely packed, finely grated carrots
1 large *chayote*, peeled and cut into ½-inch cubes
1 quart additional water, approximately
sea salt to taste

Cover the rice with very hot water and leave to soak for 10 minutes. Rinse and drain.

Meanwhile, blend together the onion, garlic, and ½ cup cold water and set aside. Heat the oil in a heavy pan, add the fresh *chiles*, and fry, turning them over from time to time, until evenly blistered. Remove and set aside.

Stir the rice into the same oil and fry over medium heat until it sounds brittle, as the local expression goes, but does not turn golden—about 10 minutes, depending on the type of pan used. Strain off any excess oil. Add the onion/garlic mixture and fry over high heat for a minute or so until it has been absorbed by the rice. Stir in the *chiles*, carrots, *chayote*, 1 quart water, and salt to taste. Bring the mixture to a boil, cover the pan, lower the heat to medium, and continue cooking until all the liquid has been absorbed—about 20 minutes.

Remove the pan from the heat and set aside, still covered, in a warm place for about 15 minutes for the rice to expand still more. Before serving, gently turn the rice over from the bottom with a fork so that the vegetables are distributed evenly—they tend to congregate at the top.

PASTA

SOPA DE ESPAGETI CON QUESO Y CREMA
(Spaghetti with Cheese and Cream)

SERVES 4 TO 6

This *sopa* is very simple and delicious but does rely on an excellent quality cream.

2 quarts water
¼ small white onion
1 garlic clove, peeled
1 small bay leaf
pinch of dried oregano, Mexican if possible
1 tablespoon safflower oil
sea salt to taste
6 ounces *spaghetti*
2 tablespoons unsalted butter
1 cup *crème fraîche*
2 to 3 ounces *queso fresco, manchego,* or medium-sharp Cheddar

Put the water into a saucepan and add the onion, garlic, bay leaf, oregano, oil, and salt. Bring to a boil and add the spaghetti. Cook over high heat until the pasta is tender—not *al dente*. Strain, discard cooking water, rinse the pasta in cold water, drain, and set aside.

Melt the butter in a deep frying pan or sauté pan, stir in the cooked pasta, and heat through, turning it over thoroughly.

Add the cream and salt to taste and heat through over low heat—about 3 minutes. Add the cheese, stir once, and serve immediately.

MACARRÓN CON JITOMATE *(Macaroni with Tomatoes)*

SERVES 4 TO 6

Macaroni broken into small lengths, *penne, spaghetti,* or *spaghettini* may be used for this recipe. It can be served either after seasoning with the tomato sauce, with the cream and cheese passed separately, or after heating it in the oven for a short period.

The pasta that is widely distributed in Mexico is commercially made on a huge scale, and it is not first-class; it tends to be rather thin. So you do not need to use the best Italian pasta for these recipes.

2 quarts water
¼ small white onion
1 garlic clove, peeled
1 small California bay leaf
pinch of dried oregano, Mexican if possible
1 tablespoon safflower oil
sea salt to taste
6 ounces *macaroni,* broken in short lengths

1 pound (about 2 large) tomatoes, roughly chopped, unpeeled
2 tablespoons finely chopped white onion
1 garlic clove, peeled and roughly chopped
2 tablespoons safflower oil or unsalted butter
2 tablespoons roughly chopped fresh parsley
½ cup *crème fraîche*
2 ounces *queso fresco* or *añejo*

In a large saucepan combine the water, onion, whole garlic clove, bay leaf, oregano, safflower oil, and salt. Bring to a boil and gradually stir in the *macaroni.* Cook over high heat until the pasta is tender—not *al dente.* Strain, reserving about ⅔ cup of the cooking water. Rinse the pasta in cold water, drain, and set aside.

Put the reserved cooking water into a blender jar; add the tomatoes, onion, and chopped garlic and blend for a few seconds to make a textured puree.

Heat the oil in a frying pan, add the tomato puree, and cook over high heat, stirring and scraping the bottom of the pan, until the sauce has reduced and thickened—about 7 minutes. Stir in the cooked pasta and parsley and adjust seasoning. Cook gently, stirring well, for about 5 minutes so that the pasta is well impregnated with the sauce. Serve immediately and pass the cream and cheese separately.

Note: As an alternative, heat the oven to 350°. Generously butter an ovenproof dish into which the pasta will fit in a layer no deeper than 1 inch. Spread with the *crème fraîche,* sprinkle with the cheese, and heat through in the oven until bubbling and the cheese is melted. Serve immediately.

SOPA DE MACARRÓN Y ACELGAS
(*Macaroni with Swiss Chard*)

SERVES 4

A silversmith who lives near me—not a rich one; he lives in very modest circumstances—is fascinated by his native food. He is always stopping me in the street or inviting me to stop by his house to see a special *chile* or to tell me about a special insect eaten by the *indios* (Indians), as he calls them. On my last visit he produced a pile of pages he had typed himself—copies of two cookbooks he had come across in Tacambaro, Michoacán. Some of the recipes I recognized, others I didn't, and of the latter I shall give a few in this book. Here is one of them: an unusual pasta casserole typical of the "dry soups" based on Italian-type pasta and a favorite in Mexican popular cooking.

Serve the dish as is or with *chipotles en adobo* or pickled *jalapeños.*

unsalted butter for baking dish
¼ pound *macaroni* or *spaghetti*
1 large scallion, both white and green parts, roughly chopped
¼ teaspoon dried oregano, Mexican if possible
sea salt to taste
½ pound Swiss chard
1 tablespoon safflower oil or unsalted butter
1 garlic clove, peeled and roughly chopped
1 tablespoon finely chopped white onion
¾ cup thick *crème fraîche*
2 ounces *queso fresco, Chihuahua,* or medium-sharp Cheddar, grated

Liberally butter an ovenproof dish about 8 by 8 by 2 inches deep. Place rack at top of oven and heat to 350°. Break pasta into pieces about 5 inches long.

Put a large pot of water over high heat, adding the scallion, oregano, and salt. When it comes to a rolling boil, add pasta and cook for about 7 minutes, depending on the quality of the pasta—it should be a little more than *al dente* but not really soft. Drain and reserve the cooking water.

Rinse the Swiss chard leaves thoroughly and drain. Remove the stems and thick fleshy part at the base of the leaf (reserve for another dish) and chop the leaves roughly. Heat the oil in a large saucepan, add the garlic and onion, and fry gently for 1 to 2 minutes or until translucent but do not brown. Add the chopped chard, the reserved cooking water, and salt to taste, cover the pan, and cook for about 5 minutes. Uncover and continue cooking until tender—about 3 minutes longer.

Put the cream into a blender jar and add the cooked chard a little at a time, blending until smooth. Mix this puree into the cooked pasta and spread evenly in the ovenproof dish. Heat through until bubbling—about 10 minutes. Sprinkle with the cheese and return to the oven for a few minutes more, until the cheese has melted but not browned.

VEGETABLES, SALADS, AND BEANS

(Legumbres, Ensaladas, y Frijoles)

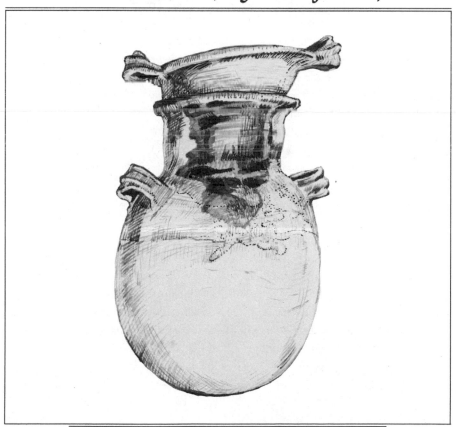

Chiles Rellenos (Stuffed Chiles)
To Prepare the Chile Poblano for Stuffing
To Prepare Dried Chiles Anchos for Stuffing
To Stuff Fresh or Dried Chiles
Coating with Batter and Frying Chiles Rellenos
Caldo de Jitomate para Chiles Rellenos (Tomato Broth for Stuffed Chiles)
Legumbres en Escabeche (Lightly Pickled Vegetables)
Sancocho de Verduras (Vegetable Relish)
Chileajo (Cold Vegetables in Chile Sauce)
Chayotes al Vapor (Steamed Chayotes)
Chayotes Guisados con Jitomate (Chayotes Cooked with Tomato)
Calabacitas (Squashes, General)
Flor de Calabaza (Squash Flowers)
Calabacitas Guisadas (Stewed Zucchini)
Torta de Calabacita (Zucchini Torte)
Budín de Elote (Corn Pudding)
Acelgas Guisadas (Stewed Swiss Chard)
Tortitas de Coliflor (Cauliflower Fritters)
Fava Beans and How to Cook Them
Habas Guisadas con Huevos (Fava Beans Cooked with Eggs)
Ensalada de Habas (Fava Bean Salad)
Tortitas de Papa (Potato Cakes)
Papas Guisadas (Potatoes Cooked with Tomato)
Papas Chirrionas (Potatoes Fried with Chile Sauce)
Camotes (Sweet Potatoes)
Hongos al Vapor ("Steamed" Mushrooms)
Tecomates con Crema (Mushrooms with Cream)
Tejamaniles con Carne de Puerco (Mushrooms with Shredded Pork)
Cuitlacoche (Corn Fungus)—To Prepare
To Cook Cuitlacoche (Corn Fungus)
Cuitlacoche Guisado con Jitomate (Corn Fungus Cooked with Tomato)
Crepas de Cuitlacoche (Crêpes Filled with Corn Fungus)
Budín de Cuitlacoche (Corn Fungus Pudding)
Nopales Asados (Grilled Cactus Paddles)
Nopales Cocidos (Boiled Cactus Paddles)
Nopales al Vapor ("Steamed" Cactus Paddles)
Nopales en Blanco ("White" Cactus Paddles)

Ensalada de Nopalitos (Salad of Cactus Pieces)
Frijoles de Olla (Pot Beans)
Frijoles Refritos (Refried Beans)
Frijoles Puercos, Michoacán ("Pork" Beans from Michoacán)
Frijoles Puercos, Colima ("Pork" Beans from Colima)
Frijoles Guisados (Cooked and Fried Beans)
Frijoles Negros a la Oaxaqueña (Oaxacan Black Beans)
Frijoles Negros con Chochoyotes (Black Beans with Dumplings)
Frijoles Colados y Fritos a la Yucateca (Yucatecan Black Bean Paste)
Garbanzos (Chick-Peas)
Lentejas en Adobo (Lentils Cooked with Chiles, Pork, and Fruit)
Cross-reference: Aluvias con Camarón Seco

VEGETABLES AND SALADS *(Legumbres y Ensaladas)*

While the concept of meat and two vegetables does not exist in the Mexican kitchen, generally speaking, fresh vegetables are used liberally in soups and stews, as an integral part of many main dishes, or served alone as a separate course. As the last they are often *guisados*—cooked with other ingredients—in fritters served in tomato sauce, pureed for vegetable puddings, or in *moles* and *pipianes* as Lenten dishes.

The simplest way of preparing vegetables in Mexico is *al vapor*. This is not in a steamer as one might suppose. After the vegetables are sautéed lightly with onion and garlic, and sometimes tomato, the pan is covered and the vegetables are left to stew briefly in their own juices. Wild greens (see below) are particularly delicious cooked this way and served with corn *tortillas* so each guest can make his or her own *tacos*.

Lightly pickled mixed vegetables like the *sancocho de legumbres* of Michoacán and the *chileajo* of Oaxaca are more than just relishes; they provide an important "filler" for meatless days and also a healthy accompaniment to other foods: pig's feet, *tamales*, a topping for *tostadas*, et al.

While markets generally, even in the small towns, are stocked with the vegetables more commonly used in the United States and Europe, they also sell a variety of seasonal herbs and wild greens, many indigenous to Mexico. Some have been domesticated and grown commercially, while others have been gathered by the local peasants: *verdolagas* (purslane, *Portulaca oleracea*), *quintoniles*, and *quelites*, of which there are several varieties (*Amaranthus hydribus, et al.*), *romeritos* (*Dondia mexicana*), *papaloquelite* (*Porophyllum coloratum* and other varieties), *vinagrera* (a wild sorrel), *epazote* (*Chenopodium* or *reloxys ambrosioides*), and many more, depending on the region and climate.

Various squashes, pumpkins, *chayotes*, and *chilacayote*, all cucurbits, are used as vegetables and in confections. There are also a number of different-colored *camotes*, types of sweet potato. Other roots are used in the Mexican cuisines, either cultivated like the *chayote* and *jícama*, or wild like those of the day lily, *Tigridia pavonia*, and a curious carmine-red-skinned tuber, *papa de agua* of the *sagitaria* species. They are subjects for endless study, both gastronomically and botanically.

Salads, as such, do not play as important a role as vegetables, although slices of tomatoes and radishes, shredded lettuce and cabbage, chopped *cilantro* and onion are used extensively on some types of *antojitos*, *enchiladas*, *tostadas*, *tacos*, etc., and are not only attractive and crunchy but provide complementary nutrients.

Beans have an introduction of their own, later in the chapter.

CHILES RELLENOS *(Stuffed Chiles)*

A dish of *chiles rellenos* (stuffed *chiles*), fried in a light batter and cooked in a tomato sauce, is one of the best-known and most popular dishes.

The most commonly used *chile* for this is the fresh *poblano*—and its dried version, the *ancho*—but there are some regional variations. In Michoacán the *manzano* is used, but it is fiercely hot; in Veracruz it's the *jalapeño,* while in the north central states the dried *pasado* can be used in the same way, and in Puebla and Oaxaca the *pasilla de Oaxaca* makes a wonderfully smoky version of the dish.

To Prepare the Chile Poblano for Stuffing

Always prepare a few more *chiles* than the number required in case they fall apart in the cleaning process.

If the *chiles* are not as fresh as they might be and have a slightly wrinkled skin, then coat them lightly with oil before charring. If you cook with electricity, then coat the *chiles* lightly with oil and place on the broiling rack about 1 inch from the heat.

Do not put them into a hot oven until they blister; the flesh will cook too much, and they will not have that pleasant charred flavor.

Do not hold a fork over a flame to peel; that will take forever.

Do not immerse in water to peel. It may sound easy, but the flavor will be diminished.

Place the whole *chile*, with stem, if any, intact onto the bare flame of a gas burner or on a grill, just above the smoldering charcoal or wood fire. Leave for a few seconds until blistered and slightly charred—do not allow the flesh to burn through. Turn the *chiles* from time to time until they are evenly blistered and charred. Transfer immediately to a plastic bag and set aside to "sweat" for about 10 minutes. Although you can start skinning immediately, this process not only helps loosen the skin but cooks the flesh just enough to bring out the sweetness.

At the end of the "sweating" period, grasp one of the *chiles* in your hand and run it down from top to tip; most of the skin will come off in your hand if you have charred the *chiles* sufficiently. Do not pick at them with your fingers, removing little bits of skin at a time; it will take forever. Wipe the outside of the *chile* with a damp cloth. If some little bits of skin remain, no matter.

Hold the cleaned *chile* on a board and make a slit from top to bottom on the side where you can see that the flesh is weakest. Open up at the top and carefully cut with a sharp paring knife through the base, or placenta, below the stalk that holds the concentration of veins and seeds. Remove the veins running down the sides of the *chile*, taking care not to leave the flesh in ribbons. (That's why it's best to have extra *chiles* to work with.) Wipe out the remaining seeds with a damp cloth and set the *chiles* on a rack to drain while you finish them all.

Note: This procedure can be done one day ahead, no more, as the juice and flavor drain out. At this point the cleaned "shells" may be frozen but for no more than a few weeks; even then, when defrosting, the *chile* loses flavor and texture.

The *chiles* are now ready to stuff. This should be done just before frying them in batter. The juice penetrates the filling and makes it watery.

To Prepare Dried Chiles Anchos for Stuffing

Always choose the largest, smoothest, and most flexible *chiles anchos* for stuffing. If they are old and completely dried out, then just heat them for a few seconds on each side on a warm *comal,* taking care that they do not scorch, until they soften and become flexible.

Using a sharp paring knife, make a slit down one side of the *chiles* from top to tip and carefully scrape out the pithy, tough placenta to which the veins and seeds are attached. Remove the veins that run down the sides of the *chiles.* If the *chiles* are old and too brittle to handle in this way, then skip the first steps.

Cover the *chiles* with boiling water, pushing them down into the water so that they are completely submerged, and leave them to soak until they have reconstituted and are full and fleshy—about 15 to 30 minutes, depending on how dry they were in the first place.

The *chiles* that were brittle in the first place can now be cleaned of veins and seeds.

Do not leave the *chiles* to soak too long, or the flavor will be left behind in the water and they will be too soft to stuff.

Do not attempt to skin them.

The *chiles* are now ready to stuff. This should be done just before frying them in the batter.

To Stuff Fresh or Dried Chiles

Always stuff the *chiles* just before you are going to fry them; otherwise the juice from them will run into the stuffing. As you were cleaning the *chiles* you will have noticed by the smell that some are much hotter than others. Mark the hot ones with a toothpick for those that like them that way. But always remember that the stuffing and the batter will dilute the heat.

Although there are many different types of stuffings, three are suggested here.

Cheese Filling: about 3 or 4 strips per *chile* at room temperature (see following page).

Chorizo and Potato Filling: see below; about ⅓ cup per *chile.*

Shredded and Chopped Pork and Raisin Filling: see recipe for *Picadillo para Chiles Rellenos* (page 249); about ⅓ cup per *chile.*

Stuff the *chiles* until they are fat and appetizing-looking, but make sure that the cut edges of the *chile* meet and overlap a little. Secure with a toothpick if you wish, although this is not absolutely necessary since the batter will seal the seam. Cover with batter, etc. (see below).

QUESO PARA CHILES RELLENOS
(Cheese for Stuffing Chiles)

Chiles poblanos, anchos, and *pasados* may be filled with cheese. In Mexico, either *queso Chihuahua, Oaxaca,* or *asadero* is used, depending on the region of the country in which the *chiles* are made. In the United States a good, not too expensive, substitute is the domestic block Muenster that has just the right melting point.

Allow about 1½ to 2 ounces for each *chile.* Cut the cheese into strips about 3 inches long and about ½ inch square.

RELLENO DE CHORIZO Y PAPA PARA CHILES ANCHOS *(Chorizo and Potato Filling for Chiles Anchos)*

MAKES ABOUT 1⅓ CUPS

1 tablespoon lard
6 ounces *chorizo,* skinned and crumbled
6 ounces potatoes, cooked, skinned, and cut into ½-inch cubes
sea salt to taste

Melt the lard in a frying pan, add the *chorizo,* and fry gently until the fat is rendered and the meat begins to brown—about 4 minutes. Add the potato cubes and fry, turning them over from time to time, until they absorb the *chile* color of the *chorizo*—about 6 minutes. Taste for salt and set aside to cool.

You will need about ⅓ cup of the filling for each *chile.*

COATING WITH BATTER AND FRYING CHILES RELLENOS

MAKES ENOUGH BATTER FOR 4 TO 6 LARGE *CHILES*

The traditional recipes for *chiles rellenos* call for them to be coated with a light batter and fried until golden in oil about 1 inch deep. Do not deep-fry, or the batter will be left sticking to the frying basket. While they are delicious and very rich, they do absorb a lot of the oil; to remedy this I like to fry the *chiles*, draining them on paper toweling, and then reheat in a 350° oven on baking sheets lined with fresh paper toweling to absorb the excess oil.

safflower oil
3 large eggs, separated
¼ teaspoon sea salt
⅓ cup flour, approximately

Heat oven to 350°. Have ready a baking sheet onto which the fried *chiles* will fit in one layer lined with a double thickness of paper toweling.

Heat oil to a depth of 1 inch in a heavy frying pan. Beat the egg whites until they form soft peaks and when the bowl is tilted they do not slide around. Add the salt and beat it in with the yolks one by one. Dry the outside of one of the *chiles* with paper toweling, lightly dust with flour, and place on a broad spatula, seam side up. Lower the *chile* into the batter and make sure it is well covered with the egg. Scrape excess egg off the underside of the spatula and lower into the hot oil (always use two spatulas to steady it so that the oil does not splash up and burn you). Fry until the underside is well set and a deep golden color; turn over and fry on the second side. Do not scoop up the fat to fry the egg coating evenly until it is well set, or it will slide off the *chile*. Once it is set, you can attend to the paler spots and turn the *chile* over as necessary, standing it on the stalk end so that the uncooked egg batter there is fried golden.

Hold the fried *chile* over the pan to drain well and then set aside on the paper toweling while you fry the rest of the *chiles*. With practice you can do several at a time, but do not overcrowd the pan, or they will be difficult to turn over neatly and the temperature of the oil will be lowered too much. While frying you may need to adjust the temperature of the oil; for instance, if you see that it is starting to smoke and cooking the batter to a deep brown too quickly, turn it down and wait for the oil to cool a little before adding the next *chile*.

Always have about four spatulas or slotted spoons ready. If you keep putting the hot ones into the batter, it will break down. When all the *chiles* have been fried, reheat as suggested in the middle of the oven for about 10 to 15 minutes, longer if you have fried the *chiles* some hours ahead, until they are sizzling and well heated through.

Chiles stuffed with cheese should be reheated for a briefer period—about 5 minutes—because the cheese will have melted in the frying process and will become tough if reheated for too long.

CALDO DE JITOMATE PARA CHILES RELLENOS
(Tomato Broth for Stuffed Chiles)

MAKES ENOUGH BROTH FOR 4 LARGE *CHILES*

In Mexico it is customary, with minor exceptions, to reheat *chiles rellenos*, or other vegetable *beignets*, in a thin tomato broth. Yes, the batter does become soft, but it absorbs the pleasant acidity of the sauce, which in turn cuts the richness of the batter.

This is the simplest version of the broth; others include a piece of cinnamon stick, a clove or peppercorns, sometimes a bay leaf or other dried herbs, such as marjoram and thyme, or occasionally a large sprig of flat-leaf parsley.

¾ pound (about 2 medium) tomatoes, roughly chopped, unpeeled
2 tablespoons finely chopped white onion
1 garlic clove, peeled and roughly chopped
½ cup water
1½ tablespoons safflower oil
2½ cups chicken broth (page 95) or pork broth (page 248)
sea salt to taste

In a blender jar, blend the tomatoes, onion, and garlic with the water until fairly smooth.

Heat the oil in a heavy pan, add the blended ingredients, and cook over fairly high heat until reduced and thickened—about 10 minutes. Add the broth, adjust seasoning, and cook for 5 minutes longer.

Add the stuffed and fried *chiles* and cook gently, turning them over once carefully, for about 10 minutes.

VEGETABLE RELISHES

LEGUMBRES EN ESCABECHE
(Lightly Pickled Vegetables)

MAKES ABOUT 10 CUPS   SEÑORA GUADALUPE MUÑIZ, ZITÁCUARO

Mixed vegetables in a light pickle are wonderful, nonfattening snacks with drinks, with pickled pig's feet (page 277), or with any cold meats for that matter. You need not use all the vegetables listed, just those that are available and very fresh.

This is another recipe that uses the soft, fruity vinegar so often made at home in Mexico out of pineapple or other fruits.

4 tablespoons safflower oil
3 medium carrots, scraped and diagonally sliced ¼ inch thick
6 *chiles jalapeños,* cut into 4 at the tip
6 large scallions or small boiling onions, peeled, tops removed
20 garlic cloves, peeled
3 small zucchini, trimmed, halved, and each piece cut into 3 lengthwise
3 cups mild vinegar or a substitute (see page 436)
8 very small waxy potatoes, parboiled for 10 minutes
½ head of cauliflower, broken into flowerets and blanched
2 medium-sized *nopales,* cut into ¼-inch strips and boiled or steamed
    (see pages 174 and 175)
2 fresh ears of corn, cut into 1-inch rounds and blanched
¼ pound green beans, trimmed, cut in half, and blanched
5 California bay leaves
3 fresh marjoram sprigs *or* ¼ teaspoon dried
sea salt to taste

Heat the oil in a large frying pan and add the carrots, fresh *chiles,* scallions, garlic, and zucchini; fry lightly until they are *just beginning* to change color—about 10 minutes. Heat the vinegar and, when it comes to a boil, add it to the fried vegetables. Stir in the remaining ingredients, season, and continue cooking for 5 minutes. Set aside in a cool place overnight. Refrigerate them (for up to 2 weeks) if the vegetables are going to be kept any length of time. Bring to room temperature and drain before using.

SANCOCHO DE VERDURAS (*Vegetable Relish*)

MAKES ABOUT 9 CUPS

SEÑORA AMALIA CHAVEZ,
SAHUAYO, MICHOACÁN

Cooks in each region of Mexico have their special ways of preserving vegetables, with somewhat rigid lines about what goes into them. This recipe is an unusual one and little known outside the area. The vegetables are "sweated" in oil and then boiled in vinegar; although cooked, they still have a crisp texture.

When I tried these vegetables for the first time, they were julienned—not very finely though—a relatively modern rendition. You can also cut each vegetable in a different way to provide many different textures.

This relish may be eaten with chicken, broiled meats, on top of rice, or—a completely unacceptable combination in practically all other areas of Mexico—with a tomato sauce over *tamales*! Although I prefer to eat this the day after making it, it can be kept for some time in the refrigerator or in carefully sealed and sterilized jars. Serve at room temperature.

It is hardly worth making a small quantity, so here goes!

½ cup safflower oil
½ pound carrots, trimmed, scraped, and julienned
½ pound turnips, trimmed, peeled, and julienned
½ pound kohlrabi, trimmed and cut into ¼-inch slices
½ pound small potatoes, unpeeled and cut into ¼-inch slices
6 garlic cloves, peeled
½ pound *jícama*, trimmed, peeled, and julienned
¾ pound cabbage, cut into ¼-inch slices
½ pound white or purple onions, cut into ¼-inch slices
¾ pound zucchini, trimmed and julienned
3 heaped tablespoons light brown sugar
10 peppercorns
1 2-inch cinnamon stick, broken into thin strips
4 whole cloves
3 California bay leaves
6 fresh thyme sprigs, *or* ½ teaspoon dried
6 fresh marjoram sprigs *or* ½ teaspoon dried
3 cups mild, fruity vinegar
1½ to 2 tablespoons sea salt

Heat the oil in a large sauté pan and add the carrots, turnips, kohlrabi, potatoes, and garlic. Cover the pan and cook for 5 minutes over medium heat, shaking the pan from time to time so that the vegetables are cooked evenly. Add the *jícama,* cabbage, and onions, cover the pan, and continue cooking for 5 minutes. Add the zucchini and cook for 5 minutes more. Add the remaining ingredients, mix well, and cook over fairly high heat, turning the vegetables over from time to time and shaking the pan, until the liquid comes to a boil. Cook at a fast simmer for 15 minutes. Transfer to a glass or china bowl and set aside to cool. Turn the vegetables over in the liquid from time to time as they cool, but carefully so as not to break them.

CHILEAJO (*Cold Vegetables in Chile Sauce*)

MAKES ABOUT 7 CUPS   OAXACA

Chileajo is a very unusual Oaxacan dish of vegetables that I suppose would best be described as a *chile* pickle. (In other parts of southern Mexico, Guerrero for instance, *chileajo* means meat in a *chile* sauce.)

Although you can find *chileajo* the year round, it is primarily a Lenten dish, often served in a bread roll. One of the most popular ways of serving it is piled on top of a *tostada* that has first been spread with Oaxacan refried black beans and topped with onion rings and crumbled *queso fresco*.

This is best eaten a day or two after it is made, to allow the flavors to blend.

HAVE READY THE FOLLOWING TENDER-COOKED VEGETABLES:
6 ounces green beans
6 ounces (about 1½) diced zucchini
½ pound (about 3 medium) diced red bliss potatoes
½ pound cauliflower flowerets
¼ pound fresh or frozen peas
6 ounces (about 3 medium) sliced carrots

THE SAUCE
¼ pound (about 18) *chiles guajillos*
½ cup mild vinegar
5 small garlic cloves, peeled
1 whole clove
2 whole allspice
1 teaspoon (or to taste) sea salt

THE TOPPING
1 cup white onion in rings
6 ounces *queso fresco*, crumbled
1 teaspoon dried oregano, Oaxacan if possible

First make the sauce. Remove the stalks from the dried *chiles*, if any. Slit them open and remove and discard seeds and veins. Toast the *chiles* briefly on a hot *comal* or griddle and rinse briefly in cold water. Cover with boiling water and set aside to soak for about 15 minutes.

Put the vinegar into a blender jar, add the garlic, spices, and salt, and blend until smooth. Gradually add the soaked *chiles* with a little of the water in which they were soaking and blend until smooth. You will need about 1½ cups of the water to blend them all. Strain the sauce (there should be about 2⅓

146

cups) into a bowl, pressing down well on the *chile* skin debris to extract as much of the flesh as possible. Put the cooked vegetables into a china or glass bowl, pour the sauce over them, taste for salt, and mix well. Set aside at the bottom of the refrigerator to marinate for 2 days. Serve topped with some onion rings and cheese and sprinkle with oregano.

CHAYOTE *(Sechium edule)*

The *chayote,* sometimes called a vegetable pear, is indigenous to Mexico and has been cultivated by the Indians for centuries; they gave it a Nahuatl name, *chayutli.*

Several varieties are grown in Mexico: small cream-colored ones, dark and light green ones with porcupinelike prickles, and then the light green, smoother variety, puckered at both ends, that is found in most Latin American and Caribbean markets in the United States as well as in the specialty vegetable sections of large supermarkets.

Only when the last variety is very tender and freshly picked can the skin be eaten; otherwise it should be discarded. But the seed, or flat almond, inside is a delicacy.

The *chayote* is a perennial climbing plant that grows profusely over the tall trees in my orchard, but it can be trained over a wire frame or *cama* when grown commercially. The tuberous root is edible and delicious, but it should be left to experts to dig it up without disturbing the reproductive part of the root system on which the following year's growth depends. The root, called *camote de chayote, chinchayote,* or *chintestle,* depending on the region, is boiled and eaten by itself or made into fritters and has a pleasant, earthy taste rather like that of the Jerusalem artichoke.

If you want to grow your own, keep a *chayote* in a dark, fairly damp place, and in the winter it will start to sprout and be ready to plant. There is a charming ceremony on the Feast of Candalaria, February 5th, in the Xochimilco church when the local country people carry their sprouted *chayotes* for the priest to bless.

There are many ways of preparing *chayote*—sweet or savory, as well as the following recipes, which happen to be favorites of mine.

CHAYOTES AL VAPOR *(Steamed Chayotes)*

SERVES 4   SIERRA DE PUEBLA

This is to my mind the most delicious way of preparing *chayotes*, and alone they make an interesting and light first course. Any variety of *chayote* could be used—the fresher the better, of course, since they will be moister and sweeter. If they are not exactly in their prime, then about ¼ cup of water should be added to the pan during the cooking time. *Al vapor* in this sense does not mean steamed in a steamer but cooked in their own juice.

Señora Fagoaga, who gave this recipe to me, cubes the *chayote*; however, I prefer to cut them into julienne strips about ¼ inch square—they cook faster and have a better texture. I am afraid I must agree with her that lard does make for more flavor, but safflower oil can be used and gives very good results.

2 tablespoons melted lard or safflower oil
1 pound *chayotes*, peeled and julienned, ¼ inch square
2 (or to taste) *chiles serranos*, finely chopped
sea salt to taste
2 heaped tablespoons roughly chopped *cilantro*

Heat the lard in a heavy pan, add the *chayote* strips and fresh *chiles*, and toss over fairly high heat for about 2 minutes. Sprinkle with salt, cover the pan, and cook over medium heat, shaking the pan from time to time, for about 8 minutes, depending on age and freshness of the *chayote*—it should still be *al dente*. Stir in the *cilantro* and continue cooking, uncovered, for 3 minutes or until just tender. Serve immediately, or it will become too wilted.

CHAYOTES GUISADOS CON JITOMATE
(Chayotes Cooked with Tomato)

SERVES 4   CENTRAL MEXICO

Chayotes are best served as soon as they are cooked as they tend to go limp if left sitting around in a warm pan. They can be served as a separate course, in which case it is best to sprinkle some finely grated cheese on top.

1 pound (about 1 medium) *chayote*
6 ounces (about 1 medium) tomatoes, broiled (see page 450)
1 garlic clove, peeled and roughly chopped
2 tablespoons safflower oil
2 tablespoons finely chopped white onion
2 (or to taste) *chiles de árbol*
¾ cup water
sea salt to taste
2 tablespoons roughly chopped *epazote* or *cilantro* leaves
2 tablespoons finely grated *queso añejo* or *sardo* (optional)

Peel the *chayote* and cut into julienne strips about ¼ inch square and 2 inches long, including the core and seed. Set aside.

Blend the unpeeled tomato and the garlic for a few seconds, until fairly smooth. Set aside.

Heat the oil in a heavy frying or sauté pan, add the onion and whole dried *chiles*, and fry gently without browning for about 2 minutes. Add the tomato puree and continue cooking, stirring and scraping the bottom of the pan, until reduced—about 3 minutes. Add the *chayote* pieces, water, and salt to taste; cover the pan and cook over medium heat, shaking the pan or stirring and turning the mixture over from time to time to prevent sticking— about 10 minutes. Stir in the *epazote* leaves, cover the pan, and cook until the *chayote* is just tender—it should be moist but not watery—10 to 15 minutes.

Sprinkle with cheese if desired and serve immediately.

CALABACITAS *(Cucurbita pepo,* var.*) (Squashes)*

Squash of different types—they vary in many regions—is a much used vegetable in Mexican cooking. And not only the squash itself is used. The flowers are stewed for soups and *quesadillas,* etc. The tender shoots, *guias,* of varieties grown in Oaxaca are used in soups and stews, while the dried and toasted seeds of the small, dark green squash grown in Yucatan that resemble the ebony squash are used in many regional dishes.

The most commonly used squash, called *calabacita italiana,* is pale green, delicately flecked with cream, and an average-sized one is about 2½ to 3½ inches long and just over 1 inch wide. (*Bonita fl.* hybrid in the United States). Another delicious little squash is the *criollo,* pale green and round; apart from being very tender and sweet, it is very attractive when stuffed. My all-out favorite is a pale green, teardrop-shaped squash that grows only in the summer rains. It is referred to as *calabacita de matón.* Pale green with four vertical ridges running down from stalk to tip, it grows, like the round variety, on a wandering vine—not a compact plant like that of the zucchini—and produces a large, fragrant flower, one of the best I know for cooking.

(Seeds of most of these varieties are available, produced by Hollar and Company in Rocky Ford, Colorado. Although this is a wholesale-only outfit, ask your local nursery for the company's seeds.)

FLOR DE CALABAZA *(Squash Flowers)*

It is curious that one never says *flor de calabacita,* always *flor de calabaza,* although the pumpkin flower is hardly ever used.

Not all squash flowers are suitable for cooking; many have too large a proportion of green—calyx and sepals—and very small petals, while a Japanese variety I once cooked was far too strongly perfumed. If you grow your own, always pick them in the morning when they are fully opened and cook them at once to capture their fresh fragrance. As afternoon approaches, they tend to close up. Make sure that you pick only the male flowers (see illustration) rather than the females, which have a round, undulating stamen. You should leave about one in 25 of the male flowers for pollination. If you buy the flowers, you have no choice, but try to get them as fresh as possible for flavor's sake.

To Prepare Squash Flowers

Cut off the stems, leaving about 1 inch attached to the calyx. Strip off the stringy sepals and the tough outside of the stem. Cut the flowers open, leaving the stamen intact, rinse quickly in cold water to get rid of any soil or sand, and shake dry. Chop the flowers—with calyx, piece of stem, and stamen—roughly with a very sharp knife and then follow the cooking instructions that follow (see photo).

Male Squash Flowers

To Cook Squash Flowers

This will seem an enormous amount of flowers in the pan, but they cook down to less than half the quantity.

Female Squash Flowers

MAKES ABOUT 1½ CUPS TO FILL 12 4-INCH *QUESADILLAS*

2 tablespoons safflower oil or unsalted butter
3 tablespoons finely chopped white onion
1 garlic clove, peeled and finely chopped
2 *chiles poblanos*, charred, peeled and cut into strips (see page 470)
1¼ pounds *flor de calabaza*, cleaned (see note above) and roughly chopped
½ teaspoon (or to taste) sea salt
1 tablespoon roughly chopped *epazote* leaves

Heat the oil in a large frying pan, add the onion and garlic, and cook gently until slightly transparent—1 minute. Add the *chile* strips and cook, stirring from time to time, for another 2 minutes—the onion and garlic must not brown. Add the flowers and salt and stir well. Cover the pan and cook over medium heat until the round calyx is tender but not soft—about 10 minutes. Remove cover, stir in the *epazote,* and reduce the juice over high heat for about 5 minutes; the mixture should be moist but not watery.

Note: If the flowers are not very fresh or have been picked too soon, they tend to be dry. In this case, add about 3 tablespoons of water to the pan and cook covered for the whole period. See also *Sopa de Flor de Calabaza.*

CALABACITAS GUISADAS (*Stewed Zucchini*)

MAKES 2½ CUPS TO SERVE 4 TO 6

The simplest of all ways of cooking small squash in Mexico.

2 tablespoons safflower oil
2 tablespoons finely chopped white onion
1 garlic clove, peeled and finely chopped
6 ounces (about 1 medium) tomatoes, finely chopped, unpeeled
1 or 2 *chiles serranos,* finely chopped
1 pound (about 4 medium) zucchini, trimmed and cut into ¼-inch cubes
sea salt to taste

Heat the oil in a frying pan, add the onion and garlic, and fry gently without browning for about 1 minute. Add the tomatoes and fresh *chiles* and cook over fairly high heat to reduce to a sauce—about 5 minutes. Add the zucchini and salt to taste, cover the pan, and cook for 5 minutes. Remove cover and cook over fairly high heat, stirring and scraping the bottom of the pan from time to time to prevent sticking, until juice has been absorbed and zucchini is well seasoned—about 5 minutes. Serve alone as a vegetable course or as follows.

Variations

Add 2 *chiles poblanos,* charred, peeled, and cut into strips (see page 470) instead of the *serranos.*
Sprinkle with ⅓ cup grated *Chihuahua* or Muenster cheese.
Add sprigs of *cilantro* or *epazote* in the last 5 minutes of cooking.

TORTA DE CALABACITA (*Zucchini Torte*)

SERVES 4 TO 5

This type of *torta* is served in the same way as the following *budín de elote,* either by itself as a separate vegetable course or with a dish of meat or chicken. However, it has a firmer, more compact consistency. It is generally topped with a layer of thick *crème fraîche* that has been beaten with salt and pepper.

¼ pound unsalted butter, plus 1 tablespoon for the baking dish
1 pound (about 4 medium) zucchini, trimmed and grated
1 cup rice flour
⅔ teaspoon double-acting baking powder
½ teaspoon (or to taste) sea salt
2 eggs
⅓ cup sugar
1 cup *crème fraîche,* beaten with sea salt and freshly ground pepper to taste
(optional)

Heat oven to 350° and place rack in the top part of the oven. Butter a 1-quart baking or *soufflé* dish.

Squeeze the grated zucchini dry in a cheesecloth and set aside. Sift the flour with the baking powder and salt and set aside. Beat the butter until creamy, then beat in the eggs one by one, beating well after each addition with a dusting of the flour mixture. Beat in the flour mixture and then stir in the zucchini and sugar. Pour the mixture into the prepared dish and bake until the *torta* is firm and springy to the touch and golden on top—about 45 to 50 minutes (depending, of course, on the material of the baking dish and the depth of the batter). Serve from the dish, smothered with the salt-and-peppered *crème fraîche* if desired.

BUDÍN DE ELOTE (Corn Pudding)

SERVES 4 TO 5

Vegetable puddings, like damp, textured *soufflés*, are served either as a separate vegetable course or to accompany plainly cooked meat or chicken. They are often served with either a tomato sauce or *crème fraîche* that has been beaten with salt and pepper.

This *budín* should, of course, be served as soon as it comes out of the oven.

While starchy field corn works best for this type of dish, ears of corn left intact that have been picked a few days earlier, for the starches to heighten, can be used.

FOR THE DISH
1 tablespoon unsalted butter
2 tablespoons toasted fine bread crumbs, approximately

FOR THE *BUDÍN*
2 cups corn kernels (see note above)
½ cup milk
5 tablespoons unsalted butter
3 eggs
1 teaspoon sugar
1 teaspoon (or to taste) sea salt
1 cup *salsa de jitomate, Sierra de Puebla* (optional) (page 339)
¾ cup *crème fraîche*, beaten with sea salt and freshly ground pepper to taste (optional)

Heat the oven to 300°. Place a heavy baking sheet on the lower rack of the oven. Butter a 1-quart baking or *soufflé* dish and sprinkle with the bread crumbs. Set aside.

Put the corn and milk into a food processor container and process for 10 to 15 seconds or until reduced to a textured puree. Beat the butter until creamy and gradually add the corn and the eggs, one by one, beating after each addition. Add the sugar and salt.

Pour the mixture into the prepared dish and bake until the mixture is firmly set and beginning to brown around the edges—about 35 minutes.

Either serve from the dish or carefully unmold onto a serving dish. Pass the tomato sauce or *crème fraîche* separately.

ACELGAS GUISADAS *(Stewed Swiss Chard)*

SERVES 4 TO 6   CENTRAL MEXICO

Swiss chard is one of the hardiest of plants, grown year-round in Mexico, even in adverse conditions. It is used in many ways in Mexican cooking (see recipes in soup chapter and *tamale* sections of corn chapter). Cooked in this way, it can be served as a separate course or used to fill *enchiladas*.

1 pound Swiss chard
2 tablespoons safflower oil
2 tablespoons finely chopped white onion
1 garlic clove, peeled and finely chopped
1 or 2 (to taste) *chiles serranos*, finely chopped
½ pound (about 1 large) tomatoes, finely chopped, unpeeled
sea salt to taste
1¼ cups water

Rinse the Swiss chard in lots of water and shake dry. Chop the stalks finely and shred the leaves roughly. Set aside.

Heat the oil in a sauté pan or shallow heavy pan and add the onion, garlic, and fresh *chiles*; fry without browning for about 1 minute. Add the tomato and cook over fairly high heat for about 3 minutes. Add the Swiss chard, salt to taste, and water, cover the pan, and cook over medium heat, shaking the pan from time to time, for about 10 minutes. Remove the lid and continue cooking over high heat until the chard is tender and the mixture moist but not watery—about 10 more minutes.

TORTITAS DE COLIFLOR (*Cauliflower Fritters*)

SERVES 4

Vegetable fritters in a tomato broth, like *chiles rellenos*, are sometimes served in a small portion as a vegetable before the main course or in a larger portion as the main course itself. Slices of cooked squash, *chayote* root, or sprigs of *huauhzontle* (see photo, page 510) sandwiched with cheese are also made into fritters and served in the same way. Occasionally they will be cooked in a light *mole*, but this is by far the most popular way of serving the fritters. Chicken broth is often added to the tomatoes for a richer flavor, but this is optional, and if it's not included, you have a good vegetarian dish.

These *tortitas* are traditionally served just with warm *tortillas*.

Like other Mexican fritters covered in this light batter, they tend to absorb a lot of oil. To avoid this I cook them at least 30 minutes ahead and drain them on several layers of paper toweling. Just before serving, I transfer them to a paper-lined tray and reheat in a 350° oven for about 10 minutes. A lot of the excess oil will then be absorbed by the paper toweling.

The batter does become soft in the sauce, and that's the way they are eaten, but you can pour the sauce/broth over them at serving time if you prefer. Serve 2 *tortitas* per person as a main course with plenty of the sauce on top and hot corn *tortillas*.

Choose a rather compact cauliflower for this recipe.

¾ pound (1 small head) cauliflower
boiling water
sea salt to taste
pinch of aniseed

THE BROTH/SAUCE
1½ pounds (about 3 large) tomatoes, roughly chopped, unpeeled
1 garlic clove, peeled and roughly chopped
1½ tablespoons safflower oil
scant ⅓ cup thinly sliced white onions
1 small California bay leaf
1 fresh marjoram sprig *or* pinch dried
1 fresh thyme sprig *or* pinch dried
2 *chiles serranos* or *jalapeños*, with a cross cut in the tip
1½ cups light chicken broth or water

safflower oil for frying
4 large eggs, separated
pinch of sea salt
½ cup flour, approximately

Have ready a tray lined with paper toweling with extra toweling for the oven.

Divide the cauliflower into 8 bunches of flowerets. Peel as much of the tough stem as you can and put into a pan. Cover with boiling water, add salt and aniseed, and bring to a boil. Cook until no longer *al dente,* but just tender—about 5 minutes. Drain and set aside to cool completely.

Meanwhile, prepare the sauce. Put the tomatoes and garlic into a blender jar and blend until you have a textured sauce—add a little water to the jar only if the tomatoes are not very juicy.

Heat the 1½ tablespoons oil in a frying pan, add the onions, and fry without browning for 2 minutes. Add the tomatoes, herbs, and fresh *chiles* and cook over fairly high heat, stirring and scraping the bottom of the pan from time to time, until reduced and well seasoned—about 5 minutes. Add the broth or water, adjust seasoning, and continue cooking for 10 minutes over medium heat. Set aside but keep warm. Heat the oven to 350°.

Heat the oil to a ¼-inch depth in a frying pan over low heat while you prepare the batter. Beat the egg whites and salt together until they form soft peaks and do not slither around in the bowl. Gradually add the yolks and beat after each addition. Lightly cover one of the cauliflower bunches with flour, dip it into the batter until evenly covered, and carefully lower, with a spatula in each hand (see technique for *chiles rellenos,* page 140), into the hot oil. Leave for a few seconds, until the bottom of the batter is a deep golden color, and carefully turn it over. Continue turning as necessary until an even golden color all over. Drain on paper toweling and continue with the rest. When all the cauliflower bunches have been fried and drained, transfer them to an oven tray covered with two layers of paper toweling. Heat through in the oven for 10 minutes. Remove and place them in the warm sauce, bring to a slow simmer, and continue simmering, turning the *tortitas* over from time to time, until they have absorbed the flavor of the sauce.

FAVA BEANS AND HOW TO COOK THEM

Fava beans, both fresh and dried, are used in Mexican dishes, especially in and around the central highland area where they are grown and are particularly prolific during the hot, dry spring months—they are an important ingredient in many Lenten dishes.

Fava beans are often picked too late, when they are starchy and have a tough skin. In that case, remove the beans from their pods and cook in boiling, lightly salted water until tender—about 5 or 6 minutes. Drain, and when cool enough to handle, slip off the outer greyish-green skin.

If they are young and tender, put the whole pods into boiling, salted water and cook for about 2 or 3 minutes, or until just tender. Drain and when cool enough to handle, remove the beans from their pods. It is not really necessary to remove the tender outer skin, which has a lot of flavor.

HABAS GUISADAS CON HUEVOS
(Fava Beans with Eggs)

SERVES 4   CENTRAL MEXICO

I like to eat this dish with pickled *chiles largos* (canned), although any pickled *chile* will do if you cannot find them locally.

    1 cup cooked and peeled fava beans (see above)
    2 tablespoons safflower oil
    3 tablespoons finely chopped white onion
    1 garlic clove, peeled and finely chopped
    10 ounces (about 2 small) tomatoes, unpeeled and finely chopped
    2 fresh mint sprigs
    sea salt to taste
    4 eggs, lightly beaten with a little sea salt

Split the beans into halves and set aside.

Heat the oil in a frying pan, add the onion and garlic, and fry without browning for about 1 minute. Add the tomatoes and cook over fairly high heat, stirring and scraping the bottom of the pan, until the mixture resembles a textured sauce—about 6 minutes. Stir in the beans and mint and add salt to taste. When the beans have heated through and the mixture is bubbling, stir in the eggs and continue stirring and scraping the bottom of the pan until they are set and the mixture is moist but not juicy.

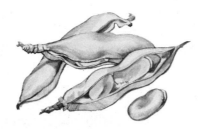

ENSALADA DE HABAS (*Fava Bean Salad*)

SERVES 4   CENTRAL MEXICO

Fava bean salad, as well as *nopal* salad, are two of the most popular in the marketplaces of central Mexico, where they are usually displayed on round, flat trays, liberally showered with *cilantro* and onion rings. You will see that the inner skin is left on, and I have learned from the vendors, and experience, that in this case the flavor is better; they are a little chewy, but it is worth it.

    2 rounded cups cooked unpeeled fava beans
    2 tablespoons finely chopped white onion
    ¾ cup finely chopped unpeeled tomatoes
    2 heaped tablespoons roughly chopped *cilantro*
    ¼ teaspoon dried oregano, Mexican if possible
    3 tablespoons fresh lime juice
    2 tablespoons olive oil
    2 *chiles jalapeños en escabeche*, cut into strips
    sea salt to taste

    THE TOPPING
    2 tablespoons roughly chopped *cilantro*, approximately
    ⅓ cup white onion rings
    chiles jalapeños en escabeche, left whole (optional)

Mix all the ingredients together, except the topping, and set aside to marinate for an hour or so before eating. Decorate with the *cilantro* and onion rings and whole *chiles* if desired. Serve at room temperature.

TORTITAS DE PAPA (*Potato Cakes*)

MAKES 10 TO 12 SMALL CAKES   MICHOACÁN

Señorita Esperanza, my herbalist friend in Zitácuaro, gave me this recipe one day when we were discussing Lenten foods. These uneven little fried cakes are unusual in that the potato is only roughly mashed, giving them an interesting texture. Surprisingly, they are often served at room temperature with a tablespoonful of *salsa mexicana* on top, although I prefer them hot. And as for *chiles rellenos*, I prefer to fry them a little ahead and then reheat them in the oven on a tray lined with paper toweling to absorb the excess oil.

Tortitas de papa make a good accompaniment for broiled fish or chicken, or they can be served, as they often are in Mexico, as an economical vegetarian first course.

safflower oil for frying
½ pound (about 3 medium) potatoes, cooked and skinned
2 heaped tablespoons finely grated *queso añejo* or Romano cheese
3 tablespoons finely chopped flat-leaf parsley
sea salt to taste (taking into account the salty cheese)
1 large egg, lightly beaten
salsa mexicana (page 351)

Heat the oven to 350°. Line a baking sheet with 2 layers of paper toweling, with extra paper on the side for the first frying. Heat oil to about a ½-inch depth in a heavy frying pan.

Crush the potatoes roughly with your hands and work in the rest of the ingredients except the sauce. Take 1 rounded tablespoon of the mixture and fry the roughly formed cake in the hot oil, turning over from time to time until it is a deep golden color. Drain on the paper toweling. When all the cakes have been fried, transfer them to the baking sheet and reheat until sizzling and a lot more of the oil has exuded—about 10 to 15 minutes.

Serve each cake topped with 1 tablespoon of *salsa mexicana*.

PAPAS GUISADAS *(Potatoes with Tomato)*

SERVES 3 TO 4   MICHOACÁN

This is one of the very simple and delicious vegetable dishes that are prepared during the Lenten period, when fish is very expensive, or when families cannot afford meat.

Although the recipe calls for peeled potatoes, I prefer them unpeeled. They should be cooked just until *al dente* so that they do not fall apart and become mushy in the tomato sauce.

While this makes a good vegetarian dish on its own, it is equally good served with broiled fish or meats.

½ pound (about 1 large) tomatoes, broiled (see page 450)
2 *chiles serranos,* broiled (see page 472) and chopped
1 garlic clove, peeled
2 tablespoons water
⅓ cup safflower oil
1 pound (about 6 medium) red bliss potatoes, cooked *al dente* and cut into
    1-inch cubes
4 tablespoons finely chopped white onion
sea salt to taste
2 ounces *queso añejo* or Romano cheese, finely grated

In a blender, blend the unpeeled tomatoes with the *chiles,* garlic, and water to make a textured sauce. Set aside.

Heat the oil in a heavy frying pan. Add the cubed potatoes and fry gently, turning them over from time to time, until they are beginning to turn golden—about 5 minutes. Add the onion and sprinkle with salt. Continue frying and turning them over so that the onion turns golden but does not burn—about 3 minutes. Pour the blended ingredients over the potatoes and mix carefully, turning the potatoes over so they do not fall apart and become mushy. Cook over low heat until some of the sauce is absorbed but the mixture is still moist—about 8 minutes. Sprinkle with the cheese and serve.

PAPAS CHIRRIONAS (*Potatoes Fried with Chile Sauce*)

SERVES 4   CENTRAL MEXICO

This is a lusty dish as its name implies—a *chirriona* is a virago—and great for those who would like their hashed-browns with a Mexican touch. This *picante* potato dish is especially good for a winter brunch along with some *chorizos*, or bacon and sausages for that matter.

Be careful not to cook the potatoes too much, or they will be mushy at the end.

I like to make this dish more *picante*, so I leave the veins—the ones attached to the flesh, not the loose central ones—in some or all of the *chiles*.

1 pound (about 6 medium) red bliss potatoes, unpeeled and cut into ½-inch cubes
sea salt to taste
3 tablespoons lard or safflower oil
½ medium white onion, finely sliced
5 *chiles pasillas*, cleaned and toasted crisp
2 small *tomate verde*, broiled (see page 451)
2 small garlic cloves, peeled and roughly chopped
⅔ cup water
3 eggs, lightly beaten with sea salt

THE TOPPING
1 heaped teaspoon dried oregano, Mexican if possible
2 heaped tablespoons finely grated *queso añejo* or Sardo cheese

Bring enough water to a boil in a saucepan to cover the potatoes, add the potatoes and salt to taste, and boil for exactly 5 minutes. Drain and set aside. Heat the lard in a heavy frying pan, add the potatoes, and fry for about 8 minutes, turning them over from time to time. Add the onion and continue frying until the potatoes are a golden brown. Crumble the dried *chiles* into a blender jar and add the *tomate verde*, garlic, and water; blend for a few seconds to make a textured sauce—it must not be too smooth. Make sure that the potatoes are well heated through before adding the sauce to the pan, then fry over very high heat until the sauce is reduced—about 4 minutes. Stir in the beaten eggs and stir until they are set—about 4 minutes more. Sprinkle with oregano and cheese before serving.

CAMOTES *(Ipomoea batatas) (Sweet Potatoes)*

Camotes are tuberous, starchy roots, a type of sweet potato indigenous to tropical America (and probably Mexico). They were an important staple in the diet of pre-Columbian Mexico.

The *camotero* walking through the streets in the evening, pushing his cart full of *camotes* cooking over a charcoal fire inside its round belly (a recycled oil drum), is still a familiar sight in the small, typical neighborhoods of Mexico City and the provincial towns. He lets you know he is coming with several mournful blasts from his steam whistle and a long, drawn-out cry, "Ca . . . m . . . oootes." In Mexico, *camotes* of different colors are cultivated: brown- and purple-skinned ones, vivid purple-fleshed ones, and my favorite of all, the brown-skinned, orange-fleshed ones. I had always thought they were rather dull eating until Señorita Esperanza, my oracle on all things sweet and an herbalist, shared her breakfast *camote* with me over a glass of milk—the perfect breakfast, she insists. It was juicy and deliciously sweet. "You never need sugar if you cook them properly," she said.

When the *camotes* are dug up in the fall, spread them out, earth-covered as they are, in the sun for 5 days, turning them over from time to time. Then scrub them clean, spread them out on a baking sheet, and bake in a 400° oven until they are soft and their syrup starts to exude—about 1 hour, depending on size.

While the *camotes* are still hot, pack them down in an earthenware casserole (in Michoacán they pack them between layers of banana leaves), cover, and let them sit overnight. The next day they should be soft and exuding plenty of syrup. Eat them skin and all.

I am sure this recipe would work with yams and sweet potatoes in the United States.

HONGOS AL VAPOR *("Steamed" Mushrooms)*

MAKES ABOUT 1½ CUPS   CENTRAL MEXICO

In the pine forest and surrounding countryside of the central plateau of Mexico, many types of wild mushrooms abound. One year I tried 30 different varieties found in the markets near Toluca in the state of Mexico. Of all the recipes for cooking them, this one, to my mind, is the simplest and most delicious—for there is nothing to mask the flavor of the mushrooms—especially when they are newly picked, juicy *chanterelles*. Cultivated mushrooms can also be used for this recipe, but they should be sliced fairly thinly and cooked for about 20 minutes over low heat to extract as much flavor as possible.

Hongos al vapor are sometimes served as a first course with corn *tortillas*. If the juice is reduced, but the mushrooms still quite moist, they serve as a filling for *tacos*, *quesadillas*, or even an omelet. Add chicken broth and you have a delicious mushroom soup; tomatoes and/or stew pork may be added for a main dish.

    ¾ pound wild or cultivated mushrooms
    2 tablespoons safflower oil
    2 tablespoons finely chopped white onion
    2 small garlic cloves, peeled and finely chopped
    2 *chiles serranos*, finely chopped
    2 tablespoons roughly chopped *epazote* leaves
    sea salt to taste

Douse the mushrooms quickly in cold water to remove any sand and particles of soil in the gills. Wipe the tops with a damp cloth to remove any dirt and cut off and discard the soiled bases of the stalks.

Heat the oil in a frying pan and add the onion, garlic, and fresh *chiles*; cook without browning for about 1 minute. Add the mushrooms, *epazote*, and salt. Cover the pan and cook over medium heat until the mushrooms are tender but not soft—about 8 minutes (20 minutes for cultivated mushrooms).

For a Taco, Quesadilla, or Omelet Filling

Remove lid from pan and reduce over high heat for about 4 minutes or until the juice has been absorbed but the mushrooms are still moist.

For a Soup

Add the mushrooms to a pan with 4 cups chicken broth (page 95) and simmer for about 5 minutes.

Variations

When the onion and garlic have been sautéed for 2 minutes, add ¼ pound (about 1 small) finely chopped, unpeeled tomato and cook for 3 minutes more over high heat before adding the mushrooms and *epazote*.

Beat in some eggs and cream and you have a good quiche filling.

Add 1 pound of stewed pork, *carne de puerco cocida y deshebrada* (see page 248), for a main dish.

TECOMATES CON CREMA (*Mushrooms with Cream*)

MAKES ABOUT 1¾ CUPS   CENTRAL MEXICO

Tecomates (*Amanita caesarea*) are large, showy mushrooms with orangey-red tops and pale yellow gills that are abundant throughout the rainy season in central Mexico. They are fleshy and have a strong flavor that lends itself to this recipe. Señora Fagoaga, who gave me this recipe and in whose house I first tried them, serves them as a first course with corn *tortillas*, but they could perfectly well be mixed with pasta or used as a filling for a quiche.

Any large, fleshy, cultivated mushrooms or *Boletus edulis* (*porcini*) can be used if *tecomates* are not available. Cook them about 1 hour ahead for the flavors to blend with the cream.

> ¾ pound mushrooms (see note above)
> 2 tablespoons safflower oil or unsalted butter
> 2 heaped tablespoons finely chopped white onion
> 2 garlic cloves, peeled and finely chopped
> 1 *chile poblano* or *chilaca*, peeled, cleaned, and cut into strips (see pages 464 and 470)
> 1 medium tomato (about 6 ounces), finely chopped, unpeeled
> ½ teaspoon (or to taste) sea salt
> ⅓ cup thick *crème fraîche*

Douse the mushrooms briefly in cold water and shake dry. Remove the soiled stalk tip and peel off the red skin (if using *tecomates*). Slice tops and stalks fairly thinly.

Heat the oil in a heavy frying pan and add the onion, garlic, and *chile* strips; fry slowly without browning for about 2 minutes. Add the tomato and cook over fairly high heat for about 3 minutes longer. Add the sliced mushrooms and salt and cook, covered, over medium heat until the mushrooms are tender but not soft—about 8 minutes. Stir in the cream and cook for 4 minutes longer.

TEJAMANILES CON CARNE DE PUERCO
(*Mushrooms with Shredded Pork*)

MAKES 1½ CUPS TO FILL 12 SMALL *TACOS*

This is an unusual filling for *tacos* made with shredded pork (beef or chicken could be used) and the cinnamon-colored wild mushrooms called *tejamaniles*. (The word *tejamanil* refers to a thin wooden slat or shingle, also *tajamanil*.) Although they appear delicate, they are quite tough, especially the stalk, and may have to be cooked first before being added to the sauce and shredded meat. Chinese tree ear mushrooms could be used, and they are much more easily obtainable now in specialty sections of greengroceries and supermarkets. If you are using more delicate tender mushrooms, lightly sauté them in oil instead of boiling them in water.

6 ounces mushrooms (see note above)
2 garlic cloves, peeled and chopped
sea salt to taste
2 tablespoons water
⅓ cup broth from cooking pork (page 248)
½ pound (about 1 medium) tomatoes, broiled (see page 450)
1 additional garlic clove
3 *chiles de árbol*, lightly toasted
2 tablespoons lard
1 cup *carne de puerco cocida y deshebrado* (page 248)

Rinse the mushrooms well to get rid of any sand or soil in the gills. Put into a small pan with the garlic, salt, and water; cover and cook over medium heat until tender—about 5 minutes. Drain and add liquid to the pork broth. Cut the mushrooms into strips, discarding the stems if they are tough.

Put the tomatoes, unpeeled, into a blender jar, crumble the dried *chiles* into it, add the garlic, and blend for a few seconds until you have a textured sauce; do not overblend. Heat the lard in a frying pan, add the tomato sauce, and fry over fairly high heat until reduced and thickened—about 3 minutes. Add the mushrooms, pork, and pork broth and continue cooking over fairly high heat until the mixture is almost dry—about 5 minutes.

CUITLACOCHE *(Corn Fungus)*

Cuitlacoche (huitlacoche) is a silvery-grey skinned black fungus that occurs on the ears of corn. It is an excrescence of enlarged and deformed kernels that form under the sheath of green husks around the ears, often forcing them open. I suppose for years farmers have been burning it in disgust—except in Mexico. Many varieties of corn are supposed to be resistant to fungi, but accidents can happen, and once it occurs it propagates easily through spores that fall to the ground and can make a nuisance of itself in an otherwise healthy crop. Botanically it is known as *Ustilago maydis,* while the Aztecs had a less than flattering name for it from the Nahuatl words *cuitlatl* (excrement) and *cochtli* (asleep). Its properties have been likened to those of the germ of the rye grain, and although people can develop an allergy to it, like any other fungus, studies done by a laboratory in Switzerland (initiated by a Mexican food writer and *cuitlacoche* enthusiast) have proved that it does not contain toxins.

Cuitlacoche is now being viewed in a new light in the United States. It is one of the "new" foods that people are discovering and talking about among the exotica introduced sporadically into the gastronomic spectrum. Although it does occur on irrigated corn during the dry season, it is at its best during the summer rainy months. You can cook it and freeze it, when available, and although after several months it does become mushy, it is certainly better than the canned stuff. Obviously it will become more readily available all over. I know of its occurring in vegetable gardens in the eastern states; of course it is prolific in Iowa, and those vegetable gardeners *par excellence,* the Chino family in Rancho Santa Fe, California, have it in limited quantities in the fall. So, if you have a garden and grow corn, one day you may have a surprise. You should be as delighted as you would be to find a trove of morels.

To Prepare Cuitlacoche

Unfurl the green husks around the ear of corn and discard. Pull off the fine strands of cornsilk and discard. Cut the fungus and corn kernels that remain off the center core as closely as you can—do not shave them off by degrees as this will spoil the texture. Remove any more stray bits of cornsilk that were tucked inside and roughly chop the fungus. Weigh at this point.

TO COOK CUITLACOCHE

MAKES ABOUT 5 CUPS

Cooked by the following method, *cuitlacoche* can be used for *crepas, quesadillas, budín,* or in plain *tacos.* Also see *Sopa de cuitlacoche* (page 105).

3 tablespoons safflower oil
2 tablespoons finely chopped white onion
2 small garlic cloves, peeled and finely chopped
rajas of 4 *chiles poblanos* (see page 471)
1½ pounds (about 6 cups) *cuitlacoche*
sea salt to taste
2 tablespoons roughly chopped *epazote* leaves

Heat the oil in a frying pan, add the onion and garlic, and fry gently until translucent—about 3 minutes. Add the *chile* strips and fry for 1 minute more. Add the *cuitlacoche* and salt, cover the pan, and cook over medium heat, shaking the pan from time to time, for about 15 minutes—the fungus should be tender, retaining some moisture, but not soft and mushy. Stir in the *epazote* and cook, uncovered, for another 2 minutes.

Note: If the *cuitlacoche* is rather dry, sprinkle on ¼ cup water before covering; if, on the other hand, it is too juicy, remove the lid before the end of the cooking time and reduce over higher heat.

CUITLACOCHE GUISADO CON JITOMATE
(Corn Fungus with Tomato)

MAKES 5 CUPS   CENTRAL MEXICO

3 tablespoons safflower oil
½ cup finely chopped white onion
3 garlic cloves, peeled and finely chopped
½ pound (about 1 large) tomato, finely chopped, unpeeled
3 *chiles serranos,* finely chopped
1½ pounds (about 6 cups) *cuitlacoche*
1 teaspoon (or to taste) sea salt
3 tablespoons roughly chopped *epazote* leaves

Heat the oil in a large frying pan, add the onion and garlic, and fry gently until translucent but not browned—about 5 minutes. Add the tomatoes and fresh *chiles* and cook over medium-high heat until some of the juice has evaporated, stirring from time to time—about 8 minutes. Add the *cuitlacoche* and salt, cover the pan, and cook over medium heat, stirring and turning the mixture over from time to time, for about 10 minutes. Remove the lid, stir in the chopped *epazote,* and cook for 5 minutes longer—the *cuitlacoche* should be tender but not soft and the mixture moist but not too juicy. If the latter, reduce a little over higher heat.

CREPAS DE CUITLACOCHE
(Crêpes Filled with Corn Fungus)

MAKES 12 CRÊPES TO SERVE 6   MEXICO CITY

The late Jaime Saldívar, a distinguished Mexican gastronome, was the first to present *cuitlacoche* in such an elegant way that the dish is now considered a classic in Mexican cuisine. Recipes, of course, vary slightly with each chef; one will use a tomato-based sauce, another *béchamel,* but to my mind this cream/ *chile* sauce provides a greater complement to the *crêpes.*

Ordinary cultivated mushrooms or the exotic ones newly arrived in many supermarkets and specialty stores can be substituted, but they won't have that inky-black extravagance of flavor. While all the component parts of this dish can be prepared ahead, it must be assembled just before it goes into the oven and eaten the moment it comes out; otherwise it tends to become a delicious but soggy, sorry mess.

1½ teaspoons unsalted butter for greasing dish
12 5-inch *crêpes*
1 recipe cooked *cuitlacoche* (page 168), kept warm
1½ cups *crème fraîche* (not sour cream)
3 *chiles poblanos,* charred, cleaned, and peeled (see page 470)
¼ teaspoon (or to taste) sea salt
4 ounces grated Chihuahua cheese or medium-sharp Cheddar
rajas of 2 *chiles poblanos,* sautéed (see page 471)

Heat the oven to 350°. Butter an ovenproof dish into which the *crêpes* will just fit in one layer. Put some of the filling along the center of each *crêpe,* roll loosely, and place on buttered dish.

Blend the cream and whole *chiles* until smooth and a pale green color (this must be done at the last minute). If the cream is too thick to blend easily, then add a little milk, but just enough to allow the blender blades to function. Stir in the salt; this must be done at the last moment because it tends to curdle the sauce. Pour the sauce over the *crêpes* and bake, loosely covered with foil, until the sauce is bubbling—about 10 to 15 minutes. Sprinkle the cheese over the top, decorate with the *chile* strips, and return to the oven only to melt the cheese, not to brown it. Serve immediately, either alone or with crusty bread to mop up the sauce.

BUDÍN DE CUITLACOCHE (*Corn Fungus Pudding*)

SERVES 4 TO 6   CENTRAL MEXICO

In Mexico this would be a "dry soup" and a delicious one at that. With a salad this *budín* makes a good lunch dish or a first course at dinner before, say, a fish course or something fairly light.

While all the component parts of this dish can be prepared ahead, the *tortillas* should be fried and the dish assembled just before going into the oven, and it should be eaten as soon as it comes out, or the *tortillas* will become soggy. *Crêpes* can be substituted for *tortillas* and mushrooms for *cuitlacoche*.

> 3 tablespoons safflower oil
> 8 4½-inch *tortillas*
> 1½ cups cooked tomato sauce (*salsa de jitomate, Sierra de Puebla*) (page 339), kept hot
> 2½ cups cooked *cuitlacoche,* with or without tomato (pages 169 and 170), kept hot
> ⅓ cup grated *Chihuahua* cheese or medium-sharp Cheddar
> ½ cup *crème fraîche*

Heat the oven to 375°. Have ready a warmed shallow ovenproof dish that will accommodate two stacks of *tortillas* side by side, plus a tray lined with paper toweling.

Heat a little of the oil—enough to coat the surface—in a small frying pan. Fry the *tortillas* lightly until heated through thoroughly but not crisp around the edge—about 3 to 4 seconds on each side—adding more oil as necessary. Drain on the paper toweling.

Dip 2 of the *tortillas* into the hot tomato sauce—it should be thick enough to coat them—and place side by side on the ovenproof dish. Spread about 1 heaped tablespoon of the cooked *cuitlacoche* over each *tortilla;* cover these with 2 more *tortillas* immersed in the sauce, and so on, until you have two stacks of 4 *tortillas,* with the filling between each pair. Pour the remaining sauce over the top *tortillas,* cover very loosely with foil, and bake until well heated through—about 10 minutes. Remove foil, sprinkle with the cheese, and return to the oven just long enough to melt the cheese—not to brown it. Just before serving, cover with the *crème fraîche* and cut into wedges.

NOPALES *(Opuntia species) (Cactus Paddles)*

The fleshy "leaves"—called *joints* or *paddles*—of various species of *nopal cactus* are cooked and eaten in Mexico. While the country people gather wild ones with large whitish thorns, there are some commercially grown, cultivated varieties that have almost invisible thorns, *aguates*, hidden inside fleshy green sheaths that form small bumps on the surface of the leaves. All of these varieties when mature yield egg-shaped fruits called *tunas*—green, yellow, or red, depending on the variety.

Nopales are now widely distributed in the United States and have joined the ranks of the "new" foods; they are sold in various stages of preparation.

Whole Nopales

You can now find whole *nopales* in either Latin American or Mexican markets throughout the United States or in the specialty vegetable sections of many supermarkets. They tend to be thin, just less than ¼ inch thick, darkish green in color, and untrimmed, with their tiny thorns intact. If you have a choice, select those that are firm and not flabby to the touch and have a smooth, unwrinkled skin. Pick them up carefully, either with tongs or a gloved hand, so that the thorns do not adhere to your fingers, causing minor but persistent irritation for a day or so. They have to be cleaned, which is a tedious job (but like all tedious jobs should be carried out to the accompaniment of music or even a cooking cassette). You will need a pair of tongs, a sharp knife, and a glove for one hand. Holding the *nopal* firmly in the tongs, shave off the tiny bumps that contain the thorns, but do not remove the whole green outer layer of the *nopal*. Rinse them well. Cut off the thick, fleshy base and discard. Then cut into ¼- to ½-inch squares. They are now ready to cook.

Prepared and Packaged

In many Mexican markets, especially on the West Coast, you can find packaged, cleaned, and diced *nopales* that are ready to use. This is fine as long as they haven't been around too long and become discolored around the edges.

Canned

The canned or bottled *nopalitos*, either in brine or in a light pickle, can be purchased in most Mexican markets. I cannot recommend those packed in brine, because they are limp and rather tasteless, while those in a light pickle could be used as a *botana*, or snack, or added to a salad (but don't make a salad of them alone).

Homegrown

If you live in the Southwest, you may have a *nopal* cactus growing out back (in Arizona it's probably in the front yard), or you may have planted them especially for eating. Even if they have dangerous-looking whitish prickles, they are edible, provided they are young and tender. About 6 inches long and about ¼ inch thick is a good size. Anything smaller than that, with a shiny, greeny-yellow skin, is too young. The dark green thick ones are too fibrous to eat.

To cut the *nopales*, arm yourself with a thick glove, a pair of tongs, and a sharp knife. Steady the paddle with the tongs and cut it cleanly—without leaving a ragged edge—from its host. (I am told by experts that this is important.) Then clean them as described above. If some of the tiny thorns have hooked themselves into your fingers, apply strong Scotch tape over the spot and pull off, and if this does not work, then do as Mexican peasants do: run your fingers through your hair several times.

There are several ways of cooking *nopales*.

NOPALES ASADOS *(Grilled Cactus Paddles)*

In the principal *nopal*-growing areas of central Mexico the popular, rustic way of cooking them is on a grill or *comal*. Clean them as described above but leave them whole. Cut into fingers, leaving them attached at the base. Heat a *comal* over very high heat and lightly grease the surface. Dip the cut *nopal* into *pulque* or beer and place on the *comal*, pressing them down flat with a spatula so that the underside sizzles and becomes speckled with brown—about 4 minutes. Turn the *nopales* over and continue cooking on the second side for 4 minutes. Chop, season with a *chile* sauce, and stuff into a hot *tortilla*.

NOPALES COCIDOS (*Boiled Cactus Paddles*)

The most common way of cooking cleaned and diced *nopales* is to boil them in salted water with some scallion tops, which, according to Mexican cooks, helps extract their viscous substance, like that of okra. Some put a copper coin or baking soda in the water to preserve the color, while others cook them in a copper *cazo*, an unlined copper pan—whatever.

Put the cleaned and diced *nopales* into boiling salted water with a few roughly chopped green scallion tops and boil fast until tender but not soft—about 10 to 15 minutes, depending on how thick they are. Drain and rinse twice in cold water if necessary to remove all the viscous juice they exude. They are now ready to use in salads, with eggs or beans, etc.

One pound of *nopales* when cleaned and diced yields about 3½ cups. This quantity will be reduced by about half in the cooking.

NOPALES AL VAPOR (*"Steamed" Cactus Paddles*)

MAKES 3 CUPS

You will in fact have *nopales* that have a better texture and color and are more nutritious if you cook them this way, taught to me by a bus driver from Otumba, a village near the pyramids of Teotihuacan.

Although *al vapor* translates as "steam," here it does not mean in a steamer; it refers to the method of stewing the *nopales* covered in their own juices. Cooked in this way, they are ready to be used in salads, with scrambled eggs, in beans, or for *taco* fillings.

2 tablespoons safflower oil
2 small garlic cloves, peeled and finely chopped
⅓ cup roughly chopped scallion tops
6 rounded cups (2¼ pounds) prepared *nopal* cactus pieces (see page 173)
1 teaspoon (or to taste) sea salt

Heat the oil in a large frying pan, add the garlic and scallion tops, and fry gently without browning—about 30 seconds. Add the *nopales* and salt, stir well, cover the pan, and cook over medium heat, shaking the pan from time to time to prevent sticking, for about 10 minutes. By this time all the juice and slimy substance will have exuded.

Note: When freshly picked, cactus pieces are very juicy; often if bought in the store they are much drier, so it may be necessary to add ½ cup water for this stage of the cooking.

Remove the lid and continue cooking, stirring and scraping the bottom of the pan from time to time to prevent sticking, until the *nopales* are almost dry and shiny—about 15 minutes. Set aside to cool.

NOPALES EN BLANCO (*"White" Cactus Paddles*)

MAKES ABOUT 2 CUPS

This simple and delicious recipe comes from *Libro Social y Familiar, para la Mujer Obrera y Campesina,* 1935. While it seems curious to refer to them as "white," it simply means that they are not cooked in a red, dried *chile* sauce. They can be served as a separate course with corn *tortillas* or with broiled meats or fish.

2 tablespoons lard or safflower oil
1 pound (about 3½ cups) *nopales,* cleaned and diced (see page 173)
2 heaped tablespoons roughly chopped scallion tops
½ teaspoon (or to taste) sea salt
2 *chiles serranos*
2 ounces *tomate verde,* cooked (page 451), plus ¼ cup of the cooking water
1 garlic clove, peeled and roughly chopped
2 tablespoons finely chopped white onion
2 tablespoons roughly chopped *cilantro*

Heat the lard in a heavy frying pan and add the *nopales,* scallion tops, and salt; cover the pan and cook over gentle heat, shaking the pan from time to time, until the sticky substance has exuded and they are tender but not soft—about 15 minutes.

Raise the heat, remove the lid, and continue cooking, stirring and scraping the bottom of the pan to prevent sticking, until the viscous juice has been absorbed and the *nopales* are beginning to fry—about 15 minutes. Add the fresh *chiles* and fry for 1 minute more. Meanwhile, put the *tomate verde* with the cooking water, garlic, and onion into a blender jar and blend until almost smooth. Add to the *nopales* and reduce over medium heat for about 5 minutes. Taste for salt, stir in the *cilantro,* cook for a few seconds, and serve.

ENSALADA DE NOPALITOS *(Salad of Cactus Pieces)*

SERVES 6

Salads as such do not play an important part in the Mexican kitchen, where there are so many fresh garnishes, pickles, and sauces to accompany the food. However, a salad of *nopalitos*, a popular food in the marketplace, does rank high. Cooked green beans or *chayote* can be substituted for *nopales*.

3 cups cooked *nopaoles,* cut into squares (page 174)
3 tablespoons finely chopped white onion
½ cup loosely packed, finely chopped *cilantro*
scant ½ teaspoon dried oregano, Mexican if possible
2 tablespoons fresh lime juice or vinegar

THE TOPPING
3 small tomatoes, unskinned, sliced
⅓ cup finely chopped *cilantro*
⅓ cup crumbled *queso fresco* or *añejo*
⅓ cup purple onion rings
3 canned *chiles jalapeños en escabeche,* cut into quarters lengthwise
1 avocado, peeled and sliced (optional)
inner leaves of romaine lettuce for the sides of the serving platter

Mix the *nopalitos* with the next four ingredients and set aside to season for 30 minutes. Stir well and adjust seasoning. Spread the *nopalitos* over the platter about 1½ inches deep. Decorate with the tomato slices and top with *cilantro*, cheese, onion rings, *chile* strips, and slices of avocado (if used). Overlap the romaine leaves around the edge of the platter and serve at room temperature.

FRIJOLES *(Phaseolus vulgaria spp.) (Dry Beans)*

The dry goods stores in Mexico that sell *chiles*, pumpkin seeds, lentils, and rice are a colorful sight with their open sacks of muticolored beans: *bayos* (bay), *flor de Mayo* (mottled with mauve), *canario* (dull yellow), *peruano* (pale yellow), *morado* (mauve), *cacahuates* (large bay-colored, mottled with reddish-mauve), shiny little *negros* (black), and small white *frijoles blanco*, to name a few. They provide a broad spectrum of regional varieties that play an important part in the nutritional value of the Mexican meal, especially in that of the *campesinos* (farm workers).

While there are slight regional differences in their preparation—with different herbs, with or without garlic, with or without *chile*, etc.—there are some general rules that govern the cooking of them. The most common and flavorful way of cooking dry beans is in an earthenware bean pot, but care has to be taken that they do not scorch. Always have ready extra hot water to add from time to time, or do as my neighbors do—put a small *cazuela* full of water on top of the bean pot. It prevents some of the evaporation and provides hot water whenever it is needed (see illustration, page 133).

In the United States I find a slow cooker (Crock-Pots, etc.) with a ceramic liner the most useful for cooking beans. I leave the beans on medium heat and let them cook all night; the water does not tend to evaporate as quickly as with other methods of cooking. (The slow cookers work much better if they have a glass rather than a plastic top.) I prefer not to use a metal pot, but if you are in a hurry, a pressure cooker is the first resort. Take care to keep the pot over very low heat and make sure there is plenty of water so the beans do not scorch.

Cooking times can never be given exactly. It will all depend on how old the beans are: *pintos*, for instance, can be cooked in a Crock-Pot on high heat in 2½ hours, but I have known some black turtle beans that have taken 7 hours, and the skins were still tough. Try to avoid this by cooking beans the day before; they are more flavorful anyway and the broth nice and soupy.

FRIJOLES DE OLLA (*Pot Beans*)

MAKES ABOUT 3½ CUPS   CENTRAL MEXICO

½ pound dry beans, such as *pinto,* California pink, or black turtle (*bayo, flor de Mayo, canario,* etc., in Mexico)
¼ white onion, roughly sliced
1 heaped tablespoon lard
sea salt to taste

Run the beans through your hands to pick out any small stones or pieces of earth, which can be found in even the best of brands. Rinse twice in cold water and drain. Put into a bean pot and cover with enough hot water to come at least 3 inches above the beans. Add the onion and lard and bring to a simmer. Continue simmering until the skins of the beans are soft, then add the salt and continue cooking until the beans are very soft and the broth soupy (see note on cooking time, page 178). Beans are always better eaten the day after they are cooked, when the flavor matures.

Frijoles de olla are usually served alone at the end of the main course, sometimes on the same plate and mopped up with a *tortilla,* or often in a small bowl apart.

Do not soak the beans first; the skin gives off an unpleasant flavor. If you do, then don't throw out the soaking water with all the minerals and flavor. Instead throw out the book that tells you to do so.

Do not add the salt until the skins of the beans are soft, or they will toughen.

Always use the bean broth—again, throw out the book that tells you to discard it (believe it or not, I have seen these instructions).

Do not leave the beans at room temperature for any length of time; they ferment easily.

FRIJOLES REFRITOS *(Refried Beans)*

MAKES ABOUT 3½ CUPS   CENTRAL MEXICO

Mashed and fried beans can appear on a Mexican table three times a day: with breakfast eggs, after the main meat course at midday, or with the evening's *tacos*. They are used to spread on *tostadas*, *raspadas*, *sopes*, and other *antojitos*. Of course, the more lard—not bacon fat, which is too strong—you use, the better they are.

A wooden bean or potato masher is best for this. I do not recommend using a blender, since the beans lose their interesting texture.

6 tablespoons lard
1 tablespoon finely chopped white onion
1 recipe *frijoles de olla* (page 179)

Heat the lard in a heavy 10-inch frying pan. Add the onion and fry over gentle heat until transparent, about 1 minute. Add a cupful of the beans and their broth and mash down over fairly high heat. As they begin to reduce, add some more and keep mashing until they have all been incorporated. Continue frying, scraping the sides and bottom of the pan to prevent sticking, until the mixture becomes a thick paste and you can see the bottom of the pan as you stir.

If you wish to prepare the beans ahead, cook them to the point where all the beans have been added and mashed. Cover tightly so that a hard crust does not form over the top. When reheating, sprinkle the surface with ¼ cup warm water, mix well, and continue with the final frying.

Bean paste freezes well, and you can always have it on hand.

FRIJOLES PUERCOS, MICHOACÁN
("Pork" Beans from Michoacán)

SERVES 6 TO 8   CENTRAL MICHOACÁN

As the name implies, these beans are rich—though not quite as rich as the Colima version that follows—and certainly to be enjoyed with all the traditional ingredients, but also certainly to be eaten in small quantities. These *frijoles* are usually prepared for a *fiesta* to accompany barbecued meats, or *carnitas*, but they sit very well on a buffet table at any time, brunch included.

This recipe was given to me by Señora Guadalupe Mendoza, who came originally to Pátzcuaro from Querétaro to marry into one of the old families there, who are so proud of their Spanish heritage. For this recipe she uses a flattish, pinky-bay-colored bean called *Ihuatzio* for the lakeside village near where it is grown. California pink or *pinto* makes a good substitute. The beans should be cooked until they are quite soft and the broth is reduced to a thickish consistency.

2 ounces bacon, cut into small squares
2 *chorizos* (about 6 ounces), skinned and crumbled
⅓ cup dried ½-inch *tortilla* squares
1 recipe *frijoles de olla* (page 179) (about 4 cups with broth)
4 canned *chiles largos* or canned *chiles jalapeños en escabeche* to taste
¼ pound *queso añejo*, Chihuahua, Romano, or Muenster
2 ounces *chicharrón*, broken into small pieces

Fry the bacon in a small frying pan over low heat so that the fat renders out, but do not allow it to brown too much and become crisp. Remove the bacon pieces with a slotted spoon and set aside. Add the crumbled *chorizo* to the bacon fat and fry gently without browning for about 5 minutes. Remove the *chorizo* with a slotted spoon and set aside. In the same fat, fry the *tortilla* squares until they are completely crisp. Drain on paper toweling.

Put the beans in a heavy, wide pan and add the whole *chiles*, bacon, and *chorizo*; heat through gently so they do not scorch on the bottom. When they just begin to bubble, add the cheese and *chicharrón*. As the cheese just begins to melt, sprinkle the top of the beans with the *tortilla* squares and serve immediately, before they become soft.

FRIJOLES PUERCOS, COLIMA
("Pork" Beans from Colima)

MAKES ABOUT 3½ CUPS   SEÑORA GUADALUPE ALCARAZ, COLIMA

Quite the richest way of cooking beans, *frijoles puercos* come from the hot country of the west central states of Michoacán, Colima, and Jalisco. In Huetamo, Michoacán, they serve them, rich as they are, with a red *mole*, in Colima with a dish of seasoned pork called *tatemadeo*. This outrageously heavy and delicious version from Colima is often served alone, on top of the fried *chiles* so that the *chiles'* flavor will merge into the damp, hot beans. *Raspadas*, very thin toasted *tortillas* (page 16), are eaten with them. I spread the *frijoles* on top like *tostadas*, but Señora Alcaraz tells me this is not done, and no doubt there are valid reasons against it.

½ pound *frijoles bayos* or *pintos de olla*, cooked until very soft (page 179), with broth
6 ounces lard
1 small dry corn *tortilla*
¼ pound pork, cooked and shredded, *carne de puerco cocida y deshebrado* (page 248)
3 ounces *chorizo*, skinned, crumbled, and fried
¼ cup *legumbres en escabeche* (page 143), finely chopped
3 ounces *queso añejo* or Romano cheese, finely grated

THE TOPPING
⅓ cup finely chopped white onion
⅓ cup sliced cooked carrots
½ cup finely shredded cabbage
2 *chiles cascabel* or *serranos sécos*, fried crisp and crumbled

Reduce the beans until they form a soft paste and all the broth has been absorbed. Set aside.

Heat the lard, add the *tortilla*, and fry until a deep golden color; remove and discard or eat. Gradually stir the beans into the lard and cook for about 2 minutes. Mash thoroughly until they form a textured paste. Add the shredded pork, crumbled *chorizo*, and vegetables and cook for about 5 minutes more, stirring and turning them over almost constantly. As the bean paste begins to shrink from the sides of the pan, stir in the cheese; as it melts, remove and serve on a hot platter topped with the onion, carrot, cabbage, and *chiles*.

FRIJOLES GUISADOS *(Cooked and Fried Beans)*

MAKES ABOUT 4½ CUPS   SEÑORA LIVIER RUIZ DE SUAREZ, VALLE DE JUAREZ

Traditionally these "semifried" beans are put on the top of *morisqueta*, boiled rice (page 124), sprinkled with crumbled *queso añejo* (or any rather dry, salty cheese), and served as a "dry soup" or a supper dish. This is a typical example of home cooking for a large family.

The beans are just reduced to a thickish sauce for *morisqueta*, but you can reduce them further and spread them on *tortillas* or *tostadas*.

½ pound *frijoles pinto, peruanos, or flor de mayo*
3 quarts hot water, approximately
¼ medium white onion, roughly sliced
3 tablespoons lard
sea salt to taste
3 (or to taste) *chiles serranos*, finely chopped
3 tablespoons finely chopped white onion

Run the beans through your hands to check for stones or lumps of earth. Rinse well in cold water and put into a bean pot. Cover with the hot water, add the sliced onion and 1 tablespoon of the lard, and bring to a simmer. Cover the pot and continue simmering until the skins of the beans are tender—from 2 to 4 hours, depending on the age of the beans. Add the salt and continue cooking until mushy—about 1 hour longer (see note, page 178).

Melt the remaining 2 tablespoons lard in a frying pan, add fresh *chiles* and chopped onion, and fry, without browning, for about 2 minutes. Add the beans and their broth (there should be about 5 cups) and start mashing with a bean or potato masher until they are roughly broken up (easy if you have cooked them enough) and resemble a textured puree. Cook over fairly high heat so that they reduce and thicken and thickly coat the back of a wooden spoon—about 15 minutes.

If you're using them for *tostadas* or refried beans, then continue cooking to a thick paste.

FRIJOLES NEGROS A LA OAXAQUEÑA
(Oaxacan Black Beans)

MAKES ABOUT 7 TO 8 CUPS

Black beans are used predominantly in the southern part of Mexico; they are small with very shiny skins like the turtle beans sold in the United States. Since one never knows how old the beans are, it is best to plan for a long cooking period. In any case, both the beans and the broth develop flavor and substance if cooked the day before being used.

1 pound black turtle beans
½ medium white onion, roughly sliced
½ small head of garlic
10 cups hot water
sea salt to taste
2 large leafy stems of *epazote*

Pick the beans over to make sure there are no small stones or other debris mixed with them. Rinse in cold water, drain, and put into a bean pot or slow cooker. Add the onion, make a superficial cut around the center of the cluster of garlic (this allows the flavor to seep out better), and cover with hot water. Cover the pot and cook at a high temperature in the slow cooker or over medium heat in a bean pot until the bean skins are soft—from 4 to 12 hours, depending on age of beans. Add salt to taste and the *epazote* and cook for 30 minutes more.

FRIJOLES NEGROS CON CHOCHOYOTES
(Black Beans with Dumplings)

SERVES 6 TO 8

This recipe typifies Oaxacan peasant cuisine: the simplest of ingredients strongly flavored with a particular herb, in this case *hierba de conejo tridax coronopiifolia* (literal translation, rabbit herb). The richness is provided by the *asiento* in the dumplings. Traditionally these soupy beans are served either after the main course—as *frijoles de olla* are in central Mexico—or to accompany some charcoal-broiled dried beef (*tasajo de hebra*). A bunch of *epazote* could be used instead of the "rabbit herb," and while it does not duplicate the flavor, it is an acceptable substitute. For those who don't like *picante* food the *chiles* can be omitted, or they can be left whole for those who do to crunch on at will. This makes a wonderfully satisfying cold weather soup.

1 small bunch of *hierba de conejo* or *epazote*
⅓ cup water
2 *chiles de árbol*, toasted
3 garlic cloves, peeled
¼ medium white onion, thickly sliced
2 tablespoons lard or safflower oil
1½ cups water
1 recipe *frijoles de olla* (page 179) using black beans (about 3½ to 4 cups with broth)
18 *chochoyotes* (page 54)

Break the herb leaves into a blender jar, discarding the main stems. Add the ⅓ cup water, dried *chiles*, garlic, and onion and blend until smooth. Heat the lard in a small frying pan, add the blended ingredients, and reduce over high heat for about 3 minutes. Add with 1½ cups water to the cooked beans and bring to a simmer over medium heat, scraping the bottom of the pan to make sure the beans do not stick. Continue cooking for about 15 minutes. Add the *chochoyotes*, making sure that the bean broth covers them, and cook until the *masa* is no longer raw-tasting—about 15 to 20 minutes. Serve in deep bowls with plenty of the broth.

FRIJOLES COLADOS Y FRITOS A LA YUCATECA
(Yucatecan Black Bean Paste)

MAKES 3 CUPS

A sieved, smooth paste of black beans is served with many of the Yucatecan dishes or as an integral part of some of their *antojitos* (*panuchos*, *garnachas*, etc.). Traditional cooks still go through the process of pressing the cooked beans through a fine strainer to remove the skins (the gassy, indigestible part, although good roughage). However, we can take a shortcut and blend them together until smooth with their broth.

½ pound dry black turtle beans
8 cups hot water, approximately
2 scallions, roughly chopped
6 to 8 tablespoons lard
sea salt to taste
1 large leafy stem of *epazote*
1 *chile habanero* or any hot green *chile*, charred

Pick over the beans to remove any stones or other debris. Rinse in cold water, put into a bean pot, and cover with hot water. Bring to a simmer and simmer until the skins are splitting open—about 2 hours, depending on the age and the dryness of the beans.

Add the scallions, 4 tablespoons of the lard, and salt to taste; continue cooking until soft and mushy—about 1 hour more.

Heat the rest of the lard in a heavy frying pan. Add about half of the beans and their broth to a blender jar and blend until smooth. Add to the frying pan. Continue with the rest of the beans and add to the pan along with the *epazote* and fresh *chile*. Reduce the puree to a thick paste over fairly high heat, stirring and scraping the bottom of the pan occasionally to prevent sticking—about 15 minutes.

Once this paste has been prepared it can be frozen indefinitely, ready to use for other occasions.

GARBANZOS *(Chick-Peas)*

MAKES 2 CUPS COOKED

Dried chick-peas (*Cicer arietinum*) are used for several Mexican soups and stews. They are also either ground to a powder or cooked and mashed for use in savory fried cakes or in fritters that are served as a dessert in syrup.

You can, of course, use canned ones, but they are precooked and tend to be a bit mushy; besides, you can't use the liquid from the can satisfactorily. If you cook them yourself, you can add the broth to the stew for extra flavor and nutrients.

1 level cup (about 6 ounces) dried *garbanzos*
sea salt to taste

Rinse the chick-peas in cold water, drain, cover with hot water, and leave to soak overnight. Put the chick-peas and their soaking water plus 2 extra cups of water into a saucepan with sea salt to taste. Bring up to a simmer and continue cooking slowly until soft but not falling apart—about 1½ hours, depending on how old and dry they are.

As an alternative, put the chick-peas, their soaking water, and the extra water, but no salt, into the pressure cooker, bring up to pressure, and cook for about 40 minutes.

Whichever method you use, when the chick-peas are cool enough to handle, rub them between your hands to loosen the papery skins and discard. They are now ready to be used, but reserve the cooking water for the soup or stew to which they are to be added.

LENTEJAS EN ADOBO
(Lentils with Chiles, Pork, and Fruit)

SERVES 4 TO 6   SEÑORA VIRGINIA RAMOS ESPINOSA

In many of the fruit-growing areas of Mexico, fruit is used as an ingredient in some of the main meat dishes: pears and peaches in Vitualla of central Michoacán, pineapple and plantain in the *mancha manteles* of Oaxaca, peaches, pears, and apples in the stuffing for *chiles en nogada* of Puebla. Much of the same fruits are used in the *caldo loco* (literally, mad broth) of the San Luis Potosi highlands. These sweet/sour, salty flavors are reminiscent of those from Moorish Spain. (However, it is interesting that in the remote country areas the peasants, at least in eastern Michoacán, will not tolerate the idea, let alone eat such a mixture.)

This recipe is a very popular way of preparing lentils in the capital and neighboring Puebla, where it would be eaten (because of the meat it contains) as a main dish. Normally a dish of lentils without meat would be served after the main course, instead of *frijoles de olla*. Lentils in Mexico are very small and greenish-brown in color; however, any other type of lentils could be used. There is, in fact, a quite indigestible version of this dish given in the *Diccionario de Cocina*, preceded by a warning: "This vegetable is best eaten only by those with strong stomachs." If they are well cooked, this advice can be ignored. It makes a delicious soup/stew for cold days, best eaten with crusty French bread and some good, strong red wine.

THE LENTILS
½ pound (1 heaped cup) lentils, brown if available (see note above)
½ small white onion
sea salt to taste

THE PORK
1 pound boneless stewing pork, cut into 1-inch cubes
sea salt to taste

THE SEASONING AND FINAL COOKING

5 small *chiles anchos,* cleaned of veins and seeds and lightly toasted (see page 475)

¼ pound tomatoes, broiled (see page 450)

1 garlic clove, peeled and roughly chopped

¼ teaspoon dried oregano, Mexican if possible

1 whole clove

1 ½-inch cinnamon stick

1 tablespoon melted lard or safflower oil

1 medium plantain (about 8 ounces), peeled and cut into ¼-inch slices

2 thick pineapple slices, peeled, cored, and cut into small triangular wedges

Run the lentils through your hands to make sure there are no stones or other foreign bodies in them. Rinse them in two changes of water and put into a pan. Add onion, salt to taste, and enough water to come about 2 inches above the surface of the lentils. Set over medium heat and bring to a fast simmer. Continue simmering until the lentils are quite soft—about 3 hours, depending on their age. Keep a pan of near-boiling water on the side, ready to add if necessary.

Put the pork pieces into a pan; add salt to taste and water to cover. Bring to a fast simmer and continue simmering until the pork is tender but not soft—about 25 minutes. Strain, reserving the broth, and set broth and meat aside.

Cover the dried *chiles* with boiling water and leave to soak for about 15 minutes, until the *chiles* have softened and become fleshy. Drain and put into a blender jar with 1 cup of the reserved pork broth, the broiled tomatoes, garlic, oregano, clove, and cinnamon; blend until smooth, adding more broth only if needed to release the blades of the blender.

Heat the lard in a small frying pan, add the blended ingredients, and fry over medium heat, stirring and scraping the bottom of the pan, until reduced and well seasoned—about 4 minutes. Add to the lentils and add the pork, remaining broth, plantain, and pineapple; simmer together for about 30 minutes. Adjust salt and add water if necessary. The mixture should be like a thick soup.

SEAFOOD

(Pescados y Mariscos)

Mexico is shaped like a cornucopia, with a coastline of thousands of miles that touches the Pacific, the gulfs of California and Mexico, and the Caribbean. It has many coastal lagoons, a few large rivers, lakes and dams, all of which—where pollution has not taken over—provide an enormous variety and plentiful supply of fish and crustaceans the year round.

The best eating will always be in those relatively isolated spots where the fish and shellfish have just been taken out of the water. Plainly grilled, or seasoned with a *chile* paste, served in a simple, crunchy sauce, or made into a *ceviche*, this seafood is superb.

In the inland cities and towns, fish cooking generally is not highly sophisticated; fish is often fried to a crisp, cooked in a tomato sauce, or cooked *en escabeche* (in a souse), and sometimes it is steamed in banana or *hoja santa* leaves, but unfortunately, too often it is overcooked except in a few expert hands.

The recipes that follow give a cross section of some of the cooking methods from different regions of the country.

PESCADO EMPEREJILADO
(Whitefish in Papillote with Parsley)

SERVES 6   PÁTZCUARO

The *pescado blanco* (whitefish, *Chirostoma estor*) is found only in Lake Pátzcuaro (and until recent years Lake Chapala) and, it is believed, nowhere else in the world. It is an elegant little fish with a pointed head and a wide silver band running down each side of it from head to tail, with an average length of 7 inches. It has no scales, and the flesh is almost transparent when raw. When cooked, the flesh is very fine, like that of sole, and has a very delicate flavor. Fillets of sole or flounder are the best substitutes.

The most popular way of cooking this fish in Pátzcuaro is to open it up and flatten it out, leaving the head intact—so you can see that it is the real thing—then cook it in a light batter such as that used for *chiles rellenos*. It is pleasant enough but tends to be rather greasy. Another method is to put it into *escabeche*—a light sauce—but that tends to toughen the flesh and overpower the flavor.

When Señora Alcocer of Pátzcuaro gave me this recipe, it came as a welcome change. In effect the fish is cooked *en papillote* (in cooking parchment), but it also echoes the Indian method of cooking seasoned fish wrapped in several layers of dried corn husks that are then placed on an earthenware *comal* or on a rack straight over a glowing wood or charcoal fire. Señora Alcocer in fact uses ordinary brown paper (like that used for grocery bags); foil, she insists, is too harsh—cooking parchment can, of course, be used. She serves it accompanied by bread rolls and a plain lettuce and tomato salad, restraining her family from using the tomato *salsa* that traditionally accompanies the fried version.

1½ pounds fish fillets (see note above), skin removed, divided into 6 portions
brown paper or cooking parchment
6 tablespoons unsalted butter, approximately
½ cup firmly packed, finely chopped flat-leaf parsley
sea salt to taste
4 tablespoons water, approximately

Remove any skin and little side bones from the fish. Since the fillets will probably vary in size, cut a rectangular piece of paper or parchment for each one, allowing the length of the fillet plus 3 inches extra on each end. The paper should be wide enough to roll the fillet tightly with an overlap to seal in the juices. Liberally smear the inside of each piece of paper with butter to the

193

size of the fillets. Place a fillet on each piece of paper. Blend the parsley, salt, and water together to form a paste and coat the top of each fillet with some of it. Roll the fish like a jelly roll lengthwise and twist the ends of the paper securely or tie if necessary, to make sure the juices will not seep out.

Meanwhile, heat a frying pan and melt 1 tablespoon of the butter—it should just lightly coat the pan. Place the packages side by side in one layer and cook over low heat, turning the packages from time to time until the paper coating is an even golden color.

Serve the closed packages of fish on each plate with salad and rolls as suggested above.

BACALAO A LA VIZCAÍNA
(Dried Cod for Christmas Eve)

MAKES ABOUT 3½ CUPS SHREDDED FISH TO SERVE 6

Bacalao, dried cod stewed in tomatoes and olive oil, a dish completely Spanish in origin, is indispensable to the traditional Christmas Eve supper in Mexico. However, it has a much milder flavor than its Spanish counterpart. It is always served with bread rolls and nothing else. Real *aficionados* always hope there will be some left over for the following day to stuff into *teleras* (flat bread rolls) or to make *empanadas,* pastry turnovers—it makes a good filling, slightly pungent but not overwhelming.

For this dish you really need a good, rich olive oil like the less refined ones of Portugal, Sicily, or Spain, and it is not necessary to go to the expense of an extra-virgin.

While you should soak the salt cod one day ahead, in fact you could cook the whole dish several days ahead—it even freezes well for several months—add the parsley at the end when reheating the dish.

Try to buy unpackaged salt cod so that you can see what you are getting— but that may be impossible, because the majority is imported from Norway and packaged in wooden boxes. Do make sure it *is* cod and so labeled. Other dried fish products on the market masquerade as cod, and while some of them are acceptable in flavor, they do not have the required rather stringy quality and turn mushy when cooked. If you are able to pick and choose, try to buy center cuts rather than the thin tail ends, which have a lot of waste in skin and bone. The color of the fish should be a greyish-white and should not have any yellowish tones that denote old age.

The soaking time will depend very much on how long the cod has been in storage, and, unfortunately, you can oversoak so that all the flavor, and salt for that matter, disappears.

I usually allow about 18 hours, changing the water about four times during that period. If it is still tough and cannot be cleaned easily, I cover it with clean water and simmer it for about 5 minutes. Carefully remove all skin and bones and shred the flesh finely.

7 tablespoons olive oil, approximately (see note on page 194)
2 pounds (about 4 large) tomatoes, finely chopped or blended, unpeeled
¼ medium white onion, finely chopped or blended
4 garlic cloves, peeled and finely chopped or blended
1 medium white onion, thinly sliced
1 pound dried salt cod (see note above), cleaned and finely shredded
2 rounded tablespoons slivered almonds
20 small green olives stuffed with red bell pepper *or* 20 small green olives,
    pitted, with 1 red bell pepper, charred, peeled, and cleaned
8 canned *chiles largos* or *jalapeños en escabeche*
4 tablespoons finely chopped flat-leaf parsley
sea salt to taste

In a heavy pan, heat 4 tablespoons of the olive oil and add the tomatoes, chopped onion, and garlic; fry over fairly high heat, stirring from time to time to prevent sticking, until the mixture has reduced and thickened (according to Mexicans, it should be *chino* or crinkly on top)—about 20 minutes. Meanwhile, in a separate pan, heat the remaining oil and cook the onion slices gently until transparent but not limp—about 2 minutes. Set aside.

Stir the shredded fish into the tomato mixture and mix well. Add the almonds, olives, *chiles*, and fried onion slices and cook over medium heat until all the flavors have blended and the mixture is almost dry—about 20 minutes. Stir in the parsley 5 minutes before the end of the cooking time. It may seem silly to say, but taste for salt.

HOW TO CLEAN SQUID

Many fish markets sell squid that has already been cleaned and is ready to cook; some sell ink—generally frozen—as well. However, you may have to, or want to, clean your own and extract the ink. Do not expect the ink to flow out profusely; there is very little of it per squid, but it is potent, and a little goes a long way.

It is always better to buy squid with bodies no more than 5 inches (approximately) long, excluding tentacles. Up to this size they are tender and cook in minutes. Also with a small squid you do not have to remove the mauvish outer skin—which incidentally is nutritious, besides looking more attractive—but on larger squid it tends to toughen on cooking.

If you want to use the ink it's particularly important to buy larger squid, not less than 5 inches long, because the ink sac—a thin, silvery sac about 1 inch long and $\frac{1}{16}$ inch wide—is more visible and manageable. It lies straight along the gelatinous mass inside the body. If more ink is needed, the small deposits behind the eyes can be used as well.

To clean the squid, pull the tentacles firmly but carefully so that they are detached from the body with eyes and gelatinous matter inside all intact. Cut the tentacles off just below the eyes and set aside. Cut off the eyes and reserve for extra ink.

Carefully remove the ink sac from the gelatinous insides, taking care not to puncture it as you do so. Pierce it and dissolve the ink in a small bowl with about $\frac{1}{4}$ cup of water or vinegar. If more ink is needed, pierce behind the eyes and squeeze out the black liquid into the same container. Discard the eyes and the gelatinous debris.

Pull out the transparent quill that holds the body rigid and discard. Rinse out the inside of the body, or to make sure it is clean, turn it inside out and rinse well. Turn it back so that the mauve-skinned side is out. The squid is now ready to cook.

CALAMARES EN SU TINTA
(Squid Stewed in Their Ink)

SERVES 4

This recipe was given to me by a lady of 80 who came from a family of excellent Yucatecan cooks. On the day she was expecting me she had not only written the recipe out in her firm hand but she had some made for me to try.

This is a very concentrated dish, so ¼ pound squid per serving should be enough. If you prefer a thinner sauce, some tomato puree may be added at the end—although I prefer it as it is. This dish is best served on a bed of plain white rice. It is also delicious served at room temperature as an hors d'oeuvre.

If you are going to clean your own squid, buy 2 pounds; the quantity will be reduced by *about* half when cleaned, depending on the amount of gelatinous substance inside the squid pockets. This recipe is best cooked in small quantities.

½ pound (about 1 large) tomatoes, unpeeled and roughly chopped
1 small white onion, roughly chopped
1 small green bell pepper, cleaned of veins and seeds and roughly chopped
¼ cup firmly packed, roughly chopped flat-leaf parsley
12 small garlic cloves, peeled
6 tablespoons fruity olive oil
1 pound cleaned squid, cut into ½-inch pieces (see page 196)
sea salt to taste
1 large California bay leaf, broken up
1 scant teaspoon sugar
1 teaspoon squid ink, approximately, diluted in 2 tablespoons vinegar
freshly ground black pepper

Put the tomatoes, onion, green pepper, parsley, and 4 of the garlic cloves into a blender jar and blend for a few seconds to make a textured puree. Set aside.

Heat the oil in a heavy frying pan or a sauté pan, add 4 garlic cloves, slivered, and fry until a very dark brown. Remove the garlic and discard. Put the remaining garlic cloves, slivered, into the pan with the squid, sprinkle with salt, and stir quickly, tossing it from time to time (really a stir-fry), for 2 to 3 minutes.

Add the tomato puree, bay leaf, sugar, squid ink, and pepper and cook quickly for about 6 minutes to reduce the sauce. The squid should be tender but still a little *al dente*. If the sauce is still a little too liquid but the squid is cooked, tip the pan to one side and reduce the sauce for 4 minutes more.

HOW TO CLEAN OCTOPUS

Many fish markets sell cleaned octopus that is ready for cooking. Some sell ink—generally frozen—as well. However, you may want to, or have to, clean and extract the ink yourself. Do not expect the ink to flow out profusely; there is a very small sac tucked inside the interior organs of the octopus— about ¼ inch in size—and the ink is very potent, a little going a long way. The sac is quite often already ruptured; don't buy if there is a big black spot of it inside the stomach.

It is best to buy an octopus that weighs about 1 pound or less; at that size it is very tender and takes only minutes to cook. It is an ideal size, too, for extracting ink, for the sac is more visible and manageable.

To clean the octopus, first make a slash across the beak and remove and discard the tortoiseshell-like pieces and the hardish ball underneath (the Mexicans say that if that bit is not removed, the octopus will remain tough no matter how long it is cooked). Cut out the eyes and discard.

Either cut open the hooded part of the octopus carefully—so as not to slash the ink sac—or turn it partly inside out and remove the membranous lining with the interior organs. Remove the ink sac and dissolve it in a small bowl with about ¼ cup of water or vinegar. If the octopus has been frozen, it is likely that the ink sac will be quite hard—*piedra* or stone, as it is called in Veracruz—but don't worry, it will gradually soften and dissolve in the water. Discard the interior organs.

Rinse the cleaned octopus; it is now ready to use.

PULPO EN ESCABECHE *(Octopus in a Light Pickle)*

This recipe comes from Señor Otilio Estrada, whom I had heard about in Mérida. Half the week he is a fisherman in his native village on the Yucatán coast, and the other half he is the cook for a well-known family in Mérida. Like all professionals, he has his likes and dislikes in the kitchen; he will not use purple onion with fish as it spoils the color of the dish, and he believes that no *recados* or seasoning pastes should be used since they overpower the fish. Like many cooks in Mexico generally, he overcooks fish, and I have cut down considerably on his cooking times.

Try to use the smallest octopus—under 1 pound each if you can. When larger than that, even with the most careful cooking, they tend to become rubbery or too soft and tasteless. Buy them cleaned or clean them yourself (see instructions and photos page 198). This recipe can be served still warm on white rice or, better still, left to season overnight and served at room temperature as an appetizer.

> 4 tablespoons fruity olive oil
> 2 pounds cleaned octopus (see above), cut into small pieces
> 4 garlic cloves, peeled and roughly chopped
> sea salt to taste
> 1 large white onion, cut into thin rings
> 1 small green bell pepper, seeds and veins removed, diced
> 1 teaspoon crumbled dried oregano, Yucatecan if possible
> 3 California bay leaves, roughly broken up
> ¼ teaspoon coarsely ground black pepper
> 1 cup mild vinegar
> 4 *chiles güeros* or Fresno or wax *chiles,* charred (see page 464) and kept whole, unpeeled

Heat the olive oil in a heavy pan, add the octopus pieces and garlic, sprinkle with salt, and toss, almost stir-frying, uncovered, for about 5 minutes. The octopus should be tender but *al dente.* Transfer half of the octopus and juice to a small, deep enamel or stainless-steel pan. Cover with half the onion rings, the green pepper, half the oregano, and the bay leaves. Cover with the rest of the octopus and the remaining ingredients. Bring to a simmer, pressing down so that the vinegar and juices cover the ingredients, and continue simmering, covered, for about 10 minutes. Taste for salt and set aside to season for at least 2 hours or overnight.

CAMARÓN SECO *(Dried Shrimp)*

Mexico produces an enormous quantity of dried shrimp, of all sizes and qualities, much of which is now finding its way into the Chinese markets in the United States.

The best ones to buy are in bulk, with head and tail intact, but they are more difficult to find. The next best choice will come with lots of heads and tails and a few bodies; they are okay since all parts of them have flavor.

Try not to buy the small packages that have a few pieces in them at a very exaggerated price. Do not buy for these recipes the tidy-looking, peeled, orangey-colored ones, for they do not have enough flavor.

Dried shrimp can be stored for months, even a year, without spoiling, provided the weather isn't too hot and sticky. I advise that before storing you set them out in one layer in a very low oven and let them dry out completely, but not turn color, before storing them in airtight containers. It is not necessary to keep them in the refrigerator, because they are dried with a lot of salt, which preserves them.

Three ounces of dried shrimp measure about 1½ rounded cups, firmly packed. When ground, this quantity will yield about 7½ tablespoons.

When grinding the shrimp, do not reduce to a powder; this is why putting a small quantity at a time in the blender jar is the best way to obtain the right texture—fine bread crumbs is about right. Traditional Mexican cooks crush and roll them on the *metate*. I do not advise using a coffee/spice grinder, because some of the shrimps are too hard and can damage the delicate blades.

Romeritos, revoltijo, tortas de camarón—whatever name is used, it refers to *the* Lenten, and particularly *the* Holy Week, dish *par excellence:* a *mole* with dried shrimp fritters and vegetables.

Cooks from in and around Mexico City and Puebla use a traditional, sweetish *mole,* which to my taste is too heavy and overpowering. And since it is such an important dish, I have chosen three lighter versions that are quite different from each other: a light red *chile* sauce flavored with *cilantro* from Jalisco, a thin dark *chile* broth with spring vegetables from eastern Michoacán, and a light, unsweet *mole* with *romeritos* from the same area.

Every cook has her own way of making the *tortas:* use only the shelled body, use everything including the head and tail, toast them first, don't toast them first, use them salty as they are, add mashed potato, add dried bread crumbs and—the advice I like best of all, although I do not follow it—remove the black eyes as they make the *tortas* bitter, a laborious job.

ROMERITOS

Romeritos (*Dondia mexicana*, Stand., or *suaeda mexicana* Torreyana) are small, somewhat stringy greens with a slightly acidic taste used in the Lenten dish called either *revoltijo, romeritos,* or *tortas de camarón* (recipes follow), which are types of *mole* with fritters of ground dried shrimp and vegetables. The leaves grouped in clusters around a fleshy stem are thin and about 1 inch in length, rather like fleshy pine needles. These little fleshy, acidy greens are called *romeritos* because they resemble rosemary, at least in shape.

To Prepare Romeritos

First they should be rinsed in two changes of water to make sure the sandy soil that tends to lodge itself in the clusters is washed out. They are then cooked in boiling water for no more than 2 minutes. After being drained well, they may be added to the *mole* and will continue cooking in the sauce.

Three cups uncooked greens will yield about 2 cups cooked.

TORTITAS DE CAMARÓN SECO
(Dried Shrimp Fritters)

MAKES ABOUT 18 FRITTERS 2 INCHES IN DIAMETER AND JUST OVER ½ INCH THICK

See notes on dried shrimp, page 200.

3 ounces (about 1½ rounded cups firmly packed) dried shrimp
2 tablespoons finely ground, toasted bread crumbs
3 eggs, separated
safflower oil for frying

Have ready a tray lined with a double layer of paper toweling.

Heat a heavy frying pan, add the dried shrimp, and toss over medium heat until they are just beginning to change color very slightly. Remove them from the heat and transfer to a dish so they do not continue to brown. Put a small quantity at a time into a blender jar and blend for a few seconds, until reduced to the texture of very fine bread crumbs, not to a powder. Continue grinding the rest in small quantities. Set aside 2 tablespoons for the sauce or *mole* (see following recipes) and mix the rest with the bread crumbs.

Beat the egg whites until firm but not dry so that when the bowl is upturned they will not slip out. Beat in the yolks and then stir in the shrimp/crumbs thoroughly.

Heat the oil (it should be a little less than ½ inch deep in the pan). By doing this after beating the eggs you give the shrimp/bread crumb mixture a little time to be absorbed by the eggs and vice versa.

When the oil is hot but not smoking, carefully put in about 4 dollops of 1 tablespoon of the mixture; the dollops should hold their shape as they go into the oil and not run about uncontrollably.

Do not overcrowd the pan; the oil tends to foam up, and if the pan is overfull, you could have a fire on your hands. When the undersides of the fritters are a deep golden color, turn them over and fry on the second side—if the oil is hot enough, it should take about 1 minute on each side. If they cook too quickly to a deep brown, lower the heat and wait until the oil has cooled a little.

Transfer them to the paper toweling to drain. As soon as the paper has absorbed a lot of oil, replace the paper and set the fritters aside while you make the *mole* or sauce. By allowing them to sit, you can extract a lot of the oil they have absorbed in the frying.

See suggestion for reheating as for *chiles rellenos* to extract even more oil (page 140).

When the *mole* or sauce is ready, about 10 minutes before serving, add the fritters and let them heat through and simmer in the sauce for about 8 to 10 minutes.

REVOLTIJO EN CALDO DE CHILE PASILLA
(A Lenten Dish of Dried Shrimp Fritters and Vegetables)

SERVES 6 TO 8

3 ounces (about 10) *chiles pasillas*
9½ cups water, approximately
2 garlic cloves, peeled
2 tablespoons safflower oil
3 tablespoons ground dried shrimp (see page 200)
1 cup cooked *nopales* (pages 174–176)
¾ cup cooked peas
1 cup cooked fava or lima beans
½ pound very small potatoes or 1½ cups cooked potatoes cut into ½-inch dice
1 recipe *tortitas de camarón seco* (page 202)
1 large leafy stem of *epazote* (optional)
sea salt to taste

Remove stems, if any, from the dried *chiles*, slit them open, and scrape out and discard seeds and veins. Cover with hot water, bring to a simmer, simmer for 5 minutes, and leave to soak for 5 minutes off the heat.

Put ½ cup of the water into a blender jar, add the garlic, and blend until smooth. Add another cup of the water and transfer the *chiles* to the blender jar with a slotted spoon, discarding the soaking water, and blend to a textured puree.

Heat the oil in a heavy pan in which you are going to cook the *revoltijo*, add the *chile* puree and ground dried shrimp, and fry over medium heat, scraping the bottom of the pan from time to time to prevent sticking—about 8 minutes. Add 8 cups water and cook for about 10 minutes more.

Add the cooked vegetables and simmer for 10 minutes. Add the *tortitas*, *epazote*, and salt to taste; simmer for another 10 minutes.

Serve in rimmed plates or shallow bowls: 3 *tortas* and 1 very full cup of broth with vegetables per portion, accompanied by hot corn *tortillas*.

TORTITAS DE CAMARÓN EN SALSA DE CHILACATE (*Shrimp Fritters in Chilacate Sauce*)

SERVES ABOUT 6   JALISCO

I first ate this version of the Lenten dish on a visit to the Sandi family in Guadalajara. It is light with some wonderfully clear flavors.

I prefer to cook the *tortitas* first and let them drain well of all excess oil before adding them to the sauce.

> 3 ounces (about 8) *chilacates* or New Mexico *chile* pods
> 5 cups water, approximately
> 3 garlic cloves, peeled and roughly chopped
> ⅛ teaspoon cumin seed
> 2 tablespoons safflower oil
> 2 tablespoons ground dried shrimp (see page 200)
> a 1½-inch ball of prepared corn *tortilla masa* (page 8) *or* 2 heaped tablespoons
>   Quaker Masa Harina
> 2 cups cooked *nopales* (pages 174–176) (about ¾ pound raw)
> 1 recipe *tortitas de camarón seco* (page 202)
> 1 small bunch of *cilantro*
> sea salt to taste

Remove the stems, if any, from the dried *chiles*, slit them open, and scrape out and discard veins and seeds. Put into a pan with hot water, bring to a simmer, and simmer for about 5 minutes. Set aside to soak off the heat for 5 minutes. Put ½ cup of the water into a blender jar, add the garlic and cumin, and blend until smooth. Set aside.

Put 1 cup of the water into the blender jar and add some of the *chiles* with a slotted spoon, discarding the soaking water. Blend as smoothly as possible and add the rest of the *chiles* (or do in two batches) with a little more of the water (just enough to make the blender blades work more effectively).

Press the sauce through a fine strainer (these *chiles* have very tough skin) and discard the debris.

Heat the oil in a heavy pan in which you are going to cook the dish, add the *chile* sauce, the blended garlic and cumin, and the ground shrimp, and cook over medium heat, scraping the bottom of the pan to prevent sticking from time to time, for about 10 minutes.

Dilute the *masa* or *masa harina* with another ½ cup of water and mix until smooth; add this with another 3 cups of water and the *nopales* and cook for about 10 minutes over fairly high heat. Add the *tortitas de camarón,* the *cilantro,* and salt if necessary and simmer for about 10 minutes.

Serve each portion with 3 *tortitas,* about ½ cup of the sauce, accompanied by some hot corn *tortillas.*

ROMERITOS *(Dried Shrimp Fritters with Greens)*

SERVES 6 TO 8   EASTERN MICHOACÁN

This is one version of the Lenten dish that is made with dried shrimp fritters and the acidy little green called *romeritos*—hence the name. They are cooked, along with *nopales* and potatoes, in a rustic, black *mole,* typical of this area of Michoacán. The recipe (also suitable for cooking with chicken) was given to me by my neighbor, Señora Anita González de Hernández. Like other cooks of the area, she eschews the adding of any sweet to a *mole*—sugar, chocolate, or raisins—as in Puebla, Oaxaca, etc. I think her *mole* goes admirably with these salty little fritters. Like other recipes of this type, the *mole* may be prepared a day or so ahead and the vegetables and fritters added during reheating. It also freezes well for weeks.

Romeritos greens can in a pinch be replaced by finely shredded sorrel.

¼ pound (about 12) *chiles pasillas*
1 *chile mulato*
1 small *chile ancho*
rounded ¼ cup sesame seed
5 cups water, approximately
1 garlic clove, peeled
2 whole cloves
3 peppercorns
rounded ¼ cup hulled raw pumpkin seeds
6 tablespoons safflower oil
5 unskinned almonds
1 dry corn *tortilla,* torn into pieces
2 tablespoons ground dried shrimp (see page 200)
1 cup cooked *romeritos* (optional) or finely shredded sorrel
1½ cups cooked diced *nopales* (pages 174–176)
½ pound potatoes, either very small seed potatoes or standards in about ¾-inch
    dice (about 1½ cups diced)
1 recipe *tortitas de camarón seco* (page 202)
sea salt to taste

Remove the stems, if any, from the dried *chiles,* slit them open, and scrape out veins and seeds. Reserve 1 tablespoon of the seeds.

Put cleaned *chiles* into a pan, cover with hot water, and bring to a simmer. Simmer for 5 minutes, remove from the heat, and set aside to soak for 5 minutes more or until fleshy and soft. Heat an ungreased frying pan, add the sesame seed, and toss over medium heat, turning them constantly, until they turn a pale golden color—about 20 seconds.

Put ½ cup of the water in a blender jar and add the toasted sesame, garlic, cloves, and peppercorns; blend to a textured puree. In the same pan, toast the raw pumpkin seeds until they swell up and just begin to turn color, *but* take care as they pop about alarmingly.

Add to the blender jar with a little more water if necessary and blend to a textured puree, from time to time loosening with a spatula the mixture that collects in the base of the jar around the blades.

Heat 2 tablespoons of the oil and fry the almonds until browned—about 2 minutes. Remove, crush lightly, and add to the blender jar. In the same oil, fry the pieces of *tortilla* until crisp and browned. Add to the blender jar with a small amount of the drained *chiles* and blend to a textured puree, adding more water only if necessary to allow the blades to work more effectively. You may have to blend the *chiles* in two batches, adding only enough water—don't dilute too much. Toss the reserved *chile* seeds in an ungreased frying pan for about 1 minute; add to blender jar.

In a heavy pan in which you will be cooking the *mole,* heat the remaining oil and that left over from frying the *tortilla,* add the *chile* puree and ground shrimp, and cook over medium heat—it should boil and reduce— scraping the bottom of the pan frequently to prevent sticking, for about 10 minutes. Like all *moles* and heavy sauces of this type, it will splatter about rather furiously. Add the rest of the water and simmer fast for 30 minutes. Pools of oil should now be forming on the surface. Add the vegetables and cook for 10 minutes more. Add the *tortitas de camarón,* salt to taste, and more water if necessary; heat through for another 10 minutes, making sure that the *tortitas* are completely submerged in the sauce.

The *mole* should be thick and coat the back of a wooden spoon well. Serve about 3 of the *tortas* with a good cupful of the sauce and vegetables and hot corn *tortillas* to accompany it.

CAMARONES ENCHIPOTLADOS
(Shrimps in Chipotle Sauce)

SERVES 3 TO 4   BRISAS DEL MAR, PORT OF VERACRUZ

There are many versions of this dish in Veracruz, but this is the one I think is most successful; it comes from the restaurant Brisas del Mar on the *malecon* (boardwalk) of the Port of Veracruz.

I have made a few adjustments to the recipe. Since seafood is almost always overcooked in Mexico, I have cooked the shrimps and sauce in two stages. I have also added oregano as an alternative to the thyme called for and softened the *chiles* with more tomato than was originally intended.

This recipe could be served as a first course or as a main course with some plain white rice; it could even be served cold. The recipe is best cooked in small quantities.

1 pound large shrimps, peeled and butterflied with tail shell left on
sea salt and freshly ground black pepper to taste
¼ cup fresh lime juice
⅓ cup light olive oil
1 medium white onion, finely sliced
¾ pound (about 2 medium) tomatoes, broiled (see page 450), or *tomate verde*,
    cooked and drained (see page 451)
4 (or to taste) *chiles chipotles adobados*
1 garlic clove, peeled and roughly chopped
⅓ cup dry white wine
¼ teaspoon dried oregano, Mexican if possible

Season the shrimps with salt, pepper, and lime juice and set aside to marinate for about 30 minutes.

Heat the oil in a frying pan; add the drained shrimp, reserving any liquid, and sliced onion and fry, shaking the pan and tossing the ingredients, for about 3 minutes. Remove shrimp and onion with a slotted spoon and set aside.

In a blender jar, blend the tomatoes, *chipotles* and their liquid, and garlic to a textured sauce. Reheat the oil, add the sauce, and fry over high heat, stirring and scraping the bottom of the pan to prevent sticking, for about 8 minutes. Add the wine, oregano, marinade, and salt to taste and cook for another minute. Add the shrimp/onion mixture and cook for about 2 minutes—the shrimps should be just cooked and still crisp.

PESCADO SARANDEADO (Barbecued Fish)

SERVES ABOUT 8   SEÑOR JESÚS VALDÉS, LOS MOCHIS, SINALOA

Of all the ways of preparing *pescado sarandeado* (*sarandeado* means "something that is turned over") on the beaches of Mexico, this is the most complicated and interesting. A whole fish is stuffed with vegetables, wrapped in *tortillas* and foil, and grilled over either a wood or charcoal fire.

You need a whole fish for this recipe but not a special one; although a red snapper would be delicious, it would be overly expensive for this type of rustic cooking. A grouper or jack would be just fine.

I usually buy a 3½-pound fish about 15 inches long, excluding the tail. It should be scaled and gutted and the fins removed, but the head and tail left intact. If you can get your fishmonger to do so, it is better to have the central part of the spine removed so that you have a larger pocket for the stuffing. You can, of course, cook this in the oven, but grilling it outside always adds something.

This dish is usually served very informally, everyone making his or her own *tacos* with extra *tortillas* (apart from those wrapped around the fish) and an optional sauce, either *salsa mexicana* (page 351) or a light tomato-based sauce and/or pickled *chile* strips. I have adjusted the recipe to sauté the tomatoes and vegetables first for a better flavor and added some chopped parsley, but this is optional.

Señor Jesús Valdés, who gave me this recipe, says that he uses oil or butter. I prefer to use a light olive oil.

HAVE READY:
a piece of heavy-duty foil large enough to wrap the whole fish well so that
    juices do not escape
1 3½-pound whole fish, cleaned (see note above)
⅓ cup light olive oil, vegetable oil, half of each
16 to 20 corn *tortillas*, ideally about 5 inches in diameter
optional sauce or *chile* strips (see note above)

THE FILLING
3 tablespoons olive oil
3 garlic cloves, peeled and finely chopped
½ pound (about 1 large) tomatoes, roughly chopped, unskinned
18 small pitted green olives, roughly chopped
sea salt to taste
½ pound carrots, diced and cooked (2 scant cups)

½ pound potatoes, peeled, diced, and cooked (1¼ rounded cups)
coarsely ground pepper to taste
¼ cup roughly chopped fresh parsley (optional)

First make the filling. Heat the oil in a frying pan and add the garlic, tomatoes, and olives with salt to taste; fry over medium heat for about 8 minutes, until the juice has been absorbed and the mixture is well seasoned. Stir in the cooked vegetables, salt, pepper, and optional parsley; cook over medium heat, stirring and turning the mixture, for another 5 minutes. Set aside while you prepare the fish.

Rinse and dry the fish. Stuff the pocket well with the filling, securing with toothpicks if necessary. Season the outside of the fish with salt and pepper. Heat the ⅓ cup of oil and quickly immerse the *tortillas*, turning them over once, but do not let them fry. Wrap the fish in two layers of *tortillas*, then cover with foil and place about 2 inches above the hot grill. Grill for about 20 minutes on each side or until the fish is cooked through.

PAN DE CAZÓN (*"Shark Bread"*)

The fish market in Campeche is the most colorful of any in Mexico, with fish of all sizes and hues, freshly caught and all slippery and shiny. Perhaps the most eye-catching of all is the number, variety, and size of the sharks, sometimes as small as 12 inches for the small *cazón* or dogfish. It is that small shark that is used in many of the traditional dishes of Campeche. In this recipe it is cooked separately and then sandwiched beween layers of *tortillas*, black bean paste, and tomato sauce, a very *picante* and popular dish, with as many recipes for it as there are cooks. Some cooks make *panuchos* (small *tortillas* made to puff up and cut to form a pocket for the fish and beans) with the beans and fish, then stack them, smothered in tomato sauce, but many take the shortcut and simply use layers of fried corn *tortillas*. Traditionally the dish is cooked with lard, but you could substitute vegetable oil or, as I do, a mixture of light olive oil and vegetable oil.

Shark is not to everyone's taste, so another white, nonfatty fish, either in fillets or in steaks, can be used perfectly well. You will need 1 pound for the former and 1½ pounds to allow for bone and skin with the latter.

This can serve 6 as a main dish or 8 as a first course.

Although the component parts of this dish can easily be cooked ahead, the frying and assembling must be done at the last moment, or it will all be very mushy. It should be eaten alone; no accompaniments are necessary.

safflower oil or melted lard for frying
12 5-inch corn *tortillas*
2½ cups *salsa de jitomate Yucateca* (page 341), approximately, kept hot
9 heaped tablespoons *frijoles colados y refritos a la Yucateca* (page 186), kept hot
the cooked and seasoned shark (see below)
3 *chiles habaneros*, charred (see page 466) and kept whole

Heat the oven to 350°. Have ready a warm serving dish into which 3 *tortillas* can be placed side by side without overlapping.

Heat the oil or lard and fry 3 of the *tortillas* lightly on each side. Dip each into the tomato sauce, which should lightly cover it, and place side by side in the serving dish. Spread each with a heaped tablespoonful of the bean paste and a good layer of the cooked fish. Repeat this layer twice more. For the final top layer, fry the *tortillas*, submerge in the sauce, and put on top of each pile. Cover with the rest of the sauce and keep warm in the oven. Fry the *chiles habaneros* lightly and put one onto each pile of *tortillas*. Cut each pile into halves and serve immediately.

MAKES ABOUT 2 CUPS

TO COOK THE SHARK
4 cups water, approximately
a few fish bones (optional)
1 small white onion, roughly sliced
4 large leafy stems of *epazote*
2 tablespoons white wine vinegar (optional)
sea salt to taste
1 pound shark or other fish fillets *or* 1½ pounds steaks (see note above)

Put the water and remaining ingredients, except the fish, into a pan, bring to a boil, and boil for about 10 minutes. Add the shark and simmer gently for about 5 minutes. Remove and drain. Clean the fish of any bones and skin and shred thoroughly, pressing out any surplus moisture.

TO SEASON THE SHARK
3 tablespoons melted lard or safflower oil
2 tablespoons finely chopped white onion
¼ pound (about 1 small) tomatoes, finely chopped, unpeeled
3 heaped tablespoons roughly chopped *epazote* leaves
1 *chile habanero* or any hot green *chile*, charred (see page 466) and left whole
the shredded fish
sea salt to taste

Heat the lard or oil and add the onion. Fry without browning for 1 minute. Add the tomato and *epazote* and continue cooking for about 3 minutes. Add the *chile habanero* and fish with salt to taste; fry well, turning the fish over to mix, for about 4 minutes. Set aside and keep hot.

OSTIONES EN ESCABECHE *(Soused Oysters)*

SERVES 4 TO 6

This recipe was given to me some years ago by my great friend from Sonora, María-Dolores Torres Izábal. It makes a refreshing first course or lunch main
dish served with crusty French rolls. I have since cooked it with shrimps, scal-
lops, lump crab, or small pieces of lotte, alone or mixed together.

This *escabeche* is best made the day before and left to marinate overnight.
It should be served at room temperature, not cold from the refrigerator.

½ cup light olive oil
⅓ cup finely sliced white onion
8 garlic cloves, peeled
½ cup finely sliced carrots, blanched
½ cup cauliflower flowerets, blanched
2 California bay leaves
3 fresh thyme sprigs *or* ¼ teaspoon dried
3 fresh marjoram sprigs *or* ¼ teaspoon dried
1½ teaspoons dried oregano, Mexican if possible
½ teaspoon peppercorns
sea salt to taste
¼ cup vinegar
2 cups shucked oysters or other seafood (see note above)
1 lime, finely sliced
strips of canned *jalapeños en escabeche* (to taste)

Heat the oil in a large frying or sauté pan. Add the onion and garlic
cloves and toss over high heat without browning for about 2 minutes. Add
the vegetables, herbs, peppercorns, salt, and vinegar; cook over high heat
until the mixture comes to a boil. Add the oysters, sliced lime, and *jalapeños*
and cook until the oysters are plump and just cooked—about 2 minutes.

Note: Jalapeños may be omitted and passed separately at the table. Set
aside to cool. Refrigerate overnight and serve at room temperature.

POULTRY
(Aves)

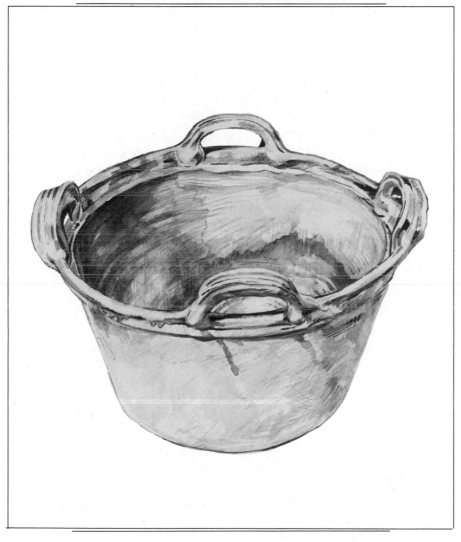

The predominant meats in any cuisine with peasant roots will be those that are raised domestically, like chicken and pork. This holds true for most of Mexico except in the North, where cattle raising is important and therefore beef tends to dominate.

Most country people raise turkeys—but they are rather stringy and have a strong flavor—mainly to go into *moles* for festive occasions, which are numerous when there are large families.

Except among those who hunt them, ducks have never been a very popular meat in regional foods, which also excludes the more sophisticated cooking of the capital.

Chickens generally—except where American rearing methods have been too enthusiastically adopted—tend to have firmer flesh and a great deal more flavor than their United States counterparts and therefore are more suitable to the method of cooking in Mexico. In traditional regional fare they are not generally grilled or roasted "dry"; they are poached, with the meat shredded for *tacos* and *enchiladas* and the broth used in *moles* and other heavily sauced dishes, or they are seasoned and pit barbecued.

For these dishes it is worthwhile to look for something better than the usual supermarket chickens. Chinatown has always led the way with better-quality chickens, and in recent years California has followed in grand style. Now dotted all over the country are small groups producing better-quality chickens that are available regionally; they are not overly fatted or slimy, and they don't fall apart at the slightest bit of heat! Try a natural foods store; if you live in a large city, there may even be a live poultry market.

HOW TO GUT AND CLEAN A CHICKEN

There are many markets even in the main cities of Mexico where you can still buy a live, or killed, uncleaned chicken with all its giblets inside. When I first went to Mexico in 1957, these were the only ones available, and I soon learned with the *marchantes* how to clean them and that nothing but the inedible parts were thrown away: feet, neck, giblets, and intestines all went into the stockpot. (When I was young I always watched and later helped my father dress the Christmas turkey, which was sold intact, including the white neck plumage, which looked so impressive hanging up in the butchers' shops at Christmastime.) But just suppose you are on your own in the country with nothing to eat but a live chicken. Well, start by getting someone else to kill it for you by wringing its neck, but if you want to make the blood recipe at the end of this chapter (which is delicious) or real *coq au vin*, pierce it in the neck below its chin and hang it upside down, with a receptacle to catch the blood, for about 30 minutes.

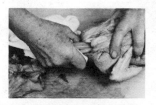

Have ready a deep container of boiling water. Plunge half of the chicken into it. Don't delay, or the skin will cook and come off with the feathers. Quickly pluck off all the feathers. Douse it again and pluck, repeating until all the feathers have come off.

Cut off the legs where the yellow skin ends. Trim off the claws. Scrape the yellow skin off the legs. If the chicken is young and tender, this should come off easily. If not, you will have to char the feet lightly over moderate heat and then peel. Set them aside for the soup.

With the chicken breast up and the head away from you, make an incision just large enough for your hand to pass through and just below the breastbones nearer the tail, as shown in the photos. Do not cut all that skin away, or there will be no place to tuck in the legs.

Plunge your hand into the cavity—if you can't bear it, put on a rubber glove—right up to the neck end and pull; all the entrails should come out. Look to make sure. Remove the chicken fat and reserve for cooking. Then sort out the entrails. Put the heart and kidney aside for the soup. Intestines are optional, but if you do decide to keep them for soup, or for the recipe on page 243, cut them open, scrape the inside, and rinse in two changes of water. Cut through the outer layer of the gizzard to the sac containing undigested food. Peel off the outside and discard the sac and its contents.

Remove and discard the greenish bile sac next to the liver. Shave off any greenish tinge that the liver may have from contact with the sac and set aside the liver for something other than the soup—it will make it bitter—such as the recipe on page 218.

As an alternative, you can remove the crop and gelatinous food pipe by pressing your hand firmly on them and dragging from the inside; however, this is not always successful unless the crop is firm with food.

Cut around the small anal passage below the tail. Turn the chicken over and slice off the small gland at the back of the tail just above the tip.

Turn the chicken around with the head facing you and the breast up. Chop off the head if it is still on. With the chicken breast down, slit open the skin of the neck and loosen the bony neck with your fingers. With a dry dishcloth, tug hard on the neck, and it should come loose from the carcass with the gelatinous food pipe. If you have not already removed the crop, feel into the neck cavity and remove the sac that lines the cavity with the crop attached. Trim off any extra useless neck skin. Rinse the cavities in cold water. The chicken is now ready to cook.

TO RENDER CHICKEN FAT

MAKES ABOUT 1 CUP

Although it is not common practice, some cooks I know in Puebla and Michoacán use chicken fat in their cooking. It is extremely good for cooking rice, potatoes, and the like.

½ pound chicken fat, approximately
⅓ cup water

Chop the fat as finely as possible. Cover with the water and let it stand at room temperature for about 2 hours. In a small, heavy frying pan set over low heat, let it cook until all the fat has rendered out, the water has evaporated, and the bits of skin are a crisp golden brown. Strain and refrigerate, uncovered. It will keep for weeks, depending on the weather.

HIGADITOS EN CHIPOTLE
(Chicken Livers in Chipotle Sauce)

SERVES 4   CENTRAL MEXICO

This is an unusual way of cooking chicken livers, but the flavors combine well. Take care not to overcook the chicken livers; they should be just pink inside.

½ pound (about 1 large) tomatoes, broiled (see page 450)
2 garlic cloves, peeled and roughly chopped
2 canned *chipotles en escabeche* or *en vinagre*
¾ pound chicken livers
3 tablespoons melted chicken fat (page 217) or safflower oil
½ medium white onion, thinly sliced
sea salt to taste

Put the unpeeled tomatoes, garlic, and *chiles* into a blender jar and blend until almost smooth; there should be a little texture to the sauce. Set aside.

Trim the livers of any connective tissue and any greenish spots from the bile duct; cut each one into six parts. Heat the fat in a frying pan, add the liver pieces and onion, sprinkle lightly with salt, and fry, tossing them almost constantly—a stir-fry if you will—for about 3 minutes over high heat. Add the blended ingredients and, still over high heat, cook for about 5 minutes or until the sauce has reduced and seasoned. Adjust seasoning.

POLLO DESHEBRADO PARA TACOS
(Poached Chicken for Tacos)

MAKES 2 CUPS

Chicken used for *antojitos* (snacks), *tacos, enchiladas, tostadas,* etc., is always cooked and shredded. I prefer to poach it in chicken broth and to enhance the flavor by leaving it to cool off in the broth.

1 large whole chicken breast with bone and skin
chicken broth (page 95) to cover

Cut the breast in half. Put the chicken into a pan with chicken broth to cover and bring to a simmer. Continue simmering until just tender but not soft, about 25 minutes. Set aside to cool off in the broth. Strain and strip the meat from the bone, discard the bone, and shred together with some of the skin for extra flavor.

TACOS DE POLLO (Chicken Tacos)

MAKES 12 TACOS   SEÑORA VERÓNICA CUEVAS, ZITÁCUARO, MICHOACÁN

These *tacos* are simple to prepare and quite delicious. They are usually served for supper in Mexico, but they can be used as a light lunch dish or as a main course to follow a *ceviche* or light soup.

THE FILLING
3 tablespoons chicken fat (page 217) or oil
½ cup finely chopped white onion
3 fresh *chiles jalapeños,* cut into thin strips with seeds and veins
1½ cups finely chopped, unpeeled tomatoes
1½ cups *pollo deshebrado para tacos* (page 218)
3 tablespoons chicken broth (page 95)
sea salt to taste

THE *TACOS*
12 5-inch corn *tortillas*
safflower oil for frying
1 cup *salsa de jitomate de Michoacán* (page 340)
2 cups finely shredded lettuce or cabbage
¾ cup *crème fraîche*
6 tablespoons finely grated *queso fresco* or *añejo*

First make the filling. Heat the oil, add the onion and *chile* strips, and fry for 1 minute; they should not brown. Add the tomatoes and cook for another 3 minutes, until some of the juice has been absorbed. Add the shredded chicken, broth, and salt and cook until the mixture is almost dry and shiny—about 8 minutes. Set aside to cool slightly. Put a little of the filling across the *tortillas,* roll, and secure with a toothpick.

Heat enough oil in a frying pan to cover liberally the bottom (it should not be deep) and put some of the *tacos*—open part down—into the oil. Fry gently, turning them from time to time; once they are sealed, you can remove the toothpick. Place 2 *tacos* on each plate. Open them a little and insert, or put over the top, some of the sauce, strew with lettuce, add a large tablespoon of cream, and sprinkle with the cheese.

POLLO CON ORÉGANO
(Grilled Chicken with Oregano)

SERVES 4 TO 6   OAXACA

This is a simple and unique way of cooking chicken with a strong garlicky-oregano flavor. It is a traditional Oaxacan dish and is accompanied invariably by *enfrijoladas* (page 34). I like to serve it with a plain *morisqueta* (boiled rice, page 124) and pickled *chile* strips. It is also an ideal picnic dish, since it can be prepared up to the coating of oregano and then finished off on an outdoor grill.

The only trick here is to have the chicken tender, but not too soft, by the time the broth has been reduced to a rich, gelatinous film—which is delicious. Some adjustments may have to be made to the amount of broth and the timing, depending on the size and quality of the chicken and the size and heaviness of the pan. A 12-inch sauté pan is ideal for this amount of chicken, and the pieces should be from a large chicken—no fryers, please!

2½ pounds large chicken pieces, *with* the skin attached
2 garlic cloves, peeled
1 small white onion, roughly sliced
1 cup reduced chicken broth (page 95)
12 additional garlic cloves, peeled and minced
3 tablespoons dried Oaxacan or Mexican oregano, stems removed and roughly crumbled
2 tablespoons additional chicken broth (page 95)
½ teaspoon (or to taste) sea salt
a little melted chicken fat (page 217) or oil for broiling

Put the chicken pieces into a sauté pan in one layer. Add the whole garlic cloves, onion, and 1 cup chicken broth and cook, covered, over medium heat, turning the pieces over from time to time, until the broth has completely reduced and the chicken is tender—about 25 minutes.

Crush the minced garlic into a mortar with the oregano, 2 tablespoons broth, and salt and work to a rough paste (or put it all into a blender jar and blend very briefly). Spread the paste over the chicken pieces, turning them so they are evenly covered; return to the pan and cover. Set aside to season for 2 hours. Heat a broiler or grill and brown lightly, brushing with a little melted chicken fat if necessary.

MOLE NEGRO OAXAQUEÑO (*Oaxacan Black Mole*)

SERVES 10 TO 12

Mole Negro, the festive dish of Oaxaca, is black, sweet, and highly complex in flavor. It differs from that of Puebla in that varying *chiles* are used—predominantly the black, sharp *chilhuacle negro*—and also a lot of dried herbs replace a variety of spices. Since *chilhuacles* are obtainable only in Oaxaca (sometimes in Mexico City), and even then less frequently than some years ago, and are expensive to boot, many cooks are resorting to using *chiles guajillos* and charring them to give the required color. You may wonder why more *mulatos* and *pasillas,* which are also black, are not used. They are much fleshier and fruitier in flavor and would not give the required sharpness.

Traditionally, Mexican cooks everywhere would have—and some still do—ground all the ingredients for their *moles* at home on the *metate.* Now they often prepare the ingredients—toasting, frying, etc.—and send them to the mill (where they grind corn for *tortillas*) to be stone-ground. But many have resorted to the blender, which is more efficient for this type of sauce than the food processor. That's okay if you take care not to swamp the ingredients with too much water and add a few ingredients at a time, blending and then adding more, with only enough water to release the blades of the blender.

In recipes like this one, where you are frying a number of ingredients, especially sesame seeds for instance, I find it better to fry and then strain them to avoid using so much oil.

When making heavy sauces of this type, always use a heavy, wide, high-sided pan—if not a *cazuela,* then something like the Le Creuset casseroles. The sauce can burn easily in a thin pan and spatters about alarmingly if the pan is too shallow.

THE CHICKEN
2 large chickens (about 3½ pounds each), cut into serving pieces, *or* 1 7-pound
   turkey
2 small heads of garlic, scored around the middle
2 small white onions, roughly sliced
6 fresh mint sprigs
sea salt to taste

THE SAUCE

¼ pound *chilhuacles negros* or *guajillos*
2 ounces *chiles pasillas* (Mexican, not Oaxacan)
2 ounces *chiles mulatos*
½ pound (about 1 large) tomatoes, broiled (see page 450)
1 cup water
3 whole cloves
3 whole allspice
6 fresh thyme sprigs, leaves only, *or* rounded ¼ teaspoon dried
6 fresh marjoram sprigs, leaves only, *or* rounded ¼ teaspoon dried
2 tablespoons Oaxacan *or* 1 tablespoon Mexican oregano
¾ cup melted lard or safflower oil
¼ cup sesame seed
¼ cup shelled peanuts
10 unskinned almonds
¼ cup raisins
1 small onion, thickly sliced
12 small garlic cloves, peeled
1 very thick 3-inch cinnamon stick, slivered
1 ripe plantain, skinned and cut into thick slices
2 crisp-fried corn *tortillas*
3 thick slices dried French bread or semisweet roll
1 2-ounce tablet Mexican drinking chocolate
sea salt to taste

Put the chicken into a saucepan with the garlic, onions, and mint. Add water to cover and salt to taste. Bring to a simmer, cover the pan, and continue simmering until the chicken is just tender—about 35 minutes. Strain, reserving the broth.

Remove stems from the dried *chiles*, if any, slit them open, and remove seeds and veins, reserving the seeds. Toast the *chiles* for about 50 seconds on each side; if you're using *guajillos*, toast them longer, until they are almost charred—about 2 minutes. Rinse the *chiles* in cold water, cover with hot water, and leave to soak for about 30 minutes. Put the reserved *chile* seeds into an ungreased frying pan and toast over fairly high heat, shaking them around from time to time so that they brown evenly. Then raise the heat and char until black. Cover with cold water and set aside to soak for about 5 minutes. Strain and put into a blender jar.

Add the broiled tomatoes, unpeeled, to the blender jar along with the water, cloves, allspice, thyme, marjoram, and oregano.

Heat some of the lard in a small frying pan and fry the sesame seed until a deep golden color—a few seconds. Strain, putting the fat back into the pan and the seeds into the blender jar, and blend as smooth as possible.

Fry the rest of the ingredients, except the *chiles* and chocolate, one by one, strain, and put into the blender jar, blending after each addition and adding water or broth as necessary to release the blades.

Heat ¼ cup of the lard in the heavy pan in which you are going to cook the *mole*, add the blended mixture, and fry over medium heat, stirring and scraping the bottom of the pan from time to time, for about 15 minutes.

Meanwhile, put a few of the *chiles* and about 2 cups of the water in which they were soaking into the blender jar and blend until smooth. When you have blended all the *chiles*, add them to the fried ingredients together with the chocolate and cook for 5 minutes longer. Add about 4 cups of the chicken broth and continue cooking for 35 minutes. (Skim the fat that forms on the top if you are going to make *tamales* or *mole*. It is added to color and flavor the *masa*.) Add more broth if necessary—the *mole* should just coat the back of a wooden spoon—along with the chicken and salt to taste; cook for 10 minutes longer.

POLLO EN MOLE RÓJO SENCILLO
(Chicken in Red Country Mole)

SERVES 6 TO 8   TUZANTLA, MICHOACÁN

This is a delicious but sharp—not at all sweet—*mole* from the hot country of eastern Michoacán. The recipe was given to me by Señora Sandoval, the owner of a small restaurant that I have frequented for some years.

This *mole* is better if made about 2 hours ahead; the flavor will develop more. It can be made with either chicken or pork and served simply with corn *tortillas*. The sauce freezes well and will keep for months.

THE CHICKEN
1 large chicken (about 3½ to 4 pounds), cut into serving pieces, with giblets
1 small white onion, roughly chopped
2 garlic cloves, peeled and roughly chopped
water or light chicken broth (page 95) to cover
sea salt to taste

THE SAUCE
2 ounces (about 11) *chiles guajillos*
2 ounces (about 7) *chiles pasillas*
2 ounces (about 5) *chiles anchos*
6 tablespoons safflower oil, chicken fat (page 217), or lard
5 ounces (1 rounded cup) hulled raw pumpkin seeds
6 to 7 cups chicken broth
3 whole cloves
5 peppercorns
4 garlic cloves, peeled and roughly chopped
sea salt to taste

Put the chicken, onion, and garlic into a pan, cover with water or a light chicken broth with salt to taste, and bring to a simmer. Continue simmering until the chicken is nearly tender (it should not be cooked through)—about 25 minutes, depending on size and age. Drain and measure the broth; if under 7 cups, make up to that amount with water.

The Sauce

Remove the stems, if any, from the dried *chiles*, slit them open, and remove and discard seeds and veins. Put the *chiles* into a pan, cover with hot water, bring to a simmer, and simmer for 5 minutes; remove from the heat and set aside to soak for about 15 minutes. Drain and discard soaking water. Meanwhile, heat 1 tablespoon of the oil in a frying pan, add the seeds, and toss in the oil over medium heat until they swell and begin to pop around. Be careful of your eyes; they pop about alarmingly. Set aside.

Put ½ cup of the broth into a blender jar, add the spices and garlic, and blend thoroughly. Add 1 cup of broth and the fried seeds and blend to a thick, textured paste.

Heat the rest of the oil in a heavy pan in which you are going to cook the *mole*, add the seed paste, and fry over medium heat, turning and scraping the bottom of the pan almost constantly to prevent sticking, for about 5 minutes. Add 1 cup broth to the blender jar and blend half of the *chiles* very thoroughly (the *guajillo* skin is very tough); add to the pan. Repeat this procedure until all the *chiles* make a thick sauce, adding more broth only if absolutely necessary to release the blades of the blender.

Cook the *mole* over medium heat, scraping the bottom of the pan from time to time, for about 15 minutes—it will be quite thick. Add the remaining broth and cook for 15 minutes longer. Add the chicken and continue cooking until the flesh is tender and the sauce a dark red with pools of deeper red oil forming on top—about 15 minutes more. If you prefer a thinner *mole*, you may add a little more broth at this stage and heat through. Serve a portion of the chicken with plenty of sauce and hot corn *tortillas*.

POLLO EN MOLE VERDE
(Chicken in Green Mole)

SERVES 6 TO 8   SEÑORA SEVERA, LA GARITA, MICHOACÁN

Practically every region of Mexico has its version of *mole* or *pipián verde*—in Oaxaca referred to as just *verde*—using ingredients that the area produces. In the eastern part of Michoacán, pumpkins abound and many market gardeners grow lettuce, chard, and herbs the year-round owing to the mild climate; sesame seeds are brought up from the hot country. This is a true *aficionado's mole*, with a roughish texture and highly complex flavor that speaks unmistakably of herbs, greens, and green *chiles*. You will be severely criticized if you do not have sufficient dark green oil floating on the surface, for therein lies the flavor, or so the local cooks aver. Without a doubt, this dish is best eaten the day it is prepared, since the greens tend to lose some of their wonderful, fresh flavor if left too long.

This *mole verde* can also be made with pork or even chicken and pork together; allow 3 pounds of meat for 6 to 8 servings.

THE CHICKEN
1 large chicken (3½ to 4 pounds), cut into serving pieces
1 small white onion, roughly chopped
1 garlic clove, peeled
sea salt to taste
light chicken broth (page 95) or water to cover

THE SAUCE
5 ounces (1 cup) sesame seeds
1½ ounces (⅓ cup) raw hulled pumpkin seeds
3 whole cloves
3 peppercorns
3 whole allspice
4 to 6 tablespoons (if you can bear it) lard or safflower oil
8 romaine lettuce leaves, roughly chopped
5 Swiss chard leaves, roughly chopped
1 large bunch of *cilantro*, with stems, roughly chopped
1 small bunch of flat-leaf parsley, roughly chopped
2 garlic cloves, peeled and roughly chopped
2 *chiles poblanos*, seeds and veins removed, roughly chopped
6 ounces (about 8 medium) *tomate verde*, roughly chopped

Put the chicken, onion, garlic, and salt into a pan, cover with chicken broth or water, and bring to a simmer. Continue simmering until the meat is tender but not soft—about 25 minutes. Strain, reserving the broth. Reduce or add water to increase broth to 6 cups. Set the chicken pieces and broth aside.

Put the sesame seeds into an ungreased frying pan and heat over medium heat, stirring and turning over constantly, until they turn a dark golden color—about 7 minutes. Spread out on a large pan to cool off. Add the pumpkin seeds to the pan and heat over medium heat, shaking the pan and stirring them until they start to swell up and pop around, but do not let them brown—about 3 minutes. Set aside to cool off.

Mix the toasted seeds with the spices and grind in an electric spice/coffee grinder, a small amount at a time, for about 5 seconds each batch, until the seeds are broken down but not ground to a powder. Transfer to a bowl and stir in ½ cup of the reserved broth to make a thick paste.

Heat the lard in a heavy pan, add the ground seed paste, and fry gently, stirring constantly for about 5 minutes, until the mixture is a rich brown.

Put 1½ cups of the broth into a blender jar and add the chopped greens, herbs, garlic, fresh *chiles*, and *tomate verde* a small quantity at a time; blend to a textured sauce. (If your blender jar is large enough, you should be able to do this in one batch; if not, divide the mixture of greens into two batches and add a little more of the broth.) Add the pureed greens to the seed paste, stir well, and cook over medium heat, stirring and scraping the bottom of the pan from time to time since the mixture tends to stick, for about 15 minutes. Add the remaining broth and cook over medium heat until the sauce has reduced and thickened and the oil is floating in little pools on the surface—about 15 to 20 minutes. Add the chicken pieces and cook for another 10 minutes, stirring from time to time. The sauce should be fairly thick, but if it dries up too much, add a little more broth or water. Serve with corn *tortillas*.

THE SEVEN MOLES OF OAXACA

The state of Oaxaca has been called the land of the seven *moles*, each one colored by distinctive *chiles* or, in the case of the green *mole*, herbs. They are *mole negro* (black *mole*); *mole colorado* (colored *mole*), a deep reddish brown; *amarillo* (yellow); *verde* (green); *chichilo* (black); *coloradito* ("little colored"), a bright orangey red; and *mancha manteles* (tablecloth strainer), a deep brickish red.

Although these *moles* used to be made exclusively with dried local *chiles*—chilcostle; black, yellow, or red *chilhuacle*; or a thin yellow *chile* similar in shape to a *costeño* (see page 510)—most cooks have substituted the cheaper and more readily available *guajillos* and *anchos*.

VERDE DE OAXACA (*Green Oaxacan Mole*)

SERVES 6 TO 8

Verde is one of the Seven *Moles* of Oaxaca, cooked with either chicken or pork and enriched with small dumplings; it is a thinnish green sauce fragrant with herbs.

Although parsley and even *epazote* are generally available—or in the case of the latter can even be grown easily—*hoja santa* is not. Where possible, avocado leaves can be substituted, and while not exactly the same flavor, they do approximate and give a true Oaxacan touch.

The recipe here is for chicken; if you wish to use pork, then 1 pound of country-style spareribs and 1 pound of boneless stewing pork should be cooked in exactly the same way as the chicken but for a little longer.

Although better eaten the same day, this *mole* can be reheated, with some loss of color and the fresh flavor of the greens; it does not freeze successfully.

The *verde* is best served in shallow bowls: some meat, 2 or 3 dumplings, and a lot of the sauce—which is more like a soup—with spoons.

Small dry white beans are often cooked and added to this *mole*; for this quantity, cook ¼ pound in the same way as *frijoles negros a la Oaxaqueña* (page 184). There should be very little broth at the end of the cooking time; reduce if necessary, then add beans and broth to the *verde*.

Some cooks in Oaxaca prefer to use half unripe red tomatoes, which are sweeter, and half *tomate verde* for this recipe. However, the former may be difficult to come by, so use all *tomate verde* and ½ teaspoon sugar.

THE CHICKEN
1 large chicken (about 3½ pounds), cut into serving pieces
1 small head of garlic, scored around the middle
1 small white onion, roughly sliced
sea salt to taste
1 recipe *chochoyotes* (page 54)

THE SAUCE
10 (about ½ pound) *tomate verde* (see note above) *or* half unripe red
    tomatoes and half *tomate verde*
1½ cups water
10 small garlic cloves, peeled
½ small white onion
1½ tablespoons Mexican oregano *or* 3 tablespoons Oaxacan
pinch of cumin seed

4 whole cloves
4 whole allspice
4 (or to taste) *chiles serranos* or *chiles de agua*
2 tablespoons melted lard or safflower oil
¼ pound (½ cup) prepared corn *tortilla masa* (page 8)
4 big leafy stems of *epazote,* roughly chopped
1 small bunch of fresh parsley, tough stalks removed, roughly chopped
8 *hoja santa* or avocado leaves
1½ cups water
sea salt to taste

Put the chicken pieces into a pan; add the garlic and onion with water to cover and salt to taste. Bring to a simmer and continue simmering until the meat is just tender. Strain, reserving the broth. Add water or reduce to make 4 cups broth.

Prepare 1 recipe *chochoyotes* and set aside.

Remove the husks from the *tomate verde,* rinse briefly, and chop roughly. Put into a blender jar with the water. Add the garlic, onion, oregano, cumin seed, cloves, allspice, and fresh *chiles* and blend until smooth.

Heat the lard in a heavy pan or sauté pan, add the blended ingredients, and fry over fairly high heat, stirring from time to time, until reduced and well seasoned—about 15 minutes.

Blend the *tortilla masa* with 1 cup of the chicken broth until smooth and stir into the pan with 2 more cups of the broth. Cook over medium heat, simmering until the sauce begins to thicken—about 10 minutes. Add the *chochoyotes* one by one, make sure they are well covered by the sauce, and simmer for a few moments while you prepare the greens.

Put the greens with 1½ cups water into a blender jar and blend as smoothly as possible. If the greens are tough and stringy, strain through a sieve into the pan, pressing the debris firmly so that all the juice and soft matter are extracted. Stir gently—you don't want to break up the dumplings—taste for salt, and cook for 10 minutes longer or until the dumpling dough is cooked.

COLORADITO *(Red Oaxacan Mole)*

SERVES 6 TO 8   OAXACA

Coloradito is one of the Seven *Moles* of Oaxaca (see page 227). The actual sauce is fairly thick, mild yet complex in flavor, and usually served with white rice and corn *tortillas*. It is customary to use the leftover sauce for *enchiladas*, accompanied by *pollo con orégano* (page 220) for brunch on the day of a wedding in Oaxaca.

Like other dishes with a sauce of this density, it is best made the day before for all the flavors to develop; the sauce freezes successfully for months.

In Oaxaca the preferred thickening agent for *moles* is the much touted *pan de yema*, a semisweet yeast roll made with egg yolks, but in fact any roll can be used, preferably one that is a day old so it is a little dry.

THE CHICKEN
1 large chicken (about 3½ pounds), cut into serving pieces
1 medium white onion, roughly chopped
1 small head of garlic, scored around the middle
4 fresh marjoram or oregano sprigs *or* ¼ teaspoon dried
4 fresh thyme sprigs *or* ¼ teaspoon dried
4 sprigs fresh flat-leaf parsley
sea salt to taste

THE SAUCE
12 *chiles guajillos* or *chilcostles*
½ pound (about 2 small) tomatoes, stewed (page 451)
4 tablespoons melted lard or safflower oil
¼ cup sesame seeds
1½ tablespoons dried oregano, Mexican if possible
2 whole cloves
2 whole allspice
1 medium white onion, thickly sliced
9 small garlic cloves, peeled
1 3-inch cinnamon stick, broken into thin strips
1 small ripe plantain, peeled and cut into thick rounds
3 slices French bread
1 ounce Mexican chocolate
sea salt to taste

Put the chicken into a pan with the onion, garlic, and herbs; cover with water and add salt to taste. Bring to a simmer and continue simmering until the chicken is *just* tender—about 20 to 25 minutes.

Remove the stems, if any, from the *chiles*, slit them open, and remove veins and seeds. Reserve the seeds for a *pipián* (page 102). Toast the *chiles* on a hot *comal* for a few seconds on each side, pressing them down until the inside flesh turns an opaque, tobacco color. Rinse the *chiles* in cold water, cover with hot water, and set aside to soak for about 15 minutes.

Put the tomatoes into a blender jar and blend briefly. Heat 1 tablespoon of the lard and fry the sesame seeds for a few seconds until a deep golden brown. Transfer with a slotted spoon, draining them as much as possible, to the blender jar; add the oregano, cloves, and allspice and blend until smooth, adding a little more of the water in which the *chiles* were soaking if necessary.

Add more lard to the pan and heat; add the onion and garlic and fry until translucent. Add the cinnamon pieces and fry until the onion and garlic are lightly browned. Transfer with a slotted spoon to the blender jar. Add the plantain and bread to the pan and fry over low heat until a deep golden color; transfer to the blender jar. Adding more *chile* water if necessary, blend until you have a smooth puree. Gradually add the soaked *chiles* with more water as necessary and blend until smooth. When all the *chiles* have been blended, dip a spoon into the bottom of the blender jar and take out a sample of the sauce to see if the rather tough *chile* skins have been blended sufficiently. If not, add a little more water, stir well, and then blend for a few seconds more.

Heat the remaining lard in a heavy pan or sauté pan, add the sauce, straining only if necessary to extract stubborn pieces of *chile* skins, add the blended sauce and chocolate, and cook over medium heat, stirring and scraping the bottom of the pan to prevent sticking, for about 15 minutes. Add 2 cups of the chicken broth and the chicken pieces, taste for salt, and cook for 15 minutes more. The sauce should be fairly thick and lightly cover the back of a wooden spoon.

Serve with white rice and *tortillas*. Or set aside and reheat carefully so that the sauce does not stick. Since the sauce tends to thicken as it sits, it may be necessary to dilute with a little more chicken broth.

AMARILLO *(Oaxacan Yellow Mole)*

SERVES 6 TO 8

Amarillo (literally yellow) is another of the famed Seven *Moles* of Oaxaca. In fact the sauce is more of a light brick red but varies with the type of *chile* used. Older recipes varied in their choice of *chiles—amarillos, chilhuacles amarillos, chilcostles, costeños* (see page 510), which are unique to Oaxaca—while latter-day recipes resort to the more easily obtainable *guajillos*. A pity, because dishes of this type tend to lose their very special regional qualities.

Amarillo is, in fact, a meat stew with a lot of vegetables and small dumplings *(chochoyotes)*, the sauce slightly thickened with *tortilla masa*. Either pork, chicken, or beef can be used, the only difference being the final flavoring herb: *hoja santa, cilantro,* or *pitiona* respectively.

The more adventurous *aficionados* who travel to Mexico and Oaxaca can always bring back *chilcostles*, which have a sharper flavor and bite than *guajillos*.

Amarillo is served in shallow bowls, with hot corn *tortillas* and a dish of *rajas con limón* and onion served separately.

While best eaten the same day, it can be held over, although I do not suggest freezing it.

THE CHICKEN
2½ pounds chicken parts
1 medium white onion, roughly sliced
1 small head of garlic, scored around the middle
sea salt to taste

THE SAUCE
12 *chiles guajillos* or *chilcostles*
½ small head of garlic (about 9 cloves), kept whole and charred (see page 439)
½ medium onion, cut into 3 pieces and charred (see page 454)
4 whole allspice
4 whole cloves
large pinch of cumin seed
1 tablespoon dried oregano, Mexican if possible
3 *tomate verde*, husks removed, rinsed and roughly chopped
2 tablespoons lard or safflower oil
¼ pound (½ cup) prepared corn *tortilla masa* (page 8)
sea salt to taste
1 small bunch of *cilantro*

THE VEGETABLES

1 large *chayote* (about ¾ pound), peeled and cut into lengthwise slices with
    core and seed
½ pound (about 3 medium) waxy potatoes, quartered, unpeeled
salted boiling water
6 ounces green beans, trimmed and halved

1 recipe *chochoyotes* (page 54)
rajas con limón (page 359)

Put the chicken pieces into a pan with the onion, garlic, salt, and water
to cover. Bring to a simmer and continue simmering until *just* tender—about
25 minutes. Strain, reserving the broth.

Meanwhile, remove the stems, if any, from the dried *chiles*, slit them
open, and remove seeds and veins (save seeds for another purpose, discard
the veins). Toast the *chiles* briefly on each side or until the inside flesh turns a
tobacco color. Rinse in cold water, cover with hot water, and set aside to
soak for about 20 minutes.

While the chicken is cooking and the *chiles* are soaking, cover the *chayote*
and potatoes with salted boiling water, bring to a boil again, and cook about
10 minutes. Add the green beans and continue cooking for about 5 minutes
longer. The vegetables should still be *al dente* since they will finish cooking in
the stew. Strain, reserving the cooking water.

Strain the *chiles*, putting half the water into a blender jar and reserving
the rest. Add the peeled garlic, onion, allspice, cloves, cumin, oregano, and
tomate verde; blend until smooth. Gradually add the *chiles* with the rest of the
soaking water and continue to blend as smoothly as possible.

Heat the lard in a heavy pan or sauté pan. Add the *chile* sauce (through a
fine strainer if there are still pieces of *chile* skins left whole) and cook over
fairly high heat, stirring and scraping the bottom of the pan, for about 8 to
10 minutes. Put 1½ cups of the reserved chicken broth into the blender jar,
add the *masa*, and blend until smooth. Stir the *masa* into the cooking sauce
with 2 more cups of the broth and cook over medium heat, stirring and
scraping, until the sauce begins to thicken. Add 1½ more cups of the broth,
the water in which the vegetables were cooked, and the cooked chicken and
vegetables; bring to a simmer and adjust seasoning. Add the *chochoyotes* and
cilantro and cook until the former are done—about 15 to 20 minutes. Serve
as suggested above.

POLLO EN SALSA DE FRESADILLA Y CHIPOTLE
(Chicken in Green Tomato and Chipotle Sauce)

SERVES 4 TO 6   ELIZABETH BORTON DE TREVIÑO

This recipe was given to me many years ago by Elizabeth Borton de Treviño, who married a Mexican from Monterrey and lived there for many years. Her book, *My Heart Lies South*, gives a vivid picture of provincial life at that time. This dish is very simple to make, far less condimented than those farther south. If the *tomate verde—fresadilla* as it is called in Nuevo Leon—is very acidy, you may need to add a little sugar to counterbalance the flavor. Serve with wheat flour *tortillas* and slices of avocado, which provides a balance for the acidity.

1 large chicken (3½ to 4 pounds), cut into serving pieces
2 garlic cloves, peeled
1 small white onion, roughly sliced
1 California bay leaf
1 fresh thyme sprig *or* a pinch of dried
1 fresh marjoram sprig *or* a pinch of dried
1 lime slice
sea salt to taste
chicken broth (page 95) or water to cover

1½ pounds (about 30) *tomate verde*, boiled (see page 454)
6 canned *chiles chipotles en adobo*
sugar if necessary
2 tablespoons lard or safflower oil

Put the chicken pieces into a pan with the garlic, onion, herbs, lime slice, salt, and broth or water to cover. Bring to a simmer and cook over gentle heat for about 20 minutes, until chicken is partially cooked. Strain and reduce broth to about 2 cups over high heat.

Put the *tomate verde* into a blender jar together with the *chiles* and blend until smooth, adding a little sugar if necessary (see note above).

Heat the lard in a heavy pan, add the sauce, and fry over fairly high heat for about 10 minutes. Add the chicken pieces and broth, adjust seasoning, and cook over medium heat, stirring from time to time, until the sauce and chicken are cooked and well seasoned, the sauce is thickened, and the fat is collecting around the sides and on top—about 20 minutes.

POLLO EN CUÑETE
(Braised Chicken with White Wine and Almonds)

SERVES 6   SEÑORA VERÓNICA CUEVAS, CIUDAD HIDALGO, MICHOACÁN

Señora Cuevas says this recipe came from her grandmother's Spanish cook many years ago in Ciudad Hidalgo. The wine, almonds, and olive oil certainly reflect the strong Spanish influence in this part of Michoacán. This is a simple and elegant dish, and with the slow cooking the sauce, although there is not a lot of it, is delicate and slightly gelatinous. Señora Cuevas serves it with crusty bread rolls and a green salad. She prefers to pass the *chiles* separately for each guest to add "the *picante*," but I prefer the flavor given to the sauce by cooking the *chiles* in it.

A heavy flameproof earthenware casserole with a tight-fitting lid is ideal for cooking this dish.

⅓ cup olive oil
1 large chicken (about 3½ to 4 pounds), cut into serving pieces
3 fresh thyme sprigs *or* ⅛ teaspoon dried
3 fresh marjoram sprigs *or* ⅛ teaspoon dried
2 California bay leaves
3 whole cloves
3 whole allspice
½ cup raisins
⅓ cup slivered almonds
1 large white onion, cut into quarters
1 small head of garlic, halved horizontally
¼ pound carrots, scraped, trimmed, and sliced
6 ounces very small new potatoes peeled and cut into ½-inch slices
1 cup water
1 cup white wine
¼ cup mild vinegar
1 teaspoon (or to taste) sea salt
6 canned *chiles largos* or *jalapeños en escabeche*

Heat the olive oil in a heavy pan, add the chicken pieces a few at a time, and sauté until a deep golden color. Add the rest of the ingredients, except the *chiles*, cover the pot tightly, and cook over very low heat. Shake the pot from time to time to prevent sticking and cook until the chicken is tender—about 1¼ hours. Add the *chiles* and cook for 5 minutes longer.

COACHALA *(Wedding Soup)*

SERVES 8   FRANCISCO DÍAZ DE SANDI, GUADALAJARA, JALISCO

Coachala is a thick soup traditionally cooked in an earthenware pot and served in deep bowls with corn *tortillas* at weddings and baptisms in the western part of Jalisco.

Instructions call for a "fat hen," but since those are few and far between in American markets, a large, solid chicken will do instead.

THE CHICKEN
1 3½- to 4-pound chicken, cut into 4 pieces
the giblets, feet, and neck (but not the liver) if possible
½ medium white onion, roughly sliced
3 small garlic cloves, peeled
½ teaspoon dried oregano, Mexican if possible
sea salt to taste

THE ADDED SAUCE
¾ pound (about 16 medium) *tomate verde* (small *tomate de milpa* preferred in Jalisco), husks removed
15 *chiles de árbol,* stalks removed
2 *chilacates,* cleaned of veins and seeds
2 tablespoons prepared corn *tortilla masa* (page 8)

Put the chicken into a deep pot and add giblets, onion, garlic, oregano, and salt. Cover well with water and bring to a simmer. Cover the pot and continue simmering until the chicken is quite tender—about 35 minutes. Strain the chicken, reserving the broth, and set aside to cool. Reduce or add water to make 6 cups broth. When cool enough to handle, remove the flesh from the bones, discarding the bones but not the skin. Shred the breast meat with skin and set aside separately from the rest of the meat.

Put the *tomate verde* and dried *chiles* into a pan, cover with water, and bring to a simmer; continue simmering for 5 minutes. Remove from the heat and leave to soak for 10 minutes more. Transfer with a slotted spoon to a blender jar and blend to a very smooth consistency, adding a little of the chicken broth if necessary for the blades to work efficiently. Set aside.

Add a little of the chicken (not the breast) to the blender jar with some of the broth and blend to a slightly grainy sauce. Repeat with more of both until all the meat has been blended—this will take about 4 cups of broth. Put this puree back into a heavy pan, add the blended *chiles* and *tomate verde,* and cook over low heat. Meanwhile, dilute the *masa* with ½ cup of the broth and add to the pot with another 1½ cups of the broth; continue cooking over low heat, stirring and scraping the bottom of the pan, for about 20 minutes. Add the shredded chicken breast, adjust seasoning, and cook for a few minutes more for the shredded meat to season. Serve in deep bowls accompanied by corn *tortillas*.

POLLO EN CIRUELA PASA
(Chicken with Prunes and Sweet Red Peppers)

SERVES 6   ANGAMACUTIRO, MICHOACÁN

This is an unusual and delicious dish that I first came across at a regional food fair in Morelia. It was surprising that such a Spanish-influenced dish should be representative of a small, remote village, Angamacutiro, in Michoacán. Nobody could explain why.

When the dish is cooked, there should be a lot of thick sauce, and the chicken should be well coated with it. It can be cooked ahead and reheated even the day after.

Traditionally it is served just with bread rolls.

Although unpitted prunes and olives were used in the original, it makes no difference if you use the pitted ones. Of course freshly roasted and peeled sweet red peppers give a far better taste than canned ones, although they are more trouble to prepare.

1 3½- to 4-pound chicken, cut into serving pieces
sea salt and freshly ground black pepper to taste
5 tablespoons olive oil
⅔ cup finely chopped white onion
5 garlic cloves, peeled and finely chopped
¾ pound (2 medium) tomatoes, chopped, unskinned
¾ pound (about 2 medium) tomatoes, blended to a smooth puree, unpeeled
15 pitted prunes
¾ cup chicken broth (page 95), if necessary
3 sweet red peppers, charred, peeled, and diced or canned, drained, and diced
15 pitted green olives

Season the chicken pieces with salt and pepper. Heat the olive oil in a heavy casserole and sauté the chicken a few pieces at a time until golden. Remove from the oil, add the onion and garlic to the pan, and fry gently without browning for about 2 minutes. Add the chopped tomatoes and fry for

3 minutes more. Return the chicken pieces to the pan and cook gently for about 10 minutes. Add the tomato puree and prunes, cover the casserole, and continue cooking until the chicken is almost tender—about 20 minutes, depending on the size and quality of the chicken. If the sauce seems rather dry, add some or all of the broth. Stir in the red peppers, olives, and salt to taste; continue cooking until the chicken is tender but not falling apart and the flavors well amalgamated.

POLLO EN ESCABECHE ROJO *(Chicken in Red Souse)*

SERVES 4 TO 5   YUCATÁN

This is a simple but surprisingly delicious Yucatecan way of preparing broiled chicken or turkey. As with many other similar dishes, it does add something special to the flavor to have a charcoal or wood grill at hand, but an ordinary broiler will do. It is a perfect diet dish.

Although this chicken is usually served with a plain tomato, lettuce, or cabbage salad, white rice goes very well and, of course, a small serving of *frijoles colados* (page 186).

6 rounded tablespoons *recado rojo* (see page 430)
5 garlic cloves, peeled and crushed
sea salt to taste
4 tablespoons Seville orange juice, a substitute (see page 456), or mild vinegar, approximately
1 3-pound chicken, cut into serving pieces
4 whole *chiles güeros, fresno,* or banana peppers, charred (see page 464)
3 small heads of garlic, charred and cloves separated but not peeled (see page 439)
1 tablespoon dried oregano, Yucatecan if possible, lightly toasted
1 cup *cebollas en escabeche* (see page 363)
3 to 4 tablespoons lard or safflower oil

Blend the *recado rojo,* crushed garlic, salt, and bitter orange juice together to a smooth paste. Spread the chicken pieces with a thin layer of the paste and set the rest aside.

Put the chicken pieces, fresh *chiles,* whole garlic cloves, and oregano into the pan, barely cover with water, add a little salt, and bring to a simmer. Continue simmering the chicken until almost tender but still a little underdone—about 20 minutes. Remove from broth. Add the onions to the broth, bring to a simmer, remove from the heat, and set aside but keep hot.

Mix the rest of the *recado rojo* mixture with the lard and set aside while you heat the grill or broiler. (If you prefer not to use lard, then just spread with the paste and brush on oil just before grilling.)

Grill the chicken pieces, turning from time to time, for about 5 minutes on each side or until cooked through and well browned. Serve with some of the hot broth and onions on top.

Alternate Way of Serving

Do not add the onions to the broth. Pour a little of the broth over the chicken, then top with the pickled onions.

BARBACOA DE POLLO
(Pit-Barbecued or Grilled Chicken)

SERVES 6 TO 8

There are some recipes that stick in your mind even after a cursory glance, and this is one of them. I read about it three years ago, and yet it stuck with me, reminiscent of a dish I had eaten years before in Guerrero.

In this case, *barbacoa* refers to pit barbecuing, the original method of simple country cooking in Guerrero and many other regions, although the recipe says it should be steamed or baked in the oven. I did both, and then I grilled the chicken, which was the most successful of all. (Since I am fortunate enough to have access to avocado and banana leaves the year round in my garden, I served the grilled chicken on a bed of slightly singed and smoking avocado leaves and let the guests help themselves to the toppings.)

If you don't have the fancy leaves on hand and want to bake or steam the seasoned chicken, just use cooking parchment to wrap the meat. But if you can get hold of, or store up, a few dry avocado leaves, they do add a very special flavor.

I have used my own special way of baking the chicken; I personally prefer not to steam it. Steaming does *not* imitate the action of a pit barbecue, as most of the flavor drops back into the water, while in the barbecue the condensed, sealed steam drops back onto the meat.

START THE DAY BEFORE
6 *chiles anchos*
6 *chiles guajillos*
1¼ cups water, approximately
6 whole cloves
10 whole allspice
pinch of cumin seed
2 peppercorns
1 1-inch cinnamon stick
2 teaspoons (or to taste) sea salt
2 teaspoons dried oregano, Mexican or Oaxacan if possible
3 garlic cloves, peeled
1½ tablespoons safflower oil, lard, or chicken fat
1 large chicken (about 3½ to 4 pounds), cut into serving pieces

2 sprays of avocado leaves (optional; see note above)
2 banana leaves or enough to wrap the chicken pieces (optional; see note above)

Bounty of a Mexican Spring

Tropical Fruits, see page 511

Pork Products, see page 510

Vegetables, Herbs And Wild Greens, see page 510

Uncommon Dried Chiles, see page 509

Common Dried Chiles, see page 509

Fresh Chiles, see page 509

Cooking *tortillas* on an earthenware *comal* over a wood fire

A collection of wild summer mushrooms from the State of Mexico

Varieties of corn with their kernels, masa, nixtamal (corn soaked in a lime solution), and cooked hominy

Grinding corn *masa* for *tortillas* on a *metate*

Patting out a corn *tortilla*

THE TOPPING
1 large avocado, peeled and cut into strips
8 thick lime slices
1½ cups finely shredded lettuce
½ cup finely sliced radishes
1 cup loosely packed, finely sliced white onion
1¼ cups *salsa verde (cruda)* (page 336), garnished with chopped *cilantro*

Slit the dried *chiles* open and scrape out and discard the veins and seeds. Toast lightly on both sides on a fairly hot *comal* or griddle. Cover the *chiles* with hot water and bring to a simmer; simmer for 5 minutes. Leave in the hot water for 10 minutes more.

Put ½ cup of the water into a blender jar and add the spices, salt, oregano, and garlic; blend until smooth. Add the rest of the water and a few of the soaked *chiles* and blend until smooth. Add the *chiles* little by little and blend after each addition. Dig to the bottom of the jar and feel the sauce to see if the *chile guajillo* skin, which is very tough, has been blended sufficiently. If not, then blend some more.

Heat the oil in a frying pan, add the sauce, and fry over medium heat, stirring from time to time to prevent sticking, for about 5 minutes. Set aside to cool.

When the paste is cool, it may still be rather loose; don't worry, it will thicken with standing. Spread all over the chicken pieces and set aside overnight in the refrigerator. Cook by one of the methods listed below.

Grilling

Make sure that the chicken is thickly and evenly coated with the *chile* paste on all sides. Place over or under the grill—depending on the type of grill and whether wood, charcoal, or gas—and grill slowly, turning over from time to time, for about 30 minutes. Garnish liberally and serve immediately.

Steaming

Make sure that the chicken is thickly and evenly covered with the *chile* paste. Lightly singe the sprays of avocado leaves (if using them) over a bare flame or hot plate and put under and on top of the chicken. Wrap in the banana leaves and place in the top of a steamer. Steam over high heat until tender—about 45 minutes to 1 hour.

Baking

Heat the oven to 350°. Prepare and wrap the chicken in the same way as for steaming. Place in one layer in a casserole with ½ cup of water in the bottom. Cover with a lid or foil and bake for about 30 minutes. Increase heat to 375°, turn the package over to baste, and return to the oven, uncovered, and bake until tender—about 20 minutes.

To Serve

If the grilling method is used, cover grilled chicken lavishly with the toppings. If the chicken is steamed or baked and covered with the leaves, open up packages and cover meat with toppings. Alternately pass toppings for diners to serve themselves.

RELLENA DE POLLO

MAKES ABOUT 3½ CUPS TO SERVE 6   ZITÁCUARO, MICHOACÁN

Rellena de pollo is one of *the* popular market foods of Zitácuaro. It is made out of the blood and intestines of chickens (misnamed *rellena*—stuffed—because of course it would be impossible to stuff the intestines with blood successfully) and prepared by a few of the local women who have cornered the market for those simple ingredients. They arrive quite early in the morning with the prepared *rellena* and do the final cooking in large *cazuelas* set over charcoal braziers. From there they dispense the bubbling, chocolate-colored contents to housewives, or their maids, sent in search of something good for *almuerzo*.

Rellena de pollo is served just with freshly made corn *tortillas* so that guests can make their own *tacos*.

1 cup chicken intestines
2 cups chicken blood
3 fresh thyme sprigs *or* ⅛ teaspoon dried
3 fresh marjoram sprigs *or* ⅛ teaspoon dried
rounded ½ teaspoon sea salt
1½ cups cold water
3 tablespoons melted chicken fat (page 217) or safflower oil
3 tablespoons finely chopped white onion
1 garlic clove, peeled and finely chopped
4 (about 3 ounces) *tomate verde* husks removed, roughly chopped
3 (or to taste) *chiles serranos*, finely chopped
1 heaped tablespoon roughly chopped mint
⅛ teaspoon cumin seed, crushed
4 peppercorns, crushed
sea salt to taste

If the intestines have not already been well cleaned, slit them open and rinse twice in lightly salted water. Cut into 1-inch lengths.

The blood will have coagulated; chop finely and put into a heavy pan with the intestines, thyme, marjoram, salt, and water; bring to a simmer over low heat. Continue simmering, scraping the bottom and sides of the pan from time to time (the blood does stick), until the intestines are tender—about 30 minutes, adding more water only if necessary. At the end of the cooking the blood should be soft and moist but not too watery. If so, reduce over slightly higher heat.

Heat the chicken fat in a frying pan, add the onion and garlic, and fry for about 10 seconds or until they are just becoming translucent. Add the *tomate verde* and fresh *chiles* and fry for about 5 minutes or until *tomate verde* are soft. Add the intestines and blood, mint, cumin, and pepper. Stir well and cook over medium heat, stirring and turning over from time to time, until the mixture is moist and shiny—about 8 minutes. Adjust salt.

THE PIG

(El Cerdo)

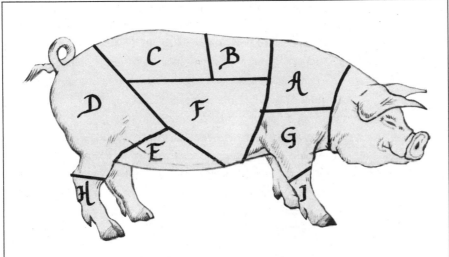

Cuts of Pork

A ~ Espaldilla ~ Shoulder
B ~ Chuletas ~ Chops
C ~ Lomo ~ Tenderloin
D ~ Pierna ~ Ham
E ~ Falda ~ Bacon ~ Saltpork
F ~ Costillita ~ Spareribs
G ~ Pecho ~ Picnic
H ~ Pata ~ Hocks
J ~ Mano ~ Pig's feet

Carne de Puerco Cocida y Deshebrada (Cooked and Shredded Pork)
Picadillo para Chiles Rellenos (Chopped Meat for Stuffed Chiles)
Pierna de Puerco Estilo Apatzingán (Leg of Pork Apatzingán)
Lomitos de Valladolid
Chilayo (Pork and Chile Stew)
Lomo Adobado Estilo Jalisco (Seasoned Pork Loin from Jalisco)
Puerco en Mole Rójo Sencillo (Pork in a Simple Red Mole Sauce)
Asado de Bodas (A Northern Wedding Dish)
Tatemado de Colima (Baked Pork for Festive Occasions, Colima)
Espinazo de Puerco con Albóndigas (Pork and Meatball Stew)
Carnitas Caseras (Home-Cooked Carnitas)
Chorizo de Huetamo (Hot-Country Sausages)
Chorizo Verde (Green Sausage)
Longaniza de Valladolid, Yucatán (Yucatecan Smoked Sausage)
Moronga Mexiquense (Blood Sausage from the State of Mexico)
Tacos de Moronga (Blood Sausage Tacos)
Moronga en Salsa Verde (Blood Sausage in Green Sauce)
Manteca de Cerdo (Pork Lard)
Manitas de Puerco en Escabeche (Pickled Pig's Feet)
Queso de Puerco (Head Cheese)
Chicharrón (Fried Pigskin)
Ensalada de Chicharrón (Fried Pigskin Salad)
Chicharrón en Salsa Verde (Fried Pigskin in Green Sauce)
Chicharrón en Salsa de Jitomate (Fried Pigskin in Tomato Sauce)
Cross-reference (For using pork as an alternative):
Verde de Oaxaca
Amarillo
Mole Verde

Without doubt pork is the most popular meat in Mexico, although perhaps not in the semi-arid north where climate and vegetation do not lend themselves to pig raising. In most peasant cultures of the world—except those that shun it for religious reasons—a pig in the backyard is a sign of affluence, and for good reason. "A pig can convert 35% of the energy of its feed to meat compared with 13% for sheep and a mere 6.5% for cattle," to quote from Marvin Harris's informative and entertaining book, *Good to Eat*; ". . . less than four months after insemination, a single sow can give birth to eight or more piglets, each of which after another six months can weigh over four hundred pounds." And although those figures do not exactly apply to the backyard Mexican pig, they come near—it is a creature cosseted with kitchen scraps, *tortillas*, whey from cheese making, and luscious fruits like *guavas* and *sapotes*.

In Mexico every part of the pig is used for human consumption except the hair—which should, but doesn't, get used for paintbrushes. As pigs are butchered in the commercial abattoirs, the *matanceros* (butchers) are accompanied by little boys or old women who deal with the innards, feet, and blood. The carcasses are sluiced well with many buckets of water and then whisked off by the butchers who have market stands. That afternoon or the next day the skinning begins. Nearly all the fat is shaved from the inside of the skin, which is then scored in a crisscross pattern and hung up overnight to dry. All of this goes to be fried in vats for the favorite Mexican snack, *chicharrón*. The head is made into *queso de puerco*, the feet are pickled, while the large intestines and blood are made into *moronga* or *rellena* (blood sausage) and the small ones reserved for *chorizo*. The tail accompanies the neck bones in stews or *frijoles*, while the organs—lungs, liver, kidneys, heart, bladder, and womb—are all cooked, fried, and chopped into savory *tacos*. The stomach is cooked too, except in the state of Mexico, where it is stuffed and irreverently called *obispo* (bishop).

Butchering of the meat differs in some respect from that of the United States (see diagram above), and many of the cuts are given a different name, depending on the region of the country. The shoulder is cut with the whole blade in it, an efficient conductor of heat to the succulent flesh around it. The loin is cut from the bone, neck chops are cut thin and then flattened for frying, while *escalopas* are cut from the leg, butterflied, and pounded out thin to be breaded and fried. The thin fleshy part hanging at the base of the loin, called *cabeza*, is also tender and has just the right amount of fat.

In a Mexican market where they butcher their own meat these cuts will be available; otherwise I have suggested a U.S. equivalent.

CARNE DE PUERCO COCIDA Y DESHEBRADA
(Cooked and Shredded Pork)

MAKES ABOUT 1 TO 1⅓ CUPS

COOKED PORK

Cooked and shredded pork is used for a taco filling, on top of *antojitos*, or, when chopped again, for *chiles rellenos*. No expensive cuts of pork need be used; boneless stewing pork with some fat left on is the best.

> 1 pound boneless stewing pork, cut into 1-inch cubes
> ⅓ medium white onion, roughly sliced
> 1 garlic clove, peeled and roughly sliced
> sea salt to taste

Put all the ingredients into a saucepan, barely cover with water, and bring to a simmer; then lower the heat and continue simmering until the pork is *just* tender, not soft—about 25 to 30 minutes. If you have the time to spare, leave the pork to cool off in the broth. Strain, reserving the broth.

SHREDDED PORK

As soon as the meat is cool enough to handle, shred it rather roughly—if it is too fine, it will lose flavor—discarding any connective tissue, gristle, etc. Set aside, ready for use.

For *chiles rellenos*, chop the shredded meat to a medium consistency.

Reserve the broth for a soup, rice, or a meat sauce.

PICADILLO PARA CHILES RELLENOS
(Chopped Meat for Stuffed Chiles)

MAKES 2 TO 2½ CUPS   SIERRA DE PUEBLA

This recipe for *picadillo* is particularly delicious as Señora Fagoaga uses it, to stuff the long, smoky-flavored *chile pasilla de Oaxaca*, but of course it can also be used with *poblano, ancho,* or Anaheim *chiles.* It is also used for her *tamales de acelgas* (page 80), a great improvement over the local, almost too simple *picadillo.*

2 pounds boneless pork with some fat, cut into 2-inch cubes
½ white onion, roughly chopped
sea salt to taste
1 pound (about 2 large) tomatoes, roughly chopped, unpeeled
2 small garlic cloves, peeled and roughly chopped
¼ small white onion, roughly chopped
2 tablespoons melted lard or safflower oil
2 whole cloves
1¼-inch cinnamon stick
2 tablespoons vinegar
20 almonds, skinned and roughly chopped
¼ cup raisins
⅓ cup loosely packed, roughly chopped flat leaf parsley
1 teaspoon sugar

Put the pork, ½ chopped onion, and salt into a saucepan, barely cover with water, bring to a simmer, and continue simmering until the meat is tender but not too soft. Strain, reserving the broth, and set the meat aside to cool. Return the broth to the saucepan and reduce over high heat to about 1¼ cups. Set aside. As soon as the meat is cool enough to handle, shred rather coarsely, removing any gristle or connective tissue but leaving the fat. Set aside.

In a blender jar, blend together the tomatoes, garlic, and ¼ chopped onion until smooth. Heat the lard, add the tomato puree, and cook over fairly high heat, stirring from time to time to prevent sticking, until reduced— about 8 minutes. Add the meat and the broth. Crush the cloves and cinnamon together with the vinegar and add to the meat mixture. Add the almonds, raisins, parsley, more salt to taste, and sugar and continue cooking until the mixture is almost dry.

PIERNA DE PUERCO ESTILO APATZINGÁN
(Leg of Pork Apatzingán)

MICHOACÁN

This is a delicious way of cooking pork and may be eaten hot or cold, thinly sliced for sandwiches or *tortas*. The recipe was given to me by Señora Aurelia, who cooks at the restaurant of the Posada de Sol in Apatzingán. She shreds this pork for her famous *tostadas* (page 26). Although Señora Aurelia prefers to use a leg of pork, I find that cut too compact and dry, so I use a pork shoulder in Mexico; the meat is succulent and a little fatty, which is good, and because of the blade across it, it cooks evenly without much shrinkage.

1 pork shoulder (about 4½ pounds)
3 *chiles guajillos*
6 ounces (about 1 medium) tomatoes, broiled (see page 450)
1 teaspoon sugar
⅓ cup fresh orange juice
2 heaped teaspoons (or to taste) sea salt
9 small garlic cloves, peeled
4 peppercorns, lightly crushed
1 large white onion, thickly sliced
1 large orange, cut into thin slices
2 California bay leaves
2 large fresh thyme sprigs *or* ¼ teaspoon dried
2 large fresh marjoram sprigs *or* ¼ teaspoon dried
1½ cups light beer

Pierce the meat all over with the point of a sharp knife and put it into a deep roasting pan or Dutch oven into which it will *just* fit (important so that the sauce does not dry out).

Heat the oven to 250°. Place a rack in the middle of the oven, allowing space, of course, for the Dutch oven.

Remove the stems from the dried *chiles*, slit them open, and scrape out and discard veins and seeds. Cover the *chiles* with boiling water and leave to soak for 15 minutes—or until they have been reconstituted and the tough skins have softened a little.

Place the unpeeled broiled tomatoes, sugar, orange juice, salt, garlic, and peppercorns in a blender jar and blend until fairly smooth. Drain the soaked *chiles* and transfer them to the blender jar; blend thoroughly until smooth.

Pour some of the sauce over the meat and turn the meat, adding sauce until it is completely covered. Distribute the onion and orange rings over the top, sprinkle the herbs around the meat, and then pour the beer over it.

Cover the pan with a lid or foil and bake for about 2½ hours or until the meat is just tender but not falling apart (cooking time will vary according to the quality and cut of meat and the heaviness of the pot). Remove lid, scrape down the sides and bottom of the pan well, and baste the meat with this residue. Raise heat to 375° and bake until the top of the meat has browned and the sauce has reduced, scraping the sides of the pan and basting from time to time—about 30 minutes. Remove meat to a platter, deglaze pan with a little hot water, reduce, and then pour over the cooling meat.

LOMITOS DE VALLADOLID

SERVES 4 TO 6   VALLADOLID, YUCATÁN

While *lomitos* translated literally means "little loins," this dish can be made with any type of meat—I always find loin too dry. It is a simple recipe, the *original* way of cooking *lomitos*, they say, in Valladolid, where they are very proud of their cooking traditions—it contrasts quite sharply with that given to me some years ago by a superlative cook in Merida, which was, however, more sophisticated.

Since tomatoes play the most important part in the dish, along with the meat, it is essential that you use the ripest ones—plum tomatoes would be great. *Chiles de árbol* can easily be substituted for the *secos*, with a slight difference in flavor, but the *chile habanero* is more difficult. In this dish it is added whole and raw to leave a unique flavor and not to add any more heat to the sauce. For appearance, if not for flavor, add a *chile güero*.

1½ pounds boneless stewing pork with some fat, cut into ½-inch cubes
1 rounded teaspoon sea salt
1½ pounds (about 4 or 5) medium tomatoes
2 small *chiles secos* or a substitute (see note above)
1 *chile habanero* or a substitute (see note above)
¼ teaspoon crumbled dried oregano, Yucatecan if possible
3 hard-cooked eggs, cut into lengthwise quarters
frijoles colados y fritos a la Yucateca as an accompaniment (page 186)

Put the meat cubes into a heavy pan into which they will just fit in no more than two layers. Sprinkle with salt and set over very low heat to dry out the moisture and then melt the fat—about 15 minutes—shaking the pan from time to time or turning the pieces over. Place the whole tomatoes on top of the meat, cover the pan, and cook again over low heat, turning once, until soft but not falling apart—about 15 minutes. Remove the tomatoes, skin them, and put them into a blender jar with the *chiles secos*. Blend until almost smooth. Put the tomato puree back into the pan, add the whole *chile habanero* and oregano, and continue cooking, uncovered, over low heat, turning the meat and scraping the bottom of the pan from time to time so that the sauce does not stick, until the meat is tender and the sauce of medium thickness (it should coat the back of a wooden spoon)—about 20 minutes. If the tomato sauce dries out too much, add a little water to the pan. Serve each portion with slices of egg, plus *frijoles* and corn *tortillas* on the side.

CHILAYO (*Pork and Chile Stew*)

SERVES 4 TO 6   COLIMA

This is a simple pork and *chile* stew and a popular way of cooking pork in the state of Colima. It is usually served on top of *morisqueta* (plain boiled rice, page 124). The use of *tomate verde* is curious and unique; they are put into the stew whole, including their papery husks. The husks give a very subtle and different flavor. *Espinazo,* the neck bones of the pork, would be used in Colima, but I suggest you use country-style spareribs cut into about 2-inch squares. *Chilayo* is simple but delicious.

2 pounds country-style spareribs, cut into 2-inch pieces
sea salt to taste
5 *chilacates or* 2 *chiles anchos* and 3 *guajillos*
1 cup water
1 garlic clove, peeled
½ medium white onion, roughly chopped
⅛ teaspoon cumin seed, crushed
6 ounces (about 8 medium) *tomate verde* with husks, well rinsed

Put the ribs into a large saucepan with water to barely cover, add salt to taste, and cook, uncovered, over medium heat for about 10 minutes.

Meanwhile, remove any stalks from the dried *chiles,* slit them open, and scrape out and discard any veins and seeds. Put into a saucepan, cover with hot water, and simmer for about 5 minutes. Set aside, off the heat, to soak for 5 minutes longer.

Put ½ cup of the water into a blender jar, add garlic, onion, and cumin seed, and blend thoroughly. Add the remaining ½ cup water and some of the *chiles,* blend well, and gradually add the rest of the *chiles,* blending well after each addition.

Add the blended ingredients to the meat. Cut the *tomate verde* into quarters, leaving the husks intact, and add to the pan. Let the meat continue cooking, uncovered, until it is tender, the sauce is reduced, and the fat has floated to the surface—about 45 minutes, depending on the pot and the quality of the meat. The sauce will be quite thick and coat the back of a wooden spoon well.

LOMO ADOBADO ESTILO JALISCO
(Seasoned Pork Loin from Jalisco)

SERVES ABOUT 6 AS A MAIN COURSE   JALISCO

In Mexico a boneless pork loin with a thin sheath of fat left on is generally used for this type of recipe. However, unless it's cooked at a low temperature with some liquid, it tends to be rather dry. This recipe is ideal because
all the flavors are well absorbed in the slow, moist cooking, and the meat remains succulent. *Lomo adobado* is used cold, thinly sliced, for *tortas de
Santuario* (page 376).

Part of the center loin can of course be used, with the bone removed
before slicing.

6 *chilacates* or California *chile* pods
4 cups water, approximately
3 garlic cloves, peeled and roughly chopped
2 peppercorns, crushed
2 whole cloves, crushed
1½-inch cinnamon stick, crushed
1 California bay leaf, broken up
2 fresh marjoram leaves *or* scant ⅛ teaspoon dried
2 tablespoons sesame seeds, lightly toasted
2 teaspoons (or to taste) sea salt
2 tablespoons mild vinegar
1 3½- to 4-pound pork loin, some fat removed (see note above)

Remove any stems from the dried *chiles*, slit them open, and scrape out
seeds and veins. Put the *chiles* into a small saucepan, cover with water, and
bring to a simmer. Cook gently for 5 minutes, remove from the heat, and
leave to soak for another 5 minutes. Strain, discarding the cooking water.

Put 1½ cups of the water into a blender jar and add the remaining
ingredients except the pork; blend until smooth. Add 2 of the soaked *chiles* at
a time to the blender jar, blending until smooth after each addition. (If *chiles*
are rather tough-skinned and blending will not puree them, pass the sauce
through a fine strainer—a messy procedure to be avoided if possible.) Pierce
the meat all over with the point of a sharp knife and cover thickly with the
seasoning paste. If you have time, set aside to season for about 2 hours.

Put the meat into a heavy pan into which it will just fit—if it is too
large, the sauce will dry up. Add 2½ cups of water, cover the pan, and cook
over fairly low heat until the meat is half cooked—about 40 minutes. Un-

cover, increase the heat slightly, and continue cooking, scraping the bottom and sides of the pan and basting the meat with the sauce, until it is reduced to a thick paste and the meat is tender but not falling apart—about 30 minutes. Set aside to cool.

Note: It is impossible to give exact cooking times as much will depend on the quality of the pork and the heat retention of the pan.

PUERCO EN MOLE ROJO SENCILLO
(Pork in a Simple Red Mole Sauce)

SERVES 6

If you wish to cook this *mole* with pork instead of chicken (page 224), choose country-style spareribs cut into 2-inch pieces with some fat on them or a proportion of these and some stewing pork. Although oil can be used for frying the sauce, lard gives a better flavor.

2½ pounds pork (see note above), cut into 2-inch cubes
1 small white onion, roughly chopped
2 garlic cloves, peeled and roughly chopped
2 peppercorns
sea salt to taste
the sauce from *pollo en mole rojo sencillo* (page 224)

Put the meat and other ingredients except sauce into a pan, cover with water, bring to a simmer, and continue simmering until the pork is almost tender but not cooked through, about 25 minutes.

Strain and measure broth; reduce to 7 cups or add water to make 7 cups if it falls short of this amount.

Prepare the sauce and finish cooking the *mole* as instructed on page 224.

ASADO DE BODAS (A Northern Wedding Dish)

SERVES 6 TO 8   SEÑORA GRACIELA MARTÍNEZ DE FLORES

Asado de bodas is little known outside Durango and Coahuila in northern Mexico. There, as its name implies, no country wedding feast would take place without it on the menu. Señora Graciela Martinez de Flores, a highly respected cooking authority in Mexico who comes from that area, provided the recipe. It is *"muy del rancho,"* she told me, and the traditional dishes are almost as much a ritual as the wedding ceremony itself. It starts, most heartily, with *siete sopas* (yes, seven soups)—"dry" and brothy ones included: rice, *macaroni*, elbow *macaroni*, pasta stars and shells, *vermicelli* in broth, and chicken *consomé*. The *asado* follows with pit-barbecued lamb and also includes *chicharrones* (although elsewhere their preparation would denote them *carnitas*) and all are eaten with corn *tortillas*. When this *asado* is served, it is unadorned.

THE MEAT
2 pounds pork with some fat, cut into 1-inch cubes
¼ medium onion, roughly sliced
2 garlic cloves, peeled
sea salt to taste

THE SAUCE
6 tablespoons lard
4 *chiles anchos*, slit open, veins and seeds removed
the pork broth
6 ounces (about 8 medium) *tomate verde*
4 garlic cloves, peeled
1 small slice dried French bread
½ dried corn *tortilla*
⅛ teaspoon cumin seed, crushed
1 ounce Mexican drinking chocolate
2 California bay leaves
¼ teaspoon oregano, Mexican if possible
thinly pared zest of 1 orange
sea salt to taste

Put the pork into a saucepan; add the onion, garlic, and salt to taste. Cover the meat with water, cover the pan, and bring to a simmer; cook slowly for about 25 minutes. Remove 1½ cups of the broth and keep warm in a bowl. Continue cooking the meat, uncovered, until it is *just* tender but not

256

soft and the water has been absorbed—about 15 minutes (cooking time will vary with the quality and cut of the meat).

Melt 3 tablespoons of the lard in a frying pan and fry the dried *chiles* very briefly on each side until they are an opaque tobacco brown inside—about 3 seconds. Remove from pan and add to the broth. Fry the *tomate verde* and garlic until golden and transfer them to the broth. Last, fry the bread and *tortilla* over very low heat until crisp and brown. Add to the broth. Set the contents of the bowl aside to soak for about 15 minutes or until the *chile* skins are soft.

Transfer the mixture to a blender jar, add the cumin seed and broken-up chocolate, and blend until smooth.

Melt the rest of the lard in a heavy pan and fry the pork pieces until golden, about 10 minutes. Add the blended ingredients, bay leaves, oregano, orange zest, and salt to taste and cook over low heat, scraping the bottom and sides of the pan until the sauce is fairly thick and the lard makes a shiny surface on the sauce—about 20 minutes. Serve with corn *tortillas*.

TATEMADO DE COLIMA
(Baked Pork for Festive Occasions, Colima)

SERVES 8 TO 10

In many parts of Mexico a *mole* is *the* festive dish for a wedding or baptism or even as a special Sunday treat, while in Colima it is a *tatemado.*

The word *tatemar* is a Hispanicized version of the Nahuatl words meaning "something to put into the fire." While nowadays it is customary to cook the meat in a covered clay pot over a fire with smoldering wood on top as well—*a dos fuegos*, with two fires—originally it must have been cooked in a pit in the ground.

Cooks in Colima seem to use *chiles anchos* (called *pasillas* there) and *guajillos* together interchangeably with *chilacates*.

In Colima the vinegar used is mild, made from the fermented palm drink called *tuba* found all along the Pacific littoral. When the meat is cooked, there should be lots of thick sauce in the pan—serve plenty of it; the sauce is as important as the meat.

4½ pounds pork shoulder with blade bone intact and some fat
2 cups mild vinegar
6 garlic cloves, peeled and crushed
1 tablespoon (or to taste) sea salt
8 peppercorns
1 fresh pork knuckle
¼ pound *chiles anchos*, approximately, and ¼ pound *chiles guajillos*, approximately *or* ½ pound *chilacates*
1 quart water
a small piece of fresh gingerroot, roughly chopped
leaves from 3 fresh thyme sprigs *or* scant ¼ teaspoon dried
1 tablespoon *chile* seeds from above *chiles*
¼ teaspoon coriander seed

FOR SERVING
cebollas encurtidas para Tatemado (page 364)
shredded lettuce
sliced radishes
corn *tortillas*

Pierce the pork shoulder all over with the point of a sharp knife and place in a deep dish. Put the vinegar into a blender jar and add the garlic, salt, and peppercorns; blend until smooth. Pour this over the meats and set aside in a cool place to marinate for 2 to 3 hours.

Heat oven to 275°.

Slit the dried *chiles* open, scraping out the veins and seeds; discard the veins and reserve 1 tablespoon of the seeds. Cover the *chiles* with boiling water and leave to soak for 20 minutes. Drain the vinegar from the meat and put into the blender jar; put the meat into a casserole. Add the *chiles* to the blender jar a few at a time, blending until smooth after each addition. Press the sauce through a fine strainer and discard the debris. Set aside. Add 1 cup of the water to the blender jar along with the ginger, thyme, *chile* seeds, and coriander seed; blend until smooth. Stir this mixture into the blended *chiles* and spread this paste over the meat.

Pour the rest of the water into the casserole, cover, and cook for 1 hour. Raise the oven temperature to 300°, turn the meat, and cook for 2 hours or until the meat is tender but not falling apart. Remove the cover; there should be a lot of sauce around the meat. Turn oven up to 400° and return meat to the oven, uncovered, fatty side up, to brown slightly and reduce the sauce a little. Serve topped with the relish, lettuce, and radishes, with hot *tortillas* on the side.

ESPINAZO DE PUERCO CON ALBÓNDIGAS
(Pork and Meatball Stew)

SEÑORITA MODESTA GARCIA,
TACÁMBARO, MICHOACÁN

SERVES 4 TO 5 GENEROUSLY

Although I always think of this as the perfect one-dish meal for a winter day, in fact I ate it for the first time on a summer day during the rainy season in the mountains of Michoacán. It was almost three o'clock in the afternoon as we drove to my friend's house in the driving rain that bent the pines low along the roadside. Hungry, we began to talk about food and conjecture about what there was for lunch. My friend said it was a secret, but he was sure I had never eaten it before today. When we were finally sitting down at the table, deep bowls of a brothy red stew of pork and meatballs, with chick-peas and vegetables topped with a mount of *morisqueta* (boiled rice, page 124), was set before us. It was a specialty of Señorita Garcia, who passed little fried cakes of dried fava beans to accompany it. Indeed, I had never eaten it before but have made it many times since.

In Mexico *espinazo*, or meaty pork neck bones, would be used, but I suggest you use country-style spareribs cut into 2-inch cubes.

THE MEATBALLS
¾ pound ground pork with some fat, medium grind
2 peppercorns, crushed
2 whole cloves, crushed
2 garlic cloves, peeled and finely chopped
sea salt to taste

THE CHILES
2 large *chiles anchos,* lightly toasted, veins and seeds removed
2 large *chiles guajillos,* lightly toasted, veins and seeds removed
⅔ cup water, approximately
1 garlic clove

THE MEAT
1½ pounds country-style spareribs, cut into 2-inch cubes
¼ medium white onion, roughly sliced
2 garlic cloves, peeled and roughly chopped
sea salt to taste

THE VEGETABLES
1 cup cooked dried chick-peas (page 187) and the cooking water
2 medium carrots, trimmed, scraped, and sliced
6 ounces green beans, trimmed and cut into halves
2 small zucchini, trimmed and cut lengthwise into eighths

First prepare the meatballs. Mix the ground pork with the peppercorns, cloves, garlic, and salt to taste. Roll into 1-inch balls and set aside.

Put the dried *chiles* into a small saucepan, cover with water, bring to a simmer, and simmer for 5 minutes. Remove from the heat and simmer for 5 minutes more. Put the ⅔ cup water into a blender jar with the garlic and soaked, drained *chiles* and blend until absolutely smooth. (If the *chiles guajillos* were rather old and the skin tough, they may not blend too well; in that case, pass the sauce through a fine strainer before adding it to the meat.) Set aside.

Put the spareribs into a large saucepan with the onion, garlic, and salt. Add water to cover; bring to a simmer and cook over low heat. Add the *chile* puree to the pan and cook for about 25 minutes. Add the meatballs, chick-peas, and vegetables and cook for about 30 minutes, by which time the meat and meatballs should be tender and the vegetables soft (no *al dente* here, please; this is a stew).

CARNITAS CASERAS (*Home-Cooked Carnitas*)

SERVES 6 TO 8   STATE OF MEXICO

Devoted as I am to the more traditional *carnitas*, succulent pieces of pork with a crisp brown crust, I have fallen for this way of preparing them. The recipe was published in *Gastronomía Mexiquense*, a collection of recipes from the state of Mexico, where it was suggested that they be served with corn *tortillas* and *guacamole*. I find this a little too heavy and prefer a *salsa mexicana*, which is fresh and crisp.

You should allow about ½ pound of meat per serving since there will be a proportion of bone. Country-style spareribs cut into 2-inch cubes and some boneless stewing pork with a little fat on it should be ideal. Preceded by a *sopa seca* of rice and followed with a salad, this quantity should serve 6 as a main course or 8 or more as an appetizer.

I have diverged from the original recipe only by leaving the onion in for the whole cooking time (instructions are to take it out) and by using a whole orange instead of just the rind.

4 tablespoons lard
3 pounds pork (see note above), cut into 2-inch cubes
½ medium white onion, roughly sliced
4 fresh marjoram sprigs *or* scant ¼ teaspoon dried, approximately
4 fresh thyme sprigs *or* scant ¼ teaspoon dried, approximately
3 California bay leaves, broken up
10 peppercorns, crushed
1 orange, cut into eighths
1 cup milk
sea salt to taste

Heat the lard in a heavy pan, add the meat, and fry, stirring and turning it over from time to time, until lightly golden—about 8 minutes. Add the onion and stir well. Cook for 8 minutes longer or until the meat is well browned (remove onion only if it has burned). Add the remaining ingredients, cover the pan, and cook over low heat until the meat is just tender, not falling apart—about 20 minutes, depending on the quality of the meat. There should be plenty of pan juices. Remove the lid, increase the heat, and fry, stirring and scraping the bottom of the pan, until the juices have been absorbed—about 10 minutes. Drain off the extra fat and serve as suggested.

These *carnitas* may be prepared ahead up to the point of the final frying, but they should be kept covered so that the meat does not dry out.

THE MEXICAN CHORIZO

The *chorizos* of Toluca have been renowned since the beginning of the eighteenth century, possibly when they were first prominently featured on the gastronomic pyramid erected in that town by the Duke of Linares to celebrate the birth of the second Bourbon king of Spain, Felipe Pedro, in 1713. The duke wanted all of the regions of New Spain to be represented by their local specialties in that monument to gluttony. Fray Jose Gil wrote some verses on that occasion titled *To the Sumptuous Paradise of Gluttony* (I can't help wondering how his ecclesiastical superiors viewed this time taken out from their devotions), in which the *chorizos* of Toluca and Metepec (a nearby town where the best earthenware *cazuelas* are made) represent "the udders of our country."!

In fact, throughout its history the Valley of Toluca, at an altitude of 8,000 feet, has been renowned for the quality of its corn, which, it was believed, had a higher nutritional value than that grown at lower altitudes. (This is not the opinion of errant friar and commentator Thomas Gage, who in the seventeenth century made as an excuse for drinking chocolate and snacking every two hours the fact that foodstuffs grown at a high altitude were not as nutritionally sustaining.) This was the area where Malinche's (Cortés's Mexican companion and interpreter) father grazed his cattle, sheep, and pigs. Malinche wrote to Cortés asking him to intercede with the king of Spain on her father's behalf so that he could own the land. It was, in fact, the first pig-raising area of importance in New Spain.

According to old cookbooks, *chorizos* were originally seasoned with herbs, ginger, *cilantro* seeds, allspice, cloves, and cumin. The meat was left to soak in salted white wine—salt should never be allowed to touch the meat directly, one was cautioned—and left to soak for 48 hours. Paprika was added for color and often *chile ancho*—called *jaral* in that area. Traditionally links of *chorizo* were made 7 to 8 centimeters (about 3 inches) long and tied with *ixtle*, a fiber from the *maguey*, or century plant, when sold by weight; for selling by the piece or for cooking with rice—an unusual distinction—they were made into smaller links.

Today there are many variations in the recipe: the addition of almonds, pine nuts, or walnuts for more luxurious versions; less *chile* and more paprika for export; the addition of *chile de árbol* for the fiery *chorizón con furia*. And then there is the "poor man's" *chorizo*, called *longaniza*, made in one long strip of inferior meats—very often pork and beef mixed together—and including *chile* veins and seeds.

There is a local saying that one eats *chorizo* three times, but all at once.

First for its ineffable and enticing aroma; second for its color, which is heightened in the cooking process; and the third time for its texture as the teeth sink into the meat. While they are usually cooked, *chorizos* can also be dried out thoroughly and eaten raw.

While *chorizos* from Toluca and the surrounding area are considered the epitome of all *chorizos* in Mexico, the usual regional rivalry exists. In the North and Northwest the meat is very finely ground, sometimes twice, and the seasoning is much less complicated. In Yucatan the *longaniza*, a specialty of Valladolid, is made of finely ground pork seasoned with *achiote* along with other spices and then smoked in thin 12-inch lengths of half-filled casings with the ends twisted and not tied.

The recipes that follow here are for that *longaniza*, a green *chorizo* from the state of Mexico that appeared only about 20 years ago, and one that I am particularly fond of from the hot country of Michoacán, since a recipe for Toluca-type *chorizos* has already been published in *The Cuisines of Mexico*.

NOTE ON SAUSAGE CASINGS

The small intestines of the pig known as sausage casings are used for the following three recipes. They usually come partially frozen, heavily packed in salt. Before using them, it is necessary to rinse them well, twice, in slightly acidulated water—approximately 1 tablespoon vinegar to 4 cups water—and leave them to soak in the second water for about 30 minutes. I find it easier at this point to cut the casings into 3- to 4-foot lengths. Submerge each length one at a time, allowing a little water to pass through; it will balloon up to show that there are no breaks or punctures. If the casing deflates at one point, cut it into two lengths at the leak. Tie a secure double knot at the end of each length and, starting at that end, press out any air or water. Hang them up to drain for about 15 minutes before starting to stuff the casings, but don't let them dry out.

You may, of course, make your *chorizo* and, instead of putting it into casings and drying it, pack it and freeze it after about 3 days of seasoning in the refrigerator. It won't have the same depth of flavor of course, and think of the gastronomic pride of having your string of *chorizos* on display in the kitchen, announcing their presence with a pleasant, herby aroma.

Plastic casings, which do not breathe, are not recommended since the fillings cannot drain or season.

To Stuff the Sausage Casing

If it has not already been done, tie a firm double knot at one end of each length of casing. Ease the open end of the casing over the funnel outlet and gradually work as much of the casing onto it as you can. Invert the funnel and press the tied end of the casing to force out any air before you begin to stuff the casing. Put some of the *chorizo* mixture into the funnel and force it down into the casing either with your fingers or with a dowel that just fits the aperture of the funnel. Stuff the casings firmly, smoothing and pressing the mixture evenly with your hand. The sausage should feel firm, but do not overstuff. Leave a short length of the casing unstuffed at the open end in order to tie a secure knot.

I find it easier not to twist the sausage into links as I go along; I prefer to tie each one at the end of the stuffing process.

Tie the *chorizo* into links of about 3½ inches, with either pieces of string or strips of dried corn husks.

Prick each link in several places with a needle so that it can drain better—although I tend to do this only in humid weather.

CHORIZO DE HUETAMO *(Hot-Country Sausages)*

MAKES 15 TO 16 3-INCH LINKS   HUETAMO, MICHOACÁN

I can never quite decide, but at the moment my favorite *chorizo* comes from a small town called Huetamo in the hot country of Michoacán. There is one *chorizo* maker there in particular who makes delicious ones, and he very kindly gave me his recipe, which he has used for many years. Of particular interest to me was the texture of the ground meat, and I noticed that the holes in the disk of his grinder were about ¼ inch in diameter.

Here are some tips:

Don't cut down on the amount of lard; you need it for flavor. Besides, most of it will render out in the cooking.

Once the casings have been filled I like to tie the links with strips of dried corn husks—it looks more picturesque. If husks are not available, then use string.

I usually dry my *chorizos* for a maximum of 3 days in a cool, airy place and then store them. If the air is humid and still, do as I did once in New York: hang them in front of a small fan by an open window overnight.

Before storing, smear the *chorizo* casings with a light coating of lard. It is better to freeze them at this stage. If left in the refrigerator they tend to dry out too much.

How often have you tried to skin a *chorizo* and had the filling stick to the casings? To remedy this, rub the outside of the *chorizo* with wet fingers. The skin will soon separate.

If you are buying ground pork from the butcher, ask him to let you see the disks so that you can choose the appropriate one and the meat will be neither too coarsely nor too finely ground. If you prefer to grind your own and have a grinding attachment to your electric mixer, you will probably have a choice of two disks (at least my KitchenAid has two), so the dilemma presents itself again: usually one is too fine and the other too coarse. So compromise. Grind first with the larger of the two disks and then use a food processor to process a small quantity at a time very briefly until you have the required medium texture. But don't process to a mush.

2 pounds ground pork (see note above)
½ pound ground pork fat
6 ounces *chiles guajillos or* 4 ounces *guajillos* (wide and mild) plus 2 ounces
    pulyas (narrow and hot)
1 cup mild vinegar, mixed with ½ cup strong vinegar
6 garlic cloves, peeled and roughly chopped
1 California bay leaf, broken up
leaves from 3 fresh marjoram sprigs *or* ¼ teaspoon dried
leaves from 3 fresh thyme sprigs *or* ¼ teaspoon dried
1 rounded teaspoon dried oregano, Mexican if possible
8 peppercorns, crushed
4 whole cloves, crushed
2 whole allspice, crushed
1¼ tablespoons coarse sea salt
7 feet of narrow pork casings, approximately, cut into 3 lengths (see note
    above)
a length of string or ⅛-inch-wide strips of dried corn husks for tying

Put the ground meat and fat into a glass, enamel, or stainless-steel bowl and set aside.

Remove stems, if any, from the dried *chiles*, slit them open, remove seeds and veins, and if you are using all wide *guajillos*, reserve some of the veins; otherwise discard. Put the *chiles* into a saucepan, cover with water, and bring to a simmer. Remove from the heat and allow to soak for 5 minutes. Drain the *chiles* and transfer them to an enamel or glass bowl. Cover with 1 cup of the vinegar and set aside to marinate for 1 hour.

Put the remaining vinegar into a blender jar together with the garlic, herbs, spices, and salt; blend until smooth. At the end of the soaking time, add about one third of the *chiles* to the blender jar and blend until smooth. Continue blending, adding more *chiles* and the vinegar in which they were soaking, until they have all been blended to a thick sauce. The sauce should be *picante*. If not, add some of the reserved veins and blend thoroughly. Add water only if it is absolutely necessary to release the blades of the blender.

Mix the *chile* paste well into the meat with your hands. Cover the bowl and set in the refrigerator overnight or for up to 18 hours, mixing and turning the mixture over from time to time. Stuff the sausage casing according to the directions on page 265.

CHORIZO VERDE (*Green Sausage*)

MAKES ABOUT 16 3½-INCH LINKS   TOLUCA

Green *chorizo* made of ground pork with herbs, greens, and *chiles* came into being in the villages around Toluca about 20 years ago—perhaps they evolved because of the skyrocketing prices of dried *chiles* and paprika; in any case, it was an inspired invention. The more rustic green *chorizos* strung up in front of the little food stands around the great recreational area La Marquesa, just outside Toluca, always tended to be overly fatty, while the commercial ones were either packed in plastic and to be avoided at all costs, tinted with artificial coloring agents, or seasoned with a poor-quality *pipián* mixture high in salts and msg. So make your own; they are delicious.

This type of *chorizo* should be eaten alone, without adornment, in a *taco* or with white rice, to appreciate all the flavors.

2 pounds ground pork (see note, page 266)
9 ounces ground pork fat
½ cup mild vinegar, mixed with ½ cup strong vinegar
6 garlic cloves, peeled and roughly chopped
1 teaspoon dried oregano, Mexican if possible
1 California bay leaf
3 whole cloves
10 peppercorns
1¼ tablespoons sea salt
¼ teaspoon cumin seed
¼ teaspoon coriander seed
2 *chiles poblanos*, veins and seeds removed
1 cup loosely packed, roughly chopped *cilantro*
1 cup loosely packed, roughly chopped flat-leaf parsley
2 cups firmly packed, roughly chopped Swiss chard leaves, stems removed
7 feet of narrow pork casings, approximately, cut into 3 lengths (see page 264)

Put the ground meat and fat into a glass, enamel, or stainless-steel bowl.

Put ½ cup of the vinegar into the blender jar and add the garlic, oregano, bay leaf, cloves, peppercorns, salt, cumin seeds, and coriander seeds; blend as finely as possible. Add the rest of the vinegar and the fresh *chiles*, blend, and gradually add the rest of the ingredients little by little until you have a smooth puree. Mix this into the meat with your hands until it is evenly distributed. Cover the bowl and refrigerate overnight to season, turning and mixing from time to time (while you are awake; don't set the alarm).

Prepare and stuff casings as for *chorizo de Huetamo* (page 266).

LONGANIZA DE VALLADOLID, YUCATÁN
(Yucatecan Smoked Sausage)

MAKES ABOUT 9 15-INCH LENGTHS

OTTO PENICHE,
CASA DE LOS ARCOS, VALLADOLID

This is a most unusual *longaniza*, highly seasoned, smoked, and formed in short, very skinny lengths. Traditionally they are made with pork, but beef is sometimes used, although it does not give such a good flavor or texture. Around Valladolid the *longaniza* is smoked over rustic, improvised smokers made out of oil drums with a bar across the top, over which the strips of *longaniza* are hung with their twisted ends hanging down over the fire so that the fat drains out. Yet you need the fat content at the beginning for flavor and texture. Green wood is burnt, and the process is slow, taking from 10 to 12 hours. The packing house that smokes my *chorizo* for me leaves it in for about 3 hours, but if you are using a home smoker—they vary tremendously in size and strength—you will have to experiment a little.

The flavor is, of course, at its peak just after the smoking, but for keeping any length of time it is advisable to coat the outside of these skinny sausages with lard and freeze them (they'll keep in the freezer for months). If you allow them to dry out too much without taking these steps, they will lose their deep red color, shrink away from the casings, and look very unappetizing.

3 ounces (scant ½ cup) *achiote* seeds
1½ tablespoons whole allspice
1 rounded tablespoon peppercorns
2 whole cloves
1 scant tablespoon dried Yucatecan oregano *or* 1 tablespoon Mexican
2 teaspoons sea salt
½ cup strong white vinegar
1 small purple onion, roughly chopped
8 small garlic cloves, peeled and roughly chopped
1¼ pounds boneless pork, thoroughly cleaned of any gristle and connective
   tissue and ground very finely twice
¼ pound pork fat, ground very finely twice
9 15-inch lengths of narrow pork casings (see page 264)

Grind the *achiote*, allspice, peppercorns, cloves, oregano, and salt a small amount at a time in an electric spice/coffee grinder. Sift through a fine sieve or strainer and grind the coarse residue a second time. Set aside.

269

Put the vinegar into a blender jar along with the onion and garlic and blend until smooth.

Put the ground meat and fat into a glass, enamel, or stainless-steel bowl and mix in the ground spices and blended ingredients thoroughly (with your hands if you can bear it; they will be stained orange, but it will wash off in a while). Cover and set aside in the bottom of the refrigerator or a cool place for 12 to 18 hours, turning and mixing from time to time.

Give the mixture a final stir before you start filling the casings. Stuff them only half full, leaving about 3 inches empty at each end of the lengths. Smooth the sausages out with your hands and then twist both ends of each length of casing firmly but not tightly. Smoke as directed above.

MORONGA MEXIQUENSE
(Blood Sausage from the State of Mexico)

MAKES ABOUT 5 POUNDS

Reading about, let alone making, *moronga* is not for the squeamish, and they should pass over the next few pages. But if you like French blood sausage, *boudin*, then its Mexican counterpart, and the recipes for preparing it for *tacos*, should be a revelation.

This *moronga* should not be confused with that offered in the more enterprising Mexican restaurants in the United States, for that, with perhaps a rare exception or two, is really Spanish *morcilla*, which I find tends to be dry and rather tasteless.

Of course, no average Mexican housewife would dream of making her own *moronga*—neither, for that matter, would the average French housewife make her own *pâtés* and *terrines*—but up until the 1930s recipes for it were included in cookbooks, presumably for country cooks who had to utilize everything that a home-butchered pig had to offer.

When the Spaniards introduced pigs into Mexico early in the colonial period and established pig farms in the Toluca Valley, traditional Spanish methods of making *chorizo* and *moronga* followed, but these have long since taken on Mexican characteristics.

Moronga, rellena, morcilla—by whatever name, they are sausages made of pork blood using the large intestines of the pig. Recipes for making them vary from region to region, but for me the most exotic of these is the *morcilla*, a specialty of Valladolid in Yucatán, where it is seasoned with *chirmole* (the *recado*, or seasoning paste of spices and burnt *chiles*) and enriched with pig's or calf's brains.

In Michoacán the *rellena* (called *zoricua* in the Tarascan language) is flavored uniquely with rue and the fragrant peel of the sweet lime (*lima*). In this case the wide casings are cut up and cooked with the blood and served like a stew in *tacos*. But recipes like these must wait for more detailed regional books.

The making of *moronga* was taught to me by Don Chabelo of Metepec, a village near Toluca, who has made them at home as a commercial enterprise for many years. It was he who showed me how to wash and reverse the intestines so that the fatty sheath covering them is turned inside to improve the flavor and richness of the *moronga*. Don Chabelo uses the tubular, narrow end of the stiff leaf of the *maguey* (see illustrations, pages 273 and 274) as a funnel to fill the casings and the sharp needle at the tip for testing to see if the *moronga* is cooked.

Don Chabelo receives his ingredients from understanding butchers, but here I was on my own facing a *mafioso* used to collecting heads, tripe, hooves, etc., daily without opposition.

My pork butcher friends all said, "Don't worry. Come to the *rastro* [slaughterhouse] at four o'clock, *en punto*, and I'll see that you get all you need." Of course I was there *en punto*; there was not a pig in sight, let alone a butcher. The water in the skinning vat was cold, only a few head of cattle were standing forlornly in the corrals, and there were lots of flies. With 4:30 came the first sign of life and a shirtless young man with a long knife tucked into his belt. "They must be here," he said, referring to pigs and men I supposed. "It is 4:30, they must be here," he repeated. He went and looked, disbelieving me, and then sat down and sharpened his knife. It was past 5:00 before the pigs began to arrive in pickups and large trucks; one by one the men who do the slaughtering began to saunter in. They couldn't start until the water was hot for the skinning; at 5:30 they started. Instead of killing one pig and eviscerating it as I had hoped, they killed several. Each one had to be skinned first and scraped thoroughly. I shifted my buckets about noisily, looked around for competition while the boys assured me, "*Ahorita, ahorita, Señora, no tardan.*" ("Right now, right now, Señora, they won't be long.") Finally the moment arrived, but just my luck, they chose to give me *las tripas* of slim young pigs with no fat. As the sun was setting at 6:30 I drove out of the *rastro* accompanied by waves and handshakes and "Anytime, *a sus órdenes, Señora.*"

Although the wide intestines (the narrow ones are kept for making *chorizo*) had been washed in the *rastro*, they were decidedly smelly. I washed them in several buckets of water, then turned them inside out, as Don Chabelo had instructed, so that the delicate fatty sheathing is inside when the *moronga* is cooked. Two more changes of water and yet a third into which I squeezed lots of bitter oranges, and then I left the skins among the casings overnight. (Limes, lemons, or vinegar can be substituted.) By morning, after another washing, they were completely odorless. *Note:* If you are leaving the casings to soak overnight, mix the ingredients into the blood and refrigerate to season.

Parts of the intestines are widened further by drapings of hundreds of little folds of skin on either side; this makes wonderfully bulbous *moronga*, quite grotesque but to the *aficionados* the best part.

Making *moronga* is not work for the fainthearted. If you do not kill your own pig, and you don't intend to go to the *rastro* for the blood, order it through your butcher; it will probably come packed, half frozen in ½-gallon containers (according to Jacques Pépin in *La Méthode*, page 208).

THE BROTH IN WHICH TO COOK THE *MORONGA*
a large pot that will hold 6 to 7 quarts of water with space to spare at the
    top
1 small bunch of fresh mint
8 scallions, with the green tops, roughly chopped
2 tablespoons sea salt

THE *MORONGA*
8 feet of large pork casings, approximately, cut into 2-foot lengths
2 quarts pig's blood
2 tablespoons sea salt
1 cup closely packed, finely chopped mint leaves
2 cups loosely packed, finely chopped green scallion tops
½ cup finely chopped white onion
1 tablespoon dried oregano, Mexican if possible
¼ cup finely chopped garlic
¾ pound pork fat, cut into strips ¼ inch square
approximately 8- to 9-inch lengths of string for tying

Heat the cooking water over low heat in a large pot, adding the mint, scallions, and salt while you prepare the *morongas*.

Run water through each length of the casings to make sure there are no leaks and no very weak parts liable to burst in cooking. If you find any, cut the casings at the weak part into two lengths. Tie one end of each length with string very firmly and hang up to drain while you mix the other ingredients, as follows.

If you are not using commercially packed blood (which will come strained), you will need to pass the blood through a coarse strainer. Discard stringy blood tissue and fat and break up the coagulated blood either with your hands

or by pressing it through the strainer into a deep bowl. Stir in the rest of the ingredients, except pork fat and string of course, and mix well.

Insert the sausage funnel into one length of casing and hold firmly—it is a loose fit and can slide off easily. Put a strip of the fat into the funnel and pour in about ½ cup of the blood mixture. Make sure that it goes to the bottom of the casing and that the greens and fat do not stick halfway—they sometimes get stuck in the folds and are difficult to dislodge. Use a dowel to make sure they get a good start down the casing and, if necessary, use a long piece of thin, blunt-tipped wood. If the lump of filling is stubborn, take both ends of the casings and swish the blood back up and down until it is dislodged. Proceed, using a piece of the fat every time you pour in a little blood. Also be careful to stir up the blood mixture every time you dip the cup into it as the leaves and other ingredients tend to drop to the bottom. *Do not overfill the casings*, or they will burst in the cooking. Leave about 2 inches unfilled at the end to allow for expansion and to tie another very tight knot with the string.

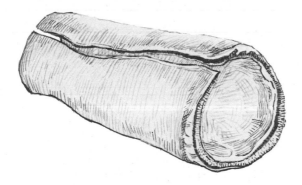

Lifting the lengths of *moronga* by both ends, place carefully in the water, which should be just breaking into a simmer. Do not let it heat any more than that. Longer, slower cooking will ensure that (unless the *moronga* are overfilled or have an undetected weak spot) the *moronga* will not burst open and will be softer and moister. Leave to cook about 1 hour for the narrower casings and up to 1¼ to 1½ hours for the more bulbous parts.

Test by pricking the skin with a coarse needle. If the liquid that comes out is a reddish-brown, continue cooking. If it's colorless, then the *moronga* is done. Remove and drain; see the following recipes for serving. It is not advisable to keep the *moronga* for more than a day or two in the refrigerator; after that time it should be frozen (for up to a month or so).

TACOS DE MORONGA *(Blood Sausage Tacos)*

MAKES 12 TACOS

Freshly made, tender *moronga* is a luxury in the city, but it's always available in the villages around Toluca in the state of Mexico. To my mind, the best way to appreciate its flavor and texture is in these simple *tacos*. They make an excellent *botana* before a traditional *comida* to accompany a glass of *tequila* with salt and lemon.

3 tablespoons lard
1 pound *moronga mexiquense* (page 270), roughly chopped with skin (skin optional)
12 4-inch warm corn *tortillas*
6 tablespoons finely chopped white onion, approximately
6 tablespoons roughly chopped *cilantro*, approximately

Melt the lard in a frying pan, add the *moronga*, and fry over very low heat, stirring from time to time, until the fat pieces in the sausage are slightly golden and exuding their lard—about 10 minutes.

Place a good 2 tablespoons of the *moronga* across a *tortilla*, sprinkle with a little of the onion and *cilantro*, roll up loosely, and eat immediately. This is pan-to-mouth food.

MORONGA EN SALSA VERDE
(Blood Sausage in Green Sauce)

SERVES 4   CENTRAL MEXICO

This is a popular, very earthy, low-budget dish in central Mexico. It is traditionally served just with freshly made corn *tortillas*.

3 tablespoons lard
1 pound *moronga mexiquense* (page 270), unskinned, cut into ½-inch slices
3 tablespoons finely chopped white onion
2 cups *salsa de tomate verde, cocida* (page 337)
sea salt to taste

Heat the lard in a frying pan, add the *moronga* slices, and cook over gentle heat until well browned on the bottom—about 5 minutes. Turn the slices over, add the onion, and continue frying and shaking the pan until browned on the second side—3 to 4 minutes. (Take care; the onion should be translucent and wilted but not browned.) Stir in the sauce, taste for salt, and reduce over fairly high heat, shaking the pan and scraping the bottom to prevent sticking—about 5 minutes. The sauce should be of a medium consistency and lightly coat the back of a wooden spoon.

ASIENTO

Asiento is the name given in Oaxaca to the residue left in the *chicharrón* (pork skin) frying vats: little bits of pork skin and fat fried to a rich dark brown in an equal volume of lard.

Asiento is used in the food of Oaxaca to enrich corn *masa*, for *chochoyotes* (page 54), for example, or to smear over *tortillas* for that rich and delicious Oaxacan snack of *Tortillas con Asiento* (page 33).

If you don't live near a *chicharrón* maker, the easiest substitute is to follow the instructions for making lard, (see page 276). Pour off the clear, light-colored liquid lard, leaving behind in the pan the little crispy bits of fat and an equal quantity of lard. Continue cooking over low heat until both are a deep *café au lait* color—about 10 to 15 minutes—taking care not to let the fat burn. Set aside to cool until the lard has thickened slightly. *Asiento* will keep indefinitely in the freezer compartment of the refrigerator.

MANTECA DE CERDO (*Pork Lard*)

MAKES ABOUT 4 CUPS, JUST UNDER 1¼ POUNDS

Pork lard is used extensively in traditional Mexican cooking, and many of the best cooks I know still insist on using it (and they are healthy and slim), even when most people have switched to vegetable oils. Be that as it may, lard is absolutely indispensable for the making of *tamales* and for frying beans, and it is preferable for frying any of the *masa antojitos*; oil can be substituted in many of the *moles* or stews or for cooking rice.

The flavor of homemade lard is incomparable, and what's more, you know you are not getting any preservatives. It is easy to make and keeps indefinitely in the refrigerator.

Paula Wolfert, in her masterpiece of a book *The Cooking of South-West France*, says, "An interesting fact I discovered in a U.S. Department of Agriculture publication—Handbook 8-4 (revised 1979)—is that rendered poultry fat (goose, duck, and chicken) contains 9 percent cholesterol, and lard contains 10 percent, compared with butter's 22 percent. Since one needs less poultry fat, oil, or lard than butter to sauté meat or vegetables, one will ingest far less saturated fat if these cooking media are used instead of butter. One needs less of these because butter breaks down and burns at a high temperature, whereas the others do not."

2 pounds unsalted fatback or pork fat pieces

Heat the oven to 325°. Have ready two heavy ovenproof skillets. Cut the fat into small cubes, discarding any pieces of tough skin. Put about one quarter of this amount into a food processor container and process for a few seconds to break it down thoroughly. (Do not force the processor by putting in too much at once.) Transfer the fat to one of the pans and continue with the rest.

Put the pans onto the top oven shelf and cook until the fat has rendered out—about 20 to 25 minutes. Do not let the lard color too much; when cold, it should be a creamy white. You may need to stir it occasionally as some fat sticks to the pan. Strain into heatproof containers and discard the crisp fatty residue (or give it to the birds). Set aside to cool.

MANITAS DE PUERCO EN ESCABECHE
(Pickled Pig's Feet)

SERVES 4 TO 6

Lightly pickled pig's feet are prepared in many parts of Mexico without those differences that mark many other regional dishes. It is best to prepare them at least one or more days before eating.

My preferred way of serving pig's feet is that of the eastern part of Michoacán, smothered with lots of pickled vegetables and accompanied by crusty rolls. A small portion of this makes a very refreshing lunch dish, an appetizer before a rather heavy *comida* such as *mole*, or a main course in hot weather. The feet can be boned and the meat chopped to put on top of *tostadas*, smothered with shredded lettuce, *chile* strips, and sliced avocado and tomato.

In this dish, as well as for many others in Mexico, a light fruity vinegar should be used.

4 pig's feet (about 3½ pounds), halved lengthwise and each piece cut into 2
1 small white onion, roughly chopped
1 garlic clove, peeled
1 tablespoon sea salt
1 tablespoon strong vinegar
3½ cups fruity vinegar
2 teaspoons dried oregano, Mexican if possible
2 California bay leaves
4 fresh thyme sprigs *or* ¼ teaspoon dried
4 fresh marjoram sprigs *or* ¼ teaspoon dried
4 canned *chiles jalapeños en escabeche*, cut into strips
2 tablespoons liquid from the can
2 medium carrots, trimmed, scraped, sliced, and blanched (optional, if not using the pickled vegetables mentioned in note above)

Scrub the feet well and put into a deep pan with the onion, garlic, salt, and strong vinegar. Cover well with water and cook over low heat until tender but not falling apart—about 2½ to 3 hours. Remember that as they get cold the gelatinous parts stiffen up, so cook long enough, but not too much, so as to retain those interesting textures.

Rinse the meat briefly, put into a glass or china bowl, and cover with the rest of the ingredients. Taste for salt and store in a cool place, stirring them and turning them over from time to time and making sure that they are immersed in the vinegar. Serve as suggested above.

277

QUESO DE PUERCO (*Head Cheese*)

Although in some areas the pig's head is used almost exclusively for making *pozole,* in the state of Mexico and neighboring regions it is turned into head cheese. The cooked and boned meat is packed down into a deep basket (see illustration) called a *tompiate* or *tompeate,* the word coming from the Nahuatl *tompiatl* and generally referring to a basket made of woven palm into which the contents "fit like a glove" (*Diccionario de Aztecismos,* 1974). The contents are pressed down with a heavy weight and left overnight to jell and become compact.

Queso de puerco is often served as a first course along with *chiles en escabeche* and lime quarters, or pickled *chipotles.* Thickly sliced, it is packed into a hefty *torta* and roughly chopped as a topping for *tostadas.*

Although *queso de puerco* can be eaten the next day, I prefer to leave it for a day or so more so that it seasons well. It will last several days in the refrigerator, provided the weather is not too hot and sticky. Because of the vinegar, it would last longer, but the meat begins to taste a little "warmed over."

You can pack this into any deep mold; I often use a *soufflé* dish when I don't have any *tompeates* on hand. If you are using a basket or other straining mold, place it, before filling it, into a mold into which it will just fit so that the head cheese can jell in the seasoned liquid that would otherwise be strained out, which would result in lost flavor.

THE HEAD
1 small or ½ large pig's head (6 to 7 pounds), cut into 8 pieces
1 medium white onion, roughly sliced
4 garlic cloves, peeled and crushed
6 peppercorns
2 fresh thyme sprigs *or* ⅛ teaspoon dried
2 fresh marjoram sprigs *or* ⅛ teaspoon dried
2 tablespoons sea salt

THE SEASONING
½ cup strong vinegar
½ cup mild vinegar
6 garlic cloves, peeled and minced
3 small California bay leaves, crumbled
4 whole cloves, crushed
20 peppercorns, crushed
leaves from 4 fresh thyme sprigs *or* scant ¼ teaspoon dried
leaves from 4 fresh marjoram sprigs *or* scant ¼ teaspoon dried
1½ cups reduced broth from cooking head
3 canned *chiles jalapeños en escabeche*, roughly chopped (optional)
2 tablespoons liquid from the *chile* can (optional)
sea salt to taste

First prepare the head for cooking. Rinse well. Scrub the skin until perfectly clean, singe off any hairs, and wash the ears out well. Put the head pieces in a deep pot with the rest of the ingredients, cover well with water, and bring to a simmer. Cook at a fast simmer until the meat can easily be slipped off the bone but is not overcooked and limp—about 2½ to 3 hours.

Drain the head pieces in a colander, reserving the broth. Strain the broth back into the saucepan and reduce over high heat to about 2 cups. Set aside.

When the head is cool enough to handle, carefully remove all the bones, making sure that no little splinters remain. Discard about two thirds of the pure fat, but of course leave the ear cartilage and the skin in with the rest of the meat; cut into roughly ½-inch squares. There should be about 7 cups of meat.

Put the meat and the rest of the seasoning ingredients, except the *chiles*, their juice, and the salt, into a pan and mix well. Heat over medium heat until the mixture comes to a boil, remove from the heat, stir in the *chiles* and their juice, and taste for salt. (Remember that cold foods need to be more highly seasoned.) Transfer the meat to a mold, cover with a plate, and put a heavy weight on top. When the meat is cool, store in the refrigerator overnight. If using a *tompeate* with a drawstring around the top, tie tightly. If there is no drawstring, just fold the basket like a package and weigh down.

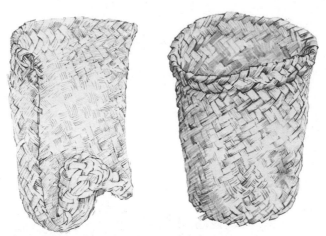

Mexican butchers often sew the top of the *tompeate* with a long, curved needle and strong cord, but this is not really necessary as the weight holds the folds of the basket well in place.

CHICHARRÓN *(Fried Pigskin)*

Puffy, crackly pork skins, called *chicharrón* in Mexico, are without doubt the most popular of *botanas* (snacks), but making them requires patience and know-how.

Every butcher who kills his own pigs or has them killed at the slaughterhouse will have a pile of undulating, golden sheets on his counter a day or so after the killing, and you will be offered a sampling as you pass, no matter how early in the morning. As soon as the pig is killed and the bristles and hairs are shaved off, it is skinned. The fat is shaved off closely at both ends, and any remaining fat in the saddle and stomach area is scored in crisscross fashion. It is then hung in any airy place to dry overnight. The next day the skins are piled into vats of boiling lard, and the long, slow cooking process takes place—2 hours, say, for a small, tender pig and 3½ to 4 hours for a big, tough one. No seasoning is added to the boiling lard. Once cooked, the skins are drained on metal screens. When cool, they are once again plunged into much hotter lard, and in moments they will have puffed up into millions of crisp little cells. Drained again, they are then ready to eat.

You can choose whether you want thin, fatless *chicharrón* from the shoulder or buttock area or the fattier middle part, the stomach and sides, while the saddle tends to have a little meat still attached. It depends on your tastes when eating them as a snack or what the recipe calls for: *en escabeche*—thin; *en salsa verde*—fattier; etc.

The quality of *chicharrón* available in the United States varies tremendously: occasionally a butcher in a Mexican market or supermarket will prepare his own with varying degrees of prowess, while some of the packaged brands can be stale and tough . . . and expensive to boot.

Apart from the following recipes, *chicharrón* can be ground to rough crumbs and added to *masa* for *gorditas*, or stuffed into *gorditas* with a *chile* sauce, or added to the ground meat for meatballs to make them rich and spongy, cooked with *frijoles de olla* (page 179), or used as a topping for a *pozole* in Guerrero.

ENSALADA DE CHICHARRÓN *(Fried Pigskin Salad)*

MAKES ENOUGH FILLING FOR 12 SMALL *TORTILLAS* TO SERVE 4

This salad can either be served alone, accompanied by warm corn *tortillas*, or as part of a mixed appetizer plate. If the *chicharrón* is broken into small pieces, it makes a good filling for *tacos*, or (untraditionally) you could wrap it in lettuce leaves as part of a mixed *hors d'oeuvre*.

The avocado for this recipe should be ripe but not too soft.

This recipe has to be prepared at the last moment and eaten almost immediately; otherwise it gets rather mushy.

1 cup (about 6 ounces) finely chopped, unpeeled tomatoes
¼ cup roughly chopped *cilantro*
2 heaped tablespoons finely chopped white onion
2 *chiles serranos*, very finely chopped, with seeds
a little sea salt
3 ounces *chicharrón*, broken into 1-inch pieces
1 medium avocado, cut into small cubes (⅔ cup)
1 tablespoon fresh lime juice (optional)

Put the tomatoes, *cilantro*, onion, and fresh *chiles* into a bowl, add a little salt, and stir well. Add the *chicharrón* and avocado pieces and, when well mixed, sprinkle with optional lime juice.

CHICHARRÓN EN SALSA VERDE
(Fried Pigskin in Green Sauce)

SERVES 4

This is one of the most popular *almuerzo* (brunch) dishes and is far less heavy in calories and cholesterol than, say, eggs Benedict. While most people enjoy thin, crispy pieces of pigskin, softening them up in a hot sauce is more of an acquired taste—but this is one of the addictive foods of Mexico.

Do not choose the thinnest *chicharrón* for this dish; you will need a little of the fat on it.

1½ pounds (about 33 medium) *tomate verde*
4 to 5 (to taste) *chiles serranos*
1 garlic clove, peeled and roughly chopped
¼ cup loosely packed, roughly chopped *cilantro*
2 tablespoons lard or safflower oil
3 tablespoons finely chopped white onion
sea salt to taste
6 ounces *chicharrón,* broken into squares about 1½ inches

Remove the husks from the *tomate verde* and rinse well. Put into a saucepan with the fresh *chiles*, cover with water, and bring to a simmer. Continue simmering until soft but not falling apart, about 10 minutes. Drain *tomate verde* and transfer with the *chiles* and ¼ cup of the cooking water to a blender jar. Add the garlic and *cilantro* and blend until smooth.

Heat the lard in a frying pan, add the onion, and fry gently, without browning, for 1 minute. Add the blended sauce and fry over high heat, stirring from time to time, until reduced and thickened—about 7 minutes. Add salt to taste and the pieces of *chicharrón* and continue cooking over medium heat until the *chicharrón* is just soft—about 5 minutes, depending on thickness and quality.

Serve with corn *tortillas* and a dollop of *frijoles refritos* (page 180).

CHICHARRÓN EN SALSA DE JITOMATE
(Fried Pigskin in Tomato Sauce)

MAKES ENOUGH FILLING FOR 12 SMALL *TACOS* TO SERVE 4

This is an equally popular recipe for *chicharrón* with tomatoes instead of *tomate verde*. It is usually served for *almuerzo* (brunch) with hot *tortillas*, but a few refried beans would not be out of place. If the *chicharrón* pieces are cut smaller, it would do as a filling for *tacos*.

The sauce can be made ahead and the *chicharrón* added about 5 minutes before serving—in any case, it is supposed to be soft and not crisp for this type of dish.

⅔ cup water, approximately
1½ pounds tomatoes, broiled (see page 450)
2 *chiles serranos*, broiled (see page 472)
1 garlic clove, peeled and roughly chopped
1 tablespoon melted lard or safflower oil
2 tablespoons finely chopped white onion
¼ pound *chicharrón*, fatty and thin (see page 280), broken up into pieces
    about 1 to 1½ inches square
sea salt to taste

Put ⅔ cup water into a blender jar and add the unpeeled tomatoes, fresh *chiles*, and garlic; blend for a few seconds to make a textured puree. Heat the lard in a deep frying or sauté pan, add the onion, and fry, without browning, for about 1 minute. Add the sauce and cook over fairly high heat, stirring and scraping the bottom of the pan to prevent sticking, until reduced and thickened—about 5 minutes. Add the *chicharrón* and stir well—the sauce should cover them; if not, add a little more water. Add salt to taste and cook for 5 minutes more or until the *chicharrón* is quite soft.

BEEF

(Res)

Cuts of Beef

A   Pescuezo ~ Shoulder
B   Diezmillo ~ Chuck
C   Pecho ~ Brisket
D   Entrecot ~ Roast Beef
E   Agujas ~ Short Ribs
F   Filete ~ Fillet Steaks
G   Falda ~ Flank
H   Aguayón ~ Steaks
J   Cuete ~ Rump
J,K Chambarete ~ Shank
L   Cola de Buey ~ Oxtail

Carne Asada a la Tampiqueña (Tampico Grilled Meat)

La Sabana ("The Sheet")

Machaca (Dried and Shredded Beef)

Carne Machaca, y con Huevo (Dried Beef Filling with Scrambled Egg)

Cocido Oaxaqueño (Oaxacan Beef Stew)

Cocido o Caldo de Res Michoacano (Brothy Beef Stew)

Ropa Vieja (Shredded Leftover Meat and Vegetables)

Salpicón de Res (Shredded Meat Cooked with Tomatoes, Chiles, and Cilantro)

Carne Enchilada (Chile-Seasoned Grilled Meat)

Chichilo Negro (Oaxacan Black Beef Stew)

Vitualla (A Stew of Beef, Rice, and Fruit)

Carnita con Chile (Beef in Green Chile Sauce)

Aporreada de Huetamo (Dried Beef Hash)

Bifsteces en Chile Pasilla (Thin Steaks in Pasilla Sauce)

Bifstek Enchorizado (Chopped Steak Flavored with Achiote)

Pacholas (Ground Meat Patties)

Carne Apache (Mexican Steak Tartare)

Riñones en Salsa de Chile Pasilla (Kidneys in Pasilla Sauce)

Panza de Res (Beef Tripe)

Panza de Res en Verde (Tripe in Green Sauce)

Panza Guisada para Tacos (Shredded Tripe for Tacos)

While beef is by far the most important meat in the northern regions of Mexico, where much of the land is devoted to cattle raising, farther south pork and chicken take over, with mutton and goat following some way behind. I am, of course, referring to the typical everyday foods, not to those of the cosmopolitan communities of the capital or those of the steakhouses dotted around the larger cities.

Beef is rarely aged—it is in fact preferred fresh—and therefore tends to be rather tough but of a very good flavor, and this is reflected in the traditional cooking methods. For instance, you would not find a grilled thick porterhouse steak (except in the steakhouses) on a provincial menu. *Bifsteks*, or *bifsteces*, are cut thin from any fleshy part of the animal and then pounded even thinner to tenderize them. Meats like brisket for soups and stews are first boiled—often in a pressure cooker; otherwise they would take ages to cook— and then *guisado* (cooked with seasonings) in a *chile* sauce or put with vegetables into a soup or shredded and seasoned for a *salpicón* (page 298).

Cecina or *tasajo* (in Oaxaca) is fresh beef cut very thinly into large strips, salted, and then air-dried for a day so that the strips are still flexible and somewhat moist. The beef is then grilled—rather leathery but with an excellent flavor—and eaten with a sauce and corn *tortillas* or shredded roughly and cooked with tomatoes, *chiles*, and eggs for *aporreada*. In the North, thinly sliced and salted beef is dried until almost stiff and then pounded to a fluff for *machaca*. It is easy to do your own—much better than buying beef jerky—and makes good ethnic picnic food.

Although kidneys and liver are used, they are not as widely popular as tripe, which is used nationally in the famous soup/stew *menudo* recipes that vary in different regions of the country. Oxtail is sold with offal as is the much touted *arrachera*, the diaphragm or skirt steak, called *fajita* in Texas. It is considered the butchers' cut; they know how to appreciate the flavor of the lesser-known pieces of meat.

To my taste, the most succulent and delicious meat of all is from a pit-barbecued cow's head. The whole head is packed neatly inside folded *maguey* leaves, and the only seasoning is salt. In eastern Michoacán it is called *rostro* (face) and is much appreciated. Many of the Mexican cuts of beef are recognizable along with their American counterparts, but the confusing thing is that in every region a cut of meat is likely to have a different name. (See illustration on page 285.)

CARNE ASADA A LA TAMPIQUEÑA
(Tampico Grilled Meat)

SERVES 6

Two of the most popular meat dishes in Mexico are undoubtedly *carne asada a la Tampiqueña* and *la sabana*, both of which were invented by the founder of the Loredo chain of restaurants, Jose Inez Loredo. Born in Tampico, he came to Mexico City in 1941 to found the Tampico Club, which was first famous for its seafood and then for these two meat dishes, using the best produce from his native region.

The recipe for *carne asada* has been interpreted in many different ways by other restaurateurs and no doubt has undergone modifications in the Loredo restaurants themselves, but here is the recipe as it is today.

A thin strip of butterflied fillet of beef is quickly seared and served with two *enchiladas verdes,* strips of *chiles poblanos,* a square of grilled *panela* cheese, with a small bowl of *frijoles charros* on the side and a *salsa mexicana* passed separately. It is perfect for the restaurant kitchen that has many of those already prepared ingredients and the happiest example that I know of a "combination plate"—usually an anathema to me.

For this recipe a thick slice of fillet steak about 3 inches wide is butterflied out to a strip about ¼ inch thick.

6 6-ounce slices *filet mignon,* cleaned of any gristle or connective tissue
salt and freshly ground pepper to taste
squeeze of fresh lime juice (optional)

With the cut side of the meat toward you and holding it firmly on top, make a horizontal cut through the center of the meat to within ¼ inch of the other side. Open meat out and cut on both sides, turning the meat (unless you are ambidextrous), and make a second cut to butterfly it on both sides. Turn meat over and cut again. Continue turning and cutting until you have an even strip of steak that is about ¼ inch thick. Season the meat lightly on

both sides, and if you're not going to cook it immediately, roll it up and set aside in a cool place.

When ready to cook, heat a very lightly greased griddle over very high heat. Lightly sprinkle water on the griddle; it should sizzle and jump fiercely when the griddle's ready. Squeeze a little lime juice on both sides of the meat and quickly sear and brown the meat on each side. It will take only about 2 minutes on each side for medium-rare.

Accompaniments

The *Chile* Strips

    4 large *chiles poblanos* or Anaheim *chiles*
    3 tablespoons safflower oil
    1 medium white onion, cut into thin crescents
    4 garlic cloves, peeled
    3 California bay leaves
    6 peppercorns
    ½ cup water
    3 tablespoons white wine vinegar
    sea salt to taste

Cut a slice off the top of the fresh *chiles*, with the stalk, if any, and discard. Do not skin the *chiles*, but cut them into halves and scrape out and discard the seeds and veins. Cut into narrow strips. Heat the oil in a frying pan and add the *chile* strips, onion crescents, garlic, bay leaves, and peppercorns; cover the pan and simmer for about 8 minutes, shaking the pan from time to time. Add the rest of the ingredients with salt to taste and cook, uncovered, for 5 minutes over medium heat. The *chiles* should still be *al dente*. Set aside to season if time permits and reheat when the meat is cooked and ready to serve.

These *chile* strips may be prepared ahead and in fact improve in flavor as they sit.

Enchiladas Verdes

    12 small corn *tortillas*
    1½ cups *salsa de tomate verde, cocida* (page 337)
    ½ cup crumbled *queso fresco, añejo*, or Romano cheese
    1 medium white onion, cut into thin crescents

Follow recipe (page 21) in *tortilla* section. After the *tortilla* has been fried and dipped into the sauce, do not fill with chicken. Double over and sprinkle with crumbled *queso fresco* and white onion cut into crescents.

Salsa Mexicana

    1½ cups *salsa mexicana* (page 351), approximately
    1 medium avocado, peeled, pitted, and diced

Sprinkle sauce with cubed avocado.

Queso Asado (Grilled Cheese)

In Mexico a square of *queso panela* is used; it has a high melting point, so it can be grilled and still hold its shape.

Cut cheese into 6 squares about 3 inches in size. Grill briefly on both sides until lightly browned just before serving the dish.

Frijoles Charros Estilo Loredo (Loredo's Charro Beans)

APPROXIMATELY 5 TO 6 SERVINGS

 3 tablespoons lard or safflower oil
 1¼ cups (about ¾ pound) roughly chopped tomatoes, unpeeled
 ¼ cup finely chopped white onion
 3 (or to taste) *chiles serranos*, finely chopped
 3½ cups black *frijoles de olla* and their broth (about ½ pound dry)
 sea salt to taste
 2 ounces *chicharrón*, broken into small pieces

Heat the lard, add the tomatoes, onion, and fresh *chiles*, and fry for about 5 minutes, stirring to prevent sticking. Add the beans and their broth a little at a time, mashing them down to a coarsely textured puree (or blend them very briefly). They should be of a soupy consistency; if not, add more water until they are. Add salt to taste. Just before serving, stir *chicharrón* pieces into each bowl.

LA SABANA (*"The Sheet"*)

SERVES 1   TAMPICO

If you order *sabana* at one of the Loredo restaurants, you will find yourself with a piece of beef fillet pounded into a super-thin oval shape about 12 inches long and 7 inches wide. It will have been cooked for one instant on a very hot griddle and served with some fried black beans and a bitingly hot *salsa arriera*.

1 6-ounce slice *filet mignon,* about 2½ to 3 inches wide
⅛ teaspoon fresh lime juice, approximately
sea salt and freshly ground pepper to taste
frijoles fritos (see below)
salsa arriera (see page 292)

Place the beef between two sheets of plastic wrap and pound, pushing it outward as you go, to a rough oval shape. Smooth the edges with a slanting thumbnail as demonstrated by the chef in the photo. Fold into a package and pound out again to the required size. Peel off the top plastic wrap and replace with wax paper. Turn meat over and replace second sheet of plastic with wax paper; set aside until ready to use.

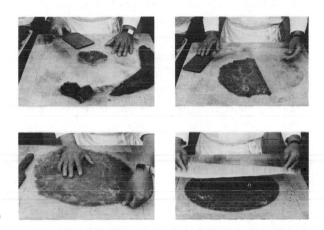

Heat a griddle. When very hot, grease lightly. Remove top paper. Sprinkle the exposed side of the meat with lime juice and salt and pepper and lay it face down, with the aid of the paper, on the griddle. Strip off the bottom paper. Cook for about 2 seconds, flip the meat over with two spatulas so it will not break in the middle, and cook for 2 seconds more. Serve immediately, flat if possible, on a large plate with the *frijoles* and the sauce passed separately.

Note: Plastic wrap does not break when pounded but does melt when heated; thus the change of paper.

Frijoles Fritos

Cook black beans *de olla* (page 179) and refry (page 180), but stop when you have a very loose paste.

Salsa Arriera (Muledrivers' Sauce)

This very hot, concentrated sauce is to be passed separately. A lot of raw fresh *serranos* are ground or very finely chopped, moistened with fresh lime juice, and seasoned with salt.

MACHACA *(Dried and Shredded Beef)*

MAKES ABOUT 1 POUND OR 4½ CUPS WHEN SHREDDED   SONORA

Carne seca or *machaca* in Sonora is made from thinly cut sirloin that is simply salted and air-dried; it has a great concentrated beef flavor and can become addictive (unless you are on a salt-free diet). It is easy to make, and the results will be superior to that made commercially on either side of the border. If there is too much humidity in the air, hang the beef in front of an electric fan or in a very low oven. Of course, if you can, it is better to use a charcoal or wood grill for the very brief cooking, but if that is impossible an ordinary broiler will do.

You may want to make a smaller quantity at first, but bear in mind that the meat's weight reduces by about half, and besides, once shredded it will last almost indefinitely.

2 pounds sirloin steak, cut about ¼ inch thick, with some fat
3 rounded tablespoons medium-ground sea salt, approximately

Trim the meat of any gristle, skin, or connective tissue and sprinkle with the salt on both sides. Pierce the slice of meat in two places at the top of the slice and hang up with string in a very airy, dry place. It will take about 3 days to dry out (see note above).

To serve, have ready a hot grill or broiler and sear the steaks for about 2 minutes on each side—the color will turn from deep mulberry red to a golden brown.

Cover the meat with cold water and leave to soak for about 30 minutes. Remove and drain. Cut the meat into approximately 1½-inch pieces and put 3 to 4 pieces, no more, into a blender jar. Blend at high speed for about 30 seconds, until the meat is reduced to fine threads. Continue with the rest and spread out to dry. When it is thoroughly dried out again, you can store it in the vegetable drawer of the refrigerator.

CARNE MACHACA, Y CON HUEVO
(Dried Beef Filling with Scrambled Egg)

MAKES 4 SCANT CUPS

Carne machaca and *machaca con huevo* are popular fillings for *burras*, (page 387) or *chivichangas* in Sonora. This quantity should be enough for 12 *burras* or 15 *chivichangas*, depending of course on the size of the wheat flour tortilla used. *Carne machaca* can be prepared ahead and just heated through with a little more water, but if you're adding eggs, do that at the last minute. *Salsa de jitomate norteña* (recipe follows) is the right accompaniment.

4 tablespoons lard or safflower oil
1 scant cup diced cooked potatoes
3 garlic cloves, peeled and finely chopped
½ cup finely chopped white onion
½ pound (about 2¼ cups) *carne seca*, (see preceding recipe)
2 Anaheim *chiles*, charred, peeled, and cut into strips (see page 472)
2 medium tomatoes, tops removed and grated
¼ cup water
freshly ground pepper to taste

CON HUEVO
3 eggs, lightly beaten

Heat the lard in a heavy frying pan, add the potatoes, and fry until a pale gold; remove from fat and set aside. Stir the garlic into the hot lard and fry for a few seconds; remove. Add the onion and fry without browning for about 30 seconds. Add the dried meat, stir well, and fry for 1 minute more. Add the fresh *chiles* and tomatoes and fry for 1 minute. Add the water, cover the pan, and cook for 3 minutes, shaking the pan from time to time to prevent sticking. Stir in the reserved potatoes and garlic, season with pepper, and heat through, stirring well, for about 1 minute.

If you're using eggs, stir in the eggs with the potatoes, garlic, and pepper and cook until the eggs are set.

SALSA DE JITOMATE NORTEÑA
(Northern Tomato Sauce)

MAKES 1½ CUPS

This is a very simple, fairly *picante* tomato sauce to be used with *burras* and *chivichangas*, especially those made with *machaca* (preceding recipe). This sauce can be made ahead and will keep for several days in the refrigerator if the weather is not too hot and humid.

1 pound (about 2 large) very ripe tomatoes
¼ cup water
3 *chiles piquin or* any dried hot *chile* to taste
2 garlic cloves, peeled and roughly chopped
sea salt to taste

Cover the tomatoes with cold water, bring to a simmer, and continue simmering until the skin is splitting and the flesh of the tomatoes is soft—about 15 minutes, depending on size. Put the water into a blender jar, add the whole *chiles* and garlic, and blend until fairly smooth. Add the drained whole tomatoes (remove the skins or not, as you like) and blend until almost smooth. Mix in salt to taste.

COCIDO OAXAQUEÑO (Oaxacan Beef Stew)

SERVES 8

Every region of Mexico has its meat and vegetable stew, with slight variations in ingredients or the way in which it is served. Oaxaca's version, preceded by a course of white rice, and accompanied by a powerful *chile* sauce, provides a wonderful autumn or winter dish for a crowd—for it is hardly worth making for two. Traditionally it is served there in courses: first the broth, then the rice (which is cooked separately), then a plate of vegetables, and finally the shredded meat with corn *tortillas* and the *chile* sauce. I always prefer to use dry chick-peas instead of the canned ones, in which case they should be put to soak the night before.

Any lean cut of meat that will shred well may be used, and I prefer to add a bone or two to give the broth more substance to back up its wonderful flavor.

THE NIGHT BEFORE
¼ pound (⅔ cup) dry chick-peas

THE NEXT DAY
2 pounds boneless stewing beef (see note on page 294)
1 piece shinbone plus a piece of porous marrow bone
1 small head of garlic, scored around the middle
1 small white onion, roughly sliced
6 large fresh mint sprigs
6 large *cilantro* sprigs
sea salt to taste
1 scant teaspoon dried oregano, Oaxacan if possible
6 ounces carrots (about 3 medium), trimmed, scraped, and cut into quarters
  lengthwise
1 medium *chayote* (about ¾ pound), peeled and cut into thick slices
4 small red bliss potatoes, cut into halves, unpeeled
1 small cabbage (about 1 pound), cut into 8 wedges
¼ pound green beans, trimmed and cut into halves
½ pound (about 2) zucchini, trimmed and cut into slices lengthwise
1 ripe plantain (about ½ pound), cut into diagonal slices, unpeeled
1 recipe *arroz blanco* (page 122)
salsa de chile pasilla de Oaxaca (page 342)
corn *tortillas*

Put the meat and bones into a large pot with the garlic, onion, mint, and *cilantro*. Strain the chick-peas and add the soaking water to the pot; tie the chick-peas loosely into a piece of cheesecloth and add to the pot. Cover with enough water to come about 2 inches above the meat. Add salt to taste, cover, and bring to a simmer. Continue simmering until the meat is tender, about 1 to 1½ hours. Strain, reserving the broth. Set the meat aside to cool. When the meat is cool enough to handle, shred, removing any connective tissue or gristle. Sprinkle with the oregano, cover, and keep warm.

The vegetables should be poached in two batches to ensure that they are cooked until just tender, neither *al dente* nor mushy—about 20 minutes for the carrots, *chayote*, and potatoes and about 8 minutes for the cabbage and green beans. Zucchini will take about 10 minutes and plantains about 15 minutes, depending on ripeness. Keep them warm on a shallow serving platter on which they can be arranged attractively. Serve immediately as suggested above or in any other order.

Note: Any shredded meat left over can be made into *salpicón* (page 298) or *ropa vieja* (page 297).

COCIDO O CALDO DE RES MICHOACANO
(Brothy Beef Stew)

SERVES 6 TO 8   SEÑORA LIVIER RUIZ DE SUAREZ

This is a hearty soup/stew made with various cuts of beef, on the bone, with a marrow bone and a piece of udder to enrich the broth. Traditionally, and that is the way I think it is best, it is cooked in a large earthenware pot. It is served in large bowls with a *picante* tomato sauce (page 340) and hot corn *tortillas*. Señora Suarez, my mentor in Michoacán cooking, says that she will often dangle a cheesecloth bag of rice, loosely packed, into the broth for a delicately flavored *morisqueta* served before the stew—another one-pot meal. The vegetables should be well stewed, not falling apart or *al dente*.

2½ pounds beef—shin, brisket, and short ribs—cut into 2-inch cubes
1 large marrow bone
1 small udder (optional; if available)
1 small white onion, roughly chopped
3 garlic cloves, peeled
sea salt to taste
1 medium *jícama* (about ¾ pound), peeled and cubed
1 medium *chayote* (about ¾ pound), peeled and cut into wedges
2 medium carrots, trimmed, scraped, and cut into 4 lengthwise
1 small cabbage, cut into wedges
6 very small potatoes, unpeeled
2 small zucchini, trimmed and cut into quarters lengthwise
8 green beans, trimmed and cut into halves
3 small ears of corn, each cut into 3 slices
3 large fresh mint sprigs

Put the meat, bone, and udder into a large soup kettle or earthenware pot. Add the onion and garlic with salt to taste. Cover with water to 3 inches above the meat and bring to a simmer. Continue cooking slowly until the meat is just about tender, about 1 hour. Add the *jícama*, *chayote*, and carrots and continue cooking for about 30 minutes, then add the rest of the ingredients and cook until tender but not too soft—about 35 minutes. Serve in deep bowls with plenty of the broth and vegetables.

ROPA VIEJA *(Shredded Leftover Meat and Vegetables)*

MAKES 2 CUPS

The literal meaning of *ropa vieja* is old clothes, an expressive name for this savory way of using up meat and vegetables left over from the preceding stew. There are, of course, other regional versions of this dish. It is usually eaten as a *taco* filling and in this case I prefer the *tacos* to be fried and served with the tomato sauce (page 340) and lots of shredded cabbage with a dollop of cream and a sprinkling of crumbled cheese.

2 tablespoons lard or safflower oil
4 tablespoons finely chopped white onion
1 garlic clove, peeled and finely chopped
1¼ cups finely chopped tomatoes
3 *chiles serranos*, finely chopped
1¼ cups shredded cooked beef from *cocido o caldo de res Michoacano* (see page 296)
¼ cup meat broth
¼ teaspoon dried oregano, Mexican if possible
sea salt to taste
1 heaped cup cooked vegetables in ¼-inch cubes (see above)
2 tablespoons roughly chopped *cilantro*

Heat the lard in a frying pan, add the onion and garlic, and fry without browning until translucent—about 2 minutes. Add the tomatoes and fresh *chiles* and cook for 3 minutes more over fairly high heat. Add the meat and broth, with oregano and salt to taste. Cook over medium heat, stirring and turning the mixture over from time to time, for about 3 minutes—the mixture should be moist but not too juicy. Add the vegetables and *cilantro* and continue cooking and stirring until the mixture is almost dry.

SALPICÓN DE RES
(Shredded Meat Cooked with Tomatoes, Chiles, and Cilantro)

SERVES 4 PORTIONS OR MAKES
ENOUGH FILLING FOR 18 *TACOS*

SEÑORA MARIA ALEJANDRE DE BRITO,
ZITÁCUARO, MICHOACÁN

Here is a simple and delicious way of cooking either flank or skirt steak. It is usually served with corn *tortillas* but can also be made into very good fried *tacos* with the usual trimmings. Served with a salad, it would make a very good lunch dish.

THE MEAT
1¼ pounds skirt or flank steak with some fat
1 small white onion, roughly chopped
3 *cilantro* sprigs
2 garlic cloves, peeled and roughly chopped
sea salt to taste

THE SEASONING
2 tablespoons lard or safflower oil
½ cup finely chopped white onion
2 garlic cloves, peeled and finely chopped
1¼ pounds tomatoes (about 4 medium), finely chopped, unpeeled
4 (or to taste) canned *chiles serranos en escabeche*
3 rounded tablespoons roughly chopped *cilantro*
¼ cup broth from cooking beef
sea salt to taste

Cut the steaks—along the grain, not against it—into 2-inch pieces. Put the meat into a saucepan with the onion, *cilantro*, garlic, and salt, barely cover with water, and simmer until tender—about 25 minutes for skirt steak and 35 for flank. Allow the meat to cool off in the broth. Strain, reserving the broth. When the meat is cool enough to handle, remove any gristle or sinew and shred roughly. Set aside.

In a heavy frying pan, heat the lard, add the onion and garlic, and fry gently without browning until translucent—about 3 minutes. Add the chopped tomatoes and continue cooking over high heat, stirring and turning it over from time to time to prevent sticking, until the mixture has reduced and thickened—about 8 minutes. Add the shredded meat, *chiles*, *cilantro*, and broth, taste for salt, and cook over medium heat, covered, for about 5 minutes longer.

CARNE ENCHILADA (*Chile-Seasoned Grilled Meat*)

SERVES 4 TO 6   GUERRERO

Thinly sliced or *aplanado* (flattened) pork or beef seasoned with a *chile* paste is a rustic favorite in many regions of Mexico, with slight variations in the recipe: many use just *chile guajillo*; others sour orange juice instead of vinegar and a different balance of herbs and spices.

Once the meat has been seasoned, it is best to let it dry out for a few days so that the meat is well infused with the flavors and the paste is not left sticking to the pan or grill. Prepared in this form, the meat is either fried or grilled, and it is best served with slices of avocado, beans, and corn *tortillas*, or a salad. This recipe is from a charming little book on the cooking of Chilapa in Guerrero, and the recipe given by Señorita Carmen Villalba, with my slightly more realistic adjustments.

2 ounces *chiles anchos*, approximately
2 ounces *chiles guajillos*, approximately
¼ cup mild vinegar
4 peppercorns
3 whole cloves
1 thin ½-inch cinnamon stick
½ teaspoon dried oregano, Mexican if possible
1 small tomato (about ¼ pound)
1½ teaspoons (or to taste) sea salt
¼ cup water, approximately
1 pound beef, cut into thin steaks

Remove stems from the dried *chiles*, if any, slit them open, and scrape out and discard veins and seeds. Put *chiles* into a pan and cover with boiling water. Soak until *chiles* are soft and fleshy; do not leave them too long, or the flavor will be left in the water—about 10 to 15 minutes, depending on how dry they are. Put the vinegar into a blender jar and add the peppercorns, cloves, cinnamon, oregano, tomato, and salt; blend until smooth. Add the water and the drained *chiles*, a few at a time, blending after each addition, to make a thick, smooth paste. Add more water only if absolutely necessary to loosen the blades of the blender. Dip the meat into the sauce; it should be fairly thickly covered. Set it on a rack to dry, either in an airy, cool place or at the bottom of the refrigerator, until the paste is dry. Grill or fry briefly on both sides.

CHICHILO NEGRO (*Oaxacan Black Beef Stew*)

SERVES 6 TO 8   OAXACA

Chichilo negro is a dramatic stew of meat and vegetables in a fragrant and complex black sauce, redolent of black *chiles* and toasted avocado leaves. It is one of the more important of the Seven *Moles* of Oaxaca and prepared in the villages of the Central Valley on festive occasions instead of the much heavier black Oaxacan *mole*.

In the past it was always made with the black, bulbous, thin-skinned *chilhuacle negro*, which in recent years have become scarcer and very expensive, so *chiles guajillos*, charred black, are now often used.

This is Mexican food at its most exotic!

Chichilo is best served in shallow bowls—meat, vegetables, and plenty of sauce, with the final touch (as if that were necessary) of *rajas con limón* (page 359). Some black beans cooked *de olla* (page 179) and corn *tortillas* accompany this dish, which is not, surprisingly, very *picante*.

THE MEAT
1½ pounds beef ribs or brisket, cut into 2-inch pieces
1 small head of garlic, scored around the middle
1 medium white onion, roughly sliced
sea salt to taste
1 pound boneless stewing pork, cut into 2-inch pieces

THE VEGETABLES
1 large *chayote* (about ¾ pound), peeled and cut into strips with core and
    seed
6 ounces green beans, trimmed and cut into halves
1 *chile pasilla de Mexico*
18 *chiles chilhuacles negros* or *guajillos*
3 medium (about ½ pound) tomatoes
3 large (about ¼ pound) *tomate verde*, approximately
12 small garlic cloves, unpeeled
1 medium white onion, quartered
the seeds from the *chiles*
2 dried corn *tortillas*
1 scant tablespoon dried oregano, Oaxacan if possible
2 whole cloves
3 whole allspice
¼ teaspoon dried marjoram

¼ teaspoon dried thyme
pinch of cumin seed
3 tablespoons lard or safflower oil
¼ pound (½ cup prepared) corn *tortilla masa* (page 8)
8 fresh or dried avocado leaves
sea salt to taste

Put the beef into a pan with the garlic, onion, salt to taste, and water to cover; bring to a simmer. Cover the pan and continue simmering for about 35 minutes. Add the pork and continue cooking until both meats are tender—about 25 minutes more. Strain, reserving broth, and set aside.

Put the *chayote* into boiling water and cook for 10 minutes, add the beans, and cook for about 10 minutes more. Drain, reserving cooking water, and set aside.

Remove the stems, if any, from the dried *chiles*. Slit them open and remove seeds but not veins; reserve the seeds. On a hot *comal* or griddle, toast the *pasillas* and *chilhuacles* for a few seconds on each side or until the inside turns an opaque tobacco brown. If you're using *guajillos*, flatten *chiles* onto the *comal* and toast for about 1 minute on each side or until they have blackened. Rinse the *chiles* in cold water, cover with hot water, and set aside to soak for about 15 minutes.

Place the whole tomatoes and *tomate verde* on a hot *comal* or griddle, and if there is room, add the garlic and quartered onion. Roast until the tomatoes are slightly charred and mushy, turning them from time to time. Char the cloves of garlic lightly until they are soft inside and char the onion quarters until soft. Set aside. Place the *chile* seeds in a small frying pan over fairly high heat, shaking and turning them over until they turn an even dark brown. Put the *tortillas* either right onto the flame or onto a hot *comal* and let them char, turning them over from time to time. When thoroughly charred, they will start to flame; don't blow it out—toss them into the frying pan with the *chiles* and put over high heat, shaking the pan until the *chile* seeds have burned black with the *tortillas*. Douse with cold water and leave to soak for 5 minutes. Drain.

Put 1 cup of the reserved vegetable water into a blender jar and gradually blend the *chiles*, drained tomatoes and *tomate verde*, peeled garlic, onion, herbs and spices, *chile* seeds, and *tortillas*, little by little, blending thoroughly with each addition and adding more vegetable water if necessary.

Heat the lard in a heavy pan or sauté pan, add the blended ingredients, and cook, stirring and scraping the bottom of the pan from time to time to prevent sticking, for about 15 to 20 minutes.

Meanwhile, put the *tortilla masa* into the blender jar with 1 cup of the meat broth and blend until smooth. Add to the contents in the pan and stir until just beginning to thicken—about 5 minutes. Add the cooked meats and vegetables along with the rest of the meat broth and continue cooking over low heat. Toast the avocado leaves for a few seconds—either over a bare flame (if in a spray) or on a hot *comal*—and add to the stew; adjust seasoning and continue cooking and stirring for 10 to 15 minutes. The sauce should be thin, hardly coating the back of a wooden spoon.

This dish may be prepared several hours ahead, refrigerated, and reheated. I would not recommend freezing it.

VITUALLA (A *Stew of Beef, Rice, and Fruit*)

SERVES 6 TO 8

This is an unusual fruity dish that has a Moroccan flavor—without, of course, the wonderful Moroccan spices. The recipe was given to me by Señora Alcocer of Patzcuaro, although it probably comes from her native Guanajuato. The name usually means "provisions for meals," while it can also mean "abundance of food," especially of meat and vegetables (*Diccionario Vox*). The *Diccionario de Cocina Mexicana* says bluntly, "We learned it [the recipe] from the Spanish." It is substantial, a meal in itself, and nothing else need be served except a dessert.

The final frying and assembling can be done in a sauté pan or shallow flameproof dish that can be taken to the table. *Vitualla* is best eaten as soon as it is cooked, as the rice tends to become a little mushy. One serving would be about 1½ to 2 cups of the rice/fruit mixture, pieces of meat on top, with a *picante* tomato sauce passed at the table.

THE DAY BEFORE
⅓ cup (2 ounces) dry chick-peas

THE MEAT
1½ pounds boneless brisket with some fat, cut into 2-inch cubes
½ pound boneless beef shin
1 large marrow bone, cut into 4 pieces
1 large piece of porous bone
1 small white onion, roughly chopped
3 garlic cloves, peeled
2 teaspoons (or to taste) sea salt
1 small cabbage, cut into wedges

THE RICE
1 cup unconverted long-grain rice
2 cups warm chicken broth (page 95)
¼ medium white onion, roughly chopped
1 garlic clove, peeled and roughly chopped

THE FRUIT
¼ cup lard or safflower oil
3 medium quinces (about 1¼ pounds), peeled, cored, and thickly sliced
3 underripe pears, peeled, cored, and thickly sliced
3 underripe peaches, unpeeled, pit removed, thickly sliced
3 tablespoons sugar
sea salt to taste
salsa de jitomate, cooked version (page 339)

In a large pot, soak the chick-peas in water to cover overnight.

The next day, put the meat, bones, onion, garlic, and salt into a deep pan. Barely cover with water and set over low heat to simmer, uncovered. Continue simmering until the meat is almost tender, about 1 hour. Place the cabbage slices on top of the meat and continue cooking until the meat and cabbage are tender—15 minutes longer. Remove the cabbage, but leave the meat in the broth and keep it warm.

Drain the chick-peas, reserving the soaking water. Rub off and discard the papery skins and put chick-peas with the water back into the saucepan. Bring to a simmer over medium heat and continue cooking at a fast simmer until all the chick-peas are tender but not falling apart—about 40 minutes. Cooking time will depend on how dry they were in the first place or how long they have been stored.

Cover the rice with hot water and soak for about 10 minutes. Drain, rinse, and put into a pot. Blend the warm broth with the onion and garlic and pour over the rice. Bring the broth to a simmer, cover, lower the heat, and cook very slowly until the water has been absorbed (see *morisqueta,* page 124). Set aside off the heat to steam, still covered. The rice should be tender but not too soft, or it will become mushy in the next step of the recipe.

In a large sauté pan or flameproof dish, heat the lard and gently sauté the fruits and sugar, shaking the pan to prevent sticking, and turn them over once so that they just begin to brown lightly. Add the chick-peas and rice with salt to taste and fry the mixture gently, turning it over, for about 5 minutes. Place the cabbage on top, cover the pan, and continue cooking over very low heat for about 5 minutes more.

CARNITA CON CHILE (*Beef in Green Chile Sauce*)

SERVES 4   FAMILIA GONZALEZ, TEQUILA, JALISCO

Carnita con chile was a favorite *almuerzo* when my Mexican friends were growing up. It is a classic example of how meat that is not hung, and therefore is tough, would have been cooked. I find the old method fascinating, and traditionalist that I am, I shall give it plus a more up-to-date cooking procedure.

Tomate de milpa are called for in the original recipe. They are very tiny *tomate verde* that grow wild among the corn, and while they have a lot of tiny seeds, they also have a distinctive flavor that has been bred out of the larger cultivated varieties.

Traditionally this dish is served with corn *tortillas* and *frijoles de olla* (page 179), *peruanos* in this case.

> ¾ pound (about 16 medium) *tomate verde*, husks removed, rinsed
> 3 or 4 *chiles de árbol*, stalks removed
> 1 garlic clove, peeled and roughly chopped
> ¾ pound thinly cut shoulder steaks (*paloma* or *aguayon* in Mexico)
> sea salt to taste
> 2 tablespoons lard or safflower oil

Put the *tomate* into a saucepan with the dried *chiles*, cover with water, and bring to a simmer. Continue cooking for about 5 minutes, no more. Drain, transfer to a blender jar, and blend with the garlic for a few seconds to make a textured sauce. Set aside.

Sprinkle the meat with the salt and put in one layer—you may have to do it in two batches—in a shallow *cazuela* or heavy pan. Set over low heat and allow the meat to sweat, turning it over once, so that the juice exudes and it changes to a lightish brown color—about 4 minutes on each side. Strain off the juice—there should be about 4 tablespoons—and set aside.

1. Pound the meat with a stone pestle and tear into pieces about 1 inch square *or*

2. Have steak pounded at the beginning and cut into pieces.

The next step may have to be done in two batches as well, depending on the size of your pan and the extension of the heat under it. Heat half the lard and fry the meat in one layer on both sides until it is browned. Remove and fry second batch with the rest of the lard. Put all the meat back into the pan, add the sauce, and cook over fairly high heat, turning it over from time to time to prevent sticking, for about 8 minutes or until the meat is tender and the sauce has reduced. If the meat is tough, cover the pan, but keep shaking it and cook longer, up to 15 minutes. Just before serving, stir in the meat juices, adjust seasoning, and serve.

APORREADA DE HUETAMO *(Dried Beef Hash)*

SERVES 4 TO 6   MICHOACÁN

Aporreada, shredded, dried meat cooked with tomato, *chile*, and eggs, is the most ubiquitous dish in the hot country around Huetamo—not to be confused with *aporreadilla* from Apatzingán. It can be eaten any time of day, from breakfast to supper. The meat used is thinly cut beef that is only partially dried after salting, and it is generally eaten with corn *tortillas* and *frijoles*. Simple food from a very hot, rather arid area that does not have an enormous variety of ingredients on hand.

THE SAUCE
1 pound (about 2 large) tomatoes, broiled (see page 450)
4 (or to taste) *chiles serranos*, broiled (see page 472)
2 garlic cloves, peeled and roughly chopped

THE MEAT
½ pound *cecina*
3 tablespoons melted lard or safflower oil
1 cup finely sliced white onion
4 eggs, lightly beaten

Put the unpeeled tomatoes, *serranos*, and garlic into a blender jar and blend for a few seconds—it should have a bit of texture (this step would be done in a *molcajete* in Huetamo). Set aside.

Grill the meat for a few seconds on each side to sear it, either over a charcoal or wood fire or on an extremely hot *comal*. Set aside to cool. When cool enough to handle, shred the meat finely, discarding any bits of sinew or gristle. This should make about 2 well-packed cups. Set aside.

Heat the lard in a heavy frying pan, add the shredded meat and sliced onion, and fry, turning it over from time to time, until the onion is translucent. Break the eggs into the mixture, or beat lightly, and stir until set— about 4 minutes. Pour in the sauce and reduce over high heat, stirring constantly until the mixture is neither too dry nor too juicy—about 8 minutes.

BIFSTECES EN CHILE PASILLA
(Thin Steaks in Pasilla Sauce)

SERVES 4

This is a simple family dish exemplifying the changing times in Mexico. When I was in Patzcuaro on a recent visit to a friend's mother who was a renowned cook in her time, there were 20 members of the family there to sit down to *comida,* the main meal of the day. Since Señora Alcocer lives alone, there is only one do-it-all maid, so compromises had to be made to reduce to a minimum the pots and plates used. The meat and sauce were cooked together in the pressure cooker and served on top of a *morisqueta* (boiled rice, page 124), thus cutting out the dry soup course. Corn *tortillas* should be served to sop up the extra sauce, and I like to put some thick slices of avocado on top to add a little richness to its rather plebeian appearance.

> 5 *chiles pasillas* (about 1½ ounces)
> ¼ pound (about 5 medium) *tomate verde*
> 1 garlic clove, peeled and roughly chopped
> ¼ small white onion, roughly chopped
> water or beef broth as necessary
> 4 thin shoulder steaks (about 1 pound) with a little fat
> sea salt to taste
> 3 tablespoons lard or safflower oil

Remove the stems from the dried *chiles,* slit them open, and scrape out and discard veins and seeds. Put into a small pan with hot water to cover and simmer for about 3 minutes. Set aside to soak for about 8 minutes.

Remove husks from *tomate verde,* cover with water, and cook over low heat until soft but not too mushy—about 8 minutes. Drain and transfer to a blender jar and add the drained *chiles,* garlic, and onion; blend until fairly smooth—it should have some texture—adding only enough water to release the blades of the blender. The sauce will be thick.

Season the steaks with salt, heat the lard in a large pan, and sear the steaks for a few seconds on each side until slightly browned. Pour the *chile* sauce over the meat and cook over medium heat until the meat is tender and the sauce reduced and thickened. Add a little more water or beef broth if the sauce is drying up too much. Adjust seasoning and serve.

Note: In Mexico, where the meat is tougher and has not been hung to tenderize it, it should be cooked covered or in the pressure cooker.

BIFSTEK ENCHORIZADO
(Chopped Steak Flavored with Achiote)

SERVES 4   YUCATÁN

This is a very simple recipe typical of the home cooking of Yucatán. It was prepared for me, among many other dishes, on my last trip to the Yucatán Peninsula by a friend and great natural cook, Señora Isela Alonso de Rodriguez.

Like many other dishes of that region, the flavor of the meat is enhanced by that touch of smoky flavor lent by the brief broiling on a charcoal or wood grill, but an ordinary broiler will do as well.

Bifstek enchorizado is generally served with plain white rice *morisqueta* (page 124) and some *frijoles colados* (page 186).

PREPARING THE MEAT
2 rounded tablespoons *recado rojo* (page 428)
2 garlic cloves, peeled and mashed
sea salt to taste
1 tablespoon bitter orange juice, a substitute (page 456), or a mild vinegar
4 tablespoons lard or safflower oil
1¼ pounds shoulder or sirloin steak with some fat, cut about ⅜ inch thick

⅓ cup finely chopped white onion
½ cup finely chopped green pepper
1 cup finely chopped, unpeeled tomatoes

Heat a grill or broiler.

Mix together the *recado rójo*, garlic, salt to taste, and orange juice. If you are using lard, mash the seasoning paste into 2 tablespoons of the lard and smear on both sides of the steaks. If you're using oil, smear the steak with seasoning paste only. Set the meat aside to season for one hour.

Once the grill or broiler is hot, place the meat just above or under the heat; if you're using oil, brush the meat with 2 tablespoons of the oil at this stage and broil for about 3 minutes on each side. The meat should be just barely cooked but not rare. Chop roughly and put into the container of a food processor. Process briefly to a roughish texture, not a smooth paste. Set aside.

Heat the remaining lard or oil, add the onion, pepper, and tomato, and cook over fairly high heat until reduced—the mixture should be moist and soft, neither dry nor juicy—about 8 minutes. Add the ground meat and cook, stirring from time to time, until the flavors have melded—about 5 minutes. Adjust salt and serve as suggested above.

PACHOLAS *(Ground Meat Patties)*

MAKES ABOUT 14 3-INCH *PACHOLAS*   FAMILIA SANDI, GUADALAJARA
ABOUT ⅛ INCH THICK

Pacholas are thin, wrinkled *"tortillas"* of ground meat, oval rather than round. The name comes from the Nahuatl word *pacholli,* meaning *tortilla.* If you have read about the *raspadas* of Jalisco on page 16, you will see that to make them, the top, uncooked layer of dough is rolled off with a metal rolling pin and forms a wrinkled oval piece of dough—that too is called *pachola.* It takes some practice, as well as a *metate,* to make these, but they are delicious, so I am suggesting a modified version.

Traditionally *pacholas* are served with *salsa de plaza* (page 348) and a lightly dressed lettuce salad, or shredded lettuce, but you can use them as a sandwich filling or take them cooked on a picnic and reheat them over charcoal. It certainly makes meat go a long way and deliciously so.

½ pound finely ground beef
½ pound finely ground pork
½ small *bolillo* (bread roll, page 367) or a 3-inch piece of French bread
⅓ cup milk
¼ small white onion, roughly sliced
3 large flat-leaf parsley sprigs, roughly chopped
1 large egg
sea salt to taste
2 Alligator Baggies
flour for the hands and Baggies
lard or safflower oil for frying

Put all the ingredients, except for the flour and lard, into the container of a food processor and process for a few seconds, until the mixture forms a soft, cohesive paste. Take 2 tablespoons of the mixture and roll into a ball—you may need to flour your hands for this. Using a *tortilla* press and two Baggies, proceed as if making *tortillas* (see page 12), lightly flouring the surface of the Baggies that will come into contact with the meat. Place the ball of meat on the bottom Baggie, place the second one on top of it, and press down lightly with the top plate of the *tortilla* press to form a disk about 4 inches in diameter.

Heat 2 tablespoons of the lard in a frying pan. Remove the top Baggie, flour your hands once again, and carefully transfer the meat to the pan— following the same procedure for *tortilla* making. Fry the *pachola* for about 2 minutes on the first side or until lightly browned, turn over, and fry on the second side for 2 minutes. Remember that the meat, being partly pork, should be cooked through and not pink when you eat it. The cooked *pacholas* will shrink to about 3 inches in diameter. Drain each one on paper toweling and keep warm. Proceed with the others, adding lard as necessary, a little at a time—when you get into the swing of it, you can be cooking 3 or 4 at once.

CARNE APACHE (Mexican Steak Tartare)

MAKES 2 CUPS   PATZCUARO

Tostadas de carne apache are one of the perennial "street" foods of Patzcuaro and points north. All the ingredients are very finely chopped to resemble the local *ceviche*, and the *tostadas* are topped with a lot of finely shredded cabbage and tomato slices. A friend of mine from the northern part of the state added some ingredients to this recipe that went into the more elaborate version her mother used to make. Her mother's *carne apache* was topped with *angulas*, canned baby eels from Spain.

½ pound finely ground beef
½ cup fresh lime juice
⅓ cup finely chopped white onion
1 cup finely chopped, unpeeled tomatoes
scant ¼ cup finely chopped *cilantro*
½ *chile peron*, seeds and veins removed, or 2 *chiles serranos*, finely chopped
2 heaped tablespoons finely chopped, pitted green olives
⅓ cup diced peeled sweet red pepper
3 tablespoons light olive oil
sea salt and freshly ground pepper to taste

THE OPTIONAL TOPPINGS
finely shredded cabbage and tomato slices
a raw egg or slices of hard-cooked egg

Put the ground meat into a glass or china bowl, stir in the lime juice, cover, and store in the refrigerator for at least 4 hours and up to a day or 2. Turn the meat over from time to time so that it "cooks" evenly. Stir in the rest of the ingredients and season to taste.

Serve piled onto *tostadas* or *raspadas* or alternatively with hot *tortillas*, plus the toppings.

RIÑONES EN SALSA DE CHILE PASILLA
(Kidneys in Pasilla Sauce)

SERVES 4   SEÑORA LIVIER RUIZ DE SUAREZ, JIQUILPAN, MICHOACÁN

When your butcher has tender veal kidneys, it is well worth making this very savory dish from the northern part of Michoacán. It is often served on top of a *morisqueta* (plain boiled rice, page 124) and served with corn *tortillas*.

1½ pounds veal kidneys
1 teaspoon sea salt (optional)
1 teaspoon vinegar (optional)
3 tablespoons melted lard or safflower oil
¼ white onion, thinly sliced
sea salt to taste
1½ recipes *salsa de chile pasilla de Michoacán* (page 343)

Remove the outer membrane from the kidneys, cut them open, and cut out the central core. Slice thinly.

Optional step for milder flavor: Cover with water and add the salt and vinegar. Set aside for 30 minutes. Then drain, discarding the soaking water, and pat the kidneys dry with paper toweling.

Heat the lard in a sauté pan, add the kidneys, onion, and salt, and fry over high heat like a stir-fry, turning it over constantly so that the water in the kidneys is absorbed and the kidneys are beginning to brown—about 2 minutes. Add the *pasilla* sauce and cook over high heat, stirring almost constantly, until the kidneys are just tender but still crisp, about 4 minutes.

PANZA DE RES (*Beef Tripe*)

It is lamentable that most people in the United States know to buy only honeycomb tripe (or are told so by recipe writers). There are, in fact, several types of tripe, all of different textures: there is a part of the stomach that looks like a textured towel (in fact called *toalla* in Yucatán); there is also a part that hangs in fringes, known as *librillo* in Mexico; and there is the thickly corded neck of the tripe. So if you are a tripe lover as I am, prod your butcher into producing more variety.

When tripe is sold in the United States, it is already blanched and deodorized, ready to use. Alas, the fat has probably been stripped off as well. But if you are lucky enough to find some with fat, leave it on for flavor.

One pound of tripe should serve about 3 to 4 people, unless you have enthusiasts like me who can dispose of ½ pound easily at a sitting. Although it tends to take a long time to cook, do not attempt to put tripe in a pressure cooker, or it will shrivel up in the sudden intense heat—it needs long, slow cooking, and for this the Crock-Pot or other slow cooker would be ideal.

2 pounds tripe, cut into 1½- to 2-inch squares
1 small white onion, roughly sliced
1 small head of garlic, scored around the middle
3 peppercorns
sea salt to taste

Put the tripe into a heavy pot or slow cooker and add enough water to come about 2 inches above the tripe. Add the rest of the ingredients and bring to a simmer. Continue simmering until tender, about 2 hours. Strain, reserving the broth in which it was cooked.

Recipes using the cooked tripe follow.

PANZA DE RES EN VERDE
(Tripe in Green Sauce)

SERVES 4   SEÑORA HORTENSIA FAGOAGA, XICÓTEPEC DE JUAREZ

Since I am an *aficionada* of tripe in most forms—except that of my native England, with white sauce and onions—I find it hard to believe that this dish, as well as the tripe *tacos,* will not find some converts. (See page 311 for selecting and cooking tripe.) The sauce, like others from this part of Puebla, is heavily textured by roughly ground pumpkin seeds. And this sauce, like many in the Mexican cuisine, plays an equal part with the meat, so serve plenty of it. This dish can be prepared well ahead and even the day before, but some of the fresh green flavor and color is lost in the reheating the next day. Serve with corn *tortillas.*

2 cups tripe broth (see page 311)
2 garlic cloves, peeled and roughly chopped
⅓ cup tightly packed, roughly chopped *cilantro*
6 to 8 (or to taste) *chiles serranos,* charred (see page 472) and roughly chopped
2 tablespoons lard or safflower oil
5 ounces (about 1 cup) hulled raw pumpkin seeds
1½ pounds tripe, cut into 1½-inch squares and cooked (see page 311)
sea salt to taste

Put 1½ cups of the broth into a blender jar, add garlic, *cilantro,* and whole *chiles,* and blend until fairly smooth. Set aside. Heat 2 teaspoons of the lard in a frying pan, stir in the seeds, until lightly coated with the lard, and heat over medium heat, turning them almost constantly, until they swell up and just begin to turn a pale golden color (do not allow to color too much, or the sauce will not look or taste as it should)—about 10 seconds. Transfer to the blender jar and blend to a rough texture—about 3 seconds. Heat the rest of the lard in a sauté pan, add the blended ingredients, and cook over medium heat, stirring and scraping the bottom of the pan from time to time, until the sauce has reduced and thickened (it will appear rough and somewhat curdled)—about 10 minutes. Add the tripe pieces, the rest of the broth, and salt to taste; cook for about 10 minutes longer or until the tripe is well infused with the flavors.

PANZA GUISADA PARA TACOS
(Shredded Tripe for Tacos)

MAKES ENOUGH FILLING FOR 6 TO 8 TACOS

Tripe cooked, cut, and seasoned in this way presents quite a change in texture and flavor from normal ways of serving it and perhaps will even be acceptable to the most hardened of non–tripe eaters. (See notes on choosing and cooking tripe, page 311.)

This quantity should be enough for 6 to 8 *tacos* made from the usual 4½- to 5-inch *tortillas*. After filling and before rolling the *tacos,* douse them with *salsa verde (cruda)* (page 336).

1 pound cooked tripe (page 311)
2 tablespoons lard or safflower oil
⅓ cup finely chopped white onion
2 (or to taste) *chiles serranos,* finely chopped
⅓ cup loosely packed *epazote* leaves
2 to 3 tablespoons tripe broth (page 311) or chicken broth (page 95), approximately
sea salt to taste

Cut tripe into narrow strips about 2 inches long and set aside. Heat the lard in a frying pan, add the onion, fresh *chiles,* and half the *epazote,* and fry gently until the onion is translucent, without browning—about 2 minutes. Add the tripe and the rest of the *epazote* and fry for another 2 minutes, stirring and turning the mixture over to prevent sticking. Add the broth and salt to taste, cover, and continue cooking over medium heat, shaking the pan from time to time, for about 5 minutes.

EGG AND CHEESE DISHES

(Platillos de Huevo y Queso)

Huevos en Salsa (Eggs in Tomato Sauce)
Huevos Rancheros ("Ranch" Eggs)
Huevos a la Hacienda (Estate Eggs)
Huevos con Chorizo y Jitomate (Eggs with Chorizo and Tomato)
Tortitas de Huevo con Chile Verde
(Rolled Omelets in Tomato Sauce with Chile Strips)
Huevos Cuauhtémoc (Emperor Cuauhtémoc Eggs)
Huevos Revueltos a la Mexicana (Mexican Scrambled Eggs)
Huevos al Albañil (Bricklayer's Eggs)
Huevos Revueltos con Col (Eggs Scrambled with Cabbage)
Requesón Revuelto con Salsa de Jitomate (Ricotta Scrambled with Tomato Sauce)
Requesón Revuelto a la Mexicana (Ricotta Scrambled Like Mexican Eggs)
Chilaquiles Michoacanos (Chilaquiles with Green Sauce and Cream)
Minguichi I (Ancho Chiles with Melted Cheese)
Minguichi II (Fried Cheese in Cream)
Minguichi III (Cheese and Chile Strips in Green Sauce)
Cross-reference:
Habas Guisadas con Huevos
Aporreada de Huetamo

The light Mexican way with eggs is very refreshing after the cloyingly rich brunch dishes like "eggs-upon-buttery-eggs" Benedict. These dishes are healthful too, adding bulk and freshness as well as contrast in flavor and texture. Using ricotta, which is low in cholesterol, instead of eggs the way some Mexican cooks do is an interesting twist, and whether old or new, nobody can tell me. In the *minguichis, chiles* provide a wonderful contrast to the melted cheese.

All of these recipes lend themselves to innovation by using up leftover ingredients and adapting them to suit your palate, purse, and diet.

HUEVOS EN SALSA *(Eggs in Tomato Sauce)*

SERVES 4   OAXACA

Throughout Mexico, eggs and tomatoes are combined in various forms very successfully. This way of preparing them is from Oaxaca. It is simple but delicious.

THE SAUCE
3 small garlic cloves, peeled
1 to 2 (to taste) *chiles serranos*, broiled (see page 472)
¾ cup cold water
1 pound (about 2 large) tomatoes, broiled or stewed (pages 450 or 451)
1 tablespoon safflower oil
2 leafy stems of *epazote*
sea salt to taste

THE EGGS
6 large eggs
3 tablespoons finely chopped white onion
sea salt to taste
2 tablespoons safflower oil

Put the garlic, fresh *chiles*, and water into a blender jar and blend until smooth. Add the unpeeled tomatoes, a few at a time, and blend until almost smooth. Heat 1 tablespoon of oil in a heavy pan, add the tomato puree, *epazote*, and salt, and cook over fairly high heat, stirring from time to time and scraping the bottom of the pan, until slightly reduced—about 5 minutes. Set aside and keep warm.

Break the eggs into a bowl and stir in the onion and salt.

Heat the oil in a large frying pan, add the eggs, and cook until set. Turn them over—should be like a broken-up omelet—and cook on the second side until firm.

Reheat the sauce and, when simmering, add the egg pieces to it and heat through, pressing them down so that the sauce covers them—about 3 minutes. Serve with hot corn *tortillas*.

HUEVOS RANCHEROS (*"Ranch" Eggs*)

SERVES 4

These eggs are perhaps the best known outside of Mexico. They make a very good brunch dish but have to be prepared at the last moment.

safflower oil for frying
4 5-inch corn *tortillas*
4 extra-large eggs
1⅓ cups *salsa ranchera* (page 338), approximately, kept hot, *or* ⅓ cup *salsa de tomate verde, cocida* (page 337), approximately, kept hot
rajas of 1 large *chile poblano* (see page 471)
4 tablespoons crumbled *queso fresco* or *añejo*

Have warm 4 small *gratin* dishes for individual portions.

Heat enough oil in a small frying pan to cover the surface by about ¼ inch. Fry the *tortillas* for about 2 seconds on each side; they should be well heated through but not crisp. Remove and drain on paper toweling, then put onto warmed plates. Fry the eggs one by one, adding oil as necessary, and place on top of the *tortillas*. Pour approximately ⅓ cup of the sauce over each egg, decorate with the *chile* strips, and sprinkle with cheese. Serve immediately.

HUEVOS A LA HACIENDA *(Estate Eggs)*

SERVES 4 (ABOUT 1½ CUPS SAUCE)

These are *huevos rancheros* with a flourish. This is a very substantial dish for brunch; 1 large egg should be sufficient per person.

THE SAUCE
¼ cup water
1 pound (about 2 large) tomatoes, broiled (see page 450)
3 *chiles serranos*, broiled (see page 472)
1 tablespoon finely chopped white onion
1 garlic clove, peeled and roughly chopped
2 tablespoons safflower oil
rajas of 3 charred and peeled *chiles poblanos* (see pages 470 and 471)
sea salt to taste

ASSEMBLING THE EGGS
safflower oil for frying
4 5-inch corn *tortillas*, approximately
4 heaped tablespoons *frijoles refritos* (page 180)
4 extra-large eggs
4 slices *Chihuahua* or Muenster cheese

Heat the oven to 350°. Warm 1 large or 4 small *gratin* dishes.

Put the water into a blender jar and add the tomatoes, unpeeled *chiles*, onion, and garlic; blend for a few seconds, until almost smooth—the sauce should have some texture and not be smooth or frothy. Heat the oil in a frying pan, add the *chile* strips and a touch of salt, and fry over medium heat, turning them over from time to time, for about 3 minutes; they will change color but should not brown. Remove one third of the strips for final garnish. Add the tomato puree and cook over high heat, stirring and scraping the bottom of the pan, until the sauce has thickened and reduced—about 4 minutes. Adjust seasoning, set aside, and keep warm.

Heat enough oil in a small frying pan to cover the surface by about ¼ inch. Fry the *tortillas* one by one for about 2 seconds on each side, until heated through but not crisp. Remove and drain on paper toweling. Spread with 1 heaped tablespoon of the bean paste and place in warmed dish. Continue with the rest, adding more oil as necessary. Fry the eggs one by one and place on the *tortillas*. Pour approximately ⅓ cup of the warmed tomato sauce over each egg, place a slice of cheese on top, and place in oven long enough for the cheese to melt, not to brown. Serve immediately.

HUEVOS CON CHORIZO Y JITOMATE
(Eggs with Chorizo and Tomato)

MAKES 2½ CUPS TO SERVE 4

Eggs cooked with *chorizo* make a popular breakfast or brunch dish in Mexico. However, if the *chorizo* is very highly seasoned, adding tomato makes it all a little lighter. If the *chorizo* contains a lot of fat, the lard or oil may be omitted.

2 tablespoons lard or safflower oil (see note above)
2 tablespoons finely chopped white onion
6 ounces *chorizos*, skinned and roughly crumbled
6 ounces (about 1 medium) tomato, unpeeled and finely chopped (about
   ¾ cup)
sea salt to taste
5 extra-large eggs, lightly beaten

Heat the lard in a frying pan, add the onion, and fry gently without browning for 1 minute. Add the crumbled *chorizo* and cook over low heat until the fat has rendered out and the meat is just beginning to brown. Raise heat, add the tomato, and cook until the juice has been absorbed— about 4 minutes. Add salt to the eggs and stir them into the tomato mixture. Cook over medium heat, stirring and turning them almost constantly, until the eggs are firm—about 5 minutes. Adjust seasoning and serve immediately with corn *tortillas*.

TORTITAS DE HUEVO CON CHILE VERDE
(Rolled Omelets in Tomato Sauce with Chile Strips)

SERVES 4   JALISCO

On a recent visit to Tequila, I was talking with one of the old families there and asking about the food of their childhood. This recipe was one of their favorites for *almuerzo*, which was a hearty meal often including meat and always *frijoles*. With *frijoles* and corn *tortillas*, one egg per person should be sufficient.

The omelets have to be thin—forget about the French and *baveuse*—so that they can be rolled and cut into small pieces. You can make single omelets or 2 larger ones.

> 1 pound (about 2 large) tomatoes
> scant ¼ cup thinly sliced white onion
> 4 tablespoons lard or safflower oil, approximately
> 4 extra-large eggs
> sea salt to taste
> *rajas* of 2 large charred and peeled *chiles poblanos* (see pages 470 and 471)
> ½ cup water

Put the tomatoes into a saucepan, cover with water, and bring to a simmer; continue simmering until the tomatoes are soft but not falling apart—about 10 minutes. Drain and transfer tomatoes, unpeeled, to a blender jar, discarding the cooking water. Add the onion and blend until fairly smooth; the mixture should have some texture. Set aside.

To make 4 separate omelets, heat 1½ teaspoons of the lard in a 6-inch frying pan. Beat one of the eggs lightly and add salt to taste. Fry until firm but not dry, roll quite tightly, and cut diagonally into 4 pieces. Continue with the rest of the eggs. Set them aside, but keep them warm.

Heat the remaining lard in a larger saucepan, add the *chile* strips, and cook over very low heat, stirring them from time to time, until they are beginning to change color—about 5 minutes. Add the tomato puree and salt to taste and cook until the sauce reduces and thickens—about 8 minutes. Add the water and bring to a simmer, add the omelet pieces, and just heat through over low heat—about 4 minutes.

Serve with *frijoles refritos* (page 180) or *de olla* (page 179) accompanied by hot corn *tortillas*.

HUEVOS CUAUHTÉMOC *(Emperor Cuauhtémoc Eggs)*

SERVES 4

Eggs, beans, and cheese are combined in an unusual way in this dish, named for the Aztec emperor. This makes a very good brunch dish; the bean mixture can be prepared ahead of time, and the final cooking of the eggs with cheese can be done at the table in a chafing dish. Although black beans are called for, in fact any beans can be used and the *epazote* omitted.

This is a very substantial dish, and one large egg should be enough for a serving. Hot corn *tortillas* are all you need to accompany it.

½ pound (about 1 large) tomatoes, broiled (see page 450)
3 tablespoons finely chopped white onion
2 garlic cloves, peeled and roughly chopped
3 tablespoons melted lard or safflower oil
2 *chiles de árbol*
2 cups pureed black beans (page 179)
1 large leafy stem of *epazote* (optional)
sea salt to taste
4 extra-large eggs
¼ pound *Chihuahua* or medium-sharp Cheddar cheese, thinly sliced or grated

Put the unpeeled tomatoes, onion, and garlic into a blender jar and blend until smooth.

Heat the lard in a frying pan, add the dried *chiles*, and fry for 1 minute, crushing them so that they open up. Add the tomato mixture and fry over high heat until reduced—about 3 minutes.

Add the bean puree and optional *epazote*, adjust seasoning, and cook gently until barely simmering (the puree should lightly cover the back of a wooden spoon). Break the eggs one at a time into the puree—or to be safe, break them onto a saucer and slide them into the mixture. Cover the pan and cook until the whites are just about to turn opaque—about 7 minutes. Put the cheese over the top of the eggs and cover the pan again until the eggs are set, or as firm as you like them, and the cheese melted.

HUEVOS REVUELTOS A LA MEXICANA
(Mexican Scrambled Eggs)

SERVES 4

This is the simplest and most popular way of cooking eggs in the Mexican manner.

6 extra-large eggs
sea salt to taste
4 tablespoons melted lard or safflower oil
1 cup finely chopped, unpeeled tomatoes
3 tablespoons finely chopped white onion
4 *chiles serranos,* finely chopped

Break the eggs into a bowl and just mix (do not beat) with the salt. Heat the lard in a large frying pan. Add the tomatoes, onions, and fresh *chiles,* stir well, and fry over medium heat, stirring from time to time, for about 3 to 4 minutes or until most of the juice has been absorbed. Stir in the eggs and continue stirring and turning them over until the eggs are set—about 4 minutes. Serve immediately with corn *tortillas.*

HUEVOS AL ALBAÑIL (*Bricklayer's Eggs*)

SERVES 4

Some years ago I was asked to do an article on Mexican breakfasts and brunches. Since I needed some rather different egg recipes, I consulted Señora María Luisa Martínez, my oracle for lesser-known dishes. She came up with this and three of the following recipes.

There is, of course, no end to the variations that bricklayers, or chefs and home cooks for that matter, can come up with when there are some stale *tortillas*, various odds and ends of sauce, and plenty of eggs around the kitchen. All that is required after that is a bit of imagination, a healthy appetite, and a somewhat earthy palate to appreciate these wonderfully rustic dishes.

Huevos al albañil should be served with a bowl of *frijoles de olla* (page 179) and corn *tortillas*.

4 *chiles pasillas*
4 *chiles guajillos* or *puyas*
1¼ cups water, approximately
2 small garlic cloves, roughly chopped
3 tablespoons finely chopped white onion
3 tablespoons lard or safflower oil
sea salt to taste
5 extra-large eggs

THE OPTIONAL TOPPINGS
4 tablespoons crumbled *queso fresco* or *añejo*
3 tablespoons finely chopped white onion

Slit the dried *chiles* open and scrape out and discard the veins and seeds. Flatten them out and toast them lightly, one by one, on a medium-hot *comal*, pressing them lightly until the inside turns an opaque tobacco color. Be careful not to burn them, or the sauce will be bitter. Cover with boiling water and leave to soak for about 15 minutes or until the *chiles* have reconstituted and the skins are soft.

Put the 1¼ cups water into a blender jar, add the garlic, onion, and drained *chiles*, and blend until almost smooth—the sauce should have some texture. Heat the lard in a large frying pan, add the sauce and salt, and cook over high heat until it is reduced and thickened and the top is crinkly with bubbles—about 5 to 6 minutes. Break up the eggs (do not beat), add more salt to taste, and stir into the sauce. Cook over medium heat, turning the mixture over, until the eggs are set. Serve at once with toppings, *frijoles*, and *tortillas* (see note above).

HUEVOS REVUELTOS CON COL
(Eggs Scrambled with Cabbage)

SERVES 4   VALLE DE JUAREZ, JALISCO

I came across this recipe when visiting a rather poor community, just inside the boundary of Jalisco, across from Michoacán. It is quite unusual and a very good way to eke out eggs—for either dietary or economic reasons. If you prefer to have the eggs more *picante* as I do, leave the veins in the dried *chiles* or use the narrow *guajillos* called *puyas*. Use lard if you can, as it makes all the difference in the flavor. Serve with hot corn *tortillas*.

> 5 extra-large eggs
> sea salt to taste
> 2 tablespoons lard or safflower oil
> 3 tablespoons finely chopped white onion
> 3 *chiles guajillos,* wiped clean, veins and seeds removed, torn into large pieces
> 3 small tomatoes (about ¾ pound), unpeeled and finely chopped
> 2½ cups tightly packed, finely shredded cabbage

Beat the eggs lightly with salt to taste. Heat the lard, add the onion and dried *chile* pieces, and fry gently without browning for about 1 minute. Add the tomatoes and cabbage and continue frying and stirring until some of the juice has been absorbed and the cabbage is wilted—about 6 minutes. Stir in the egg and cook, turning the mixture over gently until the eggs are set and almost dry (not creamy)—about 4 minutes. Adjust seasoning and serve with hot corn *tortillas* or crusty bread rolls.

REQUESÓN REVUELTO CON SALSA DE JITOMATE
(Ricotta Scrambled with Tomato Sauce)

MAKES 2½ CUPS TO SERVE 4   FAMILIA BRITO, ZITÁCUARO, MICHOACÁN

Ricotta cooked with tomato sauce or like Mexican scrambled eggs makes an appetizing alternative for a brunch menu, especially for those who cannot eat too many eggs. While *los Brito* usually prepare it with the tomato sauce, they suggested a second method (recipe follows this one) that is just as good but crunchier.

For both of these recipes the ricotta should be well drained, almost dry. If it is not, then squeeze it gently in a piece of cheesecloth to get rid of the extra moisture and then spread it out to dry a little more before using it.

While ricotta prepared in this way is normally eaten for *almuerzo* (brunch) with corn *tortillas,* it also makes an excellent fried *taco* filling.

4 tablespoons safflower oil
3 tablespoons finely chopped white onion
2½ cups firmly packed ricotta cheese
heaped ½ teaspoon (or to taste) sea salt
1¼ cups *salsa ranchera* (page 338)

Heat the oil in a frying pan, add the onion, and fry gently without browning for about 2 minutes. Add the ricotta and salt and keep stirring and turning over for about 3 minutes. Add the tomato sauce and continue cooking over medium heat, stirring almost constantly, until almost dry and when turned with a spoon the mixture comes away cleanly from the surface of the pan—4 to 5 minutes. Serve immediately with corn *tortillas.*

REQUESÓN REVUELTO A LA MEXICANA
(Ricotta Scrambled Like Mexican Eggs)

MAKES 2½ CUPS TO SERVE 4

4 tablespoons safflower oil
heaped ⅓ cup finely chopped white onion
4 to 5 (or to taste) *chiles serranos*
1¼ cups finely chopped, unpeeled tomatoes
2½ cups firmly packed ricotta cheese
heaped ½ teaspoon (or to taste) sea salt

Heat the oil in a frying pan, add the onion and fresh *chiles*, and fry gently without browning for 1 minute. Add the tomatoes and continue cooking over high heat, stirring from time to time, until the mixture is fairly dry—about 4 minutes. Add the ricotta and salt and mix well. Cook over medium heat until it begins to turn a light golden color and when turned with a spoon comes away cleanly from the surface of the pan—about 4 minutes. Serve immediately with corn *tortillas*.

CHILAQUILES MICHOACANOS
(Chilaquiles with Green Sauce and Cream)

SERVES 4   SEÑORA MARÍA LUISA MARTÍNEZ, MICHOACÁN

Señora Martínez prepared this delicious recipe for me some years ago. I remember her telling me that when she was growing up in Morelia and a day in the country was planned, the family cook would make these just before they started out, and then they would reheat them, wrapped in corn *tortillas*, over a wood fire.

For most *chilaquile* recipes the *tortillas* are half fried and become chewy in the sauce; these are fried crisp and added to the sauce at the last minute to retain their crispness. *Natas,* the scalded cream that forms a thick skin on raw milk, was usually stirred in at the last moment.

safflower oil for frying
4 stale corn *tortillas*, cut into ½-inch squares
½ pound (about 11 medium) *tomate verde,* husks removed, rinsed
4 fresh (or to taste) *chiles serranos*
2 garlic cloves, peeled and roughly chopped
sea salt to taste
5 extra-large eggs
3 tablespoons *crème fraîche* or *natas* (page 443)

Pour oil to a depth of about ½ inch into a small frying pan. Fry the *tortilla* pieces a few at a time, turning them over until light brown and very crisp. Drain on paper toweling. Set aside.

Put the *tomate verde* and whole fresh *chiles* into a small saucepan, cover with water, and bring to a simmer. Continue simmering until the *tomate* are soft but not falling apart—about 10 minutes, depending on size. Drain, reserving one third of the cooking water. Put that and the *tomate, chiles,* and garlic into a blender jar and blend to a textured sauce.

Heat 3 tablespoons of the oil in a frying pan, add the sauce, and fry over high heat, adding salt to taste, until it is reduced and thickened—about 5 minutes.

Break the eggs into a bowl, break them up (do not beat) with a fork, and season lightly with salt. Lower the heat under the sauce and gradually stir the eggs into it. Continue stirring and turning them over until they are set and the mixture is curdy. Stir in the cream and finally the crisp *tortilla* pieces. Remove from the heat and serve immediately with corn *tortillas*.

MINGUICHI *(Chiles with Cheese, Michoacán)*

MINGUICHI I *(Ancho Chiles with Melted Cheese)*

SERVES 4 TO 6   FELICIANO BÉJAR, MICHOACÁN

Minguichi is a Tarascan word used in the northern and central parts of Michoacán to refer to *chile con queso* (*chiles* and cheese). There are many variations—depending, of course, on what is on hand—the richest of them coming from Jiquilpan and Sahuayo in the very rich dairy-farming areas that border on the state of Jalisco. The dish is described in the *Diccionario de Aztequismos* as "being very tasty but almost exclusively eaten by people in the country."

Minguichi is eaten either with corn *tortillas* to sop it up or with *corundas*, both served as a dry soup course. This version was given to me by Feliciano Béjar, who loves to cook his regional dishes; he was born in Jiquilpan.

This dish is extremely rich, and much of its success depends on the quality of the cream, which should be thick and slightly soured. While traditionally it is made with *queso cotija* (*queso añejo*), which is a solid, rather dry, extremely salty cheese (and an acquired taste for many who do not live in Mexico), you can substitute a more solid domestic Muenster.

Feliciano likes to add some to a bowl of *frijoles de olla* (page 179) and sop it up with corn *tortillas*; it is a meal in itself with a salad to precede or follow.

2 *chiles anchos, pasillas,* or *guajillos*
2 tablespoons safflower oil
2 cups thick *crème fraîche*
½ pound Muenster cheese, cut into ½-inch cubes

Wipe the dried *chiles* clean with a damp cloth, slit them open, and scrape out and discard veins and seeds. Flatten them out well. Heat the oil in a frying pan, lower the heat, and fry the *chiles* very slowly on both sides until they change color inside to a light tobacco brown, taking care not to burn them—about 3 minutes on each side. Drain and set aside to cool. When cool, they should be crisp. Crumble the *chiles* into small pieces and set aside.

Add the cream to the oil in which you fried the *chiles* and reduce over medium heat, stirring from time to time, until it thickens and turns a pale coffee color—about 10 minutes. Take care that the cream does not overcook and become oily. Add the cubed cheese and, as it begins to melt, remove from the heat, stir again, and sprinkle with the *chiles*. Serve immediately.

MINGUICHI II *(Fried Cheese in Cream)*

SERVES 4 TO 6

SEÑORA LIVIER RUIZ DE SUAREZ,
MICHOACÁN/JALISCO BORDER

This recipe comes from the Sahuayo/Villa de Juarez area where Señora Suarez was born and brought up. As in the preceding recipe, traditionally a chewy *cotija* (Cotija is a town in that area where the cheese originated), which holds its shape when fried, would be used. I suggest you use a dry feta and fry it for less time than suggested. When I first tried this *minguichi*, Señora Suarez served it with *chiles serranos toreados*—charred slightly on a hot *comal*—and the second time it was with *corundas* and *chile pasilla* sauce, an incredibly rich and textured combination of flavors and textures.

1½ tablespoons unsalted butter or safflower oil
¼ pound *queso añejo* or Romano cheese, cut into ½-inch cubes
3 *chiles serranos,* finely chopped (optional)
2 cups thick *crème fraîche*

Heat the butter in a sauté or frying pan, add the cheese cubes, and fry, gently turning them over from time to time, until they are a rich golden color—about 2 minutes, adding the optional fresh *chiles* halfway through the cooking time. Add the cream and cook over moderate heat, stirring almost constantly, until it thickens. Serve with corn *tortillas* or as mentioned above.

MINGUICHI III *(Cheese and Chile Strips in Green Sauce)*

SERVES 4   URUAPAN, MICHOACÁN

This is a recipe from the Uruapan area of Michoacán, another delicious variation on the *chile con queso* theme. It is eaten in the same way as the others, with either hot corn *tortillas* or *corundas*. Add only a minimum of salt to the *chiles* and sauce until you see how salty your cheese is. Although *queso añejo* or *cotija* cheese is called for, those two hardly melt, so I use a rather dry *queso fresco*. This dish, like *Minguichi I*, will be fairly runny.

½ pound (about 11 medium) *tomate verde*, husks removed, rinsed
1 (or to taste) *chile serrano*
1½ tablespoons safflower oil
2 tablespoons finely chopped white onion
½ cup *chile poblano rajas* (page 471) (about 2 *chiles*)
pinch of sea salt
6 ounces *queso añejo* or *fresco*, cut into ½-inch cubes
½ cup thick *crème fraîche*
1 scant cup crisp-fried *totopos* (page 15)

Put the *tomate* and *chile serrano* into a saucepan, cover with water, and bring to a simmer. Continue simmering until soft but not falling apart—about 10 minutes, depending on size. Drain and transfer to a blender jar with ¼ cup of the cooking water. Blend until smooth. Set aside.

Heat the oil in a sauté pan, add the onion and *poblano* strips with a pinch of salt, cover the pan, and cook over moderate heat until both are tender but not browned—about 4 minutes. Add the sauce and cook over fairly high heat until reduced and thickened—about 4 minutes. Add the cheese and cream and heat through, stirring from time to time, and as it comes to a simmer sprinkle the top with the *totopos*. Serve immediately.

SAUCES, RELISHES, AND PICKLED VEGETABLES

(Salsas, Chiles, y Legumbres en Escabeche)

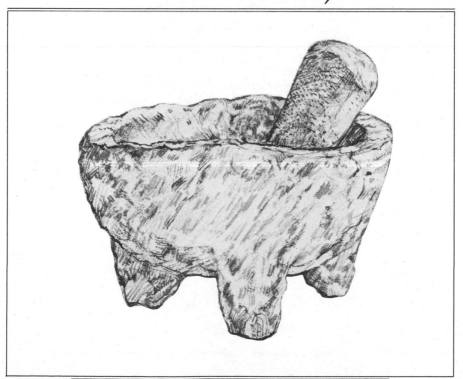

Salsa Verde (Cruda) (Raw Green Tomato Sauce)

Salsa de Tomate Verde, Cocida (Cooked Green Tomato Sauce)

Salsa Ranchera ("Ranch" Sauce)

Salsa de Jitomate, Sierra de Puebla

(Cooked Tomato Sauce, Sierra de Puebla)

Salsa de Jitomate (Raw Tomato Sauce, Michoacán)

Salsa de Jitomate Yucateca (Yucatecan Tomato Sauce)

Salsa de Chile Pasilla de Oaxaca (Oaxacan Chile Pasilla Sauce)

Salsa de Chile Pasilla de Michoacán (Cooked Michoacán Pasilla Sauce)

Salsa de Chile de Árbol (Michoacán Chile de Árbol Sauce)

Salsa de Uña (Nail Sauce)

Salsa X-ni-pek (Hot as a Dog's Nose Sauce, Yucatán)

Salsa de Suegra (Mother-in-Law Sauce)

Salsa para Tortas Ahogadas (Sauce for "Drowned Rolls")

Salsa de Plaza

Salsa para Barbacoa (Pit Barbecue Sauce)

Salsa de Chile Guajillo (Guajillo Chile Sauce)

Salsa de Chile Cascabel (Cascabel Chile Sauce)

Salsa Mexicana

Guacamole

Guacamole con Tomate Verde (Guacamole with Mexican Green Tomato)

Hongos en Escabeche (Pickled Mushrooms)

Chiles Anchos en Escabeche (Pickled Ancho Chiles)

Chiles Jalapeños en Escabeche (Pickled Jalapeños)

Chiles Chipotles en Vinagre (Pickled Chipotle Chiles)

Rajas con Limón (Chile Strips in Lime Juice)

Chile Macho

Botana de Jícama (Sliced Jícama Snack)

Pico de Gallo (Jícama and Orange Snack)

Pasta de Cacahuate (Peanut and Chile Paste)

Cebollas en Escabeche (Pickled Onions)

Cebollas Encurtidas para Tatemado (Lightly Pickled Purple Onions)

Cross-reference:

Salsa de Jitomate Norteña

Salsa Verde

It is no secret that many a Mexican travels to distant parts with cans of *chiles jalapeños, chipotles adobados,* or hot sauce stashed away in a suitcase. For many compatriots a meal is not a meal without the most important of national condiments. And they do become addictive, as I can attest after my many years in Mexico!

The *salsa de molcajete,* or table sauce—as opposed to the cooked sauce that is part of a main dish—provides not only the accent, life, and color to the food, but vitamins as well. The sauce or relish always contains *chiles* in one form or another—fresh, dried, or smoked—and with few exceptions the sauce is raw, although the ingredients in some of the sauces are either broiled or boiled in water first.

Although the sauces may be rolled up inside a *tortilla,* just that, and pickled vegetables can be served as a *botana,* or snack with drinks, both are more often put on top of rice, eaten with fried or broiled meats or fish, or used to top *antojitos* (although not *enchiladas* and *chilaquiles,* which have their own sauce). Generally they're not served with *tamales,* although Michoacán has its exceptions in *uchepos* and *corundas.* The *tamales* in the northern part of the state are served with tomato sauce and *sancocho* of vegetables on top, and the Oaxacan bean *tamales* are served with *chile pasilla* sauce.

There is no end to the regional varieties of sauces and relishes, and although large, this chapter gives a mere sprinkling of what you are likely to find when traveling around the country.

SALSA VERDE (CRUDA) *(Raw Green Tomato Sauce)*

MAKES 2 CUPS   CENTRAL MEXICO

This is a raw green table sauce; that is, it's *not* cooked before using. As an alternative, the *tomate* and *chiles* may be broiled and then blended as below for a more earthy and textured sauce. It is better still when made in a *molcajete*.

This type of sauce is always better eaten the same day it is made; it will, of course, keep a day or two under refrigeration, but it loses color, separates, and looks sort of dull the day after.

1 pound (about 22 medium) *tomate verde,* husks removed, rinsed
½ cup loosely packed, roughly chopped *cilantro*
1 large garlic clove, peeled and roughly chopped
2 tablespoons roughly chopped white onion
½ teaspoon (or to taste) sea salt

Put the *tomate* into a pan, barely cover with water, and bring to a simmer. Continue to cook until the *tomates* turn a lighter, faded green and are just soft but not falling apart—about 5 minutes. Set aside to cool.

Put ½ cup of the cooking water into a blender jar, add the *cilantro*, garlic, onion, and salt, and blend until almost smooth. Drain the *tomates* and add them to the blender jar; blend for a few seconds just to break them up roughly. The sauce should have a rough texture.

SALSA DE TOMATE VERDE, COCIDA
(Cooked Green Tomato Sauce)

MAKES ABOUT 2¼ CUPS   CENTRAL MEXICO

This is a multipurpose sauce. References are made to it in many recipes throughout the book that come from the regions of central Mexico.

1 pound (about 22 medium) *tomate verde,* rinsed, husks removed
4 *chiles serranos*
2 tablespoons roughly chopped *cilantro* (optional)
1 garlic clove, peeled and roughly chopped
1½ tablespoons safflower oil
sea salt to taste

Put the *tomate verde* and fresh *chiles* into a pan, cover with water, and bring to a simmer; continue cooking until the *tomate verde* is soft but not falling apart—about 10 minutes, depending on size. Remove from heat. Strain, reserving ⅓ cup of the cooking water.

Put the reserved cooking water into a blender jar, add the *chiles, cilantro,* and garlic, and blend until almost smooth. Add the *tomate verde* and blend for 10 seconds, no more, to make a fairly smooth sauce.

Heat the oil in a frying pan. Add the sauce and reduce over high heat until it thickens and seasons—about 8 minutes. Add salt to taste.

SALSA RANCHERA *("Ranch" Sauce)*

MAKES 1½ CUPS   CENTRAL MEXICO

This is a good basic tomato sauce used for *huevos rancheros* (page 318) or for seasoning shredded meat that is to be used in *tacos,* etc. More or fewer *chiles serranos* may be used to taste since some new varieties are not as *picante* as their smaller, narrower, older cousins.

This sauce will keep for several days in the refrigerator, depending on how hot and humid the weather is. You can freeze it (you will have to blend it again once it has defrosted), but it is not at its best then.

2 garlic cloves, peeled and roughly chopped
2 pounds (about 4 large) tomatoes, broiled (see page 450)
5 *chiles serranos,* broiled (see page 472)
2 tablespoons safflower oil
2 heaped tablespoons finely chopped white onion
½ teaspoon (or to taste) sea salt

Put the garlic, unpeeled tomatoes, and fresh *chiles* into a blender jar and blend to a slightly textured sauce. Set aside. Heat the oil in a heavy frying pan, add the onion, and cook gently until translucent—about 3 minutes. Add the blended ingredients and salt and cook over high heat, scraping the bottom of the pan from time to time, until slightly reduced and thickened— about 8 minutes. There will be flecks of brown in the sauce; that's okay, it means flavor and looks more interesting.

SALSA DE JITOMATE, SIERRA DE PUEBLA
(Cooked Tomato Sauce, Sierra de Puebla)

MAKES ABOUT 2¼ CUPS

This tomato sauce is used with many of the *antojitos* of the Sierra de Puebla—*pintos* (page 53) and *enchiladas*. It is essential to have good ripe tomatoes for this; if none are available, choose another sauce to use with your *antojitos*.

1½ pounds (about 3 large) tomatoes
4 (or to taste) *chiles serranos*
2 garlic cloves, peeled and roughly chopped
3 tablespoons safflower oil
sea salt to taste

Put the tomatoes into a pan with the fresh *chiles*, cover with water, bring to a simmer, and cook at a fast simmer until fairly soft but not falling apart—about 5 minutes, depending on size of tomatoes. Set aside.

Put the garlic, *chiles*, and ⅓ cup of the cooking water into a blender jar and blend until well broken—about 5 seconds. Add the unpeeled tomatoes and blend for a few seconds; the sauce should have a roughish texture. Heat the oil in a frying pan or *cazuela*, add the sauce, and cook over high heat, stirring from time to time and scraping the bottom of the dish, until reduced and the raw taste of garlic has disappeared—about 6 to 8 minutes. Add salt to taste.

SALSA DE JITOMATE
(Raw Tomato Sauce, Michoacán)

MAKES 2 CUPS   SEÑORITA EFIGENIA HERNANDEZ GONZALEZ, MICHOACÁN

This is a simple fresh table sauce to be eaten the same day that it is made and to be made only when tomatoes are ripe and juicy. It is better, of course, made in a *molcajete*, but if you are using a blender, be sure not to overblend; it should have some texture. The same steps apply using either of these methods.

This sauce is used as a condiment for plain shredded meat *tacos* or as a topping for *tostadas*.

2 garlic cloves, peeled and roughly chopped
4 *chiles serranos*, broiled (see page 472)
rounded ¼ teaspoon (or to taste) sea salt
1 pound (about 2 large) tomatoes, broiled (see page 450)
⅓ cup finely chopped white onion
⅓ cup loosely packed, roughly chopped *cilantro*

Blend the garlic, fresh *chiles*, and salt together to a rough paste. Gradually add the unpeeled tomatoes, grinding well after each addition. The sauce will have a roughish texture, and pieces of skin will be evident. Stir in the onion and *cilantro* and serve.

Cooked Version

To use with *uchepos*, etc., omit onion and *cilantro* and add 2 tablespoons safflower oil.

Heat oil and cook sauce over high heat to reduce and thicken—about 5 minutes.

SALSA DE JITOMATE YUCATECA
(Yucatecan Tomato Sauce)

MAKES ABOUT 1½ CUPS

There are several ways in which Yucatecan cooks prepare their tomato sauce to accompany *papadzules* (page 37) or *dzotobichayes* (page 78). Much will depend on where they come from. The Mayan cook from the village will make her *chiltomate* by roasting the tomatoes on the hot stones of the pit barbecue, the *pib*, and then grinding them roughly with *chile* in a wooden mortar called a *kokoic* (see illustration). The urban Mérida cook would probably boil the tomatoes, blend them, pass them through a fine sieve, and fry them with onion and *chile*. Yet another method is that given below, which combines the two methods with the best results.

This sauce will keep for a few days under refrigeration and can even be frozen. It is blended after defrosting as it tends to separate.

    1 pound (about 2 large) tomatoes, broiled (see page 450)
    2 tablespoons safflower oil
    ¼ small white onion, sliced
    sea salt to taste
    1 *chile habanero* or any small hot green *chile*

Blend the unpeeled tomatoes for a few seconds; they should have some texture. Heat the oil in a frying pan, add the onion, and fry for about 1 minute or until translucent—do not brown. Add the blended tomatoes, salt, and whole fresh *chile* and cook until reduced to about 1¼ cups. Serve hot.

SALSA DE CHILE PASILLA DE OAXACA
(*Oaxacan Chile Pasilla Sauce*)

MAKES 1⅔ CUPS

The predominant table sauce in Oaxaca is without doubt that made from the smoky *chile pasilla de Oaxaca* (see photo, page 509), which is very *picante* but with an unforgettable lingering flavor.

This sauce is served with broiled meats, on top of *antojitos*, with beans, and in soups. It keeps well for several days in the refrigerator, but I do not recommend freezing it.

½ pound (about 11 medium) *tomate verde* (*tomate de milpa* in Oaxaca)
3 small *chiles pasilla de Oaxaca* or *chipotles moras* or 2 *chipotle*
½ small head of garlic, charred (see page 439), the cloves separated and peeled
sea salt to taste

Remove the husks from the *tomate verde*, rinse, cut into quarters, and add water to come halfway up the *tomate*. Cover and cook over medium heat until very soft—about 10 to 15 minutes. Strain, reserving the cooking water, and add extra water if necessary to make ½ cup liquid. Put the whole dried *chiles* over a bare flame or onto a hot *comal* and toast for about 2 minutes on each side. Rinse briefly in cold water and break into small pieces into a blender jar, removing veins and seeds only if you cannot take the heat of this *chile*. Add the reserved cooking water, garlic, and salt to the blender jar and blend until smooth. Add the cooked *tomate* and blend briefly. The sauce should be of medium consistency—if too thick, add some more water; if too thin, it will thicken with sitting around.

SALSA DE CHILE PASILLA DE MICHOACÁN
(Michoacán Pasilla Sauce)

MAKES ABOUT 1¼ CUPS   SEÑORA LIVIER RUIZ DE SUAREZ, MORELIA

This sauce comes from the northern part of Michoacán that borders on Jalisco. It is earthy and delicious, served on top of *morisqueta* (boiled rice, page 124) with crumbled *cotija* cheese; with *corundas, or uchepos,* and cream; or in the *Minguichi II* (page 330) from that area; or with kidneys (page 310). It keeps well and can also be frozen.

3 *chiles pasilla*
2 tablespoons safflower oil
2 small *tomate verde,* husks removed, rinsed
¾ cup water
2 garlic cloves, unpeeled
¼ small white onion, finely chopped
¼ teaspoon (or to taste) sea salt

Remove the stalks, if any, from the dried *chiles* and discard. Wipe the *chiles* with a damp cloth to remove dust, etc. Heat the oil in a frying pan and gently fry the *chiles,* without burning, turning them around from time to time until they are just firm to the touch—about 5 minutes.

Remove the *chiles* with a slotted spoon and drain on paper toweling. In the same oil, fry the *tomate verde* and garlic until lightly browned and soft inside—about 5 minutes. Put the water into a blender jar and add the *tomate verde,* peeled garlic, and crumbled, fried *chiles* with their seeds and veins. Blend for a few seconds to a textured puree. Heat the same oil in the pan, add the onion, and fry gently until translucent, without browning—about 1 minute. Add the blended ingredients and salt and fry, stirring from time to time and scraping the bottom of the pan, until the sauce has reduced and thickened a little and is well seasoned—about 5 minutes.

SALSA DE CHILE DE ÁRBOL
(Michoacán Chile de Árbol Sauce)

MAKES ABOUT 2 CUPS   SEÑORA SEVERA NUÑEZ, LA GARITA, MICHOACÁN

This is a wonderfully rustic sauce that evokes the true earthiness of simple country food in Mexico. The charring gives it a smoky taste and the *molcajete* a rough quality. It is well worth making in this way if you have a *molcajete*, a strong hand, and time to bask in the aroma. If not, then blend but do not overblend.

Puyas can be substituted for *chile de árbol*, but they will need longer toasting. This is an example *par excellence* of an uncooked table sauce, *salsa de molcajete*.

½ pound (about 11 medium) *tomate verde*, husks removed, rinsed
8 *chiles de árbol* or 4 *puyas*
2 garlic cloves, peeled
sea salt to taste
⅓ cup warm water

Put a *comal* or heavy frying pan over medium heat and toast the *tomate verde* until they char slightly and are soft inside—about 10 minutes. Set aside. Lower the heat and place half the *chiles* onto the *comal*, turning them around every few seconds (the stem, if attached, helps); they will change to a lighter color but must not burn. Do the second batch, then crumble into the *molcajete*, shaking them to discard some of the seeds. Add the garlic, salt, and a little of the water and start grinding until the *chiles'* skins have been ground to very small pieces. Add the *tomate verde* little by little, alternating with the water, and grind them roughly; yes, there will be pieces of skin evident.

SALSA DE UÑA (*Nail Sauce*)

MAKES 2 CUPS   COLIMA

Salsa de uña is the local *salsa mexicana* with minor differences. It is used in the same way, really as a condiment with just about anything. I was told by the cook who gave me the recipe that it should be made about 2 hours before the meal so that the flavors have time to blend. It should not be kept for more than a couple of days for it loses its fresh crispness. It does not freeze well.

1½ cups finely chopped unpeeled tomatoes
½ cup finely chopped radishes
⅓ cup finely chopped white onion
3 *chiles serranos*, finely chopped
2 tablespoons finely chopped *cilantro*
½ teaspoon (or to taste) sea salt

Mix all the ingredients together and allow to macerate for about 2 hours before using. No water is necessary as the sauce creates its own juice.

SALSA X-NI-PEK (*Hot as a Dog's Nose Sauce*)

MAKES 1⅔ CUPS   YUCATÁN

This sauce is so *picante* that it will make even a dog's nose hot. It makes a nice change from *salsa mexicana*, especially with the fragrance of the *chile habanero*. Many in the West have access to sour orange trees, but if you don't, make the suggested substitute for bitter orange juice (page 456).

1 cup finely chopped unpeeled tomatoes
½ cup finely chopped purple onion
½ cup loosely packed, roughly chopped *cilantro*
1 *chile habanero or 2 serranos*, finely chopped
½ cup bitter orange juice (see note above)
sea salt to taste

Mix all the ingredients together in a china or glass bowl and set aside to season for about 30 minutes before using. It is best eaten the same day, although it will keep for about 3 days in the refrigerator.

SALSA DE SUEGRA *(Mother-in-Law Sauce)*

MAKES 2 CUPS   COLIMA

According to local lore, the cook serves this to her son-in-law because *le pica mucho* (it bites him a lot). It is very *picante*. However, if you use 3 *chiles*, it is only pleasantly *picante*.

This sauce should have a thick, rough consistency and is used with *frijoles*, rice, or broiled meats. It is best when eaten fresh but will keep for a few days in the refrigerator without spoiling. It does not freeze well.

½ pound (about 10 medium) *tomate verde*, rinsed, husks removed
6 ounces (1 medium) green (unripe) tomato
2 heaped tablespoons finely chopped scallion tops
3 *chiles serranos*, roughly chopped
2 tablespoons finely chopped *cilantro*
scant ½ teaspoon (or to taste) sea salt
⅓ cup water

Roughly chop the tomatoes, add a little at a time with the rest of the ingredients to a blender jar, and blend for a few seconds with each addition until the sauce has a rough consistency.

SALSA PARA TORTAS AHOGADAS
(Sauce for "Drowned" Rolls)

MAKES 2¾ CUPS   JALISCO

This sauce is used primarily in Jalisco to smother a bread roll stuffed with *carnitas* called *torta ahogada* (page 376), but it can be used as an all-purpose sauce, a spicy catsup if you will, with seafoods and steaks.

One of the ingredients is a local sauce called *Tamazula*. It is a popular bottled condiment originally fabricated in the small town of Tamazula in the state of Jalisco. It is pleasantly *picante* and acidy, so I suggest substituting just mild, fruity vinegar—the extra heat won't matter as the sauce is fiery-hot anyway, so a little more will not be noticed.

If you find the sauce too overpoweringly hot, reduce the number of *chiles*.

1 pound (about 2 large) tomatoes
1 cup water or *pulque*
1 California bay leaf
1 whole clove
5 garlic cloves, peeled and roughly chopped
6 peppercorns
⅛ teaspoon cumin seed
1 teaspoon prepared yellow mustard
1 tablespoon mild vinegar
2 tablespoons *Tamazula* sauce (see note on page 346) or mild vinegar
1 teaspoon sea salt
20 *chiles de árbol,* toasted

TO SPRINKLE OVER THE TOP
⅓ cup finely chopped white onion
1 heaped teaspoon dried oregano, Mexican if possible

Put the tomatoes into a pan, cover with water, and bring to a simmer. Cook until the tomatoes are fairly soft but not falling apart—about 5 to 8 minutes, depending on size. Drain and set aside.

Put the water into a blender jar and add the bay leaf, clove, garlic, peppercorns, cumin seed, mustard, vinegar, *Tamazula* sauce, and salt; blend until smooth. Remove the stems from the toasted *chiles,* shake, extracting and discarding some of the seeds, and crumble the *chiles* into the blender jar. Blend again until fairly smooth. Add the drained, unpeeled tomatoes and blend until smooth. Pass the sauce through a fine strainer, discarding the debris, and put into a serving dish. Sprinkle with the onion and oregano and serve. This sauce will keep well for several days in the refrigerator.

SALSA DE PLAZA

MAKES ABOUT 2¼ CUPS   JALISCO

This is a mild fresh tomato sauce used with *antojitos, tortas,* etc., in Jalisco. Good fresh tomatoes are a must; if they're not available, make another type of sauce.

This sauce is, of course, better eaten fresh or within a few days as it will not keep too long, especially in hot sticky weather, and does not freeze successfully.

1 pound (about 2 large) tomatoes
1 small white onion, sliced
1 *chile serrano*
1 teaspoon sugar
1 teaspoon sea salt
1 tablespoon strong vinegar
2 tablespoons liquid from canned *jalapeños en escabeche*

THE TOPPING
⅓ cup finely chopped white onion
½ teaspoon dried oregano, Mexican if possible

Put the tomatoes into a pan, cover with water, bring to a fast simmer, and cook for 5 minutes. Drain tomatoes, transfer, unpeeled, to a blender jar, and add the onion, *chile,* sugar, salt, vinegar, and liquid from *chile* can; blend until almost smooth. Transfer sauce to a serving dish and sprinkle with onion and the oregano.

SALSA PARA BARBACOA *(Pit Barbecue Sauce)*

MAKES 2¼ CUPS   SEÑORA MARIA GUADALUPE MEDINA DE ITURBE, HIDALGO

Although this sauce comes from Hidalgo, where Señora Iturbe was born, I first came across it when eating *tacos* of *barbacoa* in a small restaurant in Jungapeo, where they also serve the best *pancita,* a *menudo* made with the stomach and feet of the sheep that has been barbecued in a pit in the ground. The sauce is very *picante.*

1 pound (about 22 medium) *tomate verde,* husks removed, rinsed
5 *chiles moritas,* toasted
10 *chiles de árbol,* toasted
2 garlic cloves, peeled and roughly chopped
2 tablespoons finely chopped white onion
¼ teaspoon dried oregano, Mexican if possible
⅛ teaspoon cumin seed
½ teaspoon (or to taste) sea salt

Put the *tomate verde* into a pan, cover with water, and bring to a simmer. Continue simmering for 5 minutes. Remove from heat and set aside.

Crumble the dried *chiles* into a blender jar, taking out some of the seeds as you do so. Add the rest of the ingredients except the *tomate* and blend until smooth with ½ cup of the cooking water from the *tomate* (there will still be a few traces of *chile* skins, but that's okay). Add the cooked *tomate* and blend for about 3 seconds, just enough to break up but not to blend the *tomate.* The sauce should not be too smooth; it should be textured as though it had been made in the *molcajete.*

SALSA DE CHILE GUAJILLO (*Guajillo Chile Sauce*)

MAKES ABOUT 2 CUPS   SEÑORITA ANTONIA ORTIZ, HIDALGO

For those who don't want to go to the bother of toasting the *chiles,* here is an easy and very good sauce to use with *tacos,* with broiled meats, or on top of rice.

1 pound (about 22 medium) *tomate verde,* husks removed, rinsed
5 *chiles guajillos,* stalks removed
1 large garlic clove, peeled
1 white onion slice
sea salt to taste

Put the *tomate verde* and dried *chiles* into a pan, cover with water, bring to a simmer, and simmer for 5 minutes. Leave to soak for 5 minutes. Transfer with a slotted spoon to a blender jar. Add garlic and onion and blend briefly—about 5 seconds. Add salt to taste. The sauce should have some texture and not be overblended.

SALSA DE CHILE CASCABEL *(Cascabel Chile Sauce)*

MAKES 1¼ CUPS   WEST CENTRAL MEXICO

One of my favorite table sauces is the *chile cascabel* sauce made with red tomatoes, published in *The Cuisines of Mexico*. Here is another version, this time with *tomate verde*. What comes through in both is the nutty flavor of the toasted *chiles* and their seeds. Of course, this type of sauce is better made in the *molcajete*, but that is for the real *aficionados* who want to devote a lot of time to it. It is easier to make it in the blender, but you should take care not to overblend. If you want it more *picante*, then leave in some of the *chile* veins.

½ pound (about 11 medium) *tomate verde*, husks removed, rinsed
10 *chiles cascabel*
2 garlic cloves, peeled
scant ½ teaspoon sea salt
½ cup water

Heat a *comal* or frying pan, put the whole *tomate verde* onto it, and grill over low heat so that they cook through and the skin is browned—about 20 minutes. Set aside. Remove the stems from the dried *chiles*, if any, wipe them with a damp cloth to remove any dirt, slit them open, divide in half, and scrape out veins and seeds. Discard veins unless you want a more *picante* sauce; reserve the seeds.

Toast the *chile* pieces a few at a time, pressing down first on the outside for 2 seconds, then on the inside for 4 seconds. By this time they should be an opaque, orangey brown inside and when cooled should be crisp. Take care that the *comal* is not too hot, or the *chiles* will burn and the sauce will be bitter.

Put the garlic, salt, and water into a blender jar and crumble the *chiles* into it. Blend for a few seconds to break up the *chiles*, then add the *tomates* and reserved *chile* seeds and blend to a fairly rough texture.

SALSA MEXICANA

MAKES 1¼ CUPS

The most commonly served sauce—really more of a relish—to accompany *tacos*, rice, meats, and fish is the crisp, fresh *salsa mexicana* (referred to as *pico de gallo* in some northern areas).

This sauce should be made only when tomatoes are really red and ripe and eaten preferably the same day. A day later it looks a little sad. It does not freeze well.

¾ cup finely chopped unskinned tomatoes
⅓ cup finely chopped white onion
3 (or to taste) *chiles serranos*, finely chopped
¼ cup loosely packed, fairly finely chopped *cilantro*
salt to taste
3 tablespoons water, approximately

Mix the tomatoes, onions, *chiles*, and *cilantro* together well, add sea salt to taste, and moisten with the water. If the tomatoes tend to be dry (especially if you are using plum tomatoes), a little more water may be necessary. Set aside at room temperature to season for about 30 minutes before using.

GUACAMOLE

MAKES ABOUT 2 CUPS   CENTRAL MEXICO

The word *guacamole* derives from the Nahuatl words *ahuacatl* (avocado) and *molli* (a mixture or concoction).

Guacamole is best eaten as a *botana* of *tacos* with freshly made corn *tortillas*, and how good it is will depend very much on the quality of the avocados. Even if you leave the pit sitting in it or add lime juice—which spoils the balance of flavors—it will not keep for long, so make it at the last moment. Bring out your *molcajete* and make a show in front of your guests as they do brilliantly at Rosa Mexicano in New York. If you don't have one, resort to the blender for the base only and mash the avocados with a wooden spoon or, as they did in the old days, with your hands. It should be lumpy, not smooth.

3 tablespoons finely chopped white onion
4 *chiles serranos*, finely chopped
2 rounded tablespoons finely chopped *cilantro*
scant ½ teaspoon (or to taste) sea salt
3 large avocados (a little more than 1½ pounds)
⅔ cup finely chopped unpeeled tomato

THE TOPPING
2 tablespoons finely chopped white onion
1 heaped tablespoon finely chopped *cilantro*
2 tablespoons finely chopped tomato

If possible, use a *molcajete*. Grind the onion, fresh *chiles*, *cilantro*, and salt to a rough paste. Cut the avocados in half, remove pits (do not discard), and scoop out the flesh with a wooden spoon. Mash the flesh roughly into the base, turning the mixture over so that the seasoning is well distributed. Stir in the chopped tomato and sprinkle the top of the *guacamole* with the extra onion, *cilantro*, and tomato. Place the pits back into it for a nice effect and serve immediately, or within 15 minutes, in the *molcajete*. If you're using a blender, blend the base, turn it into a dish, and continue as above.

GUACAMOLE CON TOMATE VERDE
(Guacamole with Mexican Green Tomato)

MAKES 2 CUPS   STATE OF MEXICO

I have eaten this *guacamole* on rare occasions at homes in the state of Mexico bordering on Morelos. Although it's not my favorite, it makes an interesting change from the more popular version and is particularly suitable when tomatoes are not at their best.

3 tablespoons finely chopped white onion
4 *chiles serranos*, finely chopped
2 rounded tablespoons finely chopped *cilantro*
2 avocado leaves, toasted until crisp (optional)
scant ½ teaspoon (or to taste) sea salt
6 ounces (about 8 medium) *tomate verde*, broiled (see page 451)
3 large avocados (about 1½ pounds)

THE TOPPING
2 tablespoons finely chopped white onion
1 heaped tablespoon finely chopped *cilantro*

If possible, use a *molcajete*. Grind the onion, fresh *chiles*, *cilantro*, avocado leaves, and salt to a paste. Add the broiled *tomate verde*, a few at a time, mashing and grinding the skin as much as possible. Cut the avocados in half and remove the pits but do not discard. Scoop out the flesh with a wooden spoon and mash roughly into the base mixture, turning it over from the bottom so that the seasoning is well distributed. Put the pits back in. Sprinkle the top with onion and *cilantro* and serve immediately.

If you're using a blender, blend the base, add *tomate*, and blend very briefly—there must be some texture—then mash (do not blend) the avocado.

HONGOS EN ESCABECHE (*Pickled Mushrooms*)

MAKES ABOUT 2½ CUPS   SEÑORA HORTENSIA FAGOAGA, CENTRAL MEXICO

Once the rainy season starts in Mexico toward the end of May, we look forward to the many varieties of mushrooms that flood the market in waves, among them the various *calavaria* and *ramaria*, coral mushrooms that indeed are branched like pieces of fine coral. In Mexico they are called either *escobetilla*, because they resemble the little bunches of tough roots used to scrub pots, or *pata de pájaro*, bird's food. By far the best way to appreciate their crunchy texture is *en escabeche*. Any type of mushroom could, of course, be used with adjustments in cooking time. These mushrooms make a great snack with drinks, or they can be eaten as part of an hors d'oeuvre.

1 pound *pata de pájaro* or any other mushrooms
sea salt to taste
2 tablespoons safflower oil
1 cup sliced white onion
3 garlic cloves, peeled
2 *chiles jalapeños,* sliced lengthwise into 6 pieces
3 fresh marjoram sprigs *or* scant ¼ teaspoon dried
3 fresh thyme sprigs *or* scant ¼ teaspoon dried
2 small California bay leaves
1 cup mild vinegar
2 teaspoons sugar
2 tablespoons olive oil

Rinse the mushrooms well, trimming off the muddy stalk tips. Tear or cut the mushrooms into strips, including stems and curly tops. Put the mushrooms into a pan, add salt and water to barely cover, bring to a simmer, and continue simmering until the mushrooms are tender, about 30 minutes. Drain, reserving the cooking water. Heat the oil in a frying pan, add the onion, garlic, and fresh *chiles,* and fry over gentle heat until the onion is translucent. Add the rest of the ingredients except the olive oil and simmer for 20 minutes. Stir in the olive oil, adjust seasoning, and set aside to cool. Store in the refrigerator for at least 2 or 3 days and up to 10 days before serving them.

CHILES ANCHOS EN ESCABECHE
(Pickled Ancho Chiles)

MAKES ABOUT 9 CUPS   SEÑORA MARÍA DOLORES TORRES IZÁBAL

This is a prized family recipe very generously shared with me by my dear friend María Dolores, a wonderful cook in her own right and dedicated to the traditional cooking of Mexico. The recipe makes a lot, but you will want to make this quantity because it is so delicious on white rice, with cold cuts or broiled meats, or just for snacking, and it keeps well.

Use fine, large flexible *chiles anchos* that have not been around for too long for this dish.

1 pound *chiles anchos*
¾ cup safflower oil, approximately
¾ pound white onions, roughly sliced (about 2 cups)
24 garlic cloves, peeled
3 cups mild vinegar
¼ pound dark brown sugar or *piloncillo*, grated (about ½ rounded cup)
20 peppercorns
6 fresh marjoram sprigs *or* heaped ¼ teaspoon dried
6 fresh thyme sprigs *or* heaped ¼ teaspoon dried
6 California bay leaves
1½ tablespoons (or to taste) sea salt

Remove the stems, if any, from the dried *chiles* and wipe clean with a damp cloth. Make a slit down the side of the *chiles* and scrape out and discard veins and seeds. Open the *chiles* up and with a pair of scissors cut the rather tough rim around the base of the stem and flatten out. Cut each *chile* into 2 pieces lengthwise.

Heat a little of the oil in a frying pan and fry the pieces of *chile* one at a time, pressing them down into the oil so that the color inside changes to a light tobacco brown. If they are fleshy, they will begin to blister. Fry for about 3 to 4 seconds on each side, but do not let them burn. Remove and drain. Add a little oil to the pan as necessary while frying the *chiles*. In the same oil, fry the onion and garlic gently until the onion is translucent. Drain well and set aside.

In a separate pan, heat the vinegar and sugar together, adding the peppercorns, herbs, and salt. When the sugar has melted, bring the mixture to a simmer, then remove from the heat and set aside.

355

Spread one layer of the *chiles* into a glass or porcelain dish—a *soufflé* dish would be perfect—and add a layer of the onions and garlic. Pour over some of the vinegar mixture. Continue with the layers until the ingredients have all been used, pouring the remaining vinegar over the top. Cover loosely and set aside to season in a cool, airy place or in the bottom of the refrigerator for 8 to 10 days. Press the *chiles* down into the marinade from time to time, but do not stir or turn the mixture over.

CHILES JALAPEÑOS EN ESCABECHE
(Pickled Jalapeños)

MAKES ABOUT 8 CUPS   VERACRUZ

Ten years ago, when I was in Panuco, Veracruz, on one of my many food "expeditions," I tasted the best *jalapeños en escabeche* that I had ever eaten, prepared by a friend's son, Arnufo Perez. They had been made the day before and were still crisp, although all the flavors had combined. Señor Perez had used the thin, long-leaf oregano of the northern states, but the normal Mexican oregano can be used. I prefer to use half strong vinegar and half mild. I use small white *cebolla de rabo,* bulbous scallions; if they are not available (Texas scallions, not onions), you can use boiling onions or ordinary white onions cut into 8 pieces. If you can find fresh *jalapeños* of different shades or colors—they ripen from green through orange to red—do so, because they look more attractive.

These pickled vegetables will keep for many days in the refrigerator, although being so popular and multipurpose, they will disappear faster than you think.

> 1 pound *chiles jalapeños,* rinsed
> 1½ pounds carrots, trimmed and scraped
> 3 tablespoons sea salt
> ⅓ cup water
> 5 garlic cloves, peeled and roughly chopped
> 10 peppercorns
> 1 teaspoon cumin seed
> 4 whole cloves
> 16 California bay leaves
> leaves from 2 fresh thyme sprigs *or* ⅛ teaspoon dried
> 1½ teaspoons dried oregano, Mexican if possible
> ½ cup safflower oil
> 1 pound white onions (see note above)

3 cups mild vinegar
1 cup strong vinegar
10 garlic cloves, peeled
6 fresh thyme sprigs *or* ½ teaspoon dried
½ teaspoon granulated or brown sugar

Remove the stems from the fresh *chiles* and cut each into 4 lengthwise. Scrape out the seeds (for milder *chiles* remove the veins as well) and put into a large bowl. Slice the carrots diagonally about ⅛ inch thick and add to the *chiles*. Sprinkle with salt and toss well. Set aside to macerate for about 1 hour.

Put the water into a blender jar and add the chopped garlic, peppercorns, cumin seed, cloves, 10 of the bay leaves, the thyme leaves, and ½ teaspoon of the oregano; blend as thoroughly as possible. Heat the oil in a large, fairly deep pan. Add the blended spices and onions and fry until the liquid has evaporated and the onions are translucent, not brown—about 10 minutes. Strain the *chiles* and carrots, reserving the juice, and add to the pan. Fry over fairly high heat, stirring and turning the vegetables over for 10 minutes. Add the *chile* and carrot juice, vinegars, whole garlic cloves, 6 thyme sprigs, remaining 6 bay leaves and remaining teaspoon oregano, and the sugar. Bring to a boil and continue boiling for about 8 minutes. Transfer to a glass or ceramic bowl and set aside to cool before storing in the refrigerator.

CHILES CHIPOTLES EN VINAGRE
(Pickled Chipotle Chiles)

MAKES ABOUT 3 CUPS   CENTRAL MEXICO

Pickled *chipotles* rival *jalapeños en escabeche* for popularity in the Mexican kitchen, as either a pickle or a condiment or cooked as part of the seasoning of a dish. Either dried *chipotles mecos* (the lightish brown ones) or the slightly smaller *moras* (mulberry-colored) may be used. They should be kept for about 10 days after they are prepared, to season. When you're serving them, put several in a dish with a little of their liquid and sprinkle with oregano and 1 teaspoon olive oil as they do in Aculco, Puebla.

¼ pound (about 40 large) *chiles chipotles* or *moras*
⅓ cup safflower oil
2 cups roughly sliced onion
4 garlic cloves, peeled and slivered
4 California bay leaves
4 fresh marjoram sprigs *or* ¼ teaspoon dried
4 fresh thyme sprigs *or* ¼ teaspoon dried
2½ cups mild vinegar
1½ cups water
1½ teaspoons sea salt
6 tablespoons brown sugar or grated *piloncillo*

TO SERVE
dried oregano, Mexican if possible
olive oil

Rinse the dried *chiles* well—do not soak—and pat dry. Pierce them twice on each side with a sharp fork and set aside. Heat the oil in a frying pan, add the onion and garlic, and fry, turning them over from time to time, until they are just becoming translucent—about 20 seconds. Add the *chiles* and continue frying and turning them over for about 8 minutes. Add the herbs, vinegar, water, salt, and sugar and continue cooking and stirring over medium heat at a fast simmer for about 15 minutes longer if they are very leathery. Transfer to a glass or porcelain bowl and set aside in a cool place or in the bottom of the refrigerator for about 10 days, turning them over from bottom to top each day and pressing them down into the liquid, which should just about cover the *chiles*.

RAJAS CON LIMÓN *(Chile Strips in Lime Juice)*

MAKES ABOUT 1½ CUPS OAXACA

In Oaxaca the innocent-looking but fiercely hot *chile de agua* is charred and peeled and marinated in strips in lime juice with onion, salt, and oregano. It is used as a fresh relish with white rice, broiled meats, and stews as well as with *enfrijoladas*.

In central Mexico the fiery *chile manzano*, or *perón*, is used in the same way without the charring.

In the United States you can use any fleshy *chile* or pepper—the Anaheim, wax *chile*, banana or Italian peppers—making it hot or mild to taste. Either way, it makes a contrasting and refreshing relish.

Rajas con limón are best eaten a few hours after making them to allow time for the flavors to blend—and the acidity seems to cut the heat. They keep well in the refrigerator for several days, provided the weather is not terribly hot and damp, but do not freeze successfully.

1 cup charred, peeled, and cleaned *chile de agua strips* (see page 463)
⅓ cup thinly sliced white onion halves
⅓ cup fresh lime juice
¼ teaspoon dried oregano, Mexican if possible
sea salt to taste

Mix all the ingredients together in a glass or china bowl, and set aside to marinate for several hours.

CHILE MACHO

MAKES ½ CUP   SIERRA DE PUEBLA

Make this in small quantities as it is indeed *macho*—fearsomely strong—but does not keep well. It is used as a condiment in the Sierra, and it is particularly good on top of *pintos* (page 53).

10 *chiles serranos*, rinsed and roughly chopped
1 garlic clove, peeled and roughly chopped
¼ cup firmly packed, roughly chopped *cilantro*
½ teaspoon (or to taste) sea salt
⅓ cup water

Blend all the ingredients to a rough texture. If the *chiles* are particularly large, you may need a little more water to blend it all efficiently. The sauce should be moist but not too watery.

BOTANA DE JÍCAMA (*Sliced Jícama Snack*)

MAKES 3½ TO 4 CUPS   SEÑOR JOSÉ GARCÍA COLÍN, ZITÁCUARO, MICHOACÁN

Señor García always stations his cart outside the municipal office of the town where he does a brisk trade selling cups of brightly colored fruits. One day I noticed that he was slicing a very good-looking *jícama*, the first I had seen that fall. When I asked him where he had found it, he told me and then went on to explain that he was about to prepare a *botana* of *jícama* and peanuts that had been his *patron's* favorite when he had worked briefly in California.

1 medium *jícama* (about 1 to 1¼ pounds), peeled and sliced
2 tablespoons finely chopped white onion
3 tablespoons fresh lime juice
1 cup shelled raw peanuts, papery skin removed
4 *chiles de árbol*, toasted
2 tablespoons crumbled *queso añejo*

Spread the *jícama* slices in one layer on a platter, then sprinkle with the onion and lime juice.

Heat an ungreased frying pan and spread the peanuts in a thin layer over the surface. Over medium heat, shake and stir the peanuts until they are golden and well toasted right through—about 10 minutes. Put about ¼ cup with one of the toasted *chiles* into the blender and blend to the consistency of rough crumbs; continue with the rest in batches. (If you do them all at once, you will probably blend the bottom part to a powder, so it's better to blend in batches.)

Sprinkle the ground peanuts, cheese, and *chiles* over the *jícama* and serve with drinks.

PICO DE GALLO (*Jícama and Orange Snack*)

SERVES 4 TO 6   SEÑORA BEATRIZ TIRO, JALISCO

Cubed *jícama* and orange make up this typical *botana* from Jalisco, where it is usually served—with toothpicks—with a shot of *tequila* or beer. *Pico de gallo* is also often served at the end of a meal as dessert, salt notwithstanding, but then the *chile* powder is omitted.

Powdered *chile piquín* is available in most Mexican groceries, but hot paprika is a suitable substitute. Commercial *chile* powder mixed with other flavorings should not be used.

2 cups peeled *jícama* in ½-inch cubes
1½ cups peeled orange sections (about 4 oranges)
¼ cup fresh lime juice
¼ teaspoon sea salt
powdered *chile piquín* to taste

Mix all the ingredients except the *chile* in a glass or china bowl and leave to macerate for about 3 hours, stirring the mixture from time to time. Sprinkle with the *chile* powder and serve.

Note: This recipe name is sometimes given in the United States and along the Mexican border to a *salsa mexicana cruda.*

PASTA DE CACAHUATE (*Peanut and Chile Paste*)

MAKES 2½ TO 3 CUPS   SEÑORA HORTENSIA FAGOAGA, SIERRA DE PUEBLA

This *pasta* is in fact a crumbly condiment, *picosisimo* as the señora says, for want of a better word, that is strewn over rice, refried beans, eggs, or a freshly made corn *tortilla* slathered with *natas* or sour cream. If you don't like it as *picante*, reduce the number of *chiles*. Because of its concentrated flavor, this *pasta* will go a long way and will keep for weeks for that matter, becoming drier and stronger as it stays around.

This can be made with half or all hulled *pepita* seeds; ½ pound will measure about 1¾ cups, and *pepita* seeds will toast in about 3 minutes instead of the longer time required for the denser peanuts.

½ pound raw peanuts, shelled but brown skin left on (rounded 1½ cups)
½ ounce (well-packed ½ cup) *chiles de árbol*
⅓ cup mild vinegar
⅓ cup strong vinegar
1 large garlic clove, peeled and roughly chopped
¾ cup water
1 teaspoon (or to taste) sea salt
⅓ cup safflower oil

Heat a heavy, ungreased frying pan, add the peanuts, and gently stir over medium heat until they are well toasted and golden—about 10 minutes. Set aside.

In the same pan, toast the dried *chiles* (stalks intact) over very low heat, turning them almost constantly so that they begin to brown slightly and a strong flavor emanates from them. Take care not to burn them, or the *pasta* will be bitter. Remove stems and crumble into the blender jar.

Add the vinegars, garlic, water, and salt into the blender jar and blend for a few seconds. Add about one third of the peanuts and blend for a few seconds just to break them up. Add a second batch and do the same, loosening the blades with a spatula. Mix the third batch into the blended ingredients well and blend in spurts, stirring up the mixture from time to time until you have a grainy, textured paste.

Heat the oil in a frying pan, add the blended ingredients, and fry over medium heat, stirring and turning over the mixture constantly until it is crumbly and rather dry and has turned a dark saffron color—about 15 minutes. Store in a cool, dry place; it is not necessary to refrigerate the *pasta*.

CEBOLLAS EN ESCABECHE *(Pickled Onions)*

MAKES ABOUT 6 TO 7 CUPS   YUCATÁN

No respectable home kitchen, or restaurant for that matter, in Yucatán would be without a large jar of pickled white onion rings to go on top of *panuchos*, in a turkey or fish *escabeche*, or to accompany roasted chicken or fried fish. If they're not on hand, a Yucatecan cook will wilt the onions in hot water and then partially cover them with sour orange juice diluted with water, and finally mix with toasted oregano and some fresh *chile verde*.

Onions prepared in this way are best left for a few days to macerate for all the flavors to integrate.

2 pounds white onions, trimmed, peeled, and thinly sliced into rings
1 rounded tablespoon sea salt
4 whole cloves
4 whole allspice
1 tablespoon dried oregano, Yucatecan if possible, toasted and rubbed between the hands
2 *chiles x-cat-ik* or other large blond *chiles*, charred and left whole, unpeeled
1 whole head of garlic, outer papery peel removed only, charred, and then divided into cloves
3 cups vinegar—2 cups commercial white plus 1 cup mild and fruity
1 teaspoon peppercorns, roughly crushed

Put onions into a glass bowl, cover with water, and drain. Return to bowl, add the rest of the ingredients, and stir well before storing.

CEBOLLAS ENCURTIDAS PARA TATEMADO
(Lightly Pickled Purple Onions)

MAKES 4 CUPS   COLIMA

Although these onions traditionally decorate a plate of *tatemado* from Colima (page 258), they are very good scattered over a salad or on top of *tostadas*.

1 pound purple onions, trimmed, peeled, and thinly sliced
½ cup fresh lime juice
1½ teaspoons sea salt

Put all ingredients into a glass or porcelain bowl, mix well, and set aside to macerate for about 2 hours before using. They will keep for several weeks in the refrigerator.

BREAD, SWEET YEAST ROLLS, AND WHEAT FLOUR TORTILLAS

(Pan, Pan Dulce, y Tortillas de Harina)

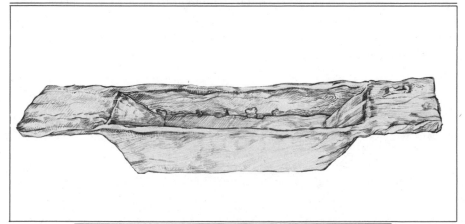

Bolillos (Bobbin-Shaped Bread Rolls)
Molletes (Bean-Stuffed Bolillos)
Teleras (Flat Bread Rolls)
Torta Mexicana (Sandwich Roll)
Galletas Marinas (Crisp Ship Crackers)
Torta de Santuario (Sanctuary Roll)
Torta Ahogada
Conchas (Sweet Rolls with Shell-Patterned Sugar Topping)
Pan de Muertos (All Saints and All Souls Day Bread)
Rosca de Reyes (Twelfth Night Ring Bread)
Tortillas de Harina (Large Wheat Flour Tortillas)
Burras
Chivichangas
Tortillas de Harina Integral (Whole-Wheat Flour Tortillas)

The first grains of wheat to be planted in Mexico came in the first ship with the *conquistadores*. They were planted in the high country around the capital and later on in the northwestern plains of Sonora. Wheat's primary use at first was for communion wafers!

Although bread making has become a highly commercialized industry in many parts of the country, many bakeries still make their own in steam ovens at the back of their shops. In country areas where hardwood, preferably oak, is available for the ovens, and the tradition of building brick or *adobe* ovens and making bread still exists, there are a number of family-run bakeries. It is mostly men who make the bread, but curiously, in Tamiahua, in the state of Tamaulipas, it is the women who perform this task, with large bread ovens most prominent in the kitchens at the back of the house.

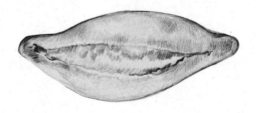

BOLILLOS *(Bobbin-Shaped Bread Rolls)*

MAKES ¾ POUND DOUGH

If there is one thing that visitors remember about food in Mexico, it is the crusty little bread rolls called *bolillos*. In large urban centers the bread is cooked in diesel-fired steam ovens, but in the small towns and villages the bread is still cooked in wood-fired *adobe* or brick ovens that not only add to the flavor but give a good crust without the aid of steam. It is sad, however, to see that they are learning some of the "fast" techniques from across the border and now use too much sugar to hurry along the rising process and form a deeper-colored crust.

In these small family bakeries the dough is mixed and left to rise on large wooden tables; there are no bowls, no thermometer in the oven, and no scales to weigh—it is all done by eye, even when using 44 kilos of flour per batch of rolls.

The flour used for *bolillos* in Mexico, at least in the central area and the South, is not a high-gluten one, so any all-purpose flour can be used.

The recipe given here was the one we used when I did my stint in a Mexico City bakery some years ago. Sugar used for the starter was minimal and could easily be left out due to the long rising period—and that was a time when master bakers cared primarily more about the development of flavor than hurrying along their bread. Each baker has his own technique for forming *bolillos*; and these techniques vary in complexity. I have given a simple, but effective method here.

If this recipe is too fussy for you, use any French bread recipe that you prefer and follow the instructions for forming the rolls.

It is hardly worth making a smaller amount of this starter; besides, it will keep for some time in the refrigerator and be useful for other batches of bread.

STARTER
¼ teaspoon crumbled cake yeast *or* ⅛ teaspoon dry yeast
1 teaspoon sugar (optional)
½ cup warm water, approximately
½ teaspoon sea salt
½ pound unbleached flour, plus extra for working surface
grease for the bowl

Cream the yeast and sugar together with 2 tablespoons of the water. Dissolve the salt in the remaining water.

Machine Mixing

Put the flour into the bowl of an electric mixer; first mix in the creamed yeast and then the salted water, reserving a little to see how much moisture you need. Beat with a dough hook until you have a smooth, rather firm, slightly sticky dough—about 2 minutes. Throw a little flour around the bowl and beat briefly so that the dough pulls away cleanly from the surface of the bowl. Lightly flour the work surface, scrape the dough from the bowl, and work it into a round cushion shape. Leave it to rest briefly while you clean and grease the bowl. Replace the dough in the bowl, cover it with greased plastic wrap and a heavy towel, and set in a cool place—about 55°—overnight or for at least 8 hours.

Hand Mixing

Place the flour in a circle on your work surface, making a well in the middle. Add the creamed yeast and work into the flour. Gradually add the salted water, reserving a little, and work it in with your hands, gathering the dough and stray flour together with a plastic dough scraper. Add the rest of the water if necessary to form the dough into a cohesive mass. Knead, sprinkling with a little more flour if necessary, until the dough "comes to life" and is smooth, very slightly sticky, and fairly firm—about 2 to 3 minutes. Form the dough into a round cushion shape. Transfer to a greased and floured baking sheet, cover with greased plastic wrap and a towel, and set aside in a cool place, about 55°, to rise overnight or for about 8 to 12 hours.

MAKES ABOUT 24 TO 26 5-INCH ROLLS

THE BREAD DOUGH
2 pounds unbleached flour, plus extra for bowl and work surface
½ pound starter (page 367)
4 teaspoons (½ ounce) crumbled cake yeast *or* 2 teaspoons dry yeast
2 cups warm water, approximately, plus extra for the yeast
2 teaspoons (or to taste) sea salt

Machine Mixing the Dough

Put the flour in the bowl of the mixer. Break the starter into small pieces and add it. Cream the yeast with 2 tablespoons of the water, pressing out any lumps with the back of a wooden spoon, and mix into the flour. Dissolve the salt in the remaining water and gradually beat it into the flour, reserving a little until you see how much the flour will absorb. Beat with a dough hook until you have a smooth, flexible, slightly sticky dough—about 2½ minutes. Throw a little flour around the bowl and beat briefly until the dough cleans itself away from the surface of the bowl.

Hand Mixing the Dough

Put the flour in a circle on your work surface and make a well in the middle. Break up the starter into small pieces and put into the well. Cream the yeast with 2 tablespoons of the water, pressing out any lumps with the back of a wooden spoon. Pour into the well and gradually work in the surrounding flour. Dissolve the salt in the water and gradually work the liquid into the flour mixture, reserving a little until you see how much moisture the flour will absorb. Keep scraping the dough together with a plastic dough scraper until it becomes a cohesive mass. Then start to knead, adding a little more flour as necessary, until you have a smooth, flexible, very slightly sticky dough—about 5 minutes.

First Rise

Form into a round cushion shape, put into a greased bowl or onto a tray, cover with greased plastic wrap and a towel, and set aside in a warm place—ideally 70°—until it has almost tripled in volume, 2½ to 3 hours.

Second Rise

Scrape onto a lightly floured work surface, punch down, and again form into a round cushion shape. Replace in the bowl or tray, cover as before, and set aside until almost triple in size, about 2 hours.

Turn out onto a lightly floured surface and work into a long sausage shape about 2 inches in diameter. Cut the dough into 24 pieces—each one should weigh just over 2 ounces. Roll each piece of dough under the palms of your hands, as illustrated, into round balls and form into *bolillos*.

First prepare baking sheets for baking the *bolillos*. You will need about 4 large ones; they should be well greased and floured. For rising method 2 you will also need a well-floured board for the rising before transferring to baking sheet. The oven should be heated to 400° about halfway through the rising period.

Forming: Method

Flattening the dough out to an oval shape, fold one third of the dough over toward the center, flatten hard, then double the dough over and flatten it out with the heel of your palm. Give the dough a roll or two under your palms to tighten, letting a little bit "escape" at each end to form the rounded ears.

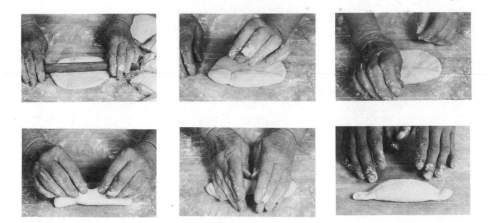

Final Rise, Slashing, and Baking

Final Rise: Method 1

When the rolls have been formed, there is a seam underneath. Turn it to the top and carefully place the *bolillos* to rise on the prepared baking sheets. In the rising and baking the seam will open as the dough expands and forms the required shape.

Set the sheets aside for the dough to rise to about half its size again—about 1 hour at 70°.

The oven by now will be heated to 400°. Bake at the top of the oven for about 15 to 20 minutes or until the *bolillos* are a pale golden color and sound hollow when tapped on the bottom.

Final Rise: Method 2

If you prefer to slash the dough in the classical fashion, place the shaped *bolillos*, seam side up, onto a floured board and set aside to rise until they have risen to about half their size again—about 1 hour at 70°. Carefully flip them over, seam side down, onto the prepared baking sheets and slash deeply as shown, either with a razor or a conventional dough slasher.

The oven will now be ready, so bake at 400° until the rolls have a good golden crust and sound hollow when tapped on the bottom—about 15 to 20 minutes.

MOLLETES *(Bean-Stuffed Bolillos)*

SERVES 6

I first ate *molletes* many years ago in Mexico City, where it was, and still is, served as an economical and satisfying brunch dish, presumably invented by a cook who wanted to use up yesterday's bread rolls and refried beans. The Mexican bobbin-shaped rolls, *bolillos,* are hollowed out, filled with refried beans, topped with melted cheese, and served with a sauce: either *salsa mexicana* (page 351), *salsa ranchera* (page 338), or *salsa verde (cruda)* (page 336). Any crusty bread rolls or 4-inch lengths of French bread can be used.

6 *bolillos* (page 367) or bread rolls
6 tablespoons unsalted melted butter, approximately
2 cups *frijoles refritos* (page 180), heated
½ pound *Chihuahua* or medium-sharp Cheddar cheese, grated
2 cups of any or all of the sauces mentioned above, approximately

Heat the oven to 375°.

Grease well a baking sheet onto which the halved rolls can be placed in one layer.

Cut the rolls in half horizontally. Lightly brush them inside with the butter. Bake until slightly crisp on the outside, about 10 minutes. Fill with plenty of the bean paste, sprinkle with cheese, and return to the oven for the cheese to melt but not brown. Serve immediately, passing the sauces separately.

TELERAS *(Flat Bread Rolls)*

Teleras are flattish bread rolls marked across the middle with a deep indentation or two with the thin rolling pin used to form them. The name came from a whole-wheat, second-class bread made in Andalusia for the day laborers, called *telera*. In Mexico it is customary to make *teleras* of the same dough as that of *bolillos* and of white flour. They are cut open horizontally and stuffed with layers of ingredients (see recipes that follow) to make the renowned Mexican *torta*.

Follow the recipe for *bolillos* up to the point of cutting the dough into 24 pieces. Then, taking one ball of the dough—you can form two at once when you have had practice—flatten it with your hand or the thin rolling pin and roll into an oval shape. Press down hard across the middle of the dough, once or twice, whichever you prefer, until you think the dough will sever, turn it upside down on the prepared baking tray, and set aside in a warm place, uncovered, at about 70° for about 1 hour. The dough should almost double in size. To bake, follow instructions for *bolillos*, flipping the *teleras* back, indented side up, for baking.

They should take about 15 to 20 minutes in a 400° oven.

TORTA MEXICANA *(Sandwich Roll)*

I know of no other "sandwich" that one could take on a picnic that gives so much pleasure and surprise to the uninitiated. It is crammed with textures and flavors. Although any foods can, in fact, be put into a *torta*, this is my favorite version.

A flat bread roll called *telera* (see page 372) is generally used, cut open horizontally, and some of the crumbs removed, but in fact any crusty bread roll or a length of hollowed-out crisp French bread can be used.

Spread one of the open faces of the roll with some refried beans (page 180) followed by some strips of *chiles jalapeños en escabeche* or *chipotles en adobo*.

ADD
a layer of sour cream
several thin layers of cooked ham, chicken, or pork
a layer of sliced tomatoes
a thick slice of cheese, any type

The other face should be thickly spread with crushed avocado with a sprinkle of salt to taste. The two sides should then be pressed together and the whole eaten with two hands and a lot of paper napkins.

GALLETAS MARINAS (*Crisp Ship Crackers*)

MAKES 25 2½-INCH CRACKERS   YUCATÁN

A block or two from where I sometimes stay in Mérida is a small bakery, Panadería Santa Teresita, where the variety of bread is modest compared with that of the bakeries in central Mexico. The Yucatecan *pan frances* (French bread) has a good yeasty flavor but is soft and pale. There are a number of puff pastry shapes filled with almond paste, pumpkin, or ham with yellow cheese that are sprinkled with sugar. But the item that I always go for is a bag of pale, crisp, round crackers made of a well-fermented bread dough, even lighter than that of breadsticks. (My predilection for crisp breads is perhaps exaggerated, but they have seen me through many a long journey.) I asked for the recipe, which they gave me accurately and without hesitation.

Cooking time may vary with your oven. The important thing is that they remain pale and yet be crisp right through. After being cooked they should be stored in an airtight container and will last for weeks, even months. Nevertheless, they do tend to lose their crispness, so just put them back into a 350° oven for about 30 minutes before using them.

These can be made with either lard or butter; I prefer to use half and half.

scant 1½ teaspoons sea salt
1 heaped tablespoon unsalted butter, softened
1 heaped tablespoon lard, plus extra for greasing trays, etc.
1¼ cups lukewarm water, approximately 110°
4 rounded teaspoons (about ½ ounce) crumbled cake yeast *or* 2 rounded
  teaspoons dry yeast
1 pound unbleached flour, plus extra for kneading

Have ready 3 large, well-greased baking sheets.

Stir the salt and fat into 1 cup of the water and keep stirring until the salt has dissolved and the butter melted. Put the crumbled yeast into a small bowl. Add 2 tablespoons of the remaining water and work to a smooth cream with the back of a wooden spoon. Form the flour in a rough circle on your work surface, making a well in the center; pour the creamed yeast into it and begin to work in the surrounding flour, sprinkling the mixture with the salted, fatty water. Mix well and gather into a rough ball. Lightly flour the board and begin kneading until the dough comes to life and is smooth and elastic— about 3 minutes.

Roll the dough into a sausage shape about 2 inches in diameter and then cut with a plastic dough scraper into 25 pieces—I usually weigh each one so they will be an even size; they should be just over 1 ounce each. Roll each piece of dough under your palms into a small ball about 1½ inches in diameter. Place the balls of dough about 2 inches apart on the greased trays. Smear the inside of your hands with more lard or butter and spread the outside of the balls with a light coating so that the outside skin of the dough will not dry out. Cover the trays with greased plastic wrap and set in a warm place, about 75° to 80°, to ferment and rise to about half their size again— about 1 hour.

Heat the oven to 325°. Again lightly grease your hands and press each ball down firmly to make a circle of the dough about 2½ inches in diameter and about ¼ inch thick. Cover with greased plastic wrap and set to rise at the same temperature for about 40 minutes. At the end of this time they will have risen slightly and be soft and puffy on top.

Bake, changing the trays from top to bottom of the oven halfway through the cooking time, until they are dry and crisp right through and a light biscuit color—about 1¼ hours.

TORTA DE SANTUARIO *(Sanctuary Roll)*

MAKES 1 FAT *TORTA*   JALISCO

This *torta* was presumably given its name because it was sold to hungry worshipers coming out of the sanctuary church after Mass.

This Jalisco version is as good as the better-known, more publicized *torta* prepared in Mexico City; they both rival and surpass any submarine sandwich I know. They are my constant standby for roadside picnics.

While a flat roll, *telera*, is used—cut horizontally, stuffed with crunchy layers, and then doused with sauce—in Jalisco any flat crusty roll may be used, or for that matter a length of hollowed-out French bread. But I stress *crusty* because you don't want any sweetish, soft, Wonder Bread type of roll, which would collapse under the weight of the filling.

There is no polite way of eating this *torta*. You need two hands and a lot of napkins to take a large bite through all the crisp layers.

While it is better freshly made, it will hold for an hour or so without becoming soggy.

> 1 *telera*, halved horizontally and some of the crumbs removed
> 2 heaped tablespoons *frijoles refritos* paste (page 180) to spread on the cut surfaces
> several thin slices *lomo adobado Estilo Jalisco* (page 254)
> a good layer of thinly shredded lettuce
> a thin layer of thinly sliced radishes
> a few slices white onion, wilted in salted water for 1 hour
> 2 or 3 tablespoons *salsa de plaza* (page 348)

TORTA AHOGADA

Split open a *telera* horizontally as you would for a *torta del santuario*; remove some of the crumbs. Stuff liberally with *carnitas* (page 262) and douse to capacity with the *salsa* of your choice.

CONCHAS
(Sweet Rolls with Shell-Patterned Sugar Topping)

MAKES ABOUT 16 BUNS 5 INCHES IN DIAMETER

If there is one sweet roll that epitomizes Mexican breakfast (or supper) bread, it is the *concha*—or *chicharrón*, depending on the pattern of the sugar topping—which I learned to make some years ago in my apprenticeship to a Mexico City bakery. The dough is slightly sweet and spongy, made with a high percentage of yeast and eggs but low in fat. Because of this, they tend to dry out rather fast when kept. Never mind; they seem to increase in flavor. To revive them I dip them quickly into a little milk and put them in a very hot oven for a few minutes. They come to life amazingly well.

Over the years I have found that no two bakers use quite the same method for risings and so on, but the proportions remain more or less the same, depending of course on the economic policy of the bakery. I still stick to this recipe, which over the years has proven itself and has certainly done so considering the sales in "my" bakery.

It is hardly worth making a smaller batch of the starter; besides, you can freeze the part that you don't use, then defrost it and allow it to rise for a future batch of *conchas*. The long rising period of the dough helps to develop flavor (in any case, any yeast bread recipe can be hurried up, or preferably slowed down, to fit into your daily routine). After forming the *conchas* and giving them their final rise, they will increase by only about half their bulk, but in the oven they will expand spectacularly.

THE STARTER
½ pound unbleached flour, plus extra for the bowl
½ ounce cake yeast *or* ¼ ounce dry yeast
2 tablespoons warm water, approximately
2 large eggs, lightly beaten

THE DOUGH
1 pound unbleached flour, plus extra for kneading
6 ounces sugar
½ teaspoon sea salt
1½ ounces (3 tablespoons) unsalted butter, softened
1 cup (about 4 large) eggs, lightly beaten
¼ cup warm water, approximately

(continued)

377

THE TOPPING
¼ pound unbleached flour
¼ pound confectioners' sugar
2 ounces (4 tablespoons) vegetable shortening or unsalted butter at room
   temperature
2 tablespoons unsweetened cocoa powder
1 tablespoon ground cinnamon

Grease and flour a baking sheet.

Sift the flour into the bowl of an electric mixer. Crumble the yeast into a small bowl, add the warm water, and mix to a smooth cream with the back of a wooden spoon. Add the creamed yeast and eggs to the flour and beat with a dough hook for about 2 minutes. The dough should be soft and sticky. Throw a little more flour around the bowl and beat for a few seconds longer so that the dough cleans itself from the surface of the bowl.

Sprinkle your work surface liberally with flour, scrape the starter onto it, and allow it to rest for a few seconds. Flour your hands and lightly pat the dough into an oval cushion shape. Transfer it to the greased baking sheet and make 3 diagonal slashes on the top. Cover with buttered plastic wrap and set aside in a warm place—80° is ideal—to double in size, about 1 to 1½ hours, depending on temperature. Cut the dough into 2 equal parts (weigh to make sure). Tear one part into pieces and put into the bowl of your mixer. Store the other half for another batch of *conchas* (see note on page 377).

Add the rest of the ingredients for the dough, except for 2 ounces of the sugar. Beat with the dough hook at high speed for about 5 minutes. Add the rest of the sugar and beat for another 3 minutes; the dough should now be soft and sticky with a shiny surface and form a cohesive mass on the dough hook. Throw a little more flour around the bowl to help the dough clean itself from the surface. Turn the dough out onto a floured surface and quickly pat it into a round cushion shape. Butter another large bowl (leaving your mixing bowl free for the long rising period), dust with flour, and place the cushion of dough into it. Cover the bowl with some buttered plastic wrap and a towel and set aside in a warm place for about 2 hours, until it has doubled in size. At the end of the rising period, place the covered bowl, with towel, into the mildest part of your refrigerator and leave it to ripen and rise slowly for at least 8 hours. (It can even be left for 16 hours.)

Just before the end of this rising period, prepare the sugar topping. Sift the flour and sugar together. Cut the fat into small pieces and rub it between your fingers into the flour/sugar mixture. Work it all together until smooth. Divide into 2 parts; mix the cocoa into one, the cinnamon into the other. Set aside, covered, so it does not dry on the outside.

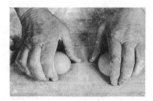

Turn the dough out onto a floured surface and quickly form into a cushion shape. Divide into 4 equal portions and each portion into 4 again, making 16 pieces of dough. I prefer to weigh each one—they should be just about 2 ounces each—to ensure an even size for the finished buns.

Butter 3 cookie sheets well. Roll each piece of the dough (see photo above) into a smooth ball and place each one onto the buttered cookie sheets, leaving a space of 3 inches between them to allow for expansion.

Divide the toppings into 8 portions each and roll into balls about 1 inch in diameter. Lightly flour the palm of your left or right hand, whichever you work best with, and press the ball of topping out onto it until it forms a circle about 3 inches in diameter. Press this topping firmly onto one of the balls of dough, flattening it out a little. Dust your palm again and continue with the next until all the balls are covered with the topping. Take your Mexican decorative cutter (see illustration), if you have one, or trace a pattern with a small sharp knife; press it down to form either the shell or *chicharrón* pattern (see photos below). Set the *conchas* aside in a warm place, uncovered, to rise until they are about half again their original size—about 2½ to 3 hours.

Set two racks in the top part of the oven and heat to 375°. When the *conchas* have risen, bake for about 12 minutes or until they are browned slightly around the edge of the topping and are springy to the touch. They are best eaten the same day. If not, see note about storing above.

PAN DE MUERTOS (All Saints and All Souls Day Bread)

For the religious and agnostic alike, observance of All Saints and All Souls—the Days of the Dead as they are commonly called in Mexico—is one of the most important events of the year. People travel hundreds of miles to take flowers and food to the graves of their departed relatives but it is no morbid affair as they eat and celebrate together. In some homes an altar will be set up and decorated with yellow flowers, *cempasuchil (Tagetes erecta)*, candles, candied skulls and fruits, *tamales, mole,* chocolate, and *pan de muerto.* In and around the capital the breads are of varying sizes, round and decorated with stylized "bones" and a round topknot representing the skull. In parts of Oaxaca the bread is formed into human shapes, and in Michoacán *monos,* small figures of animals or people, are made.

Recipes for this bread vary tremendously depending on the financial situation of the family or the predilection of the bakers. I have found no better than this one, given to me when I was apprenticed—rather informally—to one of the leading bakeries in Mexico City some years ago. The quantity will make one large one—about 11 inches in diameter, which is impressive—and about three small ones, which are always good as little presents or for hungry Halloweeners.

The oven temperature is given for a large bread; it should be increased to just under 400° for the smaller ones.

The starter can be made ahead or the day before. (Any left over can be frozen but is best used right away.) In fact, the final mixture can be kneaded and then left overnight in the refrigerator—which I do to help it develop a better flavor—and brought up to room temperature before forming and the final rising.

I am giving an exact translation from the metric weight, knowing that with bread dough a little variation here and there does not change the end product significantly.

THE STARTER
1 pound (4 scant cups) unbleached flour, plus extra for bowl and working
   surface
½ ounce (1¼ teaspoons) sea salt
2 ounces (⅓ cup) sugar
scant 1 ounce (3 scant tablespoons) crumbled cake yeast *or* 1½ scant tablespoons dry yeast
½ cup plus 2 tablespoons water
3 large eggs, lightly beaten
unsalted butter for greasing bowl

Put the flour, salt, sugar, and yeast into a mixing bowl and gradually beat in the water and eggs. (Mexican bakers do not bother to cream the yeast, knowing that it is fresh—do it if you wish.) Continue beating until the dough forms a cohesive mass around the dough hook; it should be sticky, elastic, and shiny—about 5 minutes. Turn out onto a floured board and form into a round cushion shape. Butter and flour a clean bowl. Place the dough in it and cover with greased plastic wrap and a towel and set aside in a warm place—ideally 70°—until the dough doubles in volume, about 2 hours.

THE FINAL DOUGH
the starter torn into small pieces
½ pound (1 cup) sugar
7 ounces (14 tablespoons) unsalted butter, softened, plus extra for greasing
    baking sheets
1 pound unbleached flour, plus extra for board and bowl
8 egg yolks, lightly beaten with 2 tablespoons water
¼ cup water, approximately
1 teaspoon orange flower water and/or grated rind of 1 orange

THE GLAZE
4 egg yolks, lightly beaten
¼ cup melted unsalted butter, approximately
⅓ cup sugar, approximately

Liberally grease 4 baking sheets (for both breads). Put the starter, sugar, and butter into a mixing bowl and mix well, gradually beating in the flour and egg yolks alternately. Beat in the water and flavoring—you should have a slightly sticky, smooth, shiny dough that just holds its shape (since eggs, flours, and climates differ, you may need to reduce or increase the liquid). Turn the dough out onto a lightly floured surface and form into a round cushion shape.

Wash out mixing bowl, butter and flour it, and replace the dough in it. Cover with greased plastic wrap and a towel and set aside in a warm place—ideally about 70°—for about 1½ hours, until it almost doubles in size, or set aside overnight in the bottom of the refrigerator.

Bring the dough up to room temperature before attempting to work with it. Turn out onto a lightly floured board and divide the dough into two equal pieces. Set one aside for forming later. Take three quarters of the dough and roll it into a smooth ball. Press it out to a circle about 8 inches in diameter—it should be about 1 inch thick. Press all around the edge to form a narrow ridge—like the brim of a hat—and transfer to one of the greased baking sheets. Cover loosely with greased plastic wrap and set aside in a warm place

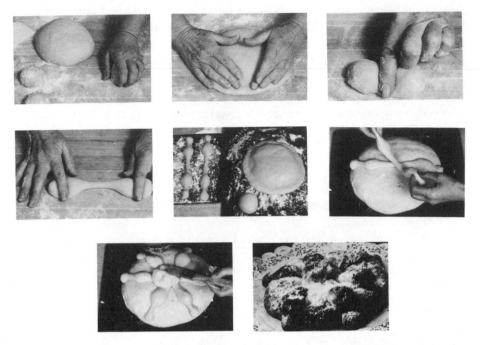

(about 70°) to rise about half its size again—about 1 hour. Taking the remaining one quarter of the dough, divide it into four equal parts. Roll one of the parts into a smooth ball. Roll the other 3 into strips about 8 inches long, forming knobs as you go (see photo) for the "bones." Transfer the four pieces to another greased tray, cover loosely with greased plastic wrap, and set aside to rise for about 1 hour.

Repeat these steps to form the second bread with the other piece of dough that was set aside. Heat the oven to 375°.

At the end of the rising period, carefully place the strips of dough forming the "bones" across the main part of the bread, place the round ball in the middle to form the "skull," and press your finger in hard to form the eye sockets. Brush the surface of the dough well with the beaten yolks and bake at the top of the oven until well browned and springy—about 15 to 20 minutes. Turn off the oven, open the door, and let the bread sit there for about 5 minutes more. Remove from the oven, brush with melted butter, and sprinkle well with sugar.

ROSCA DE REYES *(Twelfth Night Ring Bread)*

On January 6th, the Day of the Kings or Twelfth Night, it is customary in Mexico for the children to receive gifts. At supper that evening, or *merienda* (a tealike snack), a semisweet circular yeast bread is served. Hidden inside it will be one or two, depending on the size of the *rosca* and the group partaking of it, miniature dolls—they used to be made of fine imported china, but that has now given way to plastic. The person who gets the doll has to give a party on the Feast of Candelaria, February 2nd. Someone else may find a dried fava bean in the dough, and he or she will have to help the party-giver by bringing the drinks.

The dough for the *rosca* is exactly the same as for the *pan de muerto*, and the quantity will make either 2 large or 3 medium-sized *roscas*.

Crystallized fruit is used for decorating the top and sometimes added to the dough. Often sugared figs, candied orange peel, and citron peel are used; it is a matter of taste.

Baking instructions are the same as for the previous recipe.

Start from after the long rising period.

Divide the dough into 2 or 3 portions. Press each one into a tight sausage shape and join the ends by moistening with water and pressing them firmly together. Set them on the prepared baking sheets. Set aside to double in size at 70° to 80°.

Alternate Method of Forming

Form dough into a round cushion shape. Make a hole in the center with your fist and stretch the dough out to form an even circle. Allow plenty of space in the center for the dough to double in size without closing up the center space again.

crystallized fruit for decoration, optional (see page 383)
4 egg yolks, lightly beaten
3 tablespoons melted unsalted butter, approximately, to brush over the surface
½ cup sugar, approximately, to sprinkle over the top
1 recipe *pan de muertos* dough (see page 380)

Decorate the top with the fruit and set aside in a warm place to almost double in bulk.

Heat the oven to 400°. Brush the tops of the *roscas* with the beaten egg and bake until well browned—about 15 minutes. Remove, brush with butter and sprinkle with sugar, and return to the oven for 5 minutes more. Set aside to cool.

TORTILLAS DE HARINA *(Large Wheat Flour Tortillas)*

MAKES 10 15-INCH *TORTILLAS*

Sonoran food is famous for, if nothing else, its huge, membrane-thin flour *tortillas* that can measure up to 20 inches in diameter. Known as *tortillas de agua* (water *tortillas*), they are more vulgarly called *tortillas de sobaco,* which means armpit in Spanish, since they are flung with extraordinary dexterity from one arm to another, reaching to the armpits. Women in the poorer areas of Hermosillo, and I am sure in many country places, think nothing of making 2 kilos of flour into *tortillas* just before the main midday meal. They are cooked in seconds on large *comals* or electric stove burners. Once cooked, they are folded into four, like a napkin, and served as bread for either breakfast or the midday meal.

Apart from the enormous dexterity involved, it is necessary to have the right ingredients. Cooks on both sides of the border, in Arizona and Sonora, swear by Rose brand flour made of hard red winter wheat with a protein content of probably 11.8 percent, which is important. Although the older families must have used pork lard as the fat, modern cooks say that vegetable lard gives better results for this size *tortilla.* Lard, or even a mixture of lard and beef fat, can be used for the smaller *tortillas.*

Take heart: you don't have to follow what the lady in the photo is doing; you can make a modified *tortilla* as I do. It doesn't matter if it doesn't come out in a perfect circle—it takes years of practice to perfect them as it does to make superb puff pastry. If after all this you can't be bothered to make them, the supermarkets sell adequate flour *tortillas* to eat with your northern Mexican food.

    1 pound (4 scant cups) flour (see note above)
    ¼ pound (about ½ cup) softened vegetable shortening
    1 scant teaspoon finely ground sea salt
    1 cup warm water, approximately

Put the flour in a circle on your work surface or into the bowl of an electric mixer; rub in the fat with your fingertips. Dissolve the salt in the water and mix in a little at a time to see how much the flour will absorb. Gather all the extra flour into the middle of the board with a plastic dough scraper and form into a cohesive mass; knead either by hand or with a dough hook until you have a very smooth, elastic dough—about 4 or 2 minutes respectively. Divide the dough into 10 pieces, about 3 ounces each, and roll each piece into a ball about 2 inches in diameter. Cover the balls with greased plastic wrap and set aside for about 20 minutes in a warm place—70° in summer—or for about 35 minutes in a cooler place.

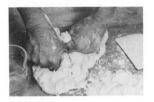  

Heat an ungreased *comal* or griddle.

Take one of the balls and flatten it on the work surface. Then, with a narrow rolling pin, or better still a dowel, roll out, using the dowel in a circular fashion as shown in the photo until you have a disk about 6 inches in diameter. Lay the *tortilla* over your cupped hands and stretch it out, gently working in circular fashion. Then, leaving it over one hand, work around the edge, gradually stretching the dough out. Repeat the stretching with both hands and then work around the edge until you have a large thin *tortilla*. Don't worry about the size.

Carefully lay the *tortilla*, or half of it, depending on the size of the griddle, onto the hot surface; it should sizzle as the dough hits the surface. After a few seconds, flip it over and cook the second side. Then, as it firms up and parts become transparent, maneuver it around so that all the raw spots are cooked. But do not leave it for more than a few seconds, because you will have a stiff, instead of pliable, *tortilla*. Fold into four and cover with a cloth to keep warm.

20 8-INCH *TORTILLAS*

(To make smaller *tortillas*, follow the recipe for mixing the dough.)
Cut the dough into 20 pieces and roll each piece into a ball about 1½ to

1¾ inches. Cover the balls with greased plastic wrap and set aside as for the preceding recipe.

At the end of the resting period, take one of the balls, leaving the rest still covered, and press it out with your hands. Then, using a dowel, start rolling in a circular fashion as shown in the photo to keep the *tortilla* as round as possible. Roll out to about 8 inches and cook on a hot *comal* or griddle as in previous recipe.

BURRAS

Burras (called *burritos* in the United States) are the *tacos* of northwestern Mexico but made with flour instead of corn *tortillas*. They are filled, rolled, and served with a simple tomato sauce, *salsa de jitomate norteña* (page 294. Traditionally *burras* were filled with dried beef cooked with red powdered *chile*, *carne seca con chile colorado*, but they can also be filled with *carne machaca* (page 292) or *carne machaca*, *y con huevo* (page 293).

Other Fillings for 12 Burras

Strips of cheese: allow 1 pound domestic Muenster cut into long strips.
Fried *chorizo*: allow 1 pound *chorizo*.
Eggs scrambled with *chorizo*: allow ½ pound *chorizo* for 7 large eggs.
Chorizo fried with potato: allow 3 cups of filling for *molotes* on page 44.
Beans and cheese: a puree of half-fried beans, page 183, with cheese melted in it at the last moment (allow ½ pound pinto beans for ¼ pound domestic Muenster or Jack cheese).

CHIVICHANGAS

Chivichangas, called *chimichangas* in the United States, are usually made out of the very large thin flour *tortillas*, which are doubled over, filled, folded like an envelope, or rolled and fried crisp. They are filled and served in the same way as the *burras*. You will need to increase the quantity of the filling for chivichangas by about one quarter.

TORTILLAS DE HARINA INTEGRAL
(Whole-Wheat Flour Tortillas)

MAKES ABOUT 10 5½- TO 6-INCH *TORTILLAS*

Whole-wheat flour *tortillas* are now being sold, packaged under a popular brand name, in Mexico. They have a very good flavor and texture and when toasted crisp make excellent *totopos* to eat with a dip, to garnish *frijoles refritos*, etc. These *tortillas* are easy to make and do not require any great expertise; it doesn't really matter if you can't—until you have had constant daily practice—get them completely round. After all, anyone who criticizes the nonroundness of your *tortillas* need not be invited back.

It is better, but not essential, to use high-gluten bread flour; simply adding some gluten flour to the mixture makes the dough pliable enough to roll out to the size required. When cooked, they should be opaque and speckled with brown. These *tortillas* freeze successfully and can be made a day or two ahead and simply reheated on a hot *comal* or griddle.

> rounded ½ teaspoon finely ground sea salt
> ½ cup warm water, approximately
> 5 ounces (about 1⅓ cups) all-purpose or bread flour
> 3 ounces (about ⅔ cup) whole-wheat flour
> 1 heaped teaspoon gluten flour (optional; see note above)
> 2 ounces (4 tablespoons) vegetable shortening, cut into small pieces and softened but not melted

Stir the salt into the warm water until dissolved. Mix the two flours together on your pastry board and gradually work in the fat with your fingertips until the mixture is crumbly. Gradually work in most of the water, reserving about 2 tablespoons until you see just how much the flour will absorb. Work the dough into a round cushion shape, adding more water if necessary to make it firm and resilient but not sticky. Knead for about 2 minutes.

Roll the dough into a sausage shape and cut into 10 equal parts. Roll each piece of the dough into an even ball about 1½ inches in diameter. Lightly grease your hands and coat the balls to keep them pliant on the outside. Cover with lightly greased plastic wrap and set aside for a minimum of 30 minutes.

Heat a *comal* or griddle over medium heat.

It should not be necessary to flour your work surface. Take one of the balls of dough and press it with your fingers to make a circle about 3 inches in diameter. (See illustrated steps, page 386.) Roll out with the narrow rolling pin in a circular motion until you have a circle about 5 inches in diameter. Then there are two methods, the first of which I find easier to preserve the round shape: gradually stretch the dough from the center on the backs of your palms and then work to the edges to form a 6-inch shape *or* continue rolling on your board. Lay the *tortilla* flat on the heated *comal*—there should be a slight sizzle as the dough touches it. If the dough burns and smokes, immediately turn down the heat and wait for a few seconds before proceeding. Cook the *tortilla* for about 10 seconds on the first side; it should be almost all opaque and slightly speckled. Turn over and cook on the second side for 8 seconds more, until opaque, but not dried out and stiff, and then for 2 seconds longer on the first side to make sure the dough is cooked. Stack them in a towel.

To reheat them at serving time, place the *tortillas* one by one on a fairly hot *comal* and heat them for about 6 to 8 seconds on each side. To toast them crisp, place them on a baking sheet in a 300° oven for about 20 minutes, depending of course on the thickness of the *tortilla*. You can also do this on the *comal*, but they need careful watching.

Note: These *tortillas* are too collapsible when toasted for making *tostadas*.

DESSERTS, ICES, AND SWEETMEATS

(Postres, Helados, y Dulces)

Flan a la Antigua (Traditional Caramel Custard)
Flan de Café (Coffee Caramel Custard)
Chongos Zamoranos (Milk Curds Cooked in Syrup)
Huevos Reales (Egg Sponge in Syrup)
Natillas de Vicki (Vicki's Egg Custard)
Queso de Nápoles (Almond Dessert)
Budín de Limón (Lime Sponge Pudding)
Torta de Piña de los Virreyes (Pineapple Rice Torte)
Basic Cocada (Shredded Coconut Filling)
Limones Rellenos de Cocada (Limes Stuffed with Coconut)
Cocada Envinada (Wine-Flavored Coconut Dessert)
Cocada con Piña (Coconut and Pineapple Dessert)
Ate de Guayaba (Guava Paste)
Membrillate (Quince Paste)
Guayabas en Almíbar (Poached Guavas in Syrup)
Nieve de Guayaba con Crema (Guava Cream Ice)
Dulce de Zapote Negro (Pureed Black Zapote)
Helado de Zapote Negro (Sorbet of Black Zapote)
Helado de Chirimoya (Cherimoya Ice)
Helado de Chicozapote (Chicozapote Ice)
Helado de Mamey (Mamey Cream Ice)
Helado de Granada China (Granada China Ice)
Helado de Mango (Mango Ice)

Traditional Mexican desserts are, almost without exception, concentrated and very sweet; they are nearly all based on the so-called "convent" desserts of Spain and Portugal, rich in almonds and pine nuts, eggs, and lots of sugar. Fruit pastes, *ates*, with their origins in the Middle East, were also introduced into Mexico via Moorish Spain, as indeed was sugar cane.

The nuns of the early part of the colonial period could be considered the chief innovators of the (then) new *criollo* cuisine tht developed when they began to experiment with ingredients found in the New World, blending them with those they had brought from Spain but using classical culinary techniques. *Camotes*, pineapples, *zapotes*, pumpkin and amaranth seeds, to name a few, were incorporated into desserts or candies that still exist in the same form today.

Apart from the desserts mentioned above, candied fruits, fruits cooked to a dark brown in raw sugar, and colorful miniature fruit forms fashioned out of almond or *pepita* marzipan are often served at *merienda,* in the late afternoon, with coffee or tea while sweet yeast rolls or sweet *tamales* are breakfast or supper food.

To my taste the perfect finish to a hearty Mexican meal is a salad of mixed tropical fruits, each cut into a different form, or fruit-based cream ices (as opposed to eggy ice creams) or *sorbets.* Here is where you can break with tradition with impunity, but you might consider adding a *flan* for those who will be disappointed not to have one.

There are no great techniques to be illustrated here; although many Mexican dessert recipes are time-consuming to make, they are, with all their furbelows, no more so than a complicated Austrian or French dessert.

FLAN A LA ANTIGUA (*Traditional Caramel Custard*)

SERVES 8

It would not be an exaggeration to say that *flan* is the most popular dessert in Mexico and one that foreigners always think of as *the* ending to a Mexican meal. They are right. Delicious as it is, it is bland and soothing after a *picante* repast, and one never seems to tire of it—provided, of course, that it is well made.

Eschew recipes that give short cuts like using canned milk or a suspicion of eggs and enjoy the rich satiny quality of this classical caramel custard.

I prefer to have a very dark, burnt caramel, which provides a great foil for the not-too-sweet custard.

If you have time, make this *flan* the day before so that it has time to set well and is easier to cut. While I use the Mexican *flan* mold for mine, you can use any sort of mold and put it in an improvised water bath. Be sure that the water is very hot when you start to cook the *flan* and that it comes at least one third of the way up the sides of the mold.

Cooking time will depend on the depth of the custard in the mold; if it is less than about 3 inches, it will probably take less cooking time.

THE CARAMEL
¾ cup sugar

THE CUSTARD
1 quart milk
pinch of sea salt
½ cup sugar
1 2-inch cinnamon stick or vanilla bean
a small piece orange or lime rind (optional)
4 eggs
6 egg yolks

Heat the sugar for the caramel in a small, heavy frying pan over low heat until it begins to dissolve. Shake the pan slightly (do not stir) until all the sugar has melted. Increase the flame and let the sugar bubble and color. Pour the caramel into the mold and quickly turn it around in all directions, tipping it up in a circular motion until the surface—bottom and about 2 inches up the sides—has been lightly coated with the caramel. If the caramel thickens and becomes sluggish, gently heat the mold in a pan of hot water or over low heat, depending on the material, and continue the coating action. Set aside to cool.

Put the milk, salt, sugar, and cinnamon or vanilla into a saucepan and bring slowly to a boil, stirring until the sugar has dissolved. Continue boiling slowly, taking care that it does not boil over, until the milk has reduced by about ⅔ cup. Set aside to cool.

Place an oven rack on the lowest rung of the oven and heat to 325°.

Beat the eggs and yolks together and stir into the tepid milk. Pour the mixture through a strainer into the *flan* mold and place it in a hot water bath in the oven. Test after 2 hours with a skewer or cake tester; if it comes out quite clean, the *flan* is cooked. Remove from the oven, but allow to sit in the water bath for about 15 minutes longer. Remove and set aside to cool completely before refrigerating.

To unmold, carefully slip a blunt-ended, thin metal spatula around the rim of the *flan* and gently tip the mold from side to side to see if the *flan* is loose. If the caramel has hardened at the bottom of the mold, place it in a pan of hot water for a short time and test again. Place the serving dish—it must have a rim to hold the syrup—on top of the mold, invert quickly, and pray that the *flan* comes out whole.

Always serve a wedge of the *flan* with plenty of the extra syrup.

FLAN DE CAFÉ *(Coffee Caramel Custard)*

SERVES 6 TO 8

Flan flavored with coffee is a delicious variation of the classic dessert. Quite untraditionally, too, I like to pour a little Kahlua over it when serving it and pass unsweetened whipped cream for those who are not on a diet. I happen to prefer a very dark caramel, which is less sweet, since it provides a good contrast to the custard.

A *flan* is always better prepared a day ahead if possible since it gives it time to firm up for unmolding. In fact it keeps very well for several days in the refrigerator.

While I use a *flanera*, a Mexican tin mold with its own water bath, any sort of mold will do in an improvised water bath of a roasting pan or any pan sufficiently deep so that the water comes at least one third of the way up the sides of the mold.

THE CARAMEL
¾ cup sugar

THE CUSTARD
1 quart milk
pinch of salt
½ cup sugar
½ teaspoon vanilla extract
2 tablespoons instant coffee powder (not decaf)
4 eggs
2 egg yolks

Heat the caramel sugar in a small, heavy frying pan over low heat until it begins to dissolve. Shake the pan slightly, but do not stir, until all the sugar has melted. Increase the heat and stir the sugar as it bubbles and takes on color. Pour the caramel into the mold and quickly turn it around in all directions, tipping it up from one side to another in a circular motion until the surface—the bottom and about 2 inches up the sides—is lightly coated with the caramel. If the caramel thickens and becomes sluggish before it reaches this point, then heat the mold over low heat until it runs more smoothly, then continue the coating action.

Put the milk, salt, and sugar into a heavy pan and bring slowly to a boil, stirring from time to time, until all the sugar has dissolved. Continue boiling—

take care it does not boil over— until the milk has reduced by about ½ cup. Stir in the vanilla extract and coffee powder and set aside to cool.

Place a rack on the lowest rung of the oven and heat the oven to 325°.

Beat the eggs and yolks together well and, when the milk is tepid, stir them into it. Pour through a strainer into the prepared *flan* mold, set in a hot water bath, and cook for about 1¾ hours. Cooking time will depend on the depth of the custard in the mold. If it is less than about 2 inches, it will probably take less time. Test by inserting a skewer or cake tester; if it comes out clean, the *flan* is cooked. Set aside to cool for 15 minutes in the water bath. Remove and cool completely before refrigerating.

To unmold, carefully slip a blunt, thin metal spatula around the rim of the *flan* and gently tip the mold from side to side to see if it is loose. If the caramel has hardened in the bottom of the mold, place it in a pan of hot water for a short time and test again. Unmold onto a serving dish with a slight rim and pour the caramel remaining in the mold around it.

CHONGOS ZAMORANOS (*Milk Curds Cooked in Syrup*)

SERVES 8

Chongos were presumably first made in Zamora, which is in the rich dairy country in the northern part of Michoacán. The word *chongo* means a little knot—hair tied into a little bun is a *chongo* in Spanish—and when cut up into small pieces *chongos* do resemble little knots by the time the long cooking period is up. You will rarely find *chongos* that are homemade; most restaurants buy them in cans, and then they are overly sweet and squeak as you chew them.

Obviously you will get the best results by using raw milk; the clabber will be firmer, and you will use less rennet. Homogenized, pasteurized milk will probably need more rennet than is recommended by the manufacturer. Buy rennet in liquid form if you can; the tablets vary enormously in strength.

If *chongos* are not cooked at a very low temperature, they will disintegrate into the whey. I use a Mexican *cazuela* for them, which is ideal, but I find the "hottest" pots—enameled metal—hold too much heat to cook them successfully.

Do not try to make these with skimmed milk. It isn't really worth making a smaller quantity of *chongos*; apart from being slightly addictive, they keep well for a few days in the refrigerator, but do not freeze them.

2 quarts milk
liquid rennet or tablets (see manufacturer's instructions)
2 tablespoons water if necessary
½ cup grated *piloncillo* or dark brown sugar
1 2-inch cinnamon stick, broken into strips

THE SYRUP
2 cups water
2 cups grated *piloncillo* or dark brown sugar
1 2-inch cinnamon stick, broken into strips

Heat the milk to 110° (or follow instructions on rennet package). If you're using tablets, crush and dissolve them in the water just as the milk reaches the right temperature, not before. Stir the rennet into the milk and continue stirring for about 20 seconds so that it is evenly distributed through the milk. Cover and set aside in a warm place. Although the milk will clabber in much less time, for this dish it is best to leave it for about 2 to 3 hours. To test whether the milk has set properly, lay a finger over the surface. The clabbered milk should not stick to the flesh but separate cleanly from it.

Cut the curd into large triangles or rectangles, sprinkle the sugar over it, and insert the slivers of cinnamon into the whey as the cut curds separate. Set the pan over very low heat; you may need to use a Flame-Tamer or asbestos pads, and cook, barely simmering, so that the bubbles do not break up the curds. Keep over low heat until the curds are almost tough and have shrunk a little—about 3 hours. Set it aside to cool completely. Remove the curds from the whey, cut into more convenient shapes if desired, and drain thoroughly.

While the *chongos* are cooking, make the syrup. Put the water into a heavy pan and stir in the sugar and cinnamon. Cook over low heat, stirring from time to time, until the sugar has melted. Bring to a boil and continue boiling until it has reduced to 1½ cups—about 15 to 20 minutes. Set aside to cool.

When the curds are completely cool and drained, set them in a shallow serving dish—they will be smoothish on top and brownish and bubbly-looking underneath. Pour the syrup around them and let them macerate for an hour or so before serving. Always store in the refrigerator.

HUEVOS REALES (*Egg Sponge in Syrup*)

SERVES 4

Huevos reales—literally royal eggs—are typical of the so-called "convent" desserts that were introduced into Mexico during the colonial period by nuns from Spain and Portugal. They used enormous amounts of eggs, almonds, and sugar in making them, and they were usually cloyingly sweet. This dessert, however, is not too sweet by those standards. It is, in fact, a flourless, unsweetened egg sponge moistened and sweetened with the syrup with which it is finally bathed.

I use my *flan* mold for this dessert, which is 5½ inches in diameter and ideal. But any mold will do, provided the beaten yolks do not spread out too much; ideally they should be approximately 1½ inches deep uncooked and from ¾ to 1 inch thick after cooking.

Make sure that the water in the bath is very hot when the filled mold is put into it, or the eggs will separate; the water should come at least one third of the way up the sides of the mold.

Huevos reales may be prepared well ahead of time; they will keep in the refrigerator very well for several days.

unsalted butter for greasing the mold

THE SPONGE
5 egg yolks
pinch of salt
1 tablespoon water

THE SYRUP
¾ cup water
½ cup sugar
1 2-inch cinnamon stick, broken into slivers
1½ tablespoons raisins
2 tablespoons dry sherry or rum
1 tablespoon pine nuts or blanched and slivered almonds

Heat the oven to 350° and place a rack on the bottom rung of the oven. Liberally butter the bottom and sides of the mold. Put the egg yolks, salt, and water into a bowl and beat with an electric beater for about 5 minutes or until the yolks hang in thick ribbons from the beater. Pour the mixture into the prepared mold, cover, and set in the hot water bath. Bake until the mixture is firm and springy to the touch—about 40 minutes.

Remove the sponge from the oven and set it aside to cool. Meanwhile, prepare the syrup. Put the water into a saucepan, add the sugar, and stir over low heat until dissolved. Add the cinnamon and bring to a boil; continue boiling fast until it thickens slightly—about 5 minutes. Using a rounded metal spatula, carefully loosen the egg sponge around the edges and along the bottom and turn it out onto a work surface. Cut the sponge into 4 or 6 triangular sections with a very sharp knife and carefully transfer them to the hot syrup so that they are in one layer. Add the raisins and heat gently so that the sponge puffs up and absorbs some of the syrup. Transfer the pieces to a shallow serving dish into which they will fit in one layer. Mix the sherry and pine nuts into the remaining syrup and pour over the *huevos reales*. Set aside to cool and macerate for about 2 hours before serving.

NATILLAS DE VICKI *(Vicki's Egg Custard)*

MAKES 5 8-OUNCE CUPS   TEQUILA, JALISCO

Vicki has a small restaurant in Tequila where one can eat good, simple food at a moderate price. The name is misleading. Strictly speaking, *natillas* refers to a custardlike *crème Anglaise,* and this should be called *jericalla,* but there it is. Whatever the name, it is a baked egg custard cooked in a water bath in the oven (improvise with a roasting pan). Vicki insists that raw milk be used, but that is not really necessary. I have reduced the cup of sugar that she uses to ¾ cup.

This dessert can be eaten lukewarm or at room temperature. It keeps very well for several days in the refrigerator, but should be brought up to room temperature to serve.

> unsalted butter for greasing the custard cups
> 1 quart milk
> ¾ cup sugar
> pinch of salt
> pinch of baking soda
> 2 eggs
> 3 egg yolks

Heat the oven to 350°. Set a rack in the lower half of the oven. Fill a roasting pan with water to a depth of 1 inch and put it in the oven to heat. Grease the custard cups.

Put the milk and sugar into a saucepan and set over low heat, stirring until the sugar has dissolved. Stir in the salt and soda. Beat the eggs and yolks together lightly and stir in about ¼ cup of the warmed milk until smooth; strain this mixture into the warmed milk and stir well. Fill the prepared custard cups and bake until set and well browned on top—approximately 1 to 1½ hours.

QUESO DE NÁPOLES *(Almond Dessert)*

SERVES 8   LA FAMILIA GONZALEZ, TEQUILA, JALISCO

This is one of those concentrated, sticky desserts so loved by the Mexicans, and it comes from the old family cookbook of one of the original Tequilero families. After being baked it will be puffy like a cake, and if well wrapped it will keep in the refrigerator for several days. While traditionally it would be eaten alone, some unsweetened whipped cream or *crème fraîche* and/or some poached fruit would not come amiss.

2 ounces (about 53) skinned almonds, roughly chopped
1½ quarts milk
¾ pound (about 1½ cups) granulated sugar
¼ teaspoon baking soda
unsalted butter for the dish
6 egg whites
15 whole almonds, skinned and split in half

Grind the chopped almonds, about one third at a time, in a coffee/spice grinder for a few seconds to produce a textured, mealy consistency. Set aside.

Put the milk, sugar, and soda into a saucepan and set over low heat, stirring until the sugar has dissolved. Increase the heat and cook at a fast simmer, stirring from time to time, until it begins to thicken slightly—about 20 minutes. Stir the ground almonds into the milk and continue cooking until it is quite thick and plops heavily from the spoon; as you stir it you should be able to see the bottom of the pan—about 30 minutes. Scrape into a large bowl and set aside to cool.

Heat the oven to 400°. Generously butter an ovenproof dish, ideally 8 by 8 by 2 inches.

When the mixture is cool, beat in the egg whites one by one, beating well after each addition. When the whites have all been incorporated, transfer to the prepared dish, decorate with the split almonds, and bake until puffy yet firm to the touch and a deep golden color—about 30 minutes. Set aside to cool, ideally overnight.

BUDÍN DE LIMÓN *(Lime Sponge Pudding)*

SERVIES 6 TO 8   *LA COCINERA POBLANA, 1877*

This is like a rich almond sponge cake rather than a pudding. If you wish to serve it as a hot dessert, I suggest you make a rather tart lime sauce to go along with it.

A deep cake tin, about 6 inches in diameter, is ideal. The mixture will puff up and then sink down to about half its original size.

¼ pound blanched almonds
6 egg yolks
1 egg white
¼ pound (½ cup) sugar
finely grated rind of 2 large limes
⅓ cup semisweet cookie crumbs
2 tablespoons unsalted butter

Butter the cake tin thoroughly. Heat the oven to 350°, placing a rack in the middle of the oven.

Put the almonds into a blender jar and grind coarsely. Beat the egg yolks and white together until they form thick ribbons on the beaters—about 5 to 7 minutes. Beat in the sugar gradually, a tablespoon at a time, then stir in the almonds and lime zest.

Pour the mixture into the prepared tin, sprinkle the top thickly with the biscuit crumbs, and dot with butter. Bake until the sponge is firm—about 20 to 25 minutes. Test by inserting a skewer into the cake; if it comes out perfectly clean, the cake is cooked. Turn the oven off and leave the cake in the oven for 5 minutes longer. Set aside to cool in a place that is free from drafts and do not attempt to unmold until it is completely cold. In any case, unmold with care as it is very delicate.

TORTA DE PIÑA DE LOS VIRREYES
(Pineapple Rice Torte)

SERVES 8 TO 10

Some years ago I was writing a commentary on a fascinating cookbook that I have in my collection, *La Cocinera Poblana,* Volumes I and II (published in Puebla, 1877) and came across this recipe, which I have reconstructed (rather than adapted). Even I, who do not particularly like sweet rice desserts (having had my fill of rice pudding as a child in England), fell for this one.

It is not as cloyingly sweet as many of the "convent" desserts of Mexico—most of which come from Spain and Portugal—and has a good crunchy texture from the pineapple and almonds.

Be careful not to overcook the rice so that it becomes mushy; nor, of course, should it be too *al dente.* When cooked, the *torta* should be about 1¾ inches high, so you will need an ovenproof dish that will accommodate it, ideally 8 by 8 by 2 inches. It can be eaten the same day that it is made, but it is also good, in fact better, after ripening for a day or so in the refrigerator. Always serve it at room temperature, not cold, and pour the syrup as you serve or 5 minutes beforehand. The syrup should also be at room temperature.

2 cups water
2 cups grated *piloncillo* or dark brown sugar
1 2-inch cinnamon stick, broken up
grated rind of ½ lime
3 cups pineapple in ¼-inch dice plus any juice that exudes
3 tablespoons fresh lime juice
1 tablespoon unsalted butter
5 ounces (about ¾ cup) unconverted short-grain rice, cooked, drained, and cooled
1 ounce (scant ⅓ cup) almonds, skinned, slivered, and toasted
2 ounces (rounded ⅓ cup) raisins
4 extra-large eggs, separated
1 egg white
1 ounce (about ¼ cup) pine nuts
1 tablespoon sifted confectioners' sugar

Put the water, sugar, and cinnamon into a saucepan and heat, stirring, until the sugar has melted. Add the lime rind and bring to a boil; continue boiling for about 10 minutes. Add the pineapple and its juice to the sugar and cook over medium heat until transparent and partially soft—about 10 minutes. Drain the pineapple and set aside to cool. Return the juice to the pan and cook over high heat with the lime juice until it has reduced to about 1¼ cups and is syrupy—about 15 minutes. Set aside to cool. Heat the oven to 375° and place a rack on the top rung. Liberally butter the ovenproof dish.

Mix the cooled rice, pineapple, almonds, and raisins together well and set aside. Beat the egg whites to soft peaks (when the bowl is turned upside down, they will not fall out), but not too dry. Beat in the egg yolks and, when mixed well, gradually stir in the rice/raisin mixture. Carefully spoon into the prepared dish, sprinkle with the pine nuts, and bake until the eggs are set and the top puffy and golden, about 20 to 25 minutes. Dust with the confectioners' sugar and set aside to cool. Serve each portion with plenty of the cool syrup (see note above).

COCO DE AGUA *(Cocos nucifera)* *(Preparing Coconut)*

You can, of course, buy good-quality unsweetened grated coconut, but occasionally for special recipes (or where it is not available) it is best to buy a whole coconut and prepare it yourself.

First you need a mature, but not dried-out, coconut, not a thin-fleshed one like those sold on tropical beaches. First look to make sure that the eyes at the top are intact. Then shake it to make sure there is plenty of water inside.

Pierce two of the eyes with a skewer—one for the air to go in, the other for the liquid to come out. Drain the water and try it. If it is rancid, the flesh will be rancid, so just throw it all away. If it is sweet, reserve it for cooking the *cocada* (recipes follow).

Heat the oven to 375°. Place the whole coconut on the top rack and bake until the shell splits open—about 15 minutes. Remove and hit firmly all over with a hammer to loosen the flesh from the shell. Break it open completely and pry off any flesh that is still adhering to the shell.

With an efficient potato peeler, peel off the tough brown outside layer and discard. Shred the white flesh to the required texture. (Use a medium grater, neither too fine nor too coarse. Do not put in a food processor with the metal blade—this will chop the flesh, and it will never make a satisfactory *cocada.*) Weigh or measure the flesh; a good-sized coconut should yield about 1 pound of flesh or 6 rounded cups loosely packed. Any flesh left over from the recipe may be frozen; any water left over may be drunk—it is a good diuretic.

Note: The liquid drained from the coconut is the water, and the milky substance squeezed out of the flesh is the milk; if you squeeze harder still and compress the finely grated flesh, you will get a cream.

BASIC COCADA *(Shredded Coconut Filling)*

MAKES ABOUT 4 CUPS

1½ cups coconut water or water
1 pound (2 cups) sugar
1 pound grated unsweetened coconut (page 406)

Put the water and sugar into a heavy pan and cook over medium heat, stirring, until the sugar has dissolved. Then boil fast, stirring as the syrup thickens to make sure it does not scorch, to the thin thread or jelly stage (230° on a candy thermometer)—about 15 minutes. Stir in the coconut, mix thoroughly until it is all well infused with the syrup, and continue cooking, stirring and scraping the bottom of the pan, until it is all transparent and the mixture pulls away from the surface of the pan—about 15 minutes.

Turn out onto a flat tray to cool and then use for stuffing limes (recipe follows).

Note: A little citrus juice and finely grated rind may also be added for extra flavor.

LIMONES RELLENOS DE COCADA
(Limes Stuffed with Coconut)

MAKES 12 STUFFED LIMES

This is quite an extraordinary and delicious dessert or sweetmeat. Not for fast-food advocates, but for those who want to preserve a culinary tradition and those who want to create something pretty to look at as well as good to eat.

I first tried these stuffed limes (apart from the commercial ones, which tend to be rather dry and artificially bright with food coloring) at the home of a great friend and cook, María Dolores Torres Izábal. It was she, her helper Alicia from Puebla, and *La Cocinera Poblana* that helped me to "perfect" this recipe. María Dolores tells me that her mother used to prepare limes in a thick syrup, but they were not stuffed—a traditional Sonoran dessert.

I always prepare 2 extra limes—just in case one splits open, and the other to try as I go along to make sure the texture is just right and that no bitterness remains.

This recipe is successful only with small, thin-skinned limes like the Mexican or Key limes. I am afraid the most commonly available thick-skinned Persian variety will not do.

If you live in a citrus-growing area of the Southwest or Florida, you will have the luxury of citrus (any type) blossoms and leaves as a flavoring and final decoration. If not, your imagination can come into play—not difficult when a dessert is as glamorous as this one.

If you have a choice, select limes that are a little underripe and very green, not those on the verge of turning yellow.

La Cocinera Poblana of 1877 advises always to keep the limes covered with water in the cooking or soaking stages as well as in the syrup; then they should turn out a deep, rich green color.

Once cooked in the syrup, the limes will keep indefinitely if covered; when exposed to the air, they dry out in a few days and become tough, especially if the air is very dry. The *cocada* can be made and kept in the refrigerator, or even frozen, and then defrosted when the limes are ready to be stuffed a few hours before serving.

14 small thin-skinned Mexican or Key limes
1½ cups sugar
¾ cup water
2 tablespoons orange flower water *or* 4 citrus blossoms and/or citrus leaves
    (optional)
1½ cups *cocada* (page 407)
12 citrus blossoms (optional; for decoration)

HAVE READY:
an enamel or stainless-steel pan into which the limes will fit when covered
    with water
a glass or china bowl into which the limes will fit when covered with water

Cut a thick slice off the stalk end of each lime and discard. Fill a pan with enough boiling water to cover the limes, add the limes, cover, and bring to a fast boil. Boil for 1 minute. Remove limes and plunge into cold water. Repeat the process, changing the water. (It is important to change water at every stage to rid the limes of their bitter, pithy taste.)

Remove the limes one by one from the cold water, squeeze out as much of the juice and seeds as possible, and return to the water. Using a pair of sharp, pointed scissors, cut around the inside of each lime to release the tough membranes that make the divisions. Then carefully turn the lime inside out and carefully pull out all the rest of the membranes adhering to the inside skin. Scrape out as much of the pith as possible—don't worry if it doesn't all come out at once; you have another chance. Replace each lime in fresh water when it has been cleaned, still inside out.

Put the cleaned limes into a pan of fresh boiling water, cover, boil for 1 minute, plunge into cold water, and then repeat this process.

Turn the limes back the right way, put into boiling water, cover, and boil for 5 minutes, then again plunge into fresh cold water. Repeat this process once again, then try a piece of the skin. It should be tender but not soft. If it is still a little tough, boil for 5 minutes longer. Remove and put into cold water while you make the syrup.

Stir the sugar and water together over low heat and keep stirring until the sugar has dissolved. Bring to a boil and boil fast so that the syrup froths up and thickens. When the syrup reaches the thin thread stage—230° on a candy thermometer—add the limes and orange flower water, cover, and cook for 5 minutes over medium heat. Remove from the heat and let the limes cool completely in the syrup. When the limes are cool, remove to a rack and drain—by now they should be infused with the syrup. Allow to dry off before filling with the *cocada*. Each lime will take about 2 tablespoons of the *cocada*. Decorate with the flowers and/or leaves and serve.

COCADA ENVINADA (*Wine-Flavored Coconut Dessert*)

SERVES 8 TO 10

This is one of those intensely sweet Mexican desserts and is just right when you want to break all the dietary rules and *have* something intensely sweet.

This is a rather soft *cocada*, but if you want it to be a little firmer, add another ¼ to ½ pound sugar to the same amount of water and coconut.

Since this is a *postre de platón*—"serving dish" dessert—it is best to use a mold that is at least 1 inch deep. It fits perfectly into a 9-inch by 9-inch mold.

Once cooked, it will keep for a month or so in the refrigerator, but it should always be served at room temperature.

1½ cups coconut water or water (p. 406)
1 pound (2⅔ cups) sugar
1 pound grated, unsweetened coconut
4 egg yolks, beaten and strained
3 tablespoons medium-dry sherry or Madeira

FOR DECORATION
⅓ cup raisins
⅓ cup pine nuts or pecans

Put the water and sugar into a heavy pan and cook over medium heat, stirring, until the sugar has dissolved. Then boil fast, stirring as the syrup thickens to make sure it does not scorch, to the thin thread or jelly stage (230° on a candy thermometer)—about 15 minutes. Stir in the coconut, mix thoroughly until it is all well infused with the syrup, and continue cooking, stirring and scraping the bottom of the pan, until it is transparent—about 10 minutes. Add about ⅔ cup of the mixture to the beaten yolks and stir in quickly. Then add the egg mixture to the pan, stirring quickly until it is all well incorporated. Continue cooking the mixture until it is stiff and pulls away from the surface of the pan. Stir in the sherry or Madeira and leave to cook for a few moments longer. Turn out into a shallow mold and smooth the surface of the mixture with a spatula—it should be about 1 inch deep.

Place the *cocada* under a hot broiler about 2 inches below the heat and broil the surface to a deep golden brown. Decorate with the raisins and nuts and set aside to cool and set.

COCADA DE PIÑA *(Coconut and Pineapple Dessert)*

SERVES 8 TO 10

This is without doubt my favorite of the coconut desserts, the pineapple providing a perfect foil for the richness of it all.

If you prefer a firmer *cocada*, increase the sugar by about ¼ pound (½ cup) and the pineapple by 1 cup.

Like the previous recipe, the *cocada* will keep for a month or so in the refrigerator but should be served at room temperature. The most suitable mold is one 9 inches by 9 inches and at least 2 inches deep.

1 large pineapple, cleaned and cored (about 2 pounds fruit)
1½ pounds (about 4 cups) sugar
1 pound grated coconut (page 406)
5 egg yolks, well beaten and strained

FOR DECORATION
⅓ cup blanched and split almonds

Chop the pineapple roughly. Add a small quantity at a time to a blender jar or food processor container and blend until almost smooth but with some texture. This should yield about 6 cups.

Put the pureed pineapple into a heavy pan and stir in the sugar over medium heat. Keep stirring until the sugar has dissolved, then raise the heat and boil until it reaches about 200° on a candy thermometer, just below the jelly stage. Add the coconut and stir until well incorporated into the pineapple syrup.

Continue cooking over high heat, stirring and scraping the bottom of the pan until the mixture thickens—about 15 minutes. Add about ⅔ cup of the mixture to the beaten eggs and stir briskly. Add this mixture to the pan, stirring it in quickly, and continue cooking over high heat, stirring constantly, until the mixture starts to dry around the edges and shrinks away from the sides of the pan—about 10 minutes more.

Turn into a mold at least 1½ inches deep, smooth the top with a spatula, decorate with the almonds, and put under a very hot broiler to brown about 2 inches below the heat. Set aside to cool well before serving.

ATE DE GUAYABA (*Guava Paste*)

MAKES ABOUT 4 1½-POUND CAKES

Most Latin Americans and some of the Caribbean countries have their *ates*, or fruit pastes. Originating in the Middle East, they were brought to the New World via Moorish Spain. Although *ates* can be made of very many types of fruit, the most popular in Mexico are those of guava and quince. A slice of *ate* by itself or with a fresh cheese is a typical dessert.

The yellow guava (*Psidium guajava*)—and I am not referring to the rather dry variety with the dark green skin—is a native of tropical America, probably Mexico and Colombia according to the eminent botanist Máximo Martínez. It is a fruit that, with rare exceptions, has a better flavor cooked than raw as the flavor tends to establish itself more firmly after cooking.

The small, roundish guavas have more flavor than the larger, more impressive varieties—they are certainly much better for *ate* making. As with any fruit preserve, the fresher the fruit, the better, not only for flavor but because the pectin content is higher and the setting point of the preserve will be reached in a shorter time.

One of the most important guava-growing areas is Michoacán with its Mediterranean type of climate (apart from the coastal plains, of course). As winter approaches and the guavas ripen, the traditional cooks take down their deep, unlined copper *cazos*, preserving pans (most of them made in the copper working village of Santa Clara de Cobre, which is about 14 miles from Pátzcuaro). Like copper pots everywhere, if they are not in constant use the surface takes on a greenish-black film that has to be cleaned off thoroughly before it's used. This they do with lime or bitter orange juice, rough salt, or ash.

All these long-cooking desserts appear more complicated than they actually are; but they are time consuming. It is hardly worth making a smaller amount; besides, once made, *ates* kept dry and cool will last for many months. I have even had some for 2 years, and they darken and intensify in flavor.

You can use any type of mold for the *ate*. I generally use wooden cheese hoops, but a springform pan or any pan with a removable bottom will do very well.

If you do not have a preserving pan, any heavy, large shallow pan can be used; if the pan is too deep, the *ate* will take forever to reduce.

6 pounds guavas
1½ quarts cold water
4½ pounds (about 12½ cups) sugar

Rinse the guavas and remove the small black shriveled remains of the flower at the base; do not peel.

Cut each guava in half horizontally and with a small spoon remove the fleshy center that contains the seeds.

Put the hollowed-out "shells" into one pan and the seedy flesh into another. Add 1 quart water to the shells and 2 cups to the flesh. Cook both over medium heat; they should simmer, not boil fast, or the setting quality of the fruit will be reduced. Simmer the pulp for 5 minutes and set aside. Simmer the "shells" for about 10 minutes—they should be quite tender but not mushy.

Strain the shells, retaining the cooking water. Transfer to the container of a food processor and process until you have a textured puree; you will need to do this in about four batches. Put the puree and the reserved cooking water into the preserving pan. Press the pulp and its cooking liquid through a fine sieve or through the fine disk of a food mill, straining out as many of the seeds as possible—a few may go through, but don't worry; they will add texture and roughage. Add the strained thick juice to the pan, discarding the debris in the sieve. Stir the sugar into the pan and set over low heat, stirring until the sugar has dissolved.

Increase the heat and cook as fast as possible, stirring at first from time to time to prevent scorching and then constantly as the mixture begins to thicken. (You will need a broad-bowled wooden spoon with a long handle as the mixture tends to splatter and can burn your skin.) When the mixture thickens and becomes harder to stir and shrinks away from the sides of the pan, the *ate* is ready. Depending on the sugar, altitude, etc., it can take up to 1½ hours.

Pour the *ate* while still hot into molds no more than 2 inches deep. Set on a rack and leave to cool and dry. As soon as they have set, remove the molds and continue to dry out the cakes in a dry, airy place, turning them over daily or more often, depending on humidity, of course; this can take from 1 to 2 weeks. Store in a cool, dry place between sheets of parchment paper or preferably on straw mats (like those from the Philippines or the French ones used for cheeses).

MEMBRILLATE *(Quince Paste)*

MAKES ABOUT 6 CAKES 4½ INCHES ACROSS AND 2 INCHES DEEP

This method of cooking quince paste was given to me by Señorita Esperanza, who is infallible when it comes to the making of preserves. Her father was the manager of several large sugar mills in the hot country where cane is grown just southwest of Zitácuaro, Michoacán. Many cooks, she told me, put in a proportion of crab apple jelly to hasten the jelling process. But if you treat the fruit with respect and bring out the best of it in the following manner, additives are unnecessary.

> 5 pounds quinces
> 9 cups cold water, approximately
> 3½ pounds (about 9¾ cups) sugar

Rinse the fruit in cold water, removing any remains of the withered flowers at the tip. Do not peel. Cut the quinces into four pieces and remove the center core with seeds, etc., and reserve. Chop the cleaned fruit roughly, cover tightly with plastic wrap, and set aside.

Chop the cores roughly. Put half of them into the container of a food processor with 1½ cups of the water and blend until they are broken up to a rough-textured puree. Repeat with the rest of the cores. Set the puree aside for at least 3 hours or overnight for the gluey juice to exude.

Strain through a fine strainer, pressing down well so that as much as possible of the juice is extracted. Discard the debris. Put the strained juice into a preserving pan (or substitute) together with the sugar and 2 cups of the water. Stir over low heat until the sugar has dissolved. Raise the heat to medium and cook, *without letting the mixture boil hard,* or the setting quality will be impaired, until the mixture has turned a light brown caramel color— about 20 to 30 minutes.

Meanwhile, put the fruit with 4 cups of the cold water into another pan and cook over medium heat until soft (*do not* allow to boil fast)—about 20 minutes. Transfer, a small batch at a time, to the container of a food processor and process to a thick, slightly textured puree. Set aside and keep warm.

When the mixture in the preserving pan is ready, stir in the fruit puree thoroughly so that it is evenly distributed in the syrup.

Cook over high heat, stirring and scraping the bottom of the pan, but take care because as it reduces it splatters and can burn your skin—wrap your arm in a towel to stir if necessary. Cook until the mixture hangs in big lumps from the wooden spoon and shrinks away from the sides of the pan—about 25 minutes.

The *ate* will be a pale reddish-brown and darken in color to a deep amber after it has been dried and stored. It will also reduce as it dries out.

Follow instructions for molding and storing in preceding recipe.

GUAYABAS EN ALMÍBAR *(Poached Guavas in Syrup)*

SERVES 4 TO 6

Guavas poached in this way, which brings out their flavor admirably, can be used in many ways: as a dessert with whipped cream, added to a compote of mixed dried fruits (prunes, apricots, etc.), added to a fruit salad, for tarts, or for my version of a cream *sorbet*. They're at their best in the fall. The scooped-out "shells" of guava are also excellent stuffed with *cocada*.

1 pound round yellow guavas (see note, page 412)
2 cups water
2 1-inch cinnamon sticks
½ cup dark brown sugar
rind of ½ lime or lemon
1 tablespoon fresh lime or lemon juice

Rinse the guavas and cut off the small black shriveled remains at the base of the fruit; do not peel.

Cut the guavas in half horizontally and set aside. Put the remaining ingredients into a heavy pan into which the guavas will fit in one layer—they can overlap slightly. Bring to a boil and boil for about 8 minutes. Place the guavas, open side down, into the hot syrup and simmer for 5 minutes. Turn them over and simmer for 5 minutes more. By this time the center part with the seeds will be bulging out, and the shells should be very tender but not mushy. Set aside to cool in the syrup.

When cool enough to handle, scoop out the center and either (1) discard or (2) press through a fine sieve and return the juice to the cooking syrup. Serve at room temperature as suggested above. I do not remove the cinnamon or lime rind.

FRUIT ICES *(Helados de Frutar)*

All types of tropical and semitropical fruits are now being imported into the United States and distributed, generally but not always, in areas where there is an ethnic group that is more likely to appreciate them.

Mexico, with its many microclimates, grows a large variety, mostly indigenous, with some introduced fruits (see photo, page 511). I have included here recipes and descriptions of the most commonly found (not only for those who see them in the grocery stores, but for those who travel to or live in Mexico).

Although some of these fruits are made into ultra-sticky desserts—for which I have not given recipes since I agree to disagree with my sweet-toothed Mexican friends—I think they are used more successfully in fruit ices. A medley of them makes a fascinating and colorful dessert. (I make a small quantity of each and have them stashed away for the right lunch or dinner.)

The amount of sugar depends very much on taste; always remember that cold detracts from flavor, sweetness, and saltiness. Although these ices may be used right away, they improve in flavor when left to ripen, anywhere from 12 to 24 hours. White of egg is optional and gives a lighter, fluffier texture. *Crème fraîche,* too, is optional in some of them and essential in others and gives a richer-bodied ice without going to the richness of a real ice cream.

If you like a more textured ice as I do, you can always chop some of the fruit instead of blending it all.

NIEVE DE GUAYABA CON CREMA
(Guava Cream Ice)

MAKES ABOUT 3½ CUPS

An ice made of uncooked guavas tastes insipid, so I came up with this unorthodox but delicious version. It is much better, of course, with the addition of the *crème fraîche*, and it's smoother if you can bear to add the raw egg white.

1 pound guavas cooked according to the preceding recipe
½ cup brown sugar
⅓ cup water
pinch of sea salt
2 tablespoons fresh lime juice
1 egg white, beaten until frothy, *and/or* ½ cup *crème fraîche* (optional)

Remove the cinnamon sticks, but not the lime rind, from the cooking liquid. Put the guavas and cooking liquid into the container of a food processor and add the sugar, water, salt, and lime juice; blend to a textured puree. Transfer to an ice cream maker. When the mixture is thoroughly chilled and the churning has started, add the egg white and cream and churn until the ice cream holds its form, following the manufacturer's instructions.

ZAPOTE NEGRO *(Black Sapodilla)*

The *zapote negro* *(Diospyros ebenaster)* or *zapote prieto* is one of several winter fruits native to tropical America that go under the name of *zapote,* although they are not all of the same botanical family of plants (see photo, page 511). It is a round, squat fruit; an average one would be about 4 inches in diameter and about 3 inches high. It has a thin, mid-green skin, and the flesh when ripe is a shiny, dark chocolaty brown with from 3 to 8 round, shiny seeds of almost the same color dispersed through the flesh. It has a delicate sweet flavor—like nothing else I know—and should be used when ripe and very soft. In Mexico the *zapote negro* is usually eaten raw, mashed with orange juice, although I prefer mixed citrus juices, including tangerine juice when in season and a proportion of lime juice, and, although not traditional, honey instead of sugar for sweetening. Some restaurants in Mexico City make a water ice or *sorbet* of this fruit, although it does not have a strong flavor. Again, I use honey, before it crystallizes, instead of the boring and usual sugar syrup.

DULCE DE ZAPOTE NEGRO *(Pureed Black Zapote)*

MAKES ABOUT 2½ CUPS

This recipe serves as the base for *helado de zapote negro* (recipe follows), but it is also eaten just as it is for dessert.

    2 pounds *zapote negro*
    ½ cup fresh orange or tangerine juice
    3 tablespoons fresh lime juice
    3 tablespoons (or to taste) transparent honey

Carefully remove the thin skin of the *zapotes*—a rather messy job. Discard the seeds and mash the pulp to a fairly smooth puree. Stir in the juices and honey and set aside at room temperature to season for 1 to 2 hours. Serve at room temperature just as it is or with some unsweetened whipped cream.

HELADO DE ZAPOTE NEGRO *(Sorbet of Black Zapote)*

MAKES ABOUT 2 CUPS

> 1½ cups *dulce de zapote negro* (preceding recipe)
> 3 tablespoons honey or to taste
> 1 egg white, beaten until frothy (optional)

Mix the pureed *zapote* with the honey and chill in an ice cream maker. Churn, following manufacturer's instructions, and when the ice cream is well chilled and just beginning to freeze, add the egg white and churn to finish ice.

CHIRIMOYA *(Annona cherimola)* *(Chirimoya)*

The *chirimoya*, often referred to in English as the custard apple, is one of the family of *annonas*—the *guanabana* and *anona* being others—that are grown and used in Mexico. They are natives of tropical America. They vary in size, a small one being about 3 inches wide and 3 inches long. It is a squat, triangular-shaped fruit with a thin, dark greenish-brown skin that darkens as it ages. The creamy white flesh is clustered around numerous dark brown seeds—I counted 28 in the size mentioned.

While the *chirimoya* is nearly always eaten raw and peeled, it makes an interesting ice, rather resembling a smooth applesauce, which needs no cream or thickeners since the texture of the fruit when blended provides sufficient body. However, all these rather sweet, dense-fleshed tropical fruits need some lime juice to bring out or complement the flavor.

Removing the seeds is a bit laborious and is easier if you have that invaluable colander attachment to the KitchenAid.

Two pounds of *chirimoya* will render approximately 1¾ cups pulp when cleaned and seeded.

HELADO DE CHIRIMOYA (*Cherimoya Ice*)

MAKES ABOUT 2½ CUPS

 2 pounds *chirimoya*
 1 rounded tablespoon sugar
 ⅓ cup water
 1 tablespoon fresh lime juice
 ¼ teaspoon finely grated lime rind

Rinse and dry the *chirimoyas*. Break them open vertically and scrape the flesh from the thin skin. (If the flesh is beginning to turn brown just under the skin, do not scrape off that part as it tends to be tough and grainy and will spoil the flavor of the fruit.) Remove the seeds and blend the flesh until smooth in the food processor (this is not necessary if you use the colander attachment to the KitchenAid). Stir the sugar into the water until it is dissolved, then add all the ingredients to the ice cream machine and follow the manufacturer's instructions.

Note: Once the ice is finished, pack it into containers and store it in the freezer section of the refrigerator. Leave it to ripen at least 24 hours before using. Remove it from the freezer at least 20 minutes before you are going to serve it (unless you live in a very hot climate).

CHICOZAPOTE *(Achras sapota)*

Chicozapote is the fruit of the gum-producing *chicle* tree, a native of tropical America. In season in winter, it is a squat, roundish fruit, an average one being 2½ inches in diameter and 2 inches high. It has a thin, pale brown, dull skin (same color as the *mamey*), and the flesh inside is cream to light brown in tone. It is moist with a slightly grainy texture and formed in circular, segmental fashion. Each fruit has one or two seeds that resemble large, skinned almonds with black burnt patches. While it is very sweet, but does not have too much flavor, a chunky ice made from it is a favorite in Mexico City.

HELADO DE CHICOZAPOTE *(Chicozapote Ice)*

MAKES ABOUT 2 CUPS

> 1½ pounds (about 6) *chicozapotes*
> 2 tablespoons light brown sugar
> ½ cup water
> 1 tablespoon fresh lime juice
> 1 egg white, beaten until frothy, *and/or* 3 tablespoons *crème fraîche* (optional)

Wipe the fruit with a damp cloth. Cut open and scoop out the flesh, discarding the seeds. Mash to desired texture—I blend about two thirds of it and roughly chop the remaining third. There should be about 2 cups flesh.

Stir the sugar into the water and add all the ingredients to the container of the ice cream machine, following the manufacturer's instructions. Transfer the ice to containers and store it in the freezer section of the refrigerator to ripen for about 12 hours. Remove it from the freezer about 10 minutes before serving.

MAMEY *(Calocarmum sapota)*

When it is at its peak, the *mamey* is a delicious and exotic fruit with light brown, rough, shell-like skin. It is oval in shape, and while sizes vary enormously, an average one would be about 5 inches long and 3 inches wide and weigh about 1 pound. The flesh is smooth, sweet with a delicate, almondlike flavor, and the color ranges from a deep salmon to pale apricot. It has a large, elongated, shiny pit.

It is difficult to choose a good, ripe *mamey* without cutting it open to see if the flesh is a good, even color. Once it has patches of brown, the flavor has been impaired. Although in Mexico some vendors will do this for you, I doubt whether distributors in the United States will accede, so always buy extra with this in mind.

It is usually eaten raw, but many sweet-toothed Mexicans prefer to make a *dulce* out of it, combining a sugar syrup, eggs, and ladyfingers. Since I think this is a wasted effort for something so innocuous and overly sweet, I have agreed to disagree with many of my friends.

Although it doesn't make a superb ice by itself, when included in a medley of tropical fruit ices it gives spectacular color and contrast. Two pounds of fruit will yield about 3 cups flesh.

HELADO DE MAMEY *(Mamey Cream Ice)*

MAKES ABOUT 3½ CUPS

> 2 pounds *mamey*
> ⅓ cup water
> 1 tablespoon sugar
> 2 tablespoons *crème fraîche*

Cut the fruit open vertically and scrape out the flesh, discarding the hard skin and pit.

Put all the ingredients into the container of a food processor and process until well mixed and fairly smooth.

Put the puree into the container of an ice cream maker and follow the manufacturer's instructions for making the ice. Transfer the ice to a container and store it in the freezer section of the refrigerator, allowing it to ripen for about 12 hours. Remove it from the freezer about 15 minutes before serving.

GRANADA CHINA *(Passiflora ligularis) (Granadilla)*

The *granada china* (golden apple in the English-speaking Caribbean and Africa) is the fruit of one of the fruit-bearing passion vines (there are also a number of non-fruit-bearing vines). It is calabash-shaped, an average one measuring 3 inches long and 2 inches wide, and has a tough, shell-like skin that turns from purplish-green to orangey-yellow as it ripens. The gelatinous white fruit pulp is clustered around small, crunchy, edible black seeds. An average-sized fruit will yield just under ¼ cup pulp.

The *granada china* is usually eaten raw or made into an *agua fresca* (a fruitade). It can also be used to make a very fresh-tasting ice. I like to leave in about half of the seeds to give a crunchy consistency, but this is optional. When strained out, the amount of pulp will be reduced by about half.

HELADO DE GRANADA CHINA *(Granada China Ice)*

MAKES ABOUT 1½ CUPS

8 *granada china*
1 tablespoon sugar
2 tablespoons water
⅛ teaspoon finely grated lime rind
½ teaspoon fresh lime juice
1 small egg white, beaten until frothy (optional)

Break the fruit open horizontally to scoop out the flesh. Press through a fine sieve to strain out the seeds if desired or put into a blender jar and blend until smooth and frothy. Stir the sugar into the water and pour all the ingredients into the container of an ice cream machine. Follow manufacturer's instructions. Transfer ice to containers and put into the freezer section of the refrigerator, allowing it to ripen for about 24 hours. Take it out of the freezer at least 10 minutes before serving.

MANGO *(Mangifera indica)*

The *mango* is a native of Ceylon, India, and Malaya and was introduced into Mexico probably during the seventeenth century. There are now many varieties grown commercially, the most sought after and luscious being the bright yellow *mango Manila* with its juicy tender flesh and slim pit. It is certainly the best for making an ice cream, but I have never seen it imported into the United States.

Taste whatever types are available before making the ice. Some tend to have stringy flesh and are oversweet. The big fat Haydens—reddish or yellowish-green—are the best of the imported ones (some varieties are probably grown in Florida), and it is better to choose slightly underripe ones for the best-flavored ice. You can either make a very smooth ice or reserve some chopped fruit to add at the end for texture.

HELADO DE MANGO *(Mango Ice)*

MAKES ABOUT 3 TO 4 CUPS

2 pounds *mangoes* (see note above)
2 tablespoons fresh lime juice
¼ teaspoon finely grated lime rind
¼ cup water
3 tablespoons (or to taste) light brown sugar
⅓ cup *crème fraîche,* lightly beaten
1 egg white, beaten until frothy (optional)

Pare the *mangoes* and cut off all the flesh from the pit—don't waste any. Chop the flesh roughly and reserve about ½ cup if you want a textured ice. Put all the ingredients except the cream and egg white into the container of a food processor and process for a few seconds, until you have a textured puree. Transfer to the container of an ice cream maker and chill. As you begin to churn, following the manufacturer's instructions, add the cream and the optional egg white. Continue churning until the ice is formed. Transfer the ice to a container and store in the freezer compartment of the refrigerator, leaving it to ripen for at least 12 hours. Remove from freezer about 10 minutes before serving.

SEASONINGS AND OTHER COMMONLY USED INGREDIENTS

A great many spices—except notably *chiles* and allspice—were introduced into Mexico early in the sixteenth century during the colonial period of its history. At that time they were used exclusively in the convents and wealthier Spanish households. Under the skillful cooking hands of the nuns they were very soon combined with native ingredients to form the beginnings of a sophisticated *mestizo* cuisine.

Needless to say, these spices were expensive, having been brought from the Orient by way of the Philippines to the West Coast of Mexico; and then they were within reach of only the privileged classes. It wasn't until 100 years or more later that they were accepted and incorporated into the less sophisticated cooking of the *pueblos*. Today the women of even the poorest villages would not dream of making their festive *moles* without at least a few of the spices required by custom, although this does not hold true of many parts of the Northwest, where food generally is not highly spiced and the *chiles* used are much milder. But even this distinction is gradually changing with migration patterns and improved transport.

Spices are used sparingly in Mexican food and in harmony so that no single one predominates. They are combined to enhance the other ingredients and create depth and complexity of flavor.

Note: In Mexican cooking, quantities are always given for whole spices, not powdered. Sometimes they are used whole and sometimes ground or crushed with other ingredients. In any case, always buy whole spices and grind them just before using them for the sake of flavor.

SPICES AND OTHER SEASONINGS

ACHIOTE AND THE YUCATECAN SEASONING PASTES
(Achiote y los Recados Yucatecos)

The Yucatán Peninsula is famed for having a very diverse cuisine, but in fact, apart from the seafood, the ingredients themselves are not that varied. It is the way in which those ingredients are prepared and, in particular, seasoned and the combination of spices for those seasonings that create this sense of diversity.

Achiote is a very hard red seed from the annatto tree (*Bixa orellana*), which is a native of tropical America. The seed is ground and used to color and flavor food. However, it should be used subtly (I have seen American versions of these sauces made out of only *achiote*, and they were strong and unpleasant). Grind the seeds in an electric coffee/spice grinder as finely as possible. Then sift and grind the residue a second time. Even then it tends to become slightly grainy when moistened.

In Yucatecan markets you can see prepared seasoning pastes, or *recados*. These red, black, or mud-colored pastes come in small, oblong packages or rolled into balls of sizes varying from ½ inch to 1½ inches in diameter. This is how most home cooks buy them. However, among those who do prepare their own, there is not one recipe exactly the same as the others or the same as those published in cookbooks on the subject. Besides, there is a bewildering number of them: for *cochinita* (small pig), beefsteak, roasts, fish, *tamales*, stews, or ducks, among others. It would be useless to give them all here, so I have chosen the most useful ones—those that apply to the recipes in this book.

It is best to make your own *recados*. The commercial ones vary in quality and balance of flavors, and some manufacturers extend them with *tortilla masa*, which can easily sour, so careful storage is necessary.

When I was last in Yucatán, my friend and great cook Isela had prepared many little piles of spices to show me the difference, but I could never quite reconcile her quantities in the recipes with those actually on the table. Anyhow, I have settled for the most practical of the lot, her *recado de toda clase* (for everything), adding *achiote* as necessary. It works perfectly well. While you are at it, always make more than you need, since you can store it in the refrigerator or freezer indefinitely.

SIMPLE RECADO ROJO *(Achiote Paste)*

MAKES ½ CUP

A simple *achiote* paste for general use and for any *pibil* recipe (although not included here) is as follows:

4 rounded tablespoons *achiote* seed
1 teaspoon crushed dried oregano, Yucatecan if possible
1 teaspoon cumin seed
½ teaspoon mild peppercorns
12 whole allspice
3 tablespoons water, approximately

Mix the spices together and grind, one third of the quantity at a time—or as much as your electric grinder can accommodate efficiently—as finely as possible. Sift through a fine strainer and grind the residue once again. Stir the water in gradually and mix well to a stiff paste.

If you are not going to use the paste immediately, form it into a round thick cake and divide into 4 pieces. Wrap well and store in the freezer compartment of the refrigerator. Storing it in this way makes it easier to take out a small piece at a time.

To dilute for use: crush this amount with about 20 small garlic cloves, and sea salt to taste and dilute to a thin cream with bitter orange juice or its substitute, a mild vinegar.

RECADO DE TODA CLASE

MAKES ABOUT SCANT ¼ CUP

This is an excellent seasoning for chicken, pork, steaks, or fish that is to be fried, broiled, or grilled and is far superior to those beautifully packaged msg- and garlic-salt-laden powders that are so hard on the palate and stomach.

2 tablespoons mild peppercorns
7 whole cloves
8 whole allspice
1 ¼-inch cinnamon stick
¼ teaspoon cumin seed
2 tablespoons lightly toasted dried oregano, Yucatecan if possible
water as necessary

Put all the ingredients except water in an electric coffee/spice grinder and grind as finely as possible. Pass through a fine strainer and grind the residue once more. Transfer to a small bowl and mix in just enough water to form a thick paste. Store until ready to use or dilute to a thin paste to spread on meat or fish.

TO USE THE *RECADO*
1 tablespoon *recado*
2 garlic cloves, peeled and crushed
1–2 tablespoons bitter orange juice or mild vinegar
sea salt to taste

Mix the *recado* and garlic together and stir in the juice. Mix well and then add salt to taste.

It is best if you can season the food for 1 or 2 hours, or even overnight, before cooking, for the flavors to penetrate.

RECADO ROJO (*Achiote Paste*)

MAKES SCANT ½ CUP

This *recado* can be used for the recipes in this book for *tamales colados* (page 68), *tamales costeños* (page 73), *pollo en escabeche rojo* (page 238), and *bifstek enchorizado* (page 307). It is always best to mix up more than you will need because it can be stored indefinitely in the refrigerator or freezer, ready for future use.

4 tablespoons ground *achiote*
2 teaspoons *recado de toda clase* (see page 429)
2 teaspoons sea salt or to taste
6 garlic cloves, peeled and crushed
4 tablespoons water, approximately, or enough to form a thick paste

Mix all the ingredients to a thick paste. At this stage it should be used for the *tamales*.

To use for spreading on meats: dilute the paste with sour orange juice or vinegar and spread a thin layer over the meat to be cooked.

Recado negro, or black seasoning, is of culinary interest since it is made with dried chiles that have been burnt black—needless to say, this operation is carried out in rather isolated places. This *recado* has a grainy texture and is used for the famous *relleno negro*—a turkey seasoned with the paste and stuffed with ground pork also seasoned with it.

I have not included a recipe for it here because some of the commercial pastes available are not good enough and I hardly think this is something that you will prepare at home. (I tried, well away from the house and the cows and the hens, but the wind changed in the middle of it all, and I nearly choked.)

Briefly, the *chiles secos* of Yucatán are seeded, soaked in alcohol, and burnt black. They are then soaked in water for 3 days, drained, and ground with charred *tortillas*, peppercorns, and garlic. Some *achiote* is added, and then it is diluted with Seville orange juice to season the meat.

ALLSPICE *(Pimenta officinalis)*

Pimienta gorda, pimienta de Jamaica, malagueta, and *pimienta de la tierra* (Tabasco) are the names given in different parts of Mexico to the allspice seed used quite extensively in southern Mexico and central Mexico to flavor sauces, stews, and pickles. The dried mid- to dark brown seeds (which should be picked before they ripen totally) vary slightly in size, an average one being about ¼ inch in diameter.

The tree belongs to the myrtle family and has shiny, elongated leaves, mid- to dark green in color and highly aromatic; the leaves are used in the cooking of Tabasco and the Yucatán Peninsula, particularly in *escabeches.*

Although generally accepted as a native of Jamaica and some of the Caribbean islands, allspice is also believed to have occurred naturally in the low-lying coastal land of Tabasco, where indeed it is called *pimienta de la tierra.* Its Nahuatl name is *xocoxochitl.*

ANISEED *(Pimpinella anisum) (Anís)*

Anís, as it is spelled in Mexico, is used mostly to flavor sugar syrups for desserts and the dough of some types of sweet rolls; it also appears as a subtle ingredient in some recipes for *mole poblano.* Curiously, I have seen a pinch of the seeds advocated for cooking with cauliflower, whose taste it subtly enhances, although I suspect that it is included to reduce the rather gassy effect of that vegetable.

CINNAMON *(Cinnamomum zeylandicum) (Canela)*

In Mexico cinnamon is *canela,* the light brown, flaky bark of a tree native to Ceylon, now Sri Lanka. Ceylon cinnamon is used extensively, but sparingly, either in whole pieces or ground up with other spices, in many sauces and stews. Whole pieces of bark are used in dessert syrups or with fruit and Mexican coffee; in powdered form cinnamon is used in and on top of puddings and sweetmeats.

This variety of cinnamon is preferred. The other, Saigon cinnamon, often more widely available outside of Mexican markets, is darker in color, not as aromatic, and very tough—which makes it much harder to grind.

CLOVE *(Eugenia aromatica) (Clavo)*

Clavo, or *clavo de especia* (in case anyone thinks you mean *nail*), is the name in Mexico for the aromatic dried flower bud of the clove tree indigenous to the Molucca Islands (Indonesia) but now extensively grown in the Caribbean. Cloves are used extensively, but sparingly, in Mexican cuisines, either whole or ground with other spices in Mexican sauces, stews, pickles, etc.

CORIANDER SEEDS *(Coriandrum sativum) (Semillas de Cilantro)*

Coriander seeds, *semillas de cilantro* as they are known are not used as extensively in the cooking of Mexico as they were at the turn of the century, although they are infrequently called for in some of the more complex sauces, such as in some recipes for *mole poblano.* The herb itself is used, however, in cooked and uncooked dishes in practically all the regions of Mexico.

Coriander is an herb native to Mediterranean Europe.

CUMIN *(Cuminum cyminum) (Comino)*

Cumin seeds, *comino* in Mexico, (never the powder), are called for in classic Mexican cooking. They are used ground with other spices in some, but not all, regions of Mexico, and then very sparingly (the amounts advocated in recipes north of the border would be totally unacceptable to the Mexican palate), for like *achiote,* when used to excess it creates a very disagreeable, overpowering flavor.

A native plant of Egypt and the Mediterranean, it is thought to have been introduced to North America by way of the Canary Islands.

PEPPERCORNS *(Piper nigrum) (Pimienta Entera)*

Pimienta negra, pimienta chica, pimienta de Castilla, and just *pimienta* are the names given in Mexico to mild black peppercorns, depending on the region in which they are used. They refer to *piper nigrum,* the dried fruit of a climbing plant native of tropical India, the East Indies, and elsewhere.

They are used extensively, if not in great quantity, with the notable exception of the *recados,* or seasoning pastes of Yucatán, where they are used in quantity. Strongly flavored peppercorns—such as Malatar or Pondicherry—should not be substituted as their sharp bite will be too overpowering.

SALT *(Sal)*

While many cooks in Mexico have fallen for the convenience of "free-flowing" salt, others have persisted in using *sal de grano* or grain salt, a lot of which is produced in Mexico either in salt lakes or on the coasts of Baja

California and the Yucatán Peninsula. Since this sea salt is saltier, you use less of it and know that it is pure.

I usually buy the medium grain in the United States and grind some finely in the coffee/spice grinder for baking. Don't use the fine grain, or kosher salt, which is not much better than ordinary table salt—try both.

SUGAR *(Azucar)*

Ordinary granulated sugar—*granulado*—is generally used in Mexican desserts and sweetmeats except where *piloncillo*, raw, cone-shaped sugar is called for. Mexico produces all of its own sugar, and a visit to a rustic sugar mill, many of which are dotted around the smaller, more isolated cane-growing areas, is fascinating. As soon as the cane is cut it is hauled by donkeys or mules to the milling shed right there in the fields and fed into the crusher. The juice is run off into large vats fired from underneath; when cooked, the syrup is poured into cone-shaped molds ranging in capacity from 100 grams to 1 kilogram, depending on the area and local demand. In Oaxaca the same sugar is called *panela* because it is molded in round, breadlike forms. The color varies from caramel to a very dark brown.

Occasionally *mascabado*, brown granulated sugar, is called for and, of course, for confectionery icing sugar, *azucar glas*.

NUTS AND SEEDS *(Nueces y Semillas)*

Nuts and oleaginous seeds have been used in the cooking of Mexico since pre-Columbian times, not only for sweetmeats but also to enrich stews and sauces.

ALMONDS *(Almendras)*

Almonds were introduced into the cuisine—although their cultivation on a large scale was prohibited—during the colonial period. Desserts of Spanish and Portuguese origin rely heavily on them, but they are also used for ground meat fillings, *picadillos*; slivered with meat, *claveteado*; or in a sauce with chicken, *pollo en cunete*. Ground with spices and *chiles*, almonds make a delicious sauce, *almendrado*, for chicken, tongue, veal, or even fish. A small quantity of fried or toasted almonds is included among the ingredients of many *mole* recipes.

PEANUTS *(Cacahuates)*

Although thought to be indigenous to South America, peanuts have been cultivated extensively in Mexico since pre-Columbian times, and in fact their name, *cacahuate*, is derived from the Nahuatl word *cacahuatl*. Toasted or boiled in their shells, shelled and fried with salt and *chile*, they are eaten as snacks. Toasted and ground with *chiles* and spices, they make a rich-tasting sauce for chicken, *encacahuatado*, and small quantities of toasted peanuts are included among the ingredients of many red or green *mole* recipes. Sweetmeats, too, are made from them: sugar-coated, they are *garapiñado*, or in hard candy they become *palanqueta*.

PECANS *(Nuez Encarcelada or Nuez Cáscara de Papel)*

Literally "imprisoned nuts" or nuts in paper shells, pecans are grown quite extensively in northern Mexico. Although eaten as snacks, either salted or sugared, and in small quantities in some regional *moles*, they are used mostly in desserts and cakes. A local variety, round and thick-shelled, grows in Oaxaca. It is called *nuez criolla*.

PINE NUTS *(Piñones)*

Pine nuts are produced in Mexico but not on a very large scale and are very expensive (cleaning them is so laborious). Their chief use is in desserts and cakes, but they are often called for in traditional recipes for ground meat fillings, *picadillos*, particularly in Puebla.

PUMPKIN SEEDS *(Pepitas)*

Many types of pumpkin seeds, either whole or hulled, have been used in the dishes of Mexico since pre-Columbian times. They vary in size considerably, from the little fat ones, *chinchilla*, about ½ inch long, to the large ones, about 1¼ inches long, edged with a light green band. Both are grown extensively in Yucatán, the latter also along the northern Gulf Coast.

Toasted, hulled *pepitas* are a favorite snack (not only in Mexico). Toasted and ground, hulled or whole, they are an important ingredient in many *moles*, green and red, *pipianes*, *pozoles* (Guerrero), and the nutritious (they contain a high percentage of vitamin E) dip in Yucatán called *sikil-p'ak*. They are mixed with a syrup for a hard candy, *palanqueta*. Washed of their green color, they are ground to make the *mazapan* (normally almond paste) of Yucatán.

SESAME SEEDS *(Sesamum orientale) (Ajonjoli)*

Sesame is *ajonjoli* (an Arabic word). Introduced into Mexico by the Spaniards early in the colonial period, they are grown and used extensively in the cuisine. They are generally used in their unhulled state, greyish instead of the pearly white of the hulled ones. Sesame seeds are indispensable for certain *moles* and *pipianes*, providing a thick, rich base for the other ingredients. They are also used on top of certain sweet rolls and some salty breads.

WALNUTS *(Nuez de Castilla)*

Walnuts were introduced from Europe and planted in the higher, colder parts of central Mexico. Like English walnuts, they are picked when the shell is still tender. And although they are also used in cakes and desserts, their outstanding function is to provide mature but tender nuts to be ground, after the thin skins have been removed, into the walnut sauce, *nogada*, for *chiles en nogada*, the classic August dish in central Mexico.

VINEGARS *(Vinagres)*

Vinegars used in Mexican cooking are usually very mild, fruity ones. Many cooks in the provinces still make their own out of pineapple and raw sugar (recipe below); in Tabasco, overripe bananas are used, while one small market stand that I deal with in Zitácuaro uses a mixture of fruits, whatever is in season, and always has on sale a delightful, light amber one. Once you have a good "mother" going (see below) you can go on making your own vinegar *ad infinitum,* with any fruit you like.

TO MAKE PINEAPPLE VINEGAR

When you are using a pineapple for other purposes, save the peelings, along with a little of the flesh. Add:

4 heaped tablespoons crushed *piloncillo* (raw sugar) or dark brown sugar
1½ quarts water

Mix well and set, uncovered, in a sunny, warm spot to ferment. It should begin to ferment in about 3 days and keep on fermenting until the sugar has been converted and the liquid becomes acidy. It may be cloudy to begin with, but as it sits it will clear and gradually turn to a dark amber color. This may take 3 weeks or more. By this time a mother—a gelatinous white disk—should be just beginning to form. Leave until it is quite solid—up to another 3 weeks—then strain the liquid and cork, ready for use. Put the mother with more sugar and water—a little more pineapple if you have it, but it is not really necessary—and leave to form more vinegar.

Yes, you need patience, but it is worth it.

While you can never quite duplicate that which you make, a good substitute would be half good-quality white wine vinegar to half mild Oriental rice vinegar.

FRESH AND DRIED HERBS *(Hierbas de Olor)*

FRESH HERBS

The regional cuisines of Mexico are full of flavor surprises, many of them owing to the abundant use of wild herbs (and greens, which are discussed in the introduction to the vegetable chapter). The more remote and mountainous the area, the more varied and interesting is the use of these herbs. Oaxaca provides a prime example. Rice and beans are flavored with *chepil (crotolaria longirostrata)* and *hierba (tridax corono piifolio) de conejo,* a *caldo de guias* (squash vine soup) with *piojo (galinsoga parviflora),* a beef stew with *pitiona* (called *tarete* in Michoacán and used only as a remedy), a minty oregano, and *hoja santa* for *tamales* and green stews. *Hoja santa (Piper sanctum),* with its heart-shaped leaf and strong anisy flavor, is very important in the cooking of Veracruz; it goes into green *moles,* wrapped around steamed fish, and for flavoring *tamales.* The wild *anis* is used for cooking fresh corn in Hidalgo and Michoacán, and rue is used for a pork dish again in Michoacán, to name just a sprinkling of examples in this very diverse spectrum of regional cuisines.

BAY LEAF *(Laurel),* THYME *(Tomillo),* AND MARJORAM *(Mejorana)*

Bay leaf *(laurel)* comes from a Mexican laurel that has a thin leaf like those in California. It is used either fresh or dried, either alone or together with the other *olores* (aromatics), marjoram and thyme, to flavor pickles, soups, stews, or cooked sauces.

If you have only the ordinary bay leaf *(Laurus nobilis),* use about half the quantity called for in the recipe.

Marjoram *(mejorana; Marjorana hortensis)* and thyme *(tomillo; Thymus vulgaris)* are both used fresh or dried, alone or together with the others for the same type of dishes.

CORIANDER *(Coriandrum sativum) (Cilantro)*

Although native to the Old World, coriander has been adopted wholeheartedly into the cuisine of Mexico, and both the fresh leaves and the seeds are used—in different ways in different dishes. The tender leaf and small stems are used in raw and cooked sauces, in some green *moles,* and with seafood, rice, and soups.

When buying coriander in the United States, always get the tender variety with lightish green leaves; there is a rather tough variety with darker leaves that does not have the same flavor and should be avoided if possible.

In Latin American and Caribbean stores, coriander is known not as *cilantro* as in Mexico, but *cilantrillo*, and the word *cilantro* is given to another herb with a tough, dark green, serrated leaf but with the same flavor. Its botanical name is *Geringium foedidum,* and in Mexico it is used chiefly in the cooking of Tabasco and can be found also in Yucatán.

Coriander leaves are delicate and should be stored with care. Buy *cilantro,* if possible, with the roots still attached—it will last longer. Wrap the roots and main stems in a damp paper towel and the leaves in a dry one, then store them in a plastic bag in the refrigerator. Remove any yellowing leaves daily.

EPAZOTE OR MEXICAN TEA OR WORMSEED
(Teloxys or Chenopodium ambrosioides) (Epazote)

Epazote is, in my opinion, the most Mexican of the culinary herbs. Although it can be found growing wild in many parts of North America and in Europe, only in Mexico does it seem to be used to the fullest extent.

The fresh leaves, or a whole stem with leaves (not the dried, which is innocuous and has lost essential air), are used extensively in the cooking of central and southern Mexico. It is a *sine qua non* for the cooking of black beans, for *tortilla* and other brothy soups, in *quesadillas,* chopped with fresh corn, and elsewhere. It is also used as a *remedio,* an herbal remedy, as an antiflatulent and a vermifuge, and the crushed leaves scattered in the path of ants will send them scurrying off within seconds.

Epazote has a pointed, serrated, mid-green leaf with a pungent, addictive flavor, and its flower/seeds are in the form of minuscule green balls clustered around the stem tips.

A source for seeds is given at the back of the book, but now many nurseries both on the West Coast and in the East sell the plants along with those of other culinary herbs.

The plants run to seed and die down in the winter but often reseed themselves. They can also be planted in window boxes and pots and kept alive under indoor plant lights.

GARLIC *(Allium sativum) (Ajo)*

Garlic is used widely in Mexican cooking but generally in moderation; there is rarely a strong garlicky flavor, except in dishes like garlic soup and fish in *mojo de ajo,* which are Spanish and not Mexican in origin. In Oaxaca and Yucatán, many recipes call for whole heads of garlic *asados;* in the first place, the heads of garlic are very small, and second, the charring process—they are then skinned—dilutes the flavor considerably.

Garlic cloves generally used in Mexico are the very small purple ones, so I have often reduced the quantity for the United States. There are also big fleshy cloves of garlic that are often interlaced with red ribbon and sold as lucky charms.

Methods of Preparing and Using

PICADO (FINELY CHOPPED):

Peeled cloves of garlic are finely chopped and fried until transparent, *acitronado,* often with onion as a base for many cooked sauces.

MACHACADO (POUNDED):

Garlic cloves are peeled and crushed in either the mortar or a blender for raw table sauces.

ASADO (BROILED, GRILLED, OR CHARRED) OR ENTERRADO (''BURIED''):

Unpeeled cloves of garlic, or whole small heads, are well charred on the outside and "steamed" inside and then used unpeeled or peeled.

FRITO (FRIED):

Occasionally a recipe—some Yucatecan ones—will call for the peeled cloves or slivers of garlic to be fried until deep brown (do not allow them to burn, or the oil will taste bitter) and then removed, but this is rare.

HOJA SANTA *(Piper auritum sanctum)*

Hoja santa is one of the distinctive cooking herbs, used mainly in southern Mexico and the eastern coastal plains. The most commonly used varieties are the *piper sanctum,* the *piper auritum* is also found in parts of Oaxaca, Yucatán, and San Luis Potosi—it is used in the same way, but it has a much larger leaf.

Hoja or *hierba santa,* *tlanepa* (Veracruz), *momo* (Chiapas), and *acuyo* or *acoyo* (Tabasco) are some of the local names given to this bush. While it more commonly grows in hot areas, it can also flourish in the climate and height of

Mexico City, and friends tell me the *auritum* species grows along the riverbanks of southern Texas.

Despite its strong medicinal taste with faint, anisy traces, it provides a wonderful complement to fish—often cooked wrapped in *hoja santa* in Veracruz and Tabasco—to the *tamales* and green *moles* of Oaxaca and Veracruz, and the *cuitlacoche* of Oaxaca. For those brought up on root beer, it is said to have a similar flavor, like that of sassafras.

Hoja santa has a large, heart-shaped leaf up to 10 inches long and 8 to 10 inches wide, dark green on the surface with a light green, heavily veined underside. The flower is long—up to 4 inches—very thin and stamenlike, with a creamy white color.

Hoja santa is always used fresh. In a pinch it can be dried, but it loses much of its character when it loses its essential oils and tends to disintegrate at a touch.

MINT *(Mentha spicata) (Yerbabuena, Hierbabuena)*

Mint is not used extensively but is considered important in some dishes in the Mexican cuisine: in meat-brothy stews, in meatballs, for cooking chicken (in Oaxaca). It is used widely as a home remedy for indigestion.

Since the leaf is tough, it can be stored for several days in a plastic bag, lined with a paper towel, in the refrigerator.

OREGANO *(Origanum vulgare) (Orégano)*

According to a study that was done some years ago when I requested information about the number of oreganos growing in Mexico, there are at least 13 varieties. The ones that I know have noticeable differences in either the shape of the leaf or the taste.

In the North there is a long-leafed oregano (*Poliomintha longiflora*), in Oaxaca a much milder minty-tasting one (*Lippia geminata* or *Lippia berlandieri*), while in Yucatán the oregano has a much larger leaf and when dried turns a dark tobacco brown. These types are all used dried, and the leaves kept whole, not rubbed to a powder. They are used in many types of sauces, fresh and cooked, to sprinkle on soups, with some broiled meats and in stews, and as a home remedy for the stomach.

There is, however, a large, juicy-leafed oregano grown and used fresh in the Yucatán Peninsula and Tabasco, mostly with fish. It is *Coleus amboinicus* (I have also seen it growing in Hawaii) and is referred to in Tabasco as *oreganón*.

Dried Mexican oregano is imported into the United States and is always available either loose or in small packages in Mexican and Latin American groceries and supermarkets. It should be used wherever possible for these recipes because the more easily found Greek oregano does not have exactly the same flavor.

In some Yucatecan recipes the oregano is toasted before using: Toss for a few seconds in an ungreased pan over medium heat just until it smells musky. Be careful; if you let it burn, it will taste bitter.

PARSLEY *(Petroselinum var. neapolitanum or carum) (Perejil)*

The flat-leaf Italian parsley is used in Mexican cooking, although sparingly, in meatballs, some rice dishes, stews, and soups.

The curly parsley is called *perejil chino* and is used mostly for international food.

Store as for mint; the leaf is rather tough and keeps well.

COOKING FATS AND OILS
(Aceites Comestibles, Manteca Vegetal)

Many types of oil are available to cooks in Mexico, made of corn, sunflower seeds, safflower, sesame, and the cheapest quality soya. But the use of pork lard for all types of cooking persists among some of the older cooks, who have not heard, or do not care to hear, about cholesterol (and for those who can afford it, because even pork fat pieces or leaf fat is quite expensive).

In some of the northern states, Sonora and Tamaulipas for instance, beef fat is used for some flour *tortillas* and corn *antojitos*, and I have heard of some cooks in Michoacán and Puebla who use chicken fat for frying rice or cooking the basic sauce of a chicken dish.

Vegetable lards are used for many of the baked goods, for the large flour *tortillas* of Sonora, and are often added to cream to give it body and stretch. A few cooks are starting to use half pork lard and half vegetable shortening for their *tamales*, but the flavor is rarely as good.

A recipe for making your own pork lard is given on page 276, and if for nothing else, use it for frying beans and *antojitos*—after all, you eat them in only small quantities.

OLIVE OIL *(Aciete de Olivo)*

Olive oil is not used to any great extent in the cooking of Mexico, with the exception of some fish dishes in Veracruz and the Yucatán Peninsula and a few other dishes like *pollo en cuñete* that have strong Spanish roots.

All the good olive oil is imported and therefore expensive, since the domestic oil is pretty poor stuff.

Green olives are used in traditional Mexican cooking.

The Spanish Sensat olive oil is often used in Mexico, but any good-quality olive oil that does not have an overpowering taste will do.

CREAM *(Crema)*

Cream in Mexico, the real thing, is thick and slightly acidy, exactly like *crème fraîche*. It is used to enrich sauces and *sparingly* on top of many *antojitos*, pasta dishes, and *tortilla* casseroles.

In the larger urban centers you can also buy a commercial *crema dulce* that is whipped for pastries and desserts.

In the rich dairying area where Michoacán and Jalisco meet, *crema* is called *jocoque* (not to be confused with the Lebanese yogurt that goes by the same name). The rich milk is left in earthenware containers in a cool place overnight. The cream is skimmed off the next morning and saved but not refrigerated. This is added to as the week goes along, thickening and souring naturally.

Unfortunately much of the cream sold in markets in Mexico is now adulterated with vegetable fats that give it body and, of course, make it go further. At the first taste you may think it is all right, but here is a test to see just how pure it is. Whip some up furiously and make butter. Wash the butter curds, strain well, and melt. Cool off in the refrigerator, and you will see how the layers separate into real butter, added fats, and coloring if any.

TO MAKE *NATAS*

Natas are essentially clotted cream like the famous Devonshire and Cornwall cream. The fresh, unhomogenized milk is set aside overnight; the cream will form a thick layer on top. Without disturbing it, set it over a low heat and scald the milk. Set aside again for the top layer of cream, now *natas*, to set—or skim off and keep in the refrigerator; it will thicken even more.

In small breakfast stands in the marketplaces you will see saucers full of this thick, matted cream set out to spread on sweet rolls. It is also used in cakes and cookies and when beaten makes a superlative butter that is germ-free since it has been scalded.

If you cannot buy a good brand of *crème fraîche*, you can make your own.

TO MAKE CRÈME FRAÎCHE

MAKES ABOUT 1 CUP

  1 cup heavy cream (*not* ultrapasteurized)
  3 tablespoons buttermilk or yogurt (not low-fat), approximately

Mix the cream and buttermilk together well and set the container in a warm place: an oven with a pilot light or near the water heater, covered with a towel. It *should* set within about 8 hours but doesn't always, depending on the quality of the cream and buttermilk. (They seem to be pasteurized to death these days.) Once it has set, put it aside in the refrigerator for another 2 days to firm it up.

I do not recommend the jars of cream marked "Mexican" or "Guatemalan"; they break down under the slightest heat and, I suspect, have been made with the reverse process of putting back together butter and milk. I stand to be corrected.

MEXICAN CHEESES *(Quesos Mexicano)*

The cheeses used in Mexican traditional cooking are relatively unsophisticated and in many cases purely regional. Among them are several semisoft cheeses that bear the name of the mold in which they are formed or other characteristics. *Queso del morral* is formed in shallow molds lined with a coarse material that resembles a *morral* or string bag and leaves its imprint on the surface of the cheese; *queso adobera* is formed in a slightly reduced *adobe*-shaped mold; *enchilado* cheese has a surface that has been heavily dusted with orangey-colored *chile* powder; and *queso panela* is in the form of a round, flattish bread or *pan*. (A raw sugar of the same shape is given that name in Oaxaca.) But the most commonly known and used ones are the following.

QUESO AÑEJO

Queso añejo (properly called *añejo de Cotija* for the farming town of Cotija on the border of Michoacán and Jalisco where it was first made) or aged cheese is a very dry, whitish, salty cheese with some acidity that comes in a barrel shape and is usually grated very finely to resemble fine bread crumbs. It is used on top of *antojitos*, *enchiladas*, soups, and pasta and does not melt.

There is one excellent brand made in the United States, near Los Angeles, with a fairly wide distribution, called simply Queso Cotija, but if it's not available in your area, use a Romano or Sardo.

QUESO ASADERO

Queso asadero is a flattish, soft, braided cheese like *mozzarella*. It is made in northern Mexico with a percentage of sour milk, has a good fat content, is pleasantly acidy, and melts well. In Sonora it is known as *queso cocido*, cooked cheese, because the curds are cooked to form the "skeins" that are then wound into balls. This cheese is used for *queso fundido* (melted cheese), for *chile con queso*, and to stuff *chiles*.

I have not found a good *asadero* in the United States, but a Jack, teleme, or domestic block Muenster can be substituted.

QUESO CHIHUAHUA

This cheese was originally made in the Mennonite communities in Chihuahua, and large wheels of it were stamped with the name of the community. The real thing is rare now as the Mennonites are migrating to other countries, but there are many passable substitutes. This cheese resembles a fairly soft Cheddar, pleasantly acidy, with a good proportion of fat, which means that it melts nicely.

Queso Chihuahua is used for stuffing *chiles*, grated on top of *sopas secas* and pastas, and for melting in *queso fundido* or *chile con queso*. The so-called *Chihuahuas* made in the United States bear little resemblance to the original, so it is best to substitute a good medium-sharp Cheddar (not the soapy packaged ones), a domestic block Muenster, or a Monterey Jack.

QUESO FRESCO

Queso fresco is a crumbly soft cheese with a pleasant acidity that melts and *hace hebra* (strings) when heated. It is made of cow's milk as are the other cheeses mentioned here (goat's milk cheeses are not very popular) and is sometimes called *queso ranchero* (not to be confused with the brand name Queso Ranchero); in one isolated village near a friend's ranch it is called *de metate* because traditionally the curds are pressed and ground on a *metate*.

Queso fresco is used in many different ways: to eat uncooked as a *botana* with drinks; crumbled, to sprinkle on top of *antojitos*, in *enchiladas*, and in soups; cut into strips for *chiles rellenos*, etc.

While several United States companies are now making this type of cheese, they fall far short of the real thing except for Cacique brand Queso Ranchero, which is the best on the market and widely available. The various types of *queso blanco* will not do; they are too white and rubbery and innocuous, so you may have to use what is available in your area.

TO MAKE QUESO FRESCO

I will include the recipe for the enthusiasts who always like to make their own. It is not hard; better, of course, if you can lay your hands on some raw milk, but if not, use what is available. You may have to use more than the rennet specified by the manufacturer. Traditionally these cheeses are formed in round cakes of different size, but a perforated mold, or better still a small round basket, can be used. As a guide a 2-cup mold, measuring 4½ inches in diameter and under 2 inches deep, is just the right size for a cheese made of 1 gallon of milk; after 2 days of draining it should weigh about 1 pound.

> 3 quarts raw milk or 3 quarts homogenized milk and ¼ cup yogurt
> rennet as necessary (either tablet or liquid form)
> 1 tablespoon water, if tablets are used
> 2 rounded teaspoons finely ground sea salt

Heat the milk to just above lukewarm—110°. When it is coming up to this temperature, but not before, crush the tablet into the water until dissolved. Stir this, or liquid rennet, into the milk and keep stirring for about 30 seconds. Cover the pan and leave in a warm place. Do not move it until it is thoroughly set—about 40 minutes, but I usually leave it for at least 1 hour.

If at the end of this time there is a wrinkled skin on the surface of the milk, it has not set properly. Either you over- or underheated the milk, or there was insufficient rennet, or the milk has been overpasteurized and the coagulating properties have been weakened. If the milk does not have the wrinkled skin on top, test to see if it is set by laying a finger on the surface. The curd will feel firm and not adhere to your finger.

Cut the clabbered milk right down to the bottom of the pan into squares about 1½ inches in size and then cut vertically to break the curds up thoroughly. Set aside for 2 hours or so longer for the curds to separate from the whey. With a perforated spoon, transfer the curds to two or three cheesecloth bags (so they dry out more quickly—do not use nylon prepackaged cheesecloth, or you will have filaments of nylon in the cheese) and hang them up to drain in a very airy place with some sort of receptacle underneath to collect the dripping whey. As the curds dry out they will become firmer. Squeeze them gently to help the dripping process along. When they become very firm and only slightly moist at the center—36 to 48 hours, depending on humidity—transfer the curds to the container of a food processor.

Add the salt and process until the curds have been broken up like fine bread crumbs. Scrape into the mold and press gently between your hands to make sure the curds are compact. Set the mold on a rack or on a shallow basket to drain. Turn the mold over after about 6 hours and continue draining. As soon as the cheese begins to feel slightly compact you can push it gently out of the mold to dry out further on the rack. Keep turning every few hours and make sure that it is in a warm, not cold, airy place for the fermentation to take place—this gives the pleasant acidity to the cheese. This process should take about 2 days. Then store it in the refrigerator to use at once or freeze it for future use.

TO MAKE RICOTTA (Requesón)

Since it is a pity to waste anything, you can make *requesón* out of the milk residues left in the whey after removing the curds.

Set the pan of whey over low heat and leave, barely simmering, until the milk residues have formed a layer on the surface of the liquid—about 2 hours. Remove from the heat and set aside for about 30 minutes.

Pour the contents of the pan through a fine cheesecloth bag, scraping the sides and bottom for any curds that have adhered to it, and hang it up to drain in an airy place for about 24 hours. As soon as these leftover curds have compacted but are still moist, they may be used or frozen for future use.

QUESILLO DE OAXACA

This is a braided, cooked cheese, made and sold in the markets of Oaxaca in all sizes, from a 1-inch ball used as a *botana* (snack with drinks), to 6 inches in diameter. Of course it is made on a large commercial scale in big blocks to be sold in Mexico City and around the country.

The *quesillo de Oaxaca* has a tougher consistency than the *asadero* and a higher melting point. It is used for *chiles rellenos, quesadillas*, etc., as well as to eat raw as mentioned above.

It is difficult to find a good substitute for this one. The usual commercial American *mozzarellas* do not have enough acidity or character but can be used in a pinch. A young Mexican chef in New York, however, has located an excellent string cheese called Laraia that acts and tastes exactly right. If it is not available in your area, use, as for *asadero*, a Jack, teleme, or domestic block Muenster (never the small, packaged kind).

QUESO PANELA

The traditional *queso panela* is a flattish, round fresh cheese marked with the weave of the basket in which the curds are set to drain. I first came across it years ago at its best, made in every household in the hot coastal area of Jalisco. The temperature there is hot enough to ferment the cheese so that it has a spongy, porous texture.

It is the simplest of all the cheeses to make. Clabber the milk in the usual way (see page 446, recipe for *queso fresco*), cut the curd into large pieces, and transfer them with a slotted spoon to a draining basket, sprinkling sea salt liberally between layers of curds. Hang up to drain overnight; when the curds are drained but still moist, set them aside on a rack for the acidity to develop for about 12 to 24 hours in a warm place.

FRUITS AND VEGETABLES *(Frutas y Legumbres)*

AVOCADO *(Persea americana* and var.*) (Aguacate)*

The avocado native to Mexico has a thin, edible skin—either blackish or green when ripe—a large pit, and thin, very fragrant flesh. Of course there are many varieties that are grafted onto this indigenous avocado, chiefly the Hass and Fuerte. In the hotter lowlands of southeastern Mexico there are huge, elongated, pear-shaped avocados with a reddish-tinged skin, and the *pagua*, a tough skin—almost like a shell—with flesh that is not as oily as the other varieties and does not therefore make a good *guacamole*.

You might say that the avocado is one of Mexico's all-purpose fruits; while principally used in *guacamole* (pages 352 and 353), it is also blended for a hot or cold soup or blended for a hot sauce with meat. It is sliced for a topping for seafood, salads, and *tortilla* dishes and even for ice cream (I have yet to find an acceptable way of making it).

Avocados come into the markets in the United States underripe and should be bought ahead and ripened in a paper bag in a warm spot in the kitchen—they can take up to 3 days to ripen. An avocado at its best has flesh that feels firm and compact and just gives to the touch.

If there is a hollow between the flesh and the skin, try the next one.

The final test: shake it. If the pit is loose, pass over that one. Even if it seems just right, you can cut one open and find the flesh mottled with brown patches; the flavor will have deteriorated. It is, therefore, always best to buy more than you need.

You never really need to peel an avocado whole, which is a messy business anyway. Cut it open, remove the pit, and scoop out the flesh with a wooden spoon.

If you are keeping half the avocado for another purpose, leave in the pit to preserve the color and wrap the avocado half tightly in plastic wrap.

To slice an avocado, cut through the skin and flesh down to the pit with a sharp paring knife, then pull the skin back; with it a section of the avocado should come cleanly away from the pit.

Avocado Leaves

Fresh or dried avocado leaves are used in some dishes in parts of Oaxaca, Puebla, and Morelos for *tamales*, for seasoning barbecued meats, or for adding to stews. The dried leaves are quickly toasted over a bare flame—they send off a wonderful fragrance. If you don't have any available, you can always prevail upon friends who do in other parts of the country to send them, as they will keep for several months dried.

TOMATOES *(Lycopersicum esculentum) (Jitomates)*

Tomatoes are called *jitomates* in central Mexico, after the Nahuatl word *xitomatl,* and *tomate rojo* in several other regions to distinguish it from the *tomate verde* described on page 451. The plant is a native of Mexico and South America. Very red, ripe tomatoes are available year-round, either the large round ones, *de bola,* or *guaje* or *guajillo,* which refers to plum tomatoes. Occasionally one comes across a recipe in Oaxaca or Campeche that calls for green (unripe) tomatoes as opposed to the green *tomate verde.* Mexican cooks will be very explicit about how tomatoes should be prepared for a certain recipe: chopped raw, boiled, grilled, stewed, skinned or unskinned.

Methods of Preparing

CRUDO (RAW):

For some raw sauces like *mexicana, uña,* etc., scrambled eggs, seafood cocktails, etc., the whole tomatoes will be chopped finely, seeds and all.

COCIDO (BOILED):

Tomatoes are covered with water and simmered until soft. The skins of the plum tomatoes tend to become even tougher with this method of cooking, and many cooks peel them before blending; however, it is not really necessary with a good blender, and besides, the sauce does not have as much body.

ASADO (BROILED, GRILLED, OR CHARRED ON A COMAL):

This method is used for many rustic table sauces that are uncooked, as well as for some of the cooked tomato sauces. The tomatoes are placed whole on an ungreased *comal* and cooked over medium heat until the skin is deep brown with charred patches and the flesh mushy. Some cooks skin them, but it adds to the flavor and texture if the skin is left on.

Tomatoes prepared in this way give the sauces a very special depth of flavor and sweetness. It is also a good method to use when tomatoes are in season and you want to store them for sauces during the winter. Choose the ripest and broil them in the following way: Line a shallow pan into which the whole tomatoes will just fit (not too large, or the juice will dry up) and broil 2 inches from the heat, turning them from time to time until the skin is blistered and browned and the flesh inside mushy. Store whole in the freezer in 1-pound batches with all the juice drained from the pan.

ENTERRADO (LITERALLY ''BURIED''):

In the villages of the Yucatán Peninsula, where cooking is still done in a *pib,* or pit barbecue, the ingredients—tomatoes, *chiles,* onions, or garlic—are put onto the hot stones at the bottom of the pit (which is not deep) and charred on the outside while the inside cooks and in fact steams. For this method you can grill or broil as described above.

ESTOFADO (STEWED):

I saw a Oaxacan cook using this method on a recent visit to that region, and it is especially good when tomatoes are on the dry side. Cut the tomatoes into 8 pieces, without skinning. Put into a saucepan with 1 table-spoon of oil and ¼ cup water (for 1½ pounds), cover the pan, and let them cook gently over low heat, shaking the pan from time to time to make sure they don't stick, until cooked through and mushy. They can then be blended for sauces.

RALLADO (GRATED):

Although no recipe is given for tomatoes prepared in this way, I have included it as a point of interest concerning the cooking methods of Sonora. Cut a slice off the top of the tomato and grate, opening the skin as you go along until you are left with the flattened skin on the palm of your hand.

MEXICAN GREEN TOMATOES *(Physalis ixocarpa) (Tomate Verde)*

One of the most fascinating ingredients in Mexican cooking is the green tomato covered with a paper husk, indigenous to Mexico. It should not be confused with the ordinary tomato. Its name varies from one region to another: *miltomate* in Oaxaca, *tomate milpero, tomate de capote* in Colima, *fresadilla* in Nuevo Leon, etc. Very rarely the very small ones are called *tomatillos*. In the state of Mexico there is a larger variety called *tomate manzano* that tends to be juicier and sweeter. In the United States, *tomate verde* are usually marketed under the name of *tomatillos*.

Whichever way you are going to prepare them, first remove the papery husk and rinse, but it is not necessary to wash off all the slightly sticky substance around the base. Do not attempt to skin them. *Tomate verde* are almost always cooked, except for some sauces in central Mexico served with barbecued meats or *carnitas*, in which the *tomates* are blended raw.

Methods of Preparing

ASADO (BROILED, GRILLED, OR CHARRED ON A COMAL):

For some sauces the *tomates* are placed whole (husks removed) onto a hot *comal* (griddle) and cooked until they're fairly soft and the skin is lightly charred. They are then ground for sauces, skin included.

COCIDO (BOILED):

By far the most common way of preparing them. Cover them with water and bring to a simmer; continue simmering until fairly soft but not mushy or breaking open—about 10 to 15 minutes, depending on size.

In Oaxaca some cooks cut them into quarters, add just a little water, not even to cover, and stew slowly. The water and juices are then used to dilute the sauce.

It is interesting to note that the papery husk has an acidic quality; when the husks are infused in water, that water can be used as a leavening for doughs such as *tamale masa*.

Tomate verde are not juicy and therefore are rather light in weight. There are about 22 medium-sized ones—approximately 1¼ to 1½ inches in diameter—to the pound.

CHICK-PEAS *(Cicer arietinum) (Garbanzos)*

Dried chick-peas are used for several Mexican soups and stews. They are also either ground to a powder, or cooked and mashed for savory fried cakes, or cooked and mashed for use in fritters that are served as a dessert in syrup.

You can, of course, use canned ones, but they are precooked and tend to be a bit mushy; besides, you can't use the liquid from the can satisfactorily. If you cook them yourself, you can use the broth to add to the stew for extra flavor and nutrients.

To Cook Chick-peas

One cup (about 6 ounces) of dried chick-peas will double its volume with cooking. Rinse the chick-peas in cold water, drain, cover with hot water, and leave to soak overnight. Put the chick-peas and their soaking water plus 2 extra cups of water into a saucepan with salt to taste. Bring to a simmer and continue cooking slowly until soft but not falling apart—about 1½ hours, depending on how old and dry they are.

Pressure Cooker Method

Put the chick-peas, their soaking water, and extra water, but no salt, into the pressure cooker, bring up to pressure, and cook for about 40 minutes.

Whichever method you use, when they're cool enough to handle, rub the chick-peas between your hands to loosen the papery skins and discard. They are now ready to be used, but reserve the cooking water for the soup or stew to which they are to be added.

PLANTAINS *(Musa paradisiaca)* *(Platano Macho)*

Plantains, or "vegetable bananas" as I have called them, are used in the cooking of some, but not all, regions of Mexico; they are a particularly popular ingredient in the southern coastal states of Veracruz, Tabasco, Chiapas, and Oaxaca.

Plantains are large, triangle-shaped, curved bananas pointed at one end and can be found in all Latin American and Caribbean markets.

In Mexico, plantains are nearly always used in their ripe state, whether the skin is still yellow or has ripened to black, when, in fact, they are at their sweetest. They are usually peeled before cooking, with an exception here and there, like some stews and notably *cocido Oaxaqueño* (page 294). Although the most common way of eating plantain is to slice it lengthwise and fry it—to accompany rice, etc.—it is also mashed to a dough (in Veracruz and Tabasco) for *empanadas* with meat filling, blended for a soup, or flattened and twice fried for a type of crisp *botana* (snack with drinks), and in Tabasco it is made into vinegar.

The smallest, sweetest plantains are the *dominica* from Tabasco, which are thin and pointed, and the small variety called *plátano de castilla* in Oaxaca.

ONIONS *(Allium cepa)* *(Cebollas)*

The most commonly used onion in Mexican cooking is the large white one, very similar to but sharper than those grown in California, widely available all over the United States. The brown onion is not grown and would, in any case, be considered too sweet.

The *cebolla de rabo*, or peasant onion as it is sometimes referred to, is a large bulbous scallion, often marked knob or Texas scallion. It is even sharper in flavor and used, with most of the green top, in the cooking of beans and *nopales* (cactus paddles), for it is believed to diminish the slimy substance they exude. Whole, with green leaves intact, it is grilled to put with the meat in *tacos del carbon*, charcoal-grilled *tacos*.

The purple or red onion, albeit small in size, is used a lot in the cooking of the Yucatán Peninsula and in some of the relishes of Jalisco and Colima.

The ordinary scallion, called *cebolla de cambrai* (*cambrai* signifying something small), is used with some pickled vegetables and chopped with part of the green leaves for fresh sauces in the western states of Colima, Jalisco, and Sinaloa. The biggest demand for these, though, is in Mexico City.

Methods for Preparing Onions

PICADA (FINELY CHOPPED):

These are used in the base of many cooked or fresh sauces and to sprinkle on top of many types of *antojitos*. They should be chopped, not minced (which leaves most of the flavor on the board), to pieces a fraction less than ¼ inch.

EN RUEDAS (IN RINGS):

The onions are finely sliced into complete rings, and then the rings are separated and used mostly for decoration.

MEDIA LUNA (HALF-MOON):

The onion is halved horizontally, and then each half is cut into thin slices to make crescents.

TAJADAS (SEGMENTS):

The onion is sliced after being cut into quarters vertically.

Methods of Cooking Onions

ACITRONADA (TRANSPARENT):

The onion is fried gently until translucent but not really wilted. It is treated like this for the base of many cooked sauces or vegetables.

FRITA (FRIED):

The onion is fried to a deep golden color, a method used in Oaxaca for a base for a sauce.

ENTERRADA (PIT-CHARRED):

A term used in Yucatán meaning to put in the earth. Whole, unskinned onions are placed on the hot stones of the *pib* or pit barbecue until they are well charred outside and the flesh is cooked (really steamed) in the middle. Of course, this can be done over a grill or on a *comal*.

ASADA (ROASTED):

Although this word means roasted in the oven, it is more often applied in Mexican cooking terms to mean cooking by charring on the outside on a *comal* or grill. The charred skin will be peeled off if tough; otherwise it is left on for flavor.

CITRUS FRUITS

Lime (Citrus aurantifolia) (Limón)

Without doubt the most ubiquitous of the citrus fruits in the Mexican kitchen is the small, thin-skinned, pale green lime (when overripe, it turns a pale yellow). It is, in fact, the same as the famous and alas scarce Key lime. It is juicier and has a more delicate flavor than the larger, dark green Persian lime so popular with fruit growers.

Limón is used in every phase of a Mexican meal: in *agua fresca* (a type of limeade), with Tecate beer, with Tequila or Mescal, in some fresh sauces, with soups, with dry soups, with seafood, with meats, and with some fresh fruits like papaya.

Although the names sound similar, it should not be confused with the yellow lemon, which is not grown in Mexico except for the occasional tree planted by *aficionados*.

Sour Lime (Citrus limetta sp.) (Lima Agria)

The sour lime is a smallish, light green lime with a pronounced nipple (sometimes referred to vulgarly as *lima chichona* for that reason). It is sour, as its name implies, and has a highly aromatic rind. Sour lime is used principally in the cooking of Yucatán, although also to some degree in that of Guerrero and part of Oaxaca. There is no real substitute, although a green, unripe Meyer lemon comes closest but still lacks some of the complexity of flavor.

Sweet Lime (Citrus limetta) (Lima)

The sweet lime is grown in central Mexico and resembles the sour variety, except that the flesh is almost without flavor but the rind is highly aromatic. I have been told (but can't substantiate it) that it is exactly the same variety of citrus but changes in character (as does grapefruit) at different altitudes and in different soil.

Limas are very popular for fruit drinks, make a delicious *tisane* when added whole, unpeeled, to the boiling water, and are the "Christmas fruit" always included with others in the interior of a *piñata* for the pre-Christmas *posadas* (parties) and for the Christmas Eve salad.

Bitter Orange (*Citrus aurantium, Citrus bigaradea, Citrus vulgaris*) (*Naranja Agria, Naranja de Cucho*)

The bitter or Seville orange, or a close relation to it, is grown and used in many parts of the Mexican Republic from Sonora to Yucatán. It looks like a smallish, squat orange with a thick, wrinkled rind usually bright orange in color—although in Yucatán it is greenish turning to yellow—and highly aromatic. The flesh is acidy and not very juicy but full of flavor.

While it is used in the cooking of many areas to a limited extent, it really comes into its own in Yucatán, where it is used to dilute many of the seasoning pastes for flavoring fish and meats and takes the place of vinegar for pickling onions, etc. It makes a wonderful orangeade and is supposed to be good for ailments of the gallbladder.

The bitter orange is available almost the year round in California and Arizona, where it is grown as an ornamental tree, and in southern Texas in the spring. Most of the imported oranges come in from the Caribbean around February and are fairly widely distributed or can be ordered specially.

If you do have access to these oranges sporadically and are addicted to Yucatecan food, then always have some of the juice, with a proportion of finely grated rind, on hand in the freezer. If not, then a substitute—although nothing can really duplicate the complex flavor of the fruit—can be made.

BITTER ORANGE SUBSTITUTE

MAKES ABOUT ½ CUP

1 teaspoon finely grated grapefruit or green Meyer lemon rind
2 tablespoons fresh orange juice
2 tablespoons fresh grapefruit or ripe Meyer lemon juice
4 tablespoons fresh lime juice

DRIED AND CANDIED FRUITS (*Frutas Secas y Cubiertas*)

In almost every Mexican marketplace—and in special sections of Mexican markets in the United States—there is a stand devoted to dried and candied fruits. Raisins and prunes are the most commonly used, although dried figs, apricots, pears, and dates appear in fairly limited quantities and are very expensive.

Candied fruits of all types outnumber the others, appealing to the very sweet tooth of the general Mexican public: orange and grapefruit peel, *chilacayote* (a member of the squash family), pumpkin, figs, papaya, cactus, and citron are among the most popular. Apart from being used in desserts and cakes, they are often eaten as a sweetmeat, on their own, for dessert after the main meal of the day.

Candied Cactus (Echinocactus grandis) (Biznaga or Acitron)

This cactus is candied in bars. Although it does not have a strong taste, when roughly chopped it adds a pleasant crunch to *picadillos*, meat stuffings, and sweet *tamales*. It is also used in sweet yeast breads and desserts.

Prunes (Ciruela Pasa)

Dried prunes are used mainly in yeast breads, cakes, and pastries, but they also appear in the odd savory dish like *pollo en ciruela pasa* (page 237) and for spiking large cuts of beef or pork for braising.

Raisins (Pasas, Pasitas)

Ordinary black raisins are used rather sparingly, just to give a touch of sweetness to *picadillos* or an occasional meat sauce such as *pollo en cuñete*.

CHILES AND HOW TO PREPARE THEM

Without doubt the apogee of *chile* cultivation and use has been reached in Mexico. Although *chile* growing is extensive in many lands—not only on the American continent but also in Europe (Hungary in particular), Asia, and Africa—Mexico produces a far greater volume and variety of *chiles*, and the per-capita consumption is far higher than in any other country.

The word *chile* in its present-day form comes from the Nahuatl word *chilli* (Nahuatl was the *lingua franca* of the inhabitants of the central highlands of Mexico when the Spaniards arrived and is in fact still spoken in a modified form today), and curiously enough, the spelling *chilli* has persisted in India since the Portuguese took them there in the sixteenth century. The Spanish and Portuguese referred to the *chile* as *pimienta de las Indias* and also used the Arawak word, *aji* or *axi*, which is still used in the Caribbean and South America today.

While many of the *chiles* are indigenous to Mexico, others come from South America. Traces of domesticated varieties and a few wild varietals have been found in the caves near Tehuacán in the state of Puebla, and others have been found in Ocampo in the state of Tamaulipas, demonstrating that their domestication predates that of tomatoes and corn.

An anonymous writer has been quoted as saying that the *chile* is the king and the soul of the Mexicans—food, drug, medicine, and solace—while Frances Toor, writing in *Mexican Folkways* in 1947, pointed out that the *chile* has been a constant factor in Mexican life from prehistoric times until the present day as a condiment, medicine, tribute, ritual object, defensive weapon, and pigment. Indeed the *chile* has played such an important role in the economic and social life of the country that many Mexicans feel their national identity would be in danger of extinction without it.

Throughout the centuries *chiles* have come under close scrutiny by botanists, but if you were to follow all of their findings and put together their various classifications the results would be confusing, to say the least. There is no complete consensus on the varieties grown in Mexico today—except of course for those grown commercially—but it is believed that most derive from the *Capsicum annum*, which is indigenous to Mexico, with the exception of the *chile habanero* (dubbed *Capsicum chinense* or *sinense* incorrectly, since they did not originate in China but probably in lowland tropical South America) and the *chile manzano* or *perón, Capsicum pubescens*, which is believed to have been introduced into Mexico from South America around the turn of the century.

At the time I was researching *Cuisines of Mexico* in the late sixties, a botanist then engaged in studying *chiles* believed that there were about 90 varieties in Mexico, but that was never substantiated because each area—especially the more remote mountainous areas—had its own *chiles* that could rarely be reproduced in different soil and climatic conditions. To add to the confusion, while most *chiles* are thought to be hermaphrodites, cross-pollination can take place.

Names are confusing too, because often the same *chile* bears a different name in a different area, even among the commercially grown ones. In parts of Michoacán the *ancho* is known as *pasilla; chile gordo* can mean a *jalapeño* in Veracruz and a *poblano* in Jalisco. In the Bajio a *guajillo* is often called a *cascabel,* and in Jalisco the *guajillo* is quite incorrectly called *mirasol,* looking at the sun, because it nearly always grows downward, not upward.

For identification purposes I have used the names used in the markets of Mexico City, the central distribution point of most, but not all, of the regional *chiles.* Don't take the distributors' labeling for granted; they are misleading and often wrongly spelled to boot. A fresh *chile poblano* is *not* a *pasilla* as they often label them. (*Pasa* is a raisin and signifies something dried and wrinkled; *ciruela pasa* for instance, is a prune, and *pasilla* also means large, along with dried and wrinkled.) You might wonder why all the fuss about names; if you use the wrong *chile,* the balance of flavors of a dish can be substantially altered.

Can we really tell how hot a *chile* is going to be? Scoville in 1911 gave us a guide by testing a range of *chiles* on some *non–chile* eaters, but long before, the Aztecs had seven words to describe the different degrees of heat of the *chiles* of their day. I am sure things have changed since 1911, with new varietal, different soils, and irrigation methods.

There is a lot of misinformation on the subject of heat, too. I would invite the author of "a *chile* with broad shoulders is not as hot" to bite into a *manzano* or *habanero.* The *chile manzano* can range from fiercely hot in Michoacán to mildly hot in Oaxaca and Chiafras. During my 30 years of regular *chile* eating, I have been constantly surprised: a batch of mild *serranos, jalapeños,* and even *habaneros* (grown in the Caribbean, not in Mexico) have come my way, as has a *poblano* so hot that it took my breath away, to mention a few exceptions.

Chile eating in Mexico is an adventure; *chiles* are not used just to make food hot, as a condiment, as in many other cuisines. Each variety has a flavor of its own, some stronger or more perfumed than others. Each is treated in a different way, or ways, and fills a different role in the cuisine: the fleshy *poblanos* as a vegetable, *piquines* as a condiment, *jalapeños* as a pickle, *serranos* fresh in a sauce, dried *anchos, mulatos,* and *pasillas* as thickeners for a sauce, adding their various colors and flavors.

Chiles can be charred and peeled, like the *poblanos* and *Anaheims;* charred and left whole to flavor sauce, like the *x-cat-ik* of Yucatán; burnt and crushed to a powder, like the *seco* of Yucatán; smoked, like the *chipotles,*

461

moras, moritas, and *pasillas* of Oaxaca; charred, peeled, and dried, like the *poblanos* and *Anaheims* of Durango and Chihuahua; or just dried for the popular *guajillos, puyas,* or *cascabeles.*

The heat of a *chile* is concentrated in the placenta—the white fleshy part at the top of the *chile* just below where the stalk joins the fruit and to which most of the seeds are joined—and the veins continuing on down the sides of the *chiles.* The seeds are not in themselves hot but acquire hotness by association with the veins and placenta. For instance, some recipes call for toasting the seeds from dried *chiles* (*moles,* for example, and *pipián* of Oaxaca) to thicken and give flavor to the sauce, not to make it hot.

I was told by the late Dr. Alfredo Barreda Marín, a well-known Mexican botanist, that not all *chiles* can be mixed; there are *chiles peleados,* or "fighting" chiles. He recounted that when his mother heard her husband returning to the house with some buddies to carouse she would hastily make up some sauce of either *pasillas* with *serranos* or *habaneros* with *chiles secos Yucatecos.* Very soon, one by one they would make their excuses and depart, looking pale and much the worse for wear.

As early as the sixteenth century, Fray Bartolome de las Casas said that without *chiles* the Indians do not consider that they have eaten.

Below I give a description of some of the *chiles,* both fresh and dried, that are used in the everyday cooking in Mexico. Each *chile* has notes on its availability in the United States. Travelers to Mexico should note that *chiles* may be carried across the border with no problems.

When working with *chiles,* take care not to touch your eyes (especially if you're wearing contact lenses) without first washing your hands thoroughly.

FRESH CHILES

CHILE DE AGUA *("Water Chile")*

This is very much a local Oaxacan *chile* and rarely exported outside the region. However, it features in an important relish in the Oaxacan cuisine and as such deserves a mention, albeit an esoteric one, for visitors to Oaxaca and *aficionados*. The *chile de agua* is a large, light green *chile* that ripens to a fiery, orangey-red. Although sizes can vary tremendously, an average one would measure about 5 to 6 inches long and about 1¾ inches wide. It has a very good fresh flavor but is extremely hot.

Chiles de agua are generally prepared for a sauce or relish by first charring, peeling, and cutting them into strips, without seeds and veins.

Although the flavor will not be the same, a good fresh relish can be made from any large hot *chile pepper*.

This *chile* is not used in its dried state. Since it is not available in the United States, any light green, large hot pepper can be substituted.

CHILACA

Chilacas are long, thin, dark to blackish-green *chiles* that ripen to a deep brown and are grown mainly in the Bajío, or central area north of Mexico City. Most of them are destined to be dried and transformed into *chile pasilla*. In their fresh green state they are used in relatively small quantities in and around Mexico City, while they are an important ingredient in the cooking of Michoacán. There they are referred to as *chile cuernillo* (big horn) or *chile para deshebrar*—the latter because they are torn into strips after being charred and peeled.

The skin of this *chile* is shiny, and the surface is formed by shallow, undulating vertical ridges. They have an excellent flavor and can be very *picante*. I have seen them on sale only once in the United States, and that was some years ago in the Los Angeles Central Market. Although sizes can vary, an average one measures about 7 inches long (not counting the stem) and ¾ to 1 inch wide.

Charred and peeled, cleaned of veins and seeds, and shredded, they are used as a vegetable or in vegetable dishes, with fried onion and potato for instance, with cheese as a filling for *tamales*, or in a tomato sauce to accompany *corundas* (page 70), and stewed pork.

To Choose

Always choose those *chiles* that are smooth and shiny, not those that have a tired-looking, wrinkled skin. Apart from losing flavor, they will be hard to peel.

To Store

If you are not going to use them right away, wrap them in two layers of paper toweling, then in a plastic bag, and store them in the refrigerator. They do not freeze when whole. After they have been prepared (see below) and torn into strips, they can be frozen, but not for more than a month or so, or they will lose their texture and flavor when defrosted.

To Prepare

With few exceptions these *chiles* are charred and peeled for use in sauces, vegetables, etc., as mentioned above. Leave the stalks intact so you can turn them more easily; place them directly onto a gas burner or outdoor charcoal or wood grill and allow them to brown and blister, turning them from time to time until they are evenly charred. Take care not to let the flesh burn through since it is not very thick. If you are using an electric stove, lightly grease the *chiles* and broil them under a hot broiler, turning them from time to time until evenly charred.

Place them in a plastic bag and set aside to "sweat" for about 15 minutes. Do not let them cool off before putting them into the bag as this will make peeling more difficult. The skin should now be slipped off easily, which should be done over a strainer because the skin is tough and can stop up the sink drainage system. Rinse the *chile* briefly; do not soak it in water, or the flavor will be impaired.

With a sharp paring knife, cut off the top with the stem attached and discard. Slit the *chile* down the side and scrape out veins and seeds and discard. Tear the *chile* into thin—about ¼-inch—strips, which are now ready to use or freeze (see note above).

CHILE GÜERO

In Mexico any pale yellow or pale green *chile* is referred to as *güero* or blond. There are several that fall into this category (listed below). They are used fresh or canned and not dried.

CHILE CERA

Also referred to as *chile caribe* or *Fresno,* this is a small triangular yellow *chile* with a smooth, waxy surface. An average one is about 2½ inches long and just over 1 inch at its widest part. It is used mostly in the northern states and Jalisco for pickling with vegetables and fruits, or whole, slashed at the bottom to be added to stews, sauces, or lentils to give flavor. It can be mild or fairly hot. In Jalisco I have seen it labeled variously *chile hungaro,* California Gold #5, or even Anaheim, none of which names I take very seriously.

This *chile* is widely available in the United States, called wax or Fresno.

CHILE X-CAT-IK

X-cat-ik means blond in the Mayan language. This is very much a locally grown and distributed Yucatecan *chile.* It is pale yellow in color, long and thin, pointed at the end, rather thin-fleshed. An average one is 4½ to 5 inches in length and ¾ inch wide; it varies from mild to fairly hot. It is generally used charred, unpeeled, and whole in sauces or in fish and chicken sauces (*escabeches*) in the Yucatecan cuisine. It is not available in the United States; an Italian or banana pepper can be substituted.

CHILE LARGO OR CARRICILLO

To my mind this is the most flavorful of the *güero chiles.* Unfortunately its distribution is very limited and seasonal, owing, I suppose, to the fact that most of the production goes to the canning industry. This is a long, curling, thin, thin-skinned *chile* with a smooth skin but undulating surface. Although grown in the central part of Mexico, it is used in the dishes of Veracruz, generally added whole for flavoring rather than for piquancy. Most of the *chiles* produced are canned in a light pickle and labeled *chiles largos,* the only form in which they reach the United States.

CHILE PARA RELLENAR AMARILLENTO
(Yellowish-Green Chile for Stuffing)

The *chile para rellenar amarillento* is shaped just like a *poblano,* but the flesh tends to be thinner and the skin a yellowy-green color. It is a very local *chile* that is not distributed widely but with a good flavor that is much appreciated in Dolores Hidalgo, in the state of Guanajuato, where it is grown. This chile is not exported to the United States.

CHILE HABANERO

The *chile habanero* plant in full production is a spectacular sight with its broad, dark green, glossy leaves and the fully ripe *chiles* hanging down in clusters like brilliant orange lanterns. When mature, the *chile* is mid-green and ripens to yellow and then orange. It looks as though it has been burnished and is almost translucent. An average-sized *chile habanero*, which is grown commercially exclusively in Yucatán with very limited distribution elsewhere, is about 1¾ inches long and about 1¼ inches wide. It is considered the hottest of the *chiles* in Mexico, although I would rate the *manzano* and *chile de árbol* in the same category. Not only are its looks exceptional but also its distinctive flavor, which is lingering and perfumed—so much so that it is often put into sauces to give flavor and not piquancy.

It is impossible to find an adequate substitute for *chile habanero*. The nearest thing to it, grown under different climatic conditions, which alters its physical appearance a little and makes for a softer flavor, is the Haitian *piment*—called Scotch bonnet in Jamaica and *chile Congo* in Trinidad—which comes into the Caribbean stores of New York.

The *chile habanero* is not used in a dried state.

To Choose

The *chile* should have a smooth, unwrinkled skin. It should be resilient, not soft, to the touch and firm around the base of the stalk.

To Store

If you are not going to use the *chiles* immediately, cover them well with two layers of paper toweling and put them into a plastic bag in the refrigerator. They will keep quite well for a week or more.

Another way of storing them for use in sauces is to char them lightly and allow them to cool off and then pack in thick wrapping for the freezer, where they will keep for about 3 months.

To Prepare

- This *chile* is used raw in fresh sauces like *x-ni-pek* (page 345) and in *cebollas en escabeche* (page 363). Simply rinse the *chile*, dry it, and chop it with seeds and veins included.
- To make a simple, very hot Yucatecan sauce, the *chile* should be charred whole, and then ground in a mortar with lime juice and sea salt. If it is for

frijoles colados (page 186) or a Yucatecan tomato sauce, it can be added whole, raw, or whole and slightly charred to release the flavor.

That lovely expression, "the *chile* takes a walk through the sauce," comes from Yucatán. A raw *chile habanero* is shredded at the pointed end and then dunked into the sauce several times just to leave behind a slight piquancy and flavor.

CHILE JALAPEÑO

Chiles jalapeños are perhaps the best-known *chiles* outside of Mexico since much of the crop is pickled and canned. There are a great many varieties of this *chile*, but their shape is unmistakable: like an elongated, blunt triangle varying from mid- to dark green, some with dark patches on them, others with a vertical brown intermittent striping. The *chile jalapeño* is called by different names according to the type and the season in which it is harvested or just local usage: *chile gordo* in Veracruz, *chilchote* in the Sierra de Puebla, or *tornachile* in old cookbooks, *cuaresmeño* in central Mexico. An average *chile jalapeño* is about 2½ inches long and just under 1 inch wide; it can range from hot to very hot. It is used either in its mature but green stage or when fully ripened and bright red in color.

Chiles jalapeños, widely available in the United States, are used mostly in strips (*rajas*), either fresh in sauces, or pickled whole or in strips. Generally speaking they will be chopped and blended for sauces only if *serranos* are not available in your area.

To Choose

The skin of these *chiles* when fresh is smooth and shiny and the flesh firm to the touch. When dull and wrinkled, they have lost their flesh flavor and crisp texture. Always make sure there is no deterioration around the base of the stem.

To Store

If you are not going to use them right away, store them as for the other fresh *chiles*, wrapping them first in paper toweling and then in plastic bags; even then it is best to keep them only about a week, for after that time the flavor and texture are impaired.

To Prepare

- First rinse the *chiles* well in case traces of insecticides remain. Wipe them dry, cut them into strips, and fry them with onion for a tomato sauce. Seeds may be removed for appearance sake.
- Fry them whole with onion and garlic for pickled *chiles* before adding herbs and vinegar.
- In Veracruz they are stuffed with tuna, sardines, or cheese—they are very potent. For these recipes (not given in this book) the *chiles* are charred over a flame as for *poblanos,* peeled, slit open, seeded, and stuffed. Occasionally they will be stuffed with meat and covered with a batter as for *chiles rellenos.*

CHILE MANZANO

The *chile manzano,* called *perón* in Michoacán and *canario* in Oaxaca, is a fleshy, bulbous *chile* with an average length of 2 inches and width of about 1¾ inches, and it is one of the hottest I know.

It is an uncommon *chile* for various reasons: the plant, which can grow into a high bush, can withstand cold and is cultivated in Michoacán, where it is *picante,* in the high country around Lake Patzcuaro, and the Chiapas highlands, where it is milder. It has a purple, rather than the normal white, flower and quite large woody seeds that are jet black in color. There are two distinct plants that I know of—as a *chile* grower—one where the green mature fruit ripens to a bright yellow, the other turning from green to a brilliant red. The real *aficionados* say they prefer the yellow because it has more flavor than the red, which they say is hotter, if that is possible.

The surface of the *chile* is smooth and shiny, and once picked it seems to keep its fresh appearance longer than other types of *chiles.* In Mexico the unpeeled *chile* is used in pickles and relishes, charred but not peeled; ground in tomato sauces; charred and peeled, it is stuffed for *chiles rellenos,* but in none of these cases are the seeds used.

The *chile manzano* is never used in a dried form and is not sold in the United States (I have seen plants in window boxes of the Latin American Mission District of San Francisco, where it is called *ricoto.*)

To Choose

Make sure that the surface is smooth and shiny and firm to the touch; when it's wrinkled and dull and soft, the best has gone out of the *chile.* Also be sure that there is no deterioration around the base of the stalk.

To Store

If you are not going to use the *chiles* right away, wrap them in paper toweling and put them into a plastic bag in the refrigerator—even then they tend to lose their crisp texture for use when raw.

To Prepare

- Rinse and dry the *chiles.* For use in fresh relishes, remove the stalk, cut open the *chile,* and remove seeds, then cut the *chile* into strips. It is usual to leave the *chiles* to macerate in lime juice with salt to cut the heat a little.
- To use a *chile manzano* in a tomato sauce, place it whole on a hot *comal* (griddle) and turn it from time to time until the skin is slightly charred and blistered. Cut it open, remove the seeds and veins, and blend the *chile* with the tomatoes—only part of one *chile* will be necessary to make the sauce *picante.*
- *Chiles manzanos* are also prepared like *poblanos* for *chiles rellenos.* They are charred and peeled in the usual way, slit open, and the seeds and veins are removed. They are then covered with hot water and simmered for about 1 minute. The water is changed, a little salt is added, and they are left to soak for 5 minutes more. They are drained, stuffed with a *picadillo* of shredded meat or with cheese, covered in an egg batter, and fried. They are served in a tomato broth, again just like *chiles rellenos.*

CHILE POBLANO

The *chile poblano* is also known by the names *chile para rellenar, chile gordo* (Jalisco), *jaral* (state of Mexico), and, most incorrectly in the United States, it is called *pasilla.*

This is a large, fleshy, triangle-shaped *chile* with a shiny, smooth, mid- to black-green color that ripens to a deep red and ranges from mild to hot with a distinctive taste. An average-sized *chile* is 4½ inches long and 2½ inches wide at the shoulder—the widest part—and is distinguished by a deep ridge around the base of the stalk. With rare exceptions it is charred and peeled, and the veins and seeds are removed before it's cooked. Used as a vegetable, it is stuffed, *chiles rellenos,* or cut into strips and fried with onion and potato, added to a tomato sauce with eggs or stewed pork, used as a garnish for soups, blended with cream for a rich sauce, or blended to add to rice. Dried when ripe, it becomes the *chile ancho;* charred and peeled when still green and then dried, it becomes *chile pasado.*

To Choose

Always choose *chiles* that are smooth and shiny and not those that have a dull, wrinkled skin. Apart from loss of flavor in this condition, they will be harder to peel.

To Store

If you are not going to use them right away, wrap them in two layers of paper toweling and then in a plastic bag; in this way they keep their moisture for a few days in the refrigerator.

They do not freeze in their raw state, but once they have been charred and peeled they can be frozen for a month, no more, or they lose their flavor and texture when defrosted.

To Prepare

As mentioned above, with few exceptions the *chile poblano* is charred or fried and peeled before using.

Leave the stalk, if any, on the *chile* intact—it makes it easier to turn the *chile*—and place it directly over an open flame of a gas stove or a wood or charcoal grill. If using electricity, then smear the *chile* with a light coating of oil and place it right up under the broiler. Turn the *chiles* from time to time to allow the skin to blister and char lightly all over. Do not allow the flesh to be burnt right through.

Place them immediately into a plastic bag and leave them to "sweat" for about 10 minutes. This helps to loosen the skin.

The skin can now be slipped off easily, and this should be done over a strainer because the little pieces are tough and can block up the sink opening. Rinse the *chile* briefly, but do not soak it in water, or the flavor will certainly be impaired.

For Chiles Rellenos

Leaving the top of the *chile* and the stem's base intact, carefully make a slit down one side. Opening it up halfway, carefully cut out the placenta (the white bulky part with the seeds and discard. Scrape out the remaining seeds and detach the veins running down the *chile* carefully so as not to tear the flesh. It is now ready to stuff. But it is best to mark any very *picante chile*, for they vary, for family or guests who like them that way. They should be used right away but can be stored overnight, no longer, or they will lose much of their juiciness and flavor. They can also be frozen, but no longer than one month, because on defrosting they lose both texture and flavor.

For Rajas (Chile Strips)

With a sharp paring knife, cut off the top of the *chile* with stem attached. Slit the *chile* down the side and scrape out veins and seeds and discard. Cut the *chile* into vertical strips about ¼ to ½ inch wide.

Chile Squares for Garnish

Follow the instructions for *chile* strips, but cut the flesh into ½-inch squares. Melt a little butter in a frying pan and sauté the *chile* squares, turning them over from time to time, for about 3 minutes. This helps to take away the raw taste and gives them a sweeter flavor.

CHILE SERRANO

The name *serrano* or *verde* for this *chile* (not to be confused with the *chile verde* of Yucatán) seems to be in general use throughout Mexico with the minor, local exception of the Sierra de Puebla, where it is often referred to as *tampiqueño*.

It is a small, mid- to dark green *chile*, depending on the variety of seed used, that ripens to bright red. The new varieties tend toward a lighter color and larger size—about 2 inches long and ½ inch wide—while the "unimproved" (but often more flavorful) *chile serrano* tends to be a darker green, more pointed at the tip, and smaller in size, an average one being 1 to 1½ inches long and ¼ inch wide.

They all have shiny, smooth skin and can range from hot to very hot. While they are generally preferred for fresh or cooked sauces in their mature but green stage, they are still used when very ripe and red.

To Choose

The skin of the *chiles* should be smooth and shiny, not dull and wrinkled. When they reach this latter stage, they have lost their crisp texture and fresh flavor and taste of earth.

Make sure that there is no deterioration in the form of black patches on the skin (there are some natural dark spots, again depending on the type of seed used), especially around the base of the stalk, and that they are firm and not soft to the touch.

To Store

If you are not going to use them right away, wrap them in two layers of paper toweling and store them in a plastic bag in the refrigerator; in this way they will not dry out. Even then they will last only about one week without losing flavor and texture.

If you wish to store them well ahead for use in cooked sauces, simmer them for 5 minutes in water, cook them, then freeze; or broil and freeze (see details below).

To Prepare

- Always rinse *chiles* well because you never know what traces of insecticides remain.
- For fresh sauces, chop or blend the *chiles* without removing seeds and veins. For a cooked sauce, with *tomate verde*, simmer the whole *chiles* with the *tomate verde* and then blend.
- For a sauce of broiled red tomatoes or *tomate verde*, broil or char the *chiles* on a *comal* (griddle), turning them until slightly charred and blistered.
- *Toreados* are *chiles serranos* that have been rolled on a hot *comal* (griddle) until they begin to color and soften; they are usually left whole and bitten into by *aficionados*.

CHILE VERDE DEL NORTE *(Anaheim Pepper)*

The large, long, skinny green *chile* used in northwestern Mexico, principally in Sonora but also in Chihuahua, is also referred to as the *chile Magdalena*, named for the town in Sonora near where it is grown in quantity. It is in fact the same as the Anaheim, or Californian, *chile* pepper. It is light green in color and can range from mild to hot. In Mexico it is usually charred and peeled; left whole with seeds and veins removed, it is often stuffed for a *chile relleno*, or it is cut into strips and used in tomato sauces and for *chile con queso* in Chihuahua.

In Chihuahua it is also charred and peeled and then dried to become the black and wrinkled *chile pasado*.

While it is usually used in its green, mature state, it is also ripened to a fiery red for drying to become the *chile seco* of the North.

DRIED CHILES

This section on dried *chiles* does not set out to be complete—it would take a whole book to do that—but it does describe some of the more commonly used *chiles*, their characteristics, their uses, and how they are prepared. There is also a brief mention of some of the lesser-known *chiles* that are very important to some of the regional cuisines and of special interest to travelers to these regions, apart from *aficionados*—among them food writers and chefs— who are on a constant quest for more information about these uniquely Mexican ingredients.

Drying *chiles* is, of course, a way of preserving them; so is smoking them, and in northern Mexico there is another method for drying *chiles pasados* that is unknown, and probably unacceptable, elsewhere. Quite apart from the preserving aspect of drying, dried *chiles* are a rich source of vitamin A.

Methods of dealing with dried *chiles* vary slightly from region to region and are set out in each recipe. For example, in some areas cooks toast *chiles* lightly before soaking and blending them for a cooked sauce, while others simmer them in water and then blend them. Proponents of the former method say that their sauce has a better flavor and is more digestible.

There are two important rules when dealing with the preparation of the fleshy *chiles* like *anchos, mulatos,* and *pasillas* for thick sauces and *moles:* they should not be soaked longer than the time specified, or their flavor will be left in the soaking water. Second, never attempt to skin the *chiles* once they have been soaked, because the skin provides flavor and color and acts as a thickening agent for the sauce.

Choosing and Storing

Always try to buy *chiles* that are loose so you can see what you are getting; all too often, dried-out, third-rate *chiles* tend to be disguised by the fancy packaging.

Do not go by the name on the package—many *chiles* are mislabeled. Study the pictures and descriptions and decide for yourself. While sizes do vary legitimately, the best-quality *chiles* should approximate the average sizes given for each type.

The best *chiles* will be of the most recent crop and still flexible. If they are damp, you know you are paying for the moisture, but no matter; let them dry out in an airy place or in the sun. But do not dry them until they're brittle; they should be just flexible. Although *chiles* that are dried out to a crisp can be used, they will have to be soaked for a longer period and *then* cleaned of veins and seeds. If you attempt to clean them before soaking them, they will break into 100 pieces.

Try to avoid buying *chiles* with transparent patches of skin; the fruit fly has been at work and eaten the flesh from the skin. It has probably also laid eggs inside and in time, with the right damp, hot conditions, little grubs will hatch out.

Stored properly, dried *chiles* will last years. It is best to store them in a cool, dry place and, if you have the space, in the refrigerator or freezer. This will prevent the fruit fly from getting at them. In any case, inspect the *chiles* every month or so to make sure they are not deteriorating. Open one up and see if it has any traces of mildew, which will spread quickly under very damp conditions. If it does, it should be thrown out or, preferably, burnt.

CHILE ANCHO

The *chile ancho*—sometimes confusingly called *pasilla roja* in parts of Michoacán—is the most commonly used *chile* throughout Mexico. (I saw it being used, but very sparingly, even in Yucatán on my last visit there.) It is in fact the *chile poblano* ripened to a deep red and then dried. It is widely available in the United States.

A good-quality *ancho* is flexible, not dried out to a crisp, with a deep reddish-brown wrinkled skin that still has some shine to it. A good, average size *chile* is 4½ inches long and about 3 inches wide. As it dries out it becomes increasingly dark in color and more difficult to distinguish from the dried *chile mulato* for one who is not thoroughly familiar with the *chiles*. To make sure, open one up and look at it through the light; it should be a reddish-brown rather than the brownish-black color of the *mulato*. Once the *chiles* are soaked it is easier to tell the difference as these tones are more pronounced. The flavor of the *ancho* is decidedly sharper and fruitier than that of the *mulato*, which is softer and more chocolaty in flavor.

Selecting and storing these *chiles* is discussed on page 473.

Preparation

There are several different methods for preparing these *chiles* for recipes in this book, and each one will be indicated specifically in the recipe.

Generally speaking the *chile ancho* is not used for fresh table sauces, or *salsas de molcajete* as they are called in Mexico, with one exception. That is more of a relish than a sauce, *salsa de tijera*—the raw *chile* is cut into strips and marinated in oil and vinegar, etc.

For Chiles Rellenos

Leaving stalk and top intact, slit the *chile* open very carefully and remove veins and seeds. Cover with hot water and leave to soak for about 15 minutes or until the *chile* is fleshy and has been reconstituted. It is then ready for stuffing with cheese, a meat filling, *chorizo* and potato, etc. (see recipe, page 140), fried in batter and served in tomato sauce in the usual way.

For Cooked Sauces, Moles, etc.

Remove stem, if any, slit the *chile* down the side, and remove seeds and veins. Flatten *chile* out as much as possible, then use one of these methods:

METHOD 1:

Cover with hot water and leave to soak until fleshy, about 15 minutes. *Note:* Soaking time will depend on how old and dry the *chile* is; 15 minutes is for a reasonably flexible *chile*. Drain and transfer to a blender jar, discarding the water.

METHOD 2:

Put the cleaned *chiles* into a pan of hot water, bring to a simmer, and continue simmering for about 5 minutes. Remove from the heat and leave to soak for 5 minutes more, until fleshy and completely reconstituted.

METHOD 3:

Heat a *comal* (griddle) over medium heat—it must not be too hot, or the *chiles* will burn and make the sauce bitter—and press the *chile*, inside down, on the *comal* as flat as possible. Leave for about 3 seconds, turn over, and repeat on the second side or until the inside flesh turns an opaque, tobacco brown—about 3 seconds (if the *chile* is fairly moist, it will blister, but that is not the sign). Remove, cover with hot water, and leave to soak for about 15 minutes.

METHOD 4:

For some *moles* the dried *chiles* should be fried. Heat enough lard or oil to cover the bottom of the frying pan. When hot—but not smoking, or the *chile* will burn—place the *chile*, inside down, as flat as possible in the hot oil. Fry for about 5 seconds, pressing down well into the oil. Turn it over and fry it on the second side for about the same time or until the inner flesh is an opaque tobacco brown. Remove and cover with water. Add more oil to the pan as you continue with the *chiles*.

METHOD 5:

For grinding *chile ancho* to a powder—which is often used in the North as a condiment to add to *menudo*, etc.—place a *comal* (griddle) over low heat, press the *chile* down as flat as possible onto the *comal*, and toast it very slowly for about 2 minutes, without burning. Turn the *chile* over and toast on the second side for about 1 minute or until the *chile* is completely dehydrated; when cool, it should be crisp. Tear the toasted *chile* into pieces into a blender jar or coffee/spice grinder and grind to a fine powder. To store it most effectively, put it into an airtight container and store it in the freezer section of the refrigerator.

CHILE MULATO

The *chile mulato* plant is essentially the same as that of the *poblano* but with slightly different genes that affect the color and taste. It is rarely used in its fresh state, since a grower can get a higher price for his crop of *mulatos* dried than fresh, and they fetch a higher price than many other types of dried *chiles*. Although size can vary considerably, an average one is 5 inches long and 3 inches wide. It is blackish-brown in color, and the skin—again in a first-class one—may be smoother than that of the *ancho*. The flavor is sweetish, rather chocolaty, and can range from quite mild to rather hot. Unfortunately many *chile* purveyors, especially those along the border, are mixing *anchos* and *mulatos* together and will swear to you that they are the same. They are not. A test to distinguish them is given under *chile ancho*. It's important to do so because, for instance, a *mole poblano* that calls for a certain proportion of *mulatos* can be altered substantially in appearance and flavor if *anchos* are used instead. *Mulatos* are widely available in the United States.

Preparation

See methods listed under *chile ancho*.

476

CHILE PASILLA

The *chile pasilla* is the dried *chilaca*, sometimes referred to as *chile negro* (black *chile*) and in Oaxaca as the *pasilla de Mexico* to distinguish it from the *chile pasilla de Oaxaca* (see page 483). It has a shiny, black, wrinkled surface with vertical ridges and a rich but sharp flavor—in contrast to the other black *chile mulato*—and can range from fairly hot to hot. An average one is 6 inches long and 1 inch wide. It is widely available in specialty stores and some supermarkets in the United States.

The *chile pasilla* is used to garnish soups, for rustic table sauces, and for *moles* or other cooked sauces.

Preparation

For many dishes it is prepared in the same way as the *chile ancho*, and methods 1 through 4 would apply. However, there are three distinctive ways in which it is used:

1. As a garnish and condiment for soup: If the *chile* has a stem, leave it intact. Wipe thoroughly with a damp cloth. Heat oil in a small frying pan to a depth of ¼ inch over medium heat. When hot—but not smoking, or the *chile* will burn—put the whole *chile* into it and fry slowly, turning from time to time, until it is shiny and crisp. If it is not punctured or broken, it will inflate impressively, which not only makes it look nice but makes it easier to fry crisp evenly. Either serve the fried *chiles pasillas* whole on top of each soup bowl or crumble them roughly with seeds and veins and pass them separately to sprinkle on the soup as a condiment.

2. As a rustic table sauce: If the *chile* has a stem, leave it intact to help turn the *chile* more easily. Wipe the *chile* thoroughly with a damp cloth. Heat a *comal* (griddle) over medium heat—it should not be too hot, or the *chile* will burn. Place the whole *chile* onto it and toast, turning from time to time, for about 5 to 7 minutes or until it is evenly crisp all around. Crumble the *chile*, with seeds and veins, into a *molcajete* or blender jar and blend briefly to a textured sauce with the other ingredients called for.

3. The veins as a condiment: When a recipe calls for the veins and seeds to be cleaned from the *chile pasilla*, save the veins, toast them on an ungreased *comal*, until a rich golden color, and crumble on soup.

CHILE GUAJILLO

The *chile guajillo* (along with the *ancho*) is the most commonly used dried *chile* in Mexican cooking, probably because it is more widely available and cheaper than many others. The *chile guajillo* has a smooth, tough skin that is a deep maroon color. It is long and thin, tapering to a point; an average one is 5 inches long and 1¼ to 1½ inches at the widest point. It can vary from fairly hot to hot and has a pleasant, sharp flavor. In the north central region of the country it is called *cascabel* (rattle) because it rattles and resembles a rattlesnake's tail. It belongs to a family of *chiles* that *when fresh* are sometimes called *mirasol* (looking at the sun)—erroneously, for the majority of these *chiles* hang down on the plant and do not point up to the sun.

While the *guajillo* is occasionally used for a table sauce, it is more often used after being soaked and blended for spreading on meat for *carne enchilada* (page 299), for *enchilada* sauces, and for thick stews. However, the sauce nearly always has to be strained since the skin is so tough and not all of it is ground sufficiently in the blender. It is widely available in the United States.

Preparation

Remove the stems, slit the *chile* open, and scrape out the veins and seeds. Follow methods 1, 2, and 3 for *chile ancho*.

METHOD 4:

When used as a substitute for the black Oaxacan *chile*, it is toasted on the *comal* (griddle) or straight on the fire until it is black and crisp. It is then rinsed twice in cold water to get rid of some of the bitterness and then soaked in hot water.

Chile Puya

The *puya*, or *guajillo puya* as it is often called, is a thinner and hotter version of the *guajillo* with an average length of 4 inches and width of ¾ inch. It is cleaned and prepared in exactly the same way as the *guajillo*. It is widely available in the United States.

CHILE DE ÁRBOL

The *chile de árbol* is not from a tree as its name implies but from a rangy, tall plant. It ripens from green to a bright red and retains its brilliant color when dried. It is a long, smooth-skinned, slender *chile* with an average length of 3 inches and width of ⅜ inch, and it is very, very hot.

While the dried *chile de árbol* is used mostly for table sauces, occasionally a few will be blended in with other, more fleshy *chiles* for a meat stew, etc. It is widely available in the United States.

Preparation

Nobody in Mexico would dream of taking the veins and seeds out of this *chile*; they know it is hot, and they like it that way.

METHOD 1:

Place the whole *chile* with stalk, if any, intact onto a fairly hot *comal* (griddle)—but not too hot, or the *chile* will burn—and keep turning it around until it is toasted to a light brown color and becomes crisp. Crumble it into a blender jar without soaking it and follow the instructions in the recipe.

METHOD 2:

Heat a little oil in a small frying pan, add the *chiles*, and fry until lightly browned and crisp, about 3 minutes. Remove, do not soak, and blend following the recipe instructions.

CHILE CASCABEL

The *chile cascabel* is in the form of a little round rattle as its name suggests. It has a smooth, tough, chocolaty-reddish-brown skin, and an average-sized *chile* measures 1¼ inches in diameter and 1 inch long. This *chile* can best be appreciated in an uncooked table sauce, although quite often it is blended with tomatoes or *tomate verde* for a cooked main dish sauce. Available in the United States.

Preparation

METHOD 1:

If it is in the form of a nice even sphere, and the flesh is not pushed in in places, then it can be toasted whole on a medium-hot *comal* (griddle), and the stem, if any, can be used to turn it around. It should be toasted slowly until crisp—about 5 minutes—but care should be taken not to let it burn, or the sauce will be bitter. Then remove the stem, cut open, remove the seeds and veins, toast the seeds (if required in the recipe), and crumble into a blender jar.

METHOD 2:

If it is not even, remove the stem, cut open, and scrape out the veins and seeds. Toast by flattening it down onto a medium-hot *comal* (griddle) until the inside of the flesh is an opaque tobacco brown. By then it should be toasted crisp. Crumble into a blender jar, unsoaked.

METHOD 3:

In the Northwest, *chile cascabel* is often just soaked or simmered in water until the tough skin begins to soften and then blended with tomatoes or green tomatoes for a cooked sauce. However, the wonderful nutty flavor of the *chile* when toasted is missing.

CHILE SECO DEL NORTE *(Dried Anaheim, California Chile Pods)*

This *chile* is also called *largo colorado* and is used exclusively in northern Mexico, particularly in Sonora. It is the dried *chile Anaheim* (or *Magdalena* on the other side of the border) and is sold in the United States labeled "California *chile* pods."

Its thin, shiny skin can best be described as a deep, burnished coppery red color. The skin is tucked around the base of the stem, forming irregular "pleats" from base to tip. It can vary from mild to fairly hot.

The *chile seco* is soaked and blended and used in sauces for *chilaquiles*, *enchiladas*, *carne con chile*, and other northern dishes. When it is ground to a powder and used for sauces, they are often thickened with lightly browned flour.

Preparation

Remove stems, slit open vertically, and remove veins and seeds. Cover with boiling salted water and simmer until soft—about 10 minutes. Then drain and follow the instructions in the recipe.

CHILACATE

The *chilacate* is grown in the Jalisco/Colima area and used, dried, in the cooking of that region. It is a smooth, shiny, tough-skinned *chile*, sweetish in flavor, that can range from mild to fairly hot. Its color could best be described as "raisin" (according to the color chart in *Webster's International Dictionary*), and an average size is 5 inches long and 2 inches at the widest part. In Colima it is used interchangeably with *anchos* and *guajillos*, mixed in a ratio of two to one respectively. You will often seen *chilacate* packaged in the United States and marked (incorrectly) *guajillo*. There is also a New Mexican dried *chile* that resembles it and can be used as a substitute. When soaked and blended, the *chilacate* is used for *enchilada* and other cooked sauces.

Preparation

Remove the stem, if any, slit open from base to tip, and remove seeds and veins. Cover with hot water and leave for about 15 minutes to soak. Drain and blend or simmer in hot water for 5 minutes and leave to soak for 5 minutes longer. The tough skin, unlike that of the *guajillo*, softens fast and blends well.

CHILE CHIPOTLE

The *chile chipotle* or *chilpocle* is the *chile jalapeño* ripened, dried, and smoked as its Nahuatl name (*chil, chile; pectli,* smoke) suggests. It is a tough, leathery, wrinkled *chile* that gives the appearance of a piece of old tobacco, although it is actually a darkish brown color highlighted with golden brown ridges. An average one—depending on the quality of the crop—is 2½ inches long and 1 inch wide at its widest part.

Canned *chipotles* are a very popular condiment, either in a light pickle or in an *adobe*—mild red *chile*—sauce. And in these forms they can be used in most dishes where *chipotles* are called for. The plain dried—and smoked—ones can be used for pickling (see recipe, page 358), to flavor soups and pasta dishes, or soaked and ground with other ingredients in a sauce for meatballs, shrimps, or meat. They are extremely hot. They are available canned or dried in the United States; don't try and remove the seeds.

Preparation

- The *chile chipotle* is always used with seeds and veins intact.
- For pickling, it is briefly stewed in water or vinegar to soften before the other ingredients are added. For sauces it (not the canned type) is often very lightly toasted and then put to soak before being blended with other ingredients, the soaking time depending on how dry it is—from 15 to 30 minutes.

CHILE MORA

In parts of Veracruz and Puebla the *chile mora* is called *chipotle,* or *chipotle mora*. It tends to be smaller than the full-blown *chipotle,* about 2 inches long and ¾ inch wide, and is a deep mulberry color as its name implies. It is extremely hot.

The *chile mora* is prepared and used in the same way as *chipotles* and is favored by the canning factories for its more convenient size. It is sometimes available in the United States, canned; don't try and remove the seeds.

CHILE MORITA

The *chile morita* is a small, dried, smoked *chile*, triangular in shape with a smooth, shiny, mulberry-colored skin. An average one is 1 inch long and ¾ inch wide. It is very *picante* and should be used with discretion. (It seems to me that they are smoking *serranos* along with the *moritas* because the shapes in the last few batches I have bought have been diverse.) It is sometimes available in the United States.

Preparation

The *chile* is either toasted lightly and blended with other ingredients or soaked in boiling water until soft, but veins and seeds are not taken out.

CHILE PASILLA DE OAXACA

The *chile pasilla de Oaxaca* is very much a local *chile* used only in the cooking of Oaxaca and part of Puebla. To me it is one of the most interesting and delicious *chiles*, and all Mexican food *aficionados* should be aware of it (and if they go to Oaxaca, they can buy and experiment with it).

It is the most wrinkled of all the *chiles*. It is smoked and is very hot. An average one is about 3½ inches long and 1¼ inches wide with shiny skin that varies from mulberry to wine red. While the *chile* is stuffed and fried in a batter like any *chile relleno*, it is also used in table and cooked sauces. The closest substitute would be the *mora*, although it would be too small for stuffing well.

Preparation

If the *chile* is to be stuffed, it is probably too dry to cut open and clean, so put it on a warm *comal* (griddle) to heat through and become flexible, then slit it open carefully, retaining the stem, if any, and scrape out the veins and seeds. Cover with hot water and simmer for about 5 minutes. If the *chile* is still *picante*, change the water and leave to soak for about 10 minutes longer. Then stuff and fry in the usual way. For sauces: toast the whole *chile* lightly on a *comal* or directly over a low flame, turning over so both sides are toasted evenly. Then tear it into pieces with seeds and veins and blend with the other ingredients for a table sauce or cooked sauce.

CHILHUACLE NEGRO, ROJO, AMARILLO

The *chilhuacles* are uniquely Oaxacan *chiles* that are gradually disappearing and quite expensive now to buy for the local people, who are substituting *guajillos* (and charring them to get the correct color for the *mole negro* of Oaxaca, for instance).

These are squat, full-bodied *chiles*, some slightly pointed at the end but most blunt, almost square; 2 inches long and 2 inches wide is an average size. The skin is matte, black, or yellow, or red, and very tough; when soaked, the flesh has a sharp licorice flavor. These *chiles* are used mostly for *moles*.

They are not available in many places outside Oaxaca, but charred *guajillo* can be used as a substitute.

Preparation

Remove seeds and veins, toast well on a *comal* (griddle) without burning, rinse in cold water, then put to soak in hot water for about 20 minutes. They can also be cleaned, rinsed, and fried, then blended without soaking, depending on the recipe.

CHILE PIQUÍN

Chile piquín, pequín, chiltepe (Puebla), *chiltepin* (Sonora), *chile max* (Yucatán), *amashito* (Tabasco): they are all very small, very hot *chiles*. Triangular, round, or cylindrical in shape, they are generally either pickled in vinegar or ground dry as a condiment. Usually no more than ½ inch long and ¼ inch wide—the round ones are about ¼ inch in diameter—they have shiny skins that range from orangey to deep red in color.

CHILE SECO YUCATECO

I have included the *chile seco* of Yucatán because it is an interesting one and significant in the Yucatecan cuisine. It is in fact the dried *chile verde* of Yucatán—a small, thin, light green *chile* that has a unique flavor. It ripens and dries to a golden orangey color and has a shiny, transparent, tough skin with an average length of 2 inches and width of ¾ inch. It is very hot.

In Yucatán it is ground to a powder and used as a condiment, but perhaps most interesting of all, it is charred black and ground with other spices to a paste used for the black *chilmole* and *rellenos negros* seasoning. While the *chile* is not available in the United States—use hot paprika as a substitute—the black seasoning pastes are.

COOKING EQUIPMENT

ELECTRICAL

BLENDER:

A good heavy blender is absolutely necessary (not the built-in countertop type with a plastic jar). The jars should be of glass, straight-sided if possible, with detachable blades and base for easy cleaning. In fact it is more practical to have two jars and sets of cutting blades since some recipes call for two separate sauces.

For finer blending—especially for dried *chile* sauces—the blender is superior to the food processor, which comes into its own for other types of preparations.

COFFEE/SPICE GRINDER:

An indispensable piece of equipment for these recipes; for grinding nuts, whole spices—especially *achiote* seeds—sesame seeds and pumpkin seeds, etc.

FOOD PROCESSOR:

Useful and time-saving for grinding certain ingredients to a rougher texture, such as curds for *queso fresco*, cooked fruits for *ates*, fresh corn for *tamales*, grinding meat to a very fine texture, etc.

GRAIN MILL:

Not absolutely essential, but wonderful if you are a start-from-scratcher and grind your own wheat and dried/prepared corn for *tamale* flour.

ICE CREAM MAKER:

A luxury but well worthwhile for quick, varied (and impressive) fresh desserts. Simac's Il Gelataio is my choice.

MIXER:

The KitchenAid mixer with attachments is to my mind the best-designed and most efficient of all. The meat grinder, dough hook, and colander are the most useful attachments for these recipes.

SLOW COOKER OR CROCK-POT:

Not essential but will save you time "watching" the pot and prevent many burnt beans. Buy one with a ceramic liner and a glass (not plastic) top, which is more efficient.

COOKWARE

CASSEROLES:

The enameled, cast-iron cookware of Le Creuset is the most versatile for cooking rice, stews, and *moles*. Because of its quality and weight, it is the most efficient (except for the frying pans and saucepans, which scorch easily). The most useful are the round 10- and 11½-inch-diameter sizes and for whole chickens the oval 11½-inch casseroles.

FRYING AND SAUTÉ PANS:

Frying pans of varying sizes are useful for this type of cooking. I favor the heavy cast-iron ones of 6-, 8-, and 10-inch diameters. Heavy sauté pans of 10- and 12-inch diameters with lids are also very useful.

GRIDDLE:

A cast-iron griddle, 8-inch diameter, can be used as a substitute for a *comal* in *tortilla* making.

OVENWARE:

Round or oval ceramic or china bakers, or *gratin* dishes—with sides at least 2 inches high—are necessary for various recipes, including casseroles of layered *tortillas*, or *tamales*, whole fish cooked in a sauce, etc.

PRESSURE COOKER:

Used with discretion, a pressure cooker can be a time-saver in the kitchen, especially for long-cooking items such as chick-peas, corn for *pozole*, pig's feet—and beans, *in an emergency only*; the flavor suffers. A 4-quart-capacity cooker is a most useful size.

MISCELLANEOUS UTENSILS

CUP MEASURES:

Standard glass measuring cups for liquids and stainless-steel cups for solids are indispensable. Avoid those that come in fancy plastic shapes and colors. A straight-sided, clear plastic cup for degreasing broth is invaluable.

KNIVES:

Good-quality classic chef's knives, 12- and 14-inch lengths, a paring knife, and a good-quality steel and/or knife sharpener are essential (unless you use a Chinese cleaver for all types of cutting). Learn how to sharpen your own knives. You can spend a lot of money on having knives "professionally" sharpened, but they are not *well* sharpened.

ROLLING PINS:

Apart from the standard fat rolling pin, it is necessary to have a 12-inch dowel (¾ inch in diameter) for rolling out wheat flour tortillas, forming *teleras*, etc.

RULER:

A 12-inch ruler is useful to familiarize yourself with the sizes of certain *antojitos*, banana leaf wrappers, etc.

SCALE:

A workmanlike scale is a boon, more accurate and faster than using measuring cups for certain ingredients, such as flour. Avoid the bouncy, wall-type scale and those that are neatly designed but difficult to read with a badly balanced container, like those of so many popular brands. I use a 2-kilo Ade-Oken scale, made in Mexico, which measures ½ ounce accurately.

SPOONS:

When buying measuring spoons, always buy the standard metal ones (not the shallow shiny ones made in Japan or the fancy plastic ones) since they tend to be more consistently accurate. Broad-bowled wooden spoons and scrapers with flat bottoms are a necessity for stirring heavy sauces like the *moles*. Besides, they don't set your teeth on edge while you're scraping the pot, nor do they scratch the surface.

TRADITIONAL MEXICAN COOKING UTENSILS

EARTHENWARE CASSEROLES AND POTS *(Cazuelas y Ollas)*

The highly glazed dark brown earthenware *cazuelas* (see illustrations, pages 213 and 507) are still used by traditional and country cooks who swear that the flavor of the food cooked in them is superior to that cooked in metal pots—and, of course, I tend to agree. They can be used over direct heat if you're cooking with gas, wood, or charcoal. If you have an electric stove, the *cazuela* should be isolated with the thin metal ring used under glass coffeepots, and even then the heat should be low to medium and never high.

In my opinion, the best-quality and most attractive earthenware cooking pots come from the small town of Metepec in the state of Mexico a few miles from Toluca, but they are rarely, if ever, seen beyond the border towns. If you are in Mexico and want to buy one, first tap it sharply; there should be a ring, not a dull sound, which would indicate a hairline crack almost invisible to the eye.

Before you cook with a *cazuela* or *olla*, it has to be cured. Although every cook has her own method of curing, this is the one I learned during my apprentice days. Fill the pot with cold water and add a whole head or two, depending on the size of the pot, of unpeeled garlic. Set over low heat and leave to simmer gently until the water has evaporated—this can take some hours. Wash the pot and, to be absolutely sure that you have got rid of that raw earthenware taste, repeat the process.

Cazuelas can be used for cooking Mexican rice, *moles*, or other sauces with meat and vegetables, etc. *Ollas* I use for *morisqueta* (plain boiled rice), chicken broth, beef broth and stew, or for heating milk or chocolate.

Caution: It is advisable not to store food overnight in these glazed pots or to cook anything highly acidic; in either case some lead might leach into the food from the glaze.

VOLCANIC ROCK MORTAR AND PESTLE *(Molcajete y Tejolote)*

One of the oldest pieces of kitchen equipment in the New World, along with the *metate*, is the *molcajete*, a black or grey basalt mortar, with its pestle or *tejolote* of the same material (see illustration, page 335). They are still used widely today for making *guacamole*, for crushing whole spices, or for table sauces, referred to as *salsas de molcajete*. And sauces made with them are superior in texture and flavor, for they crush out the flavor of the ingredients, rather than chopping them finely, which gives a truly rustic quality to the sauce.

A *molcajete* should be chosen with care, either in Mexico or in the United States (they can be found in large Mexican groceries and markets). It should be heavy and not too porous. Grind briefly with the pestle; if the stone seems soft and an inordinate amount of dust is formed, then pass on to the next one. The final test is to put some water into it. If the water leaks out—often through the legs—pass on to the next. The *molcajete* has to be "cured" before you use it. Grind about ¼ cup of dry rice in it; when it has been transformed into a greyish powder, rinse and repeat. This process should be repeated about five times; each time the rice should be a lighter color. Give it a final rinse, and it is ready to use. The first one or two sauces may be a little gritty—no matter; it means added natural minerals.

To wash it out, scour with a brush, but don't use strongly scented detergents or soap powders, which will leave behind an artificial taste.

GRINDING STONE AND MULLER *(Metate y Mano)*

The *metate* or grinding stone with its muller, *mano,* are made of the same material as the *molcajete,* and instructions for choosing, curing, and cleaning are the same. Only the most valiant of traditional cooks still use them today as it is a backbreaking, knee-aching job to grind the corn or *chiles* and other ingredients for *moles* and *pipianes* on it.

BEAN MASHER

A wooden bean masher is useful not only for mashing refried beans but also for pushing ingredients through a sieve. Any flat- or curved-bottomed potato masher will do, although the flat wire-meshed ones do not really work well.

GRIDDLE *(Comal)*

This is described in the equipment needed for making *tortillas.*

CORN GRINDER

This is described and illustrated on page 10.

TAMALE STEAMER

This is described in the *tamale* section (page 63).

SOURCES FOR MEXICAN INGREDIENTS

During my years of traveling and teaching, I have personally visited many of the following sources for ingredients, but some, of necessity, have been supplied by *aficionados* of Mexican food. Since change is constant—especially where small specialty businesses are concerned—and while we have done our best to bring the information up to date at the time of writing, there may very well be discrepancies owing to very recent changes. If in doubt, check your local yellow pages in the telephone directory or make inquiries at neighboring Mexican restaurants. While *epazote* and *hoja santa* can be found growing wild, if you cannot identify them, check with local nurseries as many, all over the country, have these plants for sale.

The list that follows, in alphabetical order by state, followed by listings for Canada and the United Kingdom, is not meant to be all-inclusive. Supermarkets and specialty shops in all areas of the country are sure to have many of the ingredients necessary for Mexican cooking.

ARIZONA

Phoenix Area

Estrella Tortilla Factory and Deli, 1004 S. Central Ave., Phoenix, AZ 85003; 602-253-5947

Mi Ranchito Mexican Food Products, 3217 W. McDowell Rd., Phoenix, AZ 85009; 602-272-3949

El Molino, 117 S. 22nd St., Phoenix, AZ 85304; 602-241-0364

Carol Steele Co., 7303 E. Indian School Rd., Scottsdale, AZ 85251; 602-947-4596

La Tolteca, 609 E. Washington, Phoenix, AZ 85004; 602-253-1511

Safeway and Alpha Beta supermarkets carry several types of fresh *chiles* and other Mexican produce.

Flores Bakery, 8402 S. Avenida del Yaqui, Guadalupe, AZ 85283; 602-831-9709 Corn *masa* and *tortillas*, flour *tortillas*, some canned goods, dried *chiles*, and Mexican spices (not a great range).

Mercado Mexico, 8212 S. Avenida del Yaqui, Guadalupe, AZ 85283; 602-831-5925 Mexican cooking equipment, dried *chiles*, *achiote*, and other spices.

CALIFORNIA

Claremont

Many of the large supermarkets in this area carry a variety of Mexican ingredients, including corn and wheat flour *tortillas* and fresh produce. Seville orange and banana trees are abundant for those interested in Yucatecan cooking.

Fresno

Chihuahua Tortilleria, 718 F St., Fresno, CA 93706

Chihuahua Inc., 1435 Fresno St., Fresno, CA 93706; PO Box 12304, Fresno, CA 93777; 209-266-9964

Los Angeles Area

Tianguis supermarkets. All have an extensive range of Mexican groceries, canned goods, produce, dried *chiles*, *tortillas*, and corn *masa*. Regina Cordova at the El Monte store is very knowledgeable about sources and producers.

3610 North Peak Rd, El Monte, CA; 818-443-0498

1201 Westwood Air Blvd., Montebello, CA 90640

7300 N. Atlantic, Cudahay, CA

El Mercado, First Ave. and Lorena, Los Angeles, CA 90063; 213-268-3451

Central Market, Broadway (downtown), Los Angeles, CA; 213-749-0645

Liborio Market, 864 S. Vermont Ave. (near 9th), Los Angeles, CA; 213-386-1458

La Luz del Dia, 624 N. Main (near Sunset), Los Angeles, CA; 213-972-9578

Mercado Cali Mex, 2377 Pico Blvd. (near Vermont), Los Angeles, CA; 213-384-9387

Peter Pan Market, 2791 Pico Blvd. (near Normandie), Los Angeles, CA; 213-737-3595

Los Cinco Puntos, 3300 Brooklyn Ave., East Los Angeles, CA; 213-261-4084

Cotija Cheese Co., 15130 Nelson Ave., City of Industry, CA 91744; 818-968-2284 (wholesale cheese)

Modesto

Don Juan Foods, 1715 Crows Landing Rd., Modesto, CA 95351; 209-538-0817

Oakland

Mi Rancho, 464 Seventh St., Oakland, CA 94607; 415-451-2393

Redwood City

Mario's Food Market, 2835 Middlefield Rd., Redwood City, CA 94063; 415-364-9524

Mission Bell Bakery, 2565 Middlefield Rd., Redwood City, CA 94063; 415-365-7001

Sacramento

Casa Grande, 1730 Broadway, Sacramento, CA 95818; 916-443-5039

Farmer's Market on Franklin Blvd. and La Esperanza Mexican Bakery next door (916-455-0215) carry dried *chiles* and spices plus a good range of Mexican produce.

Jalisco, 318 12th St., Sacramento, CA.; 916-448-3175

La Hacienda, 5029 Franklin, Sacramento, CA; 916-452-2352

Maxis Supermarket, 5814 Stockton Rd., Sacramento, CA; 916-452-6661

Sakai Oriental Grocery downtown sells banana leaves and a limited variety of spices, etc.

Salinas

Sal-Rex Foods, 258 Griffin St., Salinas, CA 93901

San Diego Area

Casa Magui, S.A., Av. Constitucion 932, Tijuana, B.C., Mexico; 5-7086

El Indio Shop, 3695 India St., San Diego, CA 92103; 714-299-0333

El Nopalito Tortilla Factory, 560 Santa Fe Dr., Encinitas, CA 92024; 714-436-5775

Fruteria Jacaranda, Stand 90, Interior Mercado, Tijuana, B.C., Mexico

Main market (Revolucion), Tijuana, B.C., Mexico

Woo Chee Chong, 633 16th St., San Diego, CA 91001; 714-233-6311

San Francisco

Casa Lucas Market, 2934 24th St., San Francisco, CA 94110; 415-826-4334

Casa Sanchez, 2778 24th St., San Francisco, CA 94110; 415-282-2400

La Favorita, 2977 24th St., San Francisco, CA 94110

La Tapatia Tortilleria, 411 Grand Ave., South, San Francisco, CA 94080; 415-489-5881

La Palma, 2884 24th St., San Francisco, CA 94110; 415-MI8-5500

Latin American Imports, 3403 Mission Ave., San Francisco, CA 94110; 415-648-0844

Mi Rancho Market, 3365 20th St., San Francisco, CA 94110; 415-647-0580

San Jose

Cal-Foods, 195 S. 28th St., San Jose, CA 95116; 408-292-4296

Santa Ana

Potato Bin Rancho Market, 1605 West St., Santa Ana, CA 92703; 714-547-8497

El Toro, 1340 W. First St., Santa Ana, CA 92703; 714-836-1393

Santa Barbara

La Tolteca, 614 E. Haley St., Santa Barbara, CA 93101; 805-963-0847

Santa Cruz Market, 605 N. Milpas St., Santa Barbara, CA 93101

Villareal Market, 728 E. Haley St., Santa Barbara, CA 93101; 805-963-2613

COLORADO

Denver

Casa Herrera, 2049 Larimer St., Denver, CO 80205

El Molino Foods, 1078 Sante Fe Dr., Denver, CO 80204; 303-623-7870

El Progreso, 2282 Broadway (near corner at Larimer), Denver, CO 80205; 303-623-0576

Johnnie's Market, 2030 Larimer St., Denver, CO 80205; 303-297-0155

Safeway Supermarket, 2660 Federal Blvd., Denver, CO 80219; 303-477-5091

CONNECTICUT

Gilbertie's Herb Gardens, Sylvan Ln., Westport, CT 06880; 203-227-4175

Hay Day, 907 Post Rd. E., Westport, CT 06880; 203-227-4258
A large selection of fresh produce for Mexican cooking, including *chiles poblanos.*

GEORGIA

Atlanta

Rinconcito Latino, Ansley Square Mall, 1492B Piedmont Ave. NE, Atlanta, GA 30309; 912-874-3724

ILLINOIS

Chicago

El Pelicano, 1911 S. Blue Island Ave., Chicago, IL 60608; 312-226-4743

La Casa del Pueblo, 1810 S. Blue Island Ave., Chicago, IL 60608; 312-421-4640

La Unica, 1515 W. Devon Ave., Chicago, IL 60660; 312-274-7788

Supermercado del Rey, 1714 W. 18th St., Chicago, IL 60608; 312-738-1817

KENTUCKY

Louisville

Abrigo Oriental Foods, 423 W. Chestnut St., Louisville, KY 40202; 502-584-4909

Mendoza Mexican Grocery, 4608 Gravois Ave., Louisville, KY; 502-353-9955

MASSACHUSETTS

Boston Area

Garcia Superette, 367 Centre Ave., Jamaica Plain, MA 02130; 617-524-1521

Harbar Corporation, 30 Germania St., Jamaica Plain, MA 02130; 617-524-6107
Sell exclusively *tortillas*, corn *masa* of excellent quality. Will ship.

India Tea & Spice Inc., 9-B Cushing Ave., Cushing Square, Belmont, MA 02178; 617-484-3737

Ricardo y Maria's Tortillas, 30 Germania St., Jamaica Plain, MA 02130; 617-524-6107

Star Market, 625 Mt. Auburn St., Cambridge, MA 02138; 617-491-3000

Stop and Shop, 390 D St., East Boston, MA 02128; 617-463-7000

MICHIGAN

Detroit

Algo Especial, 2628 Bagley, Detroit, MI 48216; 313-963-9013

La Colmena Supermercado, Bagley at 17th St., Detroit, MI 48216; 313-237-0295

La Jalisciense, 2634 Bagley, Detroit, MI 48216; 313-237-0008

MINNESOTA

St. Paul

El Burrito Mexican Foods, 196 Concord Ave., St. Paul, MN; 612-227-2192

Joseph's Food Market, 736 Oakdale Ave., St. Paul, MN 55107

La Tortilleria Coronado, 197 Concord, St. Paul, MN; 612-292-1988

Morgan's Mexican Lebanese Foods, 736 S. Robert St., St. Paul, MN; 612-291-2955

MISSOURI

St. Louis

    Soulard Market, 730 Carroll St., St. Louis, MO; 314-421-2008

    Tropicana Market, 5001 Lindenwood, St. Louis, MO; 314-353-7326

NEW MEXICO

Santa Fe

    Theo. Roybal Store, Rear 212, 214, 216 Galisteo St., Santa Fe, NM 87501

NEW YORK

New York City and Vicinity

Midtown

    International Groceries and Meat Market, 529 Ninth Ave. (between 39th & 40th Streets), New York, NY 10018; 212-279-5514

    Latin American Products, 142 West 46th St., New York, NY 10036; 212-302-4323 Limited range of Mexican products at the time of writing but will be bringing in more canned goods, general groceries, and dried *chiles.*

Downtown

    The Green Markets in Union Square on Wednesdays and Saturdays and the World Trade Center on Tuesday and Thursday.
    A large range of fresh *chiles, epazote,* and other herbs as well as squash flowers and other very fresh produce.

    Pete's Spice, 174 First Ave., New York, NY 10009; 212-254-8773
    Limited range of Mexican products but has variety of dried *chiles, tortillas,* etc.

    Trinacria Importing Co., 415 Third Ave., New York, NY 10016; 212-532-5567

Uptown (East)

    La Marqueta, Park Ave. between 112th & 116th Streets, New York, NY

Uptown (West)

    Hummingbird Foods and Spices, 2520 Broadway, New York, NY 10025

    Latin American Grocery, 2585 Broadway, New York, NY 10025

Vicinity

Special orders for *chiles* can be accepted by the Blew family in New Jersey; 201-782-9618

L. A. Barbone Inc., 170 W. Main St., Goshen, NY 10924; 914-294-9711

Laraia's Cheese Co., Nanuet, NY 10954; 914-627-2070 (wholesale string cheese)

OHIO

Cincinnati

Bolti's Market, 1801 Vine, Cincinnati, OH 45210; 513-579-1721

Cleveland

Danny Boy Farm Market, 24579 Lorain Rd., Cleveland, OH; 216-777-2338
A large range of fresh *chiles* and Mexican produce.

La Borincana Foods Inc., 2127 Fulton Rd., Cleveland, OH 44113; 216-651-2351
A fair range of Mexican products, dried *chiles, tortillas*, etc.

Rico Imported Latin Foods, 4506 Lorain, Cleveland, OH 44102; 216-961-4993
A good selection of Mexican groceries, canned goods, dried *chiles, tortillas*, etc. Some fresh produce.

OKLAHOMA

Oklahoma City

Mayphe's International Foods, 7519 N. May Ave., Oklahoma City, OK 73116; 405-848-2002

OREGON

Portland

Corno & Son, 711 S.E. Union Ave., Portland, OR 97214

PENNSYLVANIA

Philadelphia and Area

J&J Food Imports, 1014 Federal St., Philadelphia, PA 19147; 215-334-0914

La Cantina, 6140 Brockton Rd., Hatboro, PA 19040; 215-487-1360

TEXAS

Brownsville

The Mexican Kitchen, PO Box 214, Brownsville, TX 78520; 512-544-6028

Dallas

Danal's Stockyards Stores
#1 4800 Columbia Ave., Dallas, TX 75219; 214-821-2934
#2 10544 Harry Hines, Dallas, TX 75220; 214-357-0241
#3 5011 Lemmon Ave., Dallas, TX 75209; 214-528-8570

Hernandez Mexican Foods, 2120 Alamo St., Dallas, TX 75202; 214-742-2533

Horticultural Enterprises, PO Box 34082, Dallas, TX 75234

Super Mercado Mexico
#1 501 S. Rosemont Ave., Dallas, TX; 214-941-6293
#2 2008 Greenville Ave., Dallas, TX; 214-821-0171
#3 1235 S. Buckner Blvd., Dallas, TX; 214-391-5831
#4 5535 Columbia Ave., Dallas, TX; 214-698-9986
#5 1314 W. Davis St., Dallas, TX; 214-924-1225

Fort Worth

Danal's Stockyards Store, 2469 N. Houston, Ft. Worth, TX 76106

Houston

Antone's Import Co., 807 Taft, 8111 South Main, and 1639 South Voss Rd., Houston, TX

Mexicatessen, 302 W. Crosstimbers, Houston, TX 77018; 713-691-2010

Rice Food Market, 3700 Navigation Blvd., Houston, TX 77003

Manchaca

It's About Thyme, PO Box 878, Manchaca, TX 78652; 512-280-1192
A large variety of Mexican herbs.

San Antonio

Alamo Masa, 1603 N. Laredo, San Antonio, TX 78209

Chicago Tortilleria, 2009 Blanco, San Antonio, TX

El Mercado, San Antonio, TX

Frank Pizzini, 202 Produce Row, San Antonio, TX 78207; 512-227-2082

H.E.B. Food Stores, 4821 Broadway, San Antonio, TX

WASHINGTON

Seattle and Area

El Mercado Latino, 1514 Pike Pl., Seattle, WA 98101; 206-623-3240
A large range of Mexican products, canned goods, *tortillas*, *masa*, fresh produce, and *chiles*, including *chiles habaneros*.

El Ranchito, 1313 E. 1st Ave., Zillah, WA 98953

Herb Farm, 32804 Issaquah, Fall City Rd., Fall City, WA 98024

Sanchez Mexican Grocery, 1914 Pike Place Market, Seattle, WA 98104; 206-682-2822

Wapato

Krueger Pepper Gardens, Rt. 1, Box 1086-C, Wapato, WA 98951; 509-877-3677
A large selection of fresh *chiles*, including *habaneros*.

WASHINGTON, D.C., AREA

Americana Grocery, 1813 Columbia Rd. NW, Washington, DC 20009; 202-265-7455

Arlington Bodega, 6017 N. Wilson Blvd., Arlington, VA 22205; 703-532-6849

Bethesda Ave. Co-op, 4937 Bethesda Ave., Bethesda, MD 20014; 301-986-0796

Casa Lebrato, 1729 Columbia Rd., NW, Washington, DC; 202-234-0099

Casa Pena, 1636 17th St., NW, Washington, DC 20009; 202-462-2222

Safeway, 1747 Columbia Rd., NW, Washington, DC 20009; 202-667-0774

WISCONSIN

Milwaukee

Casa Martinez, 605 S. 5th St., Milwaukee, WI 53204

CANADA

Alberta

Calgary

Lori's Gourmet Delikatessen, 314 10th Street N.W., Calgary, AB, Canada T2N 1V8; 403-270-4464
A good selection of Mexican groceries and canned goods, dried *chiles*, and some Mexican produce, including fresh *chiles*. Will special-order ingredients and mail-order.

British Columbia

Vancouver

Que Pasa Mexican Foods, 530 W. 17th Ave., Vancouver, BC, Canada V5Z 1T4; 604-874-0064
Large selection of Mexican groceries and canned, dried, and fresh *chiles*, fresh produce, *tortillas*, and corn *masa*. Will mail-order and accept special orders.

Victoria

Las Flores Restaurant, 536 Yates St., Victoria, BC; 604-386-6313
A limited stock of Mexican groceries, dried *chiles*, etc.

Ontario

Ottawa

El Mexicano Food Products, Ltd., 285-A St. Patrick St., Ottawa, ON K1N 5K4, Canada; 613-238-2391; 613-224-9870

Toronto

Dinah's Cupboard, 9 Yorkville Ave., Toronto, ON, Canada

El Capricho Espanol, 312 College St., Toronto, ON, Canada; 416-967-6582

El Sol de Espana, College St. at Ossington, Toronto, ON, Canada

Home of the Gourmet, 550 Yonge St., Toronto, ON, Canada; 416-921-2823

New Portuguese Fish Store, Augusta St., Toronto, ON, Canada

Sanci Fruit Company, 66 Kensington Ave., Toronto, ON, Canada; 416-368-6541

Wong Yung's, 187 Dundas St. W., Toronto, ON, Canada; 416-368-3555

UNITED KINGDOM

England

Liverpool

El Macho, Mexican Foods Ltd., 8 Spindus Rd., Speke Hall Industrial Estate, Liverpool L24 9HE, England; 651-486-8742

METRIC CONVERSION CHART

CONVERSIONS OF QUARTS TO LITERS

Quarts (qt)	Liters (L)
1 qt	1 L*
1½ qt	1½ L
2 qt	2 L
2½ qt	2½ L
3 qt	2¾ L
4 qt	3¾ L
5 qt	4¾ L
6 qt	5½ L
7 qt	6½ L
8 qt	7½ L
9 qt	8½ L
10 qt	9½ L

*Approximate. To convert quarts to liters, multiply number of quarts by 0.95.

CONVERSIONS OF OUNCES TO GRAMS

Ounces (oz)	Grams (g)
1 oz	30 g*
2 oz	60 g
3 oz	85 g
4 oz	115 g
5 oz	140 g
6 oz	180 g
7 oz	200 g
8 oz	225 g
9 oz	250 g
10 oz	285 g
11 oz	300 g
12 oz	340 g
13 oz	370 g
14 oz	400 g
15 oz	425 g
16 oz	450 g
20 oz	570 g
24 oz	680 g
28 oz	790 g
32 oz	900 g

*Approximate. To convert ounces to grams, multiply number of ounces by 28.35.

CONVERSIONS OF POUNDS TO GRAMS AND KILOGRAMS

Pounds (lb)	Grams (g); kilograms (kg)
1 lb	450 g*
1¼ lb	565 g
1½ lb	675 g
1¾ lb	800 g
2 lb	900 g
2½ lb	1,125 g; 1¼ kg
3 lb	1,350 g
3½ lb	1,500 g; 1½ kg
4 lb	1,800 g
4½ lb	2 kg
5 lb	2¼ kg
5½ lb	2½ kg
6 lb	2¾ ikg
6½ lb	3 kg
7 lb	3¼ kg
7½ lb	3½ kg
8 lb	3¾ kg
9 lb	4 kg
10 lb	4½ kg

*Approximate. To convert pounds into kilograms, multiply number of pounds by 453.6.

CONVERSIONS OF FAHRENHEIT TO CELSIUS

Fahrenheit	Celsius
170°F	77°C
180°F	82°C
190°F	88°C
200°F	95°C
225°F	110°C
250°F	120°C
300°F	150°C
325°F	165°C
350°F	180°C
375°F	190°C
400°F	205°C
425°F	220°C
450°F	230°C
475°F	245°C
500°F	260°C
525°F	275°C
550°F	290°C

*Approximate. To convert Fahrenheit to Celsius, subtract 32, multiply by 5, then divide by 9.

CONVERSION OF INCHES TO CENTIMETERS

Inches (in)	Centimeters (cm)
1/16 in	1/4 cm*
1/8 in	1/2 cm
1/2 in	1½ cm
3/4 in	2 cm
1 in	2½ cm
1½ in	4 cm
2 in	5 cm
2½ in	6½ cm
3 in	8 cm
3½ in	9 cm
4 in	10 cm
4¼ in	11½ cm
5 in	13 cm
5½ in	14 cm
6 in	15 cm
6½ in	16½ cm
7 in	18 cm
7½ in	19 cm
8 in	20 cm
8½ in	21½ cm
9 in	23 cm
9½ in	24 cm
10 in	25 cm
11 in	28 cm
12 in	30 cm
13 in	33 cm
14 in	35 cm
15 in	38 cm
16 in	41 cm
17 in	43 cm
18 in	46 cm
19 in	48 cm
20 in	51 cm
21 in	53 cm
22 in	56 cm
23 in	58 cm
24 in	61 cm
25 in	63½ cm
30 in	76 cm
35 in	89 cm
40 in	102 cm
45 in	114 cm
50 in	127 cm

*Approximate. To convert inches to centimeters, multiply number of inches by 2.54.

BIBLIOGRAPHY

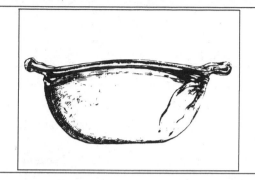

Almazan, Ma. Teresa de la Rosa, ed. *Gastronomía Mexiquense*. Pub. Gobierno del Estado de Mexico, Toluca, undated.

Bourchier, E.M., and Roldan Parrodi, Jose. *Plants for Pot and Body*. Private Publication, Mexico City, 1962.
Herbs. Private Publication, Mexico City, 1961.

Cabrera, Luis. *Diccionario de Aztequismos*. Ediciones Oasis, Mexico City, 1974.

Cossio y Soto, Guadalupe. *Cocina Mexicana*. Private Publication, Tulancingo, Hidalgo, 1901.

Diaz-Bolio, Jose. *La Chaya, Planta Maravilloso, Vol. I: Crónica Etnobotánico*. Gobierno de Quintana Roo, Mérida, Yucatán, 1974.

Diccionario de Cocina. various, Pub. Mariano Galvan Rivera, Mexico City, 1845.

Guzman de Vazquez Colmenares, Ana Maria. *Tradiciones Gastronómicas Oaxaqueñas*, 2nd Edition. Private Publication, Oaxaca, Oaxaca, 1982.

Harris, Marvin. *Good to Eat*. Simon & Schuster, New York, 1985.

Hernandez, Ana María. *Libro Social y Familiar, para la Mujer Obrera y Campesina*. Private Printing (Printer A. del Bosque), Mexico City, 1935.

Kennedy, Diana. *The Cuisines of Mexico*. Harper & Row, New York, 1972, Revised Edition 1986.
The Tortilla Book. Harper & Row, New York, 1975.
Mexican Regional Cooking (original title *Recipes from the Regional Cooks of Mexico*). Harper & Row, New York, 1978, Revised 1984.
Nothing Fancy. Dial Press, New York, 1984. Revised 1989, North Point Press.

La Cocinera Poblana, Vols. 1 and 2. Collection published Libreria del Editor, Narciso Bassols, Puebla, 1877.

Lomeli, Arturo. *El Chile y Otros Picantes.* Editorial Prometeo Libre, Mexico, D.F., 1986.

Long-Solis, Janet. *Capsicum y Cultura, La Historia del Chilli.* Fondo del Cultura Economica, Mexico City, 1986.

Martinez, Maximino. *Plantas Utiles de la Flora Mexicana.* Ediciones Botas, Mexico City, 1959.

Novo, Salvador. *Cocina Mexicana.* Editorial Porrua, S.S., Mexico City, 1967.

Ramos Espinosa, Virginia. *Recetas para la Buena Mesa.* Editorial Jus, Mexico City, 1960.

Recetario de Cocina de "La Casa de la Mujer Tabasquena." Ediciones del Gobierno de Tabasco, Villahermosa, Tabasco, 1963.

Sanchez Garcia, Alfonso. *Toluca del Chorizo, Apuntes Gastronómicos.* Pub. Gobierno del Estado de Mexico, Toluca.

Santamaria, Francisco J. *Diccionario de Mejicanísmos,* 2nd Edition. Editorial Porrua, Pub. S.A., Mexico City, 1972.

Toklas, Alice B. *Aromas and Flavours.* Michael Joseph, London, 1959.

Valdes-Villarreal, Familia. *Manuscrito de Recetas.* Coahuila, Coahuila, 1910.

Vidal, Francisco. *Cocina Tradicional de Chilapa.* Institute Guerrerense de la Cultura, Chilpancingo, Guerrero, 1984.

Wolfert, Paula. *The Cooking of South-west France.* Dial Press, New York, 1983.

DESCRIPTIONS OF COLOR PHOTOGRAPHS

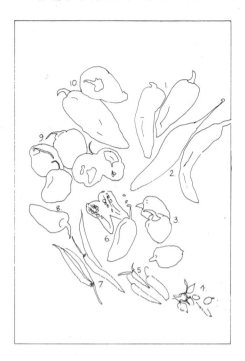

FRESH CHILES
1. Chile de Agua (Oaxaca)
2. Chilaca
3. Chile Habanero
4. Chile Piquín
5. Chile Serrano
6. Chile Jalapeño
7. Chile de Árbol
8. Chile Güero
9. Chile Peron
10. Chile Poblano

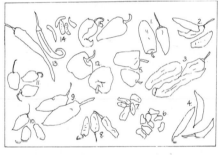

COMMON DRIED CHILES
1. Pasilla
2. Guajillo
3. Pulla
4. Mulato
5. Chile Catarina
6. Chile Piquín
7. Morita
8. Mora
9. Chipotle
10. Cascabel
11. Chile le Árbol
12. Ancho
13. Chilacate (Jalisco)

UNCOMMON DRIED CHILES
1. Tabiche
2. Amarillo
3. Seco Norteño
4. Chile De Onza
5. Chilhuacle Amarillo (Oaxaca)
6. Comapeño
7. Pico de Pájaro (Hidalgo)
8. Costeño
9. Chile Pasilla (Oaxaca)
10. Chile Seco (Yucátan)
11. Chile Seco (Hidalgo)
12. Chilhuacle Negro (Oaxaca)
13. Chilcostle (Oaxaca)
14. Chiltepe (Oaxaca)
15. Chilhuacle Rojo (Oaxaca)

PORK PRODUCTS

1. Longaniza de Valladolid
2. Pickled Pig's Feet (Manitas de Puerco en Escabeche)
3. Blood Sausage (Moronga)
4. Head Cheese (Queso de Puerco)
5. Red and Green Chorizo
6. Chicharrón

VEGETABLES, HERBS AND WILD GREENS

1. Jícama
2. Oreganón
3. Chilacayote (Para Dulce)
4. Guía de Calabacita
5. Romeritos
6. Chepiche
7. Papaloquelitze
8. Huauzontle
9. Chilacayote
10. Flor de Calabaza
11. Calabacita Criolla
12. Calabacita de Guía
13. Guajes
14. Quintonil
15. Verdolagas
16. Epazote
17. Hoja Santa
18. Chayotes

TROPICAL FRUITS

1. Aqua Fresa de Naranja Agria (Bitter Orangeade)
2. Limónes Rellenos de Cocada
3, 16. Mamey
4. Guanabana
5. Zapote Negro
6. Limón
7, 12. Chicozapote
8. Guayabas en Almíbar
9. Helados de Frutas Tropicales (Fruit Ices)
10. Ciruela Criolla
11. Ciruela Criolla
13. Lima Dulce
14. Granada China
15. Guava
17. Anona
18. Mangoes
19. Guanabana

INDEX

INDEX

Glenview Public Library
1930 Glenview Road
Glenview, Illinois